SMOKER BEYOND THE SEA

SMOKER BEYOND *the* SEA

The Story of Puerto Rican Tobacco

Juan José Baldrich

University Press of Mississippi / Jackson

The University Press of Mississippi is the scholarly publishing agency of the Mississippi Institutions of Higher Learning: Alcorn State University, Delta State University, Jackson State University, Mississippi State University, Mississippi University for Women, Mississippi Valley State University, University of Mississippi, and University of Southern Mississippi.

www.upress.state.ms.us

The University Press of Mississippi is a member of the Association of University Presses.

Copyright © 2022 by University Press of Mississippi
All rights reserved

First printing 2022
∞

Library of Congress Cataloging-in-Publication Data

Names: Baldrich, Juan José, author.
Title: Smoker beyond the sea : the story of Puerto Rican tobacco / Juan José Baldrich.
Description: Jackson : University Press of Mississippi, 2022. | Includes bibliographical references and index.
Identifiers: LCCN 2022031694 (print) | LCCN 2022031695 (ebook) | ISBN 9781496842107 (hardback) | ISBN 9781496842114 (trade paperback) | ISBN 9781496842121 (epub) | ISBN 9781496842138 (epub) | ISBN 9781496842145 (pdf) | ISBN 9781496842152 (pdf)
Subjects: LCSH: Tobacco industry—Puerto Rico—History. | Tobacco workers—Puerto Rico—History. | Tobacco—Puerto Rico—History. | Tobacco—Social aspects—Puerto Rico.
Classification: LCC HD9144.P82 B35 2022 (print) | LCC HD9144.P82 (ebook) | DDC 338.1/7371097295—dc23/eng/20220815
LC record available at https://lccn.loc.gov/2022031694
LC ebook record available at https://lccn.loc.gov/2022031695

British Library Cataloging-in-Publication Data available

To Estelle,
Isabel,
Melanie,
and Manuel

CONTENTS

PREFACE

Half a century ago, José Rivero Muñiz published *Tabaco*, a detailed history of Cuban tobacco from the beginnings of Spanish colonization to World War II. A decade has gone by since José Chez Checo and Mu-kien Sang's extensive *El tabaco: Historia general en la República Dominicana.*[1] Puerto Rico is the only major tobacco-producing island in the Antilles lacking an encompassing history.

This book presents the transformations and structural changes in the Puerto Rican tobacco world and its overseas markets during five centuries. It spans from early Spanish use of local tobacco as a medicine during the sixteenth century to current small-time farming, buckeyes, *chinchales*, and the large Consolidated Cigar factory. Most themes explored in tobacco's voyage have been the subject of precious little scholarship. Consequently, this volume offers a detailed exploration through generally uncharted waters with a strong reliance on primary sources.

Chapter 1 presents tobacco agriculture, early forms of manufacture, and trade from the onset of Spanish colonization to the first half of the nineteenth century. First used for its medicinal properties, Europeans then employed it mostly for pipe smoking and chewing. A colonial product generally eschewed by the Spaniards but prized by the Dutch, it became a mainstay of intense contraband until the end of the Napoleonic wars, when it became the subject of free trade.

As discussed in chapters 1 and 2, during the nineteenth century, cigars first and cigarettes later accrued gains that eventually displaced snuff, pipe smoking, and chewing tobacco as the dominant forms of consumption in Europe, the Americas, and elsewhere. In time, Havana cigars and Vuelta Abajo leaf (from western Cuba) displaced Barinas canasters (from modern-day Venezuela) to become the standard to judge a superior tobacco.[2] Manufacturers, merchants, and growers attempted to reproduce them elsewhere with varying degrees of success. Chapter 2 covers the successes and difficulties of the diffusion of the Cuban paradigms in a period marked by deep changes that set the ground for new relations among those who made their living from tobacco in Puerto Rico. It seeks to place local events in a wider, at times regional or global, context in the diffusion of the Havana and Vuelta Abajo models in the Caribbean and elsewhere.

Tobacco agriculture experienced a mid-nineteenth century readaptation, from the inexpensive filler for cigars and cut tobacco for the pipes of Britain, the Netherlands, Hamburg, Bremen, and France to specialize in a superior filler exported to Cuba and the economical *boliche* for Spanish cigarettes. New areas in the highlands, around Aibonito, Cayey, and Comerío, proved more suitable for Cuban-style leaf than the traditional growing areas in the northwest, close to Isabela, or in the southwest, near Yauco.

Cigar manufactures for the local market, already present in small artisanal shops, in time expanded to a factory setting in which some employed more than a hundred workers by the century's end. Chapter 2 also documents how some larger undertakings experienced vertical integration that, at times, included growing their own leaf, manufacture, and export. By the end of the Spanish colonial regime, three manufacturing firms had established steam-driven cigarette factories.

While the commission merchant, who financed small-time farmers, remained paramount, the change paved the way for the beginnings of the specialized leaf dealer, like José Rodríguez Fuentes, and some fair-sized operations in tobacco growing, like those of the Rucabado Hermanos. Nevertheless, cigar and cigarette manufacture remained oriented almost exclusively to the local market.

The intervention of the United States in the second Cuban war for independence and the Filipino insurrection led to Spain's prompt defeat in 1898, provoking the complete loss of the Spanish and Cuban tobacco leaf markets. Afterward, as presented in chapters 3 and 6, manufacturers and leaf dealers, the latter in substitution of the traditional commission merchant, entered the US leaf and cigar markets, where both products became major export staples. The aftermath of the war witnessed an abundance of US investments that included the powerful American Tobacco Company (ATC), the tobacco trust that, in effect, arrested local bourgeois development when it bought the two largest cigarette manufacturers.

Chapter 3 documents how tobacco interests, independent of the trust, developed a cigar called the Porto Rico that held some sway in the US market to a lesser extent than the Havana and the Manila. It examines the changes in the nature and ownership of the factories and the strategies employed to market local cigars in the United States. The tactics ranged from singling the geographic provenance of the cigars as a sign of prestige to associating them with the Havana cigar and to marketing them as a generic merchandise, with no reference to their origin. In a matter of a few years the Porto Rico cigar came to have its own distinct characteristics that set it apart from other incarnations of the cigar.

Chapters 4 and 5 follow the Porto Rican–American Tobacco Company (PRATCO) and its subsidiaries, factories, and plantations from its incorporation in 1899 to its shuttering in 1939. Chapter 4 examines the local operations of the tobacco trust, from a cigarette manufacturer in 1899 to an agribusiness by 1911. PRATCO started with the creation of monopoly conditions by absorbing the two major domestic cigarette factories. When the ATC entered, in earnest, into the US cigar trade, PRATCO initiated an enormous expansion that soon led to it becoming the largest tobacco enterprise. The scarcity and desirable qualities of a light-colored wrapper for cigars became a powerful incentive for the ATC, the tobacco trust, to venture into farming in Cuba and Puerto Rico. Chapter 4 documents how a local trust subsidiary, the Porto Rican Leaf Tobacco Company (PRLTC) brought experts of diverse origins to grow this type of tobacco.

Chapter 5 starts with the 1911 court-mandated dissolution of the trust, leaving PRATCO as an independent enterprise and the PRLTC as a jointly owned one. A decade after the incursion of the trust in the cigar trade, PRATCO and its subsidiaries gave employment to twelve thousand men and women in agriculture and manufacturing. During the twenties, however, the firm faced a reduced demand for its cigars in the United States and a debilitating cigarette war with the ATC, capped by the degeneration of its wrapper leaf growing in the Cordillera that together led to a loss of profitability. PRATCO tackled these obstacles with a pyrrhic court victory over the ATC and by selling its participation in the PRLTC. PRATCO sought revenue by gaining control of other cigar manufacturers. For some time, the dividends from the new subsidiaries covered its own losses. The firm closed its major factory in the Puerta de Tierra barrio of San Juan, leaving about one thousand workers jobless, mostly women who stemmed leaves, operated cigar and cigarette machines, and the like. It went bankrupt in 1939, two years later after closing its flagship plant—twelve thousand jobs lost in a quarter century that ended "sailing close to the wind."

After two chapters dedicated to the trust and its local successor companies, chapter 6 returns to the independent firms and individuals that served as intermediaries between the growers and the manufacturers. It examines the rise of a merchant almost exclusively dedicated to the tobacco trade during the twentieth century. Leaf dealers, stemmers, and tobacco merchants experienced a consolidation into a few firms during the same period.

Chapter 7 traces the notable expansion of tobacco growing in the highlands at the expense of coffee during the first decades of the twentieth century. In addition to the small farmer, it examines the development and twilight of an hacendado class in tobacco agriculture. While most gender studies of this industry have focused on manufacture, this chapter addresses the generally overlooked gendered division of labor that drew thousands of women to family patches, haciendas, and corporate plantations.

Chapter 8 examines strikes and trade unions in tobacco manufacture with emphasis on the articulation of both. The earliest strikes during the 1890s were generally not union led. While the roots of labor organizations in manufacture lie in the nineteenth century, the broad expansion of cigar making that followed saw an enormous growth in militancy and deep and profound changes to the nature of the strike and its eventual subordination to the trade unions. Thus followed a strong and vigorous spate of union-led strikes. The chapter discusses, at times, tense articulation between both forms of organization. By the 1920s, the decomposition of the cigar-making craft into simpler tasks first, and the mechanization of manufacture later, decimated the number of cigar makers. Acting from a position of strength, PRATCO initiated an aggressive challenge to the unions that ultimately broke their control over the strike. The last major cigar makers' strike in 1927 was spontaneous, not union led but union supported.

Chapter 9 examines a social movement, the Hermanos Cheos, born and bred in the tobacco patch. The US invasion in 1898, the 1899 hurricane, the crisis of Catholicism, and the collapse and reorientation of tobacco markets all contributed to the breakdown of normalcy in tobacco agriculture that created a favorable environment for their strong apocalyptical message. The subsequent expansion of the tobacco leaf market to the United States seems to have been a crucial component in the diffusion of the movement. Lastly, the Cheos gained influence when the disruptions of order dissolved, at least partially, the bonds that tied smallholding peasants, sharecroppers, and peons to tobacco hacendados, leaf dealers, and credit merchants.

In the mid-twentieth century, the introduction of the mechanical leaf stemmer and the thresher had dire consequences for hand stemmers as it had decades before for cigar makers. Chapter 10 documents the massive unemployment that visited the women stemmers who worked for behemoths like the Consolidated Cigar Corporation, the Utuado Tobacco Growers cooperative, and individual leaf dealers like Luis Rivera, Serafín Inclán, and Belarmino Suárez.

After PRATCO's shuttering in 1939, no major cigar manufacturing firm had local operations for fourteen years. In 1953 the Consolidated Cigar Corporation established a factory in Caguas followed by the General Cigar Company in 1965 with a factory in Utuado and others elsewhere. As documented in chapter 10, Consolidated Cigar moved all its manufacturing operations to Cayey, where it still maintains a significant presence, while General Cigar ceased all its operations in 1979. In a sharp reversal, both firms broke away from the Havana paradigm in a situation where General Cigar did not even employ local leaf.

Chapter 10 also explores the unraveling of tobacco growing during the second half of the twentieth century. The chapter documents the displacement of agriculture into a niche of small farms worked by unpaid family members with very little wage labor and almost no sharecroppers as in earlier years. Gone are the tobacco hacienda and corporate plantation.

Sections of this book have appeared previously and are reprinted with permission. Chapter 2 is a revision of "From Handcrafted Tobacco Rolls to Machine-Made Cigarettes: The Transformation and Americanization of Puerto Rican Tobacco, 1847–1903" in *CENTRO: Journal of the Center for Puerto Rican Studies* 17, no. 2 (2005): 144–69 and as "Del tabaco hilado a mano a los cigarrillos a máquina: La transformación y americanización del tabaco puertorriqueño, 1847–1903," in

El tabaco en la historia económica: Estudios sobre fiscalidad, consumo y empresa (siglos xvii–xx), ed. Luis Alonso Álvarez, Lina Gálvez Muñoz, and Santiago de Luxán (Madrid: Fundación Altadis, 2006), 461–88. Chapter 4 is an expanded version of "The 'Tobacco Trust' in Puerto Rico, from Cigarette Manufacturing to Agribusiness, 1899–1911," *Agricultural History* 89, no. 1 (2015): 34–56.

LIST OF ABBREVIATIONS

AFL—American Federation of Labor
AGPR—Archivo General de Puerto Rico
ATC—American Tobacco Company
AWITCO—American West Indies Trading Company
CGT—Confederación General de Trabajadores
CMIU—Cigar Makers International Union
FLT—Federación Libre de Trabajadores
FTC—Federal Trade Commission
GPO—Government Printing Office
NARA—National Archives and Records Administration
PN—Protocolos Notariales
PRACO—Puerto Rico Agricultural Company
PRATCO—Porto Rican-American Tobacco Company
PRIDCO—Puerto Rico Industrial Development Company
PRLTC—Porto Rican Leaf Tobacco Company
UPR—Universidad de Puerto Rico

SMOKER BEYOND THE SEA

CHAPTER ONE

The Foundations

Despite the historical importance of tobacco to the Puerto Rican economy, most themes explored in its voyage through half a millennium have been the subject of precious little scholarship. This volume offers a detailed exploration through mostly uncharted waters with a strong reliance on primary sources. A discussion of tobacco farming, manufacture, consumption, and markets before 1850 identifies relevant parts of the complex matrix of relations that had been centuries in the making, while setting the foundations for the following chapters.

Consumption morphed from Native American societies to tobacco's overseas markets in Europe during the early stages of colonization. Sailors and soldiers picked up the vice, however, divesting it from its milieu, and initiated others in their homelands with the small amounts carried in their personal belongings. Acquired through barter with Native Americans, they diffused consumption by informal trade most likely carried on in European taverns.[1]

By the mid-sixteenth century and with widening markets in Europe, the Spanish were planting the much-cherished Nicotiana tabacum. At the end of the century, the Iberians were organizing its cultivation in both Cuba and Trinidad.[2] While this early trade failed to show up in the ledgers that registered merchandise from the Americas, it did not escape chroniclers and other keen observers.[3]

The expanding trade in tobacco had powerful repercussions beyond its lands of origin that included unimpressive modifications like the mid-seventeenth-century Amsterdam merchants stimulating its planting, in Utrecht and Gelderland, as an attempt to undercut imports.[4] Other changes were enduring and pervasive, like that of the Spanish crown, in anticipation of its importance as a source of revenue, imposing a tax on tobacco (1616) and centralizing its manufacture in Seville (1620) to organize a state-run monopoly in 1636.[5]

With Puerto Rico conquered soon after the European discovery of America, the local transition from Taíno ceremonial practices to more secular habits included healing powers that European scientists and physicians hastily documented on both shores of the Atlantic.[6] A sixteenth-century memoir identifies an infusion derived from tobacco that served as a cure for rigor, *pasmo*, but bears no mention of recreational practices.[7] Nevertheless, the leaf caught the attention of other chroniclers and government officials during the seventeenth century. Its trade must have been salient enough that Enrique Enríquez, governor of Puerto Rico, started taxing, *estanco*, it in 1632.[8] Canon Diego Torres de Vargas identified 1636 in what is one of the earliest dates given for commercial tobacco agriculture and exports. The canon qualified Puerto Rican leaf as superior to that from Havana but of lesser quality than that grown in Barinas.[9]

Local tobacco planting generally followed the same paths reported elsewhere in the Caribbean. In 1646, an inspector, Melchor Fernández de Tejada, described the island's crop as limited and suggested that "only poor people" planted it. Other contemporaries stressed that tobacco agriculture was in the hands of small-time farmers, whom some wealthier residents derided as owners of "ten plantains and half a dozen dogs."[10]

The domination of the smallholding was, however, far from universal.[11] Ambrosio Jusino in 1658 is an early case in point. This mayor of San Germán owned 5,000 feet of tobacco, 2,500 feet of cacao, and a herd of 800 pigs.[12] Upon studying the seasonal patterns of marriages of enslaved people in eighteenth century Yauco and Coamo, two tobacco-growing municipalities, David Stark documents higher nuptiality rates after the harvest. Furthermore, he adds that the largest slave holders in the same municipalities maintained their preference for tobacco despite the inroads posed by coffee.[13]

EARLY PATTERNS OF CONSUMPTION

Local consumption patterns are not clear cut during the seventeenth and eighteenth centuries. Other than medicinal uses, did they include snuff, chewing, pipes, cigars, or cigarettes? Difficult as it is, the type of packaging for the export trade offers a limited insight in the ways that consumers might have employed the leaf.

According to Jaime O'Daly and Johan Peter Nissen, two knowledgeable sources and longtime residents of the Antilles, exports consisted of rolls made from a rope of "twisted leaves" forming a cylinder from which consumers either smoked or chewed. O'Daly consistently recognized the roll as the packaging unit but failed to identify the dominant mode of consumption at the end of the eighteenth century or earlier.[14]

Elsewhere, Jacob M. Price suggests that tobacco rolls diffused from Brazil to the Caribbean and Europe, strongly emphasizing that consumers preferred them for chewing.[15] Despite Price's suggestion, the Dutch, who also chewed, preferred cutting roll tobacco into small pieces fit for a pipe. Jan Steen, a Dutch Golden Age painter, documents the inclination in two oil paintings of tavern scenes.

One presents a peasant cutting the tobacco from a roll segment, while the other includes the knife, a piece of roll that is several inches long, a white clay pipe, and the smoker.[16] The Dutch mixed local tobacco with that of other origins in their pipes.[17] Manuel A. Alonso's richly ethnographic *El jíbaro* identified the countryfolk with chewing quids, *mascaúra*, and cigars, *jumazos*, while excluding other forms of consumption.[18]

In a deeply stratified society, patterns of consumption generally followed social class and ethnic lines. The elites considered chewing tobacco as a lower-class marker, favoring cigars themselves.[19] Overall, the countryfolk had little use for the pipe (locally called *cachimba* in a word of Kimbundu origin), save among those of African origin in a practice that may have diffused from the Eastern Caribbean.[20] Summing up, chewing was the dominant form of consumption, followed by pipes and cigars, until the twentieth century, when smoking tobacco displaced the former.

While rolls were not the only means of export from the Americas, they were part and parcel of the Atlantic trade. Brazilian tobacco rolls already had a small, if steady, market before the establishment of the Spanish monopoly in 1636.[21] Venezuelan tobacco rolls, called canasters, made it to the Dutch Republic.[22] As early as 1684, French peasants cut quids of rope from rolls spun in the French Caribbean.[23]

CONTRABAND

From its early days, the Spanish monopoly privileged Cuba and later tobacco from Virginia and Brazil, making little use of Puerto Rican leaf or that from other domains of the empire.[24] However, imperial economic policy required the shipment of all exports to Spain, where local leaf had few takers. So, from its beginnings, the island's tobacco exports became mainly the province of Dutch smugglers and those of other nationalities up to the end of the Napoleonic Wars.[25]

During the War of the Spanish Succession (1701–1714), French corsairs captured three Dutch sloops in the port of San Germán, loaded with oil, hides, and tobacco traded on the island. In addition, the Spanish attempted to curtail contraband by granting letters of marque that authorized seamen to capture both enemy vessels and those engaged in illegal traffic. Following this practice, Miguel Enríquez, who was an enterprising mixed-race shoemaker, born and raised in San Juan, entered the new trade to sail the Caribbean during the early years of the eighteenth century.[26] For instance, in February 1705 he commanded a brigantine and a sloop that captured a ten-cannon sloop off the island's south coast. The ship, like many others, carried tobacco, hides, annatto, and shells.[27] He became a wealthy merchant and invested some proceeds from his seafaring activities into more vessels and in a sugar mill manned by fifty-eight enslaved workers.[28]

Maintaining the practice in the waning decades of the century, privateers in the service of the Real Compañía Guipuzcoana de Caracas frequently set sail for two-month voyages across the eastern Caribbean, navigating as far north as Puerto Rican waters, where they frequently captured armed ships laden with tobacco and other tropical commodities. For example, in the 1770s, Manuel Antonio de Urtesábel commanded the sloops *Nuestra Señora de Aránzazu* and *La Borbón* when they seized fifteen vessels in a single voyage. Urtesábel and his men captured five ships off Puerto Rican waters, where *La Jamaica*, an English sloop; *El León*, a Danish brigantine; and *El Águila*, a Danish sloop, carried tobacco and other products.[29]

On the receiving end of contraband stood some well reputed firms. For instance, before its liquidation in 1783, the firm of Courtiau, La Coste, and Pascal freighted ships in Amsterdam, where some of their vessels carried on contraband in the Hispanic Caribbean. Ironically, the firm also served as providers to the Spanish navy.[30]

Suffice it to say that, up to the latter decades of the eighteenth century, local residents consumed a small portion of the crop while the bulk went overseas through contraband with little space in the Spanish markets. Tobacco was the major export crop up to the 1780s, when coffee displaced it.[31] Attempting to gain the upper hand over such pervasive contraband, the Spanish crown chartered the Compañía Guipuzcona de Caracas in 1728 and the Compañía de La Habana in 1740.[32]

FREE TRADE

Shortly before 1781, Jean Courtiau, a Frenchman, joined two Basques, Manuel de Echenique and Manuel Sánchez Toscano, in a society domiciled in the Dutch Republic but having agents in Cádiz y Bilbao.[33] The firm had a wide range of operations, which included loans to banking houses in Paris and the Spanish crown while serving as consultants for the latter's interests in the tobacco trade.[34] In 1781, Courtiau, Echenique, and Sánchez requested authorization from José de Gálvez, the minister of Indies, to establish warehouses in Puerto Rico for exporting the local commodity and tobacco from Caracas.[35] In 1785, the crown selected the firm to manage the newly established Real Factoría de Tabacos to give a legal character to what had, until then, been mostly Dutch contraband.[36]

During the planning stages, Jaime O'Daly was instrumental in documenting the feasibility of legal trade between San Juan and Amsterdam for the crown and Courtiau, Echenique, and Sánchez.[37] Understandably, he became the Factoría's local representative in 1785. Before his arrival in 1776, O'Daly attended business from Sint Eustatius, a nearby Dutch island, where he charged the crown more than 34,000 pesos that a business associate, Ricardo Downing, had lent for the repair of two Spanish warships. In compensation, a royal order allowed O'Daly to sell Puerto Rican products on the Dutch island.[38]

The Factoría received tobacco and other products of the land directly from the growers in warehouses in San Juan, San Germán, and Arecibo.[39] It would store the goods until a frigate arrived from Amsterdam with merchandise that, at times, included iron pots and luxury items like English hats that proved expensive and posed difficulties in exchange for the tropical commodities.[40] The ship would return to the Dutch Republic to sell the goods and realize a gain or a loss. The crown received a guaranteed 25 percent of the price of the sold merchandise.[41]

In 1786, Manuel Sánchez Toscana bought for the firm a 320- to 330-ton frigate in Pamplona, rechristened *El Marqués de Sonora* after the title bestowed on José de Gálvez.[42] Tobacco and coffee were the most valuable cargo on the *Sonora*'s first return voyage to Amsterdam in 1787. In time, tobacco became the most valuable commodity shipped, but coffee exports proved more profitable as tobacco contributed only 9 percent of the earnings between 1787 and 1790.[43] A rise in shipments peaked between 1789 and 1791, when three vessels set sail for Amsterdam every year. However, 1790 was the top year for tobacco exports, when they reached thirty-five thousand arrobas.[44]

The Real Factoría faced strong opposition from social groups that, more than once, resulted in serious loss of property. Under never-resolved circumstances, arsonists burned to the ground two properties of the Factoría: a warehouse in San Germán in 1790 with 6,000 pesos in tobacco and, two years later, a warehouse in Arecibo with cotton and tobacco. Antonio Mejías, the treasury official in charge of the investigation, reported to the governor that he suspected the locals, *moradores*. The growers were not satisfied with the low grades that the Factoría accorded to their leaf.[45] It also faced strong opposition from the merchants who denounced the privileged position that the Dutch enjoyed when selling their wares and products.[46] Jaime O'Daly and the Factoría's personnel had a long and intense conflict with some treasury officials, which ended with the death of one of the officials.[47]

In 1793, the *Sonora* foundered off Calais, leaving six surviving crew members, which, with renewed war between the French revolutionary government and the Spanish monarchy, brought the Atlantic trade to an end, thus infusing renewed vigor to contraband and corsairs. For a couple of years afterward, the Factoría traded some excess tobacco that it could not ship to Amsterdam with merchants in the non-Hispanic Caribbean, which notably included Saint Thomas.[48]

While in Amsterdam, Juan Ángel de Múzquiz, a ship captain, wrote to his wife in the Basque Country that, in spite of the Factoría, the tobacco trade was not free from contraband.[49] In 1795, a high government official, an *intendente*, in Puerto Rico echoed Múzquiz's observation, adding that the Factoría's merchandise was about 40 percent more expensive than similar wares bought from smugglers.[50] According to Birgit Sonesson, Dutch statistics lend more credence to contraband's relevance during the times of the Factoría. Nevertheless, despite its failure to uproot contraband, the "privileged trading company" turned out to be a profitable venture.[51]

Consequently, in 1794 Hamburg, Bremen, and Magdeburg merchants bought the island's tobacco from importers based in Copenhagen, Amsterdam, and England who had, in turn, purchased it in Saint Thomas and to a lesser extent in Sint Eustatius. The purchases were mostly the product of contraband that remained deeply entrenched in the social and economic fabric. Merchants bought the tobacco in rolls as in earlier times but also in packages.[52]

The Napoleonic wars, the War of 1812, and the wars for Spanish-American independence provided fertile ground for an upsurge of privateering and piracy in the Americas that now included corsairs from Buenos Aires and Cartagena.[53] Upon the restoration of peace, during the 1820s, strong maritime powers in the region, like the United States, sought to suppress piracy and the remnants of privateering by deploying five specially designed schooners well suited to sail close to the wind.[54]

Foreign commercial interests and international peace, important as they were, were not the sole influences for the end of privateering and contraband. Remittances, known as the *situado*, from the Viceroyalty of New Spain, which had long subsidized the colonial government, ended with Mexico's war for independence. The loss of the *situado*, together with the insistent petitions of the propertied, led the Spanish crown to allow a greater opening of commerce with foreign interests that had already started with the Real Factoría, as discussed, and sugar during the war for US independence.[55] While the Cédula de Gracias of August 1815 provided the legal basis for economic development, it codified much of what were already standard practices.[56]

Tobacco shipping registries bear an eloquent testimony to the widening legal commerce. The port of Isabela—which served a rich tobacco hinterland intercropped with rice, corn, and other staples—documented a single outbound shipment in 1820. The pirogue *Sirena*, under captain Antonio de Liz, left Isabela for San Juan loaded with 81 tobacco rolls and 61 hides. Five years later, the same port experienced a transformation. In January 1825, a boat returned to Aguadilla with 108 tobacco rolls. In May, a sloop of Spanish registry sailed for Saint Thomas with 80 hundredweights of *boliche*, an inexpensive tobacco leaf. Another Saint Thomas–bound schooner set sail in June with 80 hundredweights of *boliche*, and a sloop sailed for Arecibo with 40 hundredweights of *boliche*. In July, two sloops, of Spanish and Dutch registries, left for nearby Aguadilla, respectively carrying 114.5 hundredweights and 100 hundredweights of *boliche*. During the same month, a Dutch schooner departed for Aguadilla with a shipment of 250 hundredweights of *boliche*. In August, two sloops sailed from Aguadilla, returning to the same port with 1,058 and 1,834 tobacco rolls.[57]

In consonance with the Isabela shipments, Antonio Viscovich from Cabo Rojo sailed for Curaçao on three occasions, in a short time span, during 1825. In April, his ship carried provisions. Upon returning in May, he sailed again on 4 June with a shipload of tobacco, and on 26 June with agricultural produce.[58] Despite the legality of the trade and that the tobacco was for European consumption, the ports of call, Saint Thomas and to a lesser extent the Dutch island of Curaçao, remained in the Caribbean as in the heyday of contraband.

The early 1820s witnessed a notable increase in privateering and piracy that, in Puerto Rico, relied on small sailing ships often armed with less than half a dozen cannons, with notable exceptions like the *Panchita*, a brigantine that carried sixteen guns and a crew of 120.[59] A case in point took place late in October 1823 when Roberto Cofresí cruised the Mona Passage near Desecheo Island aboard a ten-ton schooner armed with a single swivel gun and a crew of seven. They spotted the *John*, an eighty-six-ton schooner, with Newburyport registry, carrying provisions, tobacco, and tar to Mayagüez, a west coast port. Armed with muskets and cutlasses, Cofresí and his men boarded the *John* and robbed the merchandise, including its mainsail and square rig. After the fact, Daniel Knight, the *John*'s captain, anchored in Mayagüez to denounce and seek redress for his predicament.[60]

A strong reaction from neutral powers, who held the privateers to be pirates toward the end of the Spanish-American wars of independence, led Spanish authorities, in 1823, to begin the revocation of the letters of marque and the refitting of the same vessels as merchant ships. However, without legal protection for privateering, several turned to outright piracy.[61]

As of 1832, at the end of piracy and privateers and the eclipse of contraband, Saint Thomas remained the main port of departure for Hamburg-bound tobacco traffic. Nonetheless, in anticipation of the future, Mayagüez and Aguadilla already had foreign-born merchants with strong commercial ties in Altona, Hamburg, and Bremen.[62] For instance, in 1849 Norman Hesse, an Altona merchant, bought tobacco directly in Ponce. During the 1850s, other Altona merchants bought tobacco and, for the first time, cigars.[63]

Gustav Adolph Schröder and his business associates provide another instance of the presence of foreign merchants among exporters. Arriving in 1824, he established Schröder y Cía. with Francisco Quevedo, a merchant hacendado from Isabela, and Karl F. Schomburg, a German resident of Aguadilla.[64] The partnership, according to Sonesson, originally specialized in coffee and tobacco exports and had correspondents in Hamburg, among them relatives such as Christian Matthias Schröder. In 1842, Carl Reichard became a partner and managed the recently opened Mayagüez branch and the original one in Aguadilla.[65] In 1840, the firm was the main taxpayer in Aguadilla, and in 1853, it tied with Francisco Sardá y Cía. for first place. Brother Wilhelm managed the Mayagüez branch during the late 1840s and 1850s. In consonance with the developing trend, the partnership had no known branches in Saint Thomas.[66] The firm dissolved itself and sold its assets in 1858.[67] Schröder y Cía. seems to have been the major Schröder business on the island.

However, Gustav Adolph joined several partnerships of unequal capitalization and duration. Earlier, in 1825, he, a Dane, and another German established a short-lived commercial firm, also in Aguadilla.[68] During the 1830s, another partnership, Schröder and Kuster, became wholesalers and financed agricultural production in the same area.[69] In the same decade, Gustav Adolph and his recently arrived brother, Wilhelm, established Schröder Hnos.[70]

Since some Schröder family members owned shipping lines in Hamburg and Bremen, it is no accident that the corvette *Wilhelm Schröder* sailed between Aguadilla, Mayagüez, Newburyport, and Boston during the early 1840s.[71] Unfortunately, only one of five trips examined identifies the cargo, which consisted of provisions and wood when it set sail from Aguadilla to Mayagüez on 2 January 1841. The vessel also sailed from Aguadilla to Newburyport in September 1841, and from Mayagüez to Boston in January 1841.[72] Neither of the two Massachusetts ports had known importers of local tobacco, but they were at the receiving end for sugar, another mainstay of the Schröder family businesses.[73] In 1848, the *Wilhelm Schröder*, this time identified as a "Bremen barque," had been buying tobacco along the north coast when it sank off Manatí.[74]

As in earlier times, local tobacco left its imprint in European markets. Around 1841, 7.2 and 8.1 percent of the leaf manufactured in Magdeburg and the Grand Duchy of Brunswick respectively originated in Puerto Rico.[75] Beginning in 1845, the United Kingdom became an important factor in local tobacco, but its purchases exhibited considerable variations from year to year. London merchants forwarded a substantial part of their purchases to German manufacturers.[76]

The deepening free trade had trendsetting consequences in the tobacco commerce. West Indian ports in Saint Thomas, Sint Eustatius, and Curaçao lost their dominance and came to share the export trade with direct shipping to European ports like Altona, Bremen, Hamburg, and London. Until the second half of the nineteenth century, local tobacco was never an important factor in Spanish markets.

MID-NINETEENTH CENTURY

Despite the enormous changes associated with the opening of the colonial markets to foreign commerce, the planting and growing of tobacco had not changed much. George Flinter, an acute observer who spent some time on the island during the 1830s, held that growers still dedicated about one-fourth to one-half acre of their farmland to tobacco.[77]

Although Flinter gives no details, for all practical purposes, he might have been describing Antonio Agustín, who, by 1851, owned thirteen cuerdas in barrio Salto Arriba of Utuado, where he planted the staples of subsistence farming with two cuerdas of plantains; one of corn; half of coffee; and three-fourths, divided in equal shares, of sweet potatoes, yams, and *malangas*.[78] Agustín, who was an African-born freeman since 1841, also kept a tobacco patch and planted some sugarcane. The tobacco possibly satisfied the needs of his household but could have been a cash source. Six cuerdas were scrubland. He also kept a horse, a cow, and two calves in two cuerdas of pasture, where only the horse and a calf were his property.[79] While David Stark, as indicated earlier, documented a limited use of slave labor in eighteenth-century tobacco plantations, Flinter, in contrast, held unequivocally that it was a free people's crop.

Flinter offers one of the earliest accounts of the relations that bonded growers and buyers in which "shopkeepers furnish clothes and money in advance at an enormous interest to the poor cultivators, on condition that they sell them their whole crop at a certain price, always less than half its value."[80] While not identifying the relation by name, he was referring to *refacción*, the crop lien, common among tobacco growers in the US South, Cuba, the Dominican Republic, and the island's sugarcane growing areas.[81] Chapters 4 and 6 explore the pervasiveness and centrality of the lien in financing tobacco growing.

The decline of contraband, and the resulting channeling of tobacco through legal means, led to the development of networks and the deepening of existent ones. The crop lien tied the grower to the village shopkeeper, who, in turn, served as agent for a commission merchant with foreign contacts.

Porrata Hermanos from Isabela might have been one of Flinter's leaf buyers. Their partnership maintained a warehouse in town for their trading operations and farmland equipped for planting of sugarcane, its cultivation, and rum distilling. In 1846, when the brothers mortgaged all their properties to Schröder y Cía. for 47,291 pesos, the assets included 154 hundredweights of tobacco that were the likely results of purchases from farmers, presumably on the scale of Antonio Agustín.[82]

The packing of tobacco leaves for export experienced a profound transformation between the end of the eighteenth century and the first half of the nineteenth. Tobacco rolls ceased to be the most common way of readying the leaf. By then, exporters shipped most tobacco in bales. Hamburg, Altona, and Bremen manufacturers, the major recipients of the leaves, found bales very handy in the preparation of cigars that were displacing cut tobacco, as in earlier days with Dutch pipes.[83] Nevertheless, during the late 1830s, manufacturers in the Duchies of Mecklenburg-Schwerin and Mecklenburg-Strelitz employed Puerto Rican leaf mostly for pipe smoking in a throwback to earlier times.[84]

CHAPTER TWO

From Handcrafted Tobacco Rolls to Machine-Made Cigarettes, 1847–1903

The most reputed tobacco-growing district of Cuba, Vuelta Abajo, became the major theater of operations during the 1897 and 1898 campaigns of the second war for Cuban independence (1895–1898). The conflict dislocated production, and the relocation policies of the Spanish regime severely constrained the time that growers and farmhands could dedicate to the plantations.[1] At the end of the war, large areas of the heavy and sandy clay soils were barren and laid to waste.[2] Seed for the 1898–99 harvest was scarce and needed to be imported from other areas as corporate and individual planters required excellent seed to supply their markets and maintain the international reputation of their leaf. According to the authoritative Ángel González del Valle, growers generally imported it from Puerto Rico.[3]

Following the invasion, many US residents surveyed Puerto Rico for their newspapers, for business opportunities, and for government agencies. One of these appraised tobacco factories extant in 1898–1899 as follows:

> Rucabado and Portela are the owners of *La Flor de Cayey* cigars and cigarettes, manufactured in Cayey, and *La Ultramarina* cigar and *La Colectiva* cigarette factories in San Juan. The machinery and equipment are of the most modern classes, employing *La Colectiva* factory machinery as good as that of any other factory in Puerto Rico.
>
> In Ponce, Toro and Company operate a factory dedicated exclusively to cigars and in Playa de Ponce they have a very large one for cigars and cigarettes. With over 500 laborers and the most up to date machinery, Toro and Company can produce 1,000,000 cigarettes and 25,000 cigars daily.[4]

These observations identify a lively and modern tobacco industry and even suggest some degree of industrial concentration where large factories had a considerable output and employed a sizable work force. Both firms reviewed had crossed the threshold from the hand-rolled commodity to the capital-intensive, machine-made cigarette, and besides, the bulk of the machinery was state of the art.

During the 1850s the situation was noticeably different. The quality of Puerto Rican leaf was poor, "unworthy for a good cigar," and was similar to the ill-reputed exports from the neighboring Dominican Republic.[5] At mid-century, the literature holds no known references to cigar or cigarette factories and mechanization. Perhaps the best illustration of this state of affairs is Rafael Cordero (1790–1868), revered to this day as the great nineteenth-century educator of the wealthy and the poor alike.[6] Figure 2.1 presents a detail of a canvas, done by Francisco Oller during the 1890s, of the maestro at home with his students. It discreetly reproduces his trade in the cigar maker's bench with finished cigars beside a keg with filler leaf and other artifacts of the craft. On one hand, part-time artisans hand rolled cigars in "the backrooms of retail shops and small grocery stores." On the other, the major medium of tobacco consumption remained in rolls, known as *tabaco hilado*, which the growers prepared themselves in their own homes. Rolls consisted of twisted tobacco leaves in the shape and length of a rope, then, marketed in cylindrical rolls from which the seller would cut a quid or chaw, a *mascadura*, chewed for its juices.[7]

Tobacco leaf was the third leading export before the invasion and, soon after, it would be second only to sugar. Besides, the men and women who toiled in tobacco factories became a vital element in anarchist groups, the trade union movement, and the Socialist Party. However, historians have not researched changes in leaf quality, the development of the factory system, or the penetration of US capital in the tobacco industry at the end of the nineteenth century and early years of the twentieth.

Thus, this chapter seeks to document the expansion of leaf production and the veritable transformation of its attributes during the second half of the nineteenth century. When Puerto Rican growers gained awareness of the bonanza obtained by the leaf from the Vuelta Abajo region of Cuba, many shifted their planting to a type of tobacco with similar properties. A second goal is to examine the displacement of small artisanal shops, run by independent cigar or cigarette makers, by the factory system employing wage labor. While this industrial capacity was not export oriented, it contributed to the substitution of Havana cigars and Cuban cigarettes with domestic ones. The third aim is to document the halt of a developing entrepreneurial class in the manufacture of cigars and cigarettes. At the turn of the century, the ATC, the tobacco trust, bought into the most technologically sophisticated of all tobacco manufacturing sectors, cigarettes. Cigar manufacturers faced stiff competition from the trust when it attempted to monopolize the trade. The chapter also seeks to interpret the transformation of the island's tobacco industry with reference to changes in the Caribbean and elsewhere in

Figure 2.1. Francisco Oller, *La escuela del maestro Rafael Cordero* (detail). Colección Ateneo Puertorriqueño.

the Americas and Europe. It holds that Cuban leaf and Havana cigars became the standard to judge domestic products.

TOBACCO AND THE CUBAN STANDARD

During much of the eighteenth century the dominant forms of tobacco consumption were snuff and pipes in Europe, chewing tobacco in the United States, and cigars and cigarettes in some Iberian colonies. From the Americas, cigars and cigarettes first spread to Spain, where they posted small gains, eventually surpassing snuff by the end of the eighteenth century.[8] Imports from Havana and Spanish Santo Domingo, with the production of the Royal Factories in Seville and Cádiz, attended the demand.[9] Philippine tobacco farming started in the last quarter of the sixteenth century, and the commercial manufacture of cigars took off sometime before the establishment of the monopoly's factory in 1782.[10]

Cigar smoking seems to have diffused to Britain during the Seven Years' War, when the British occupied Havana in 1762, and later to the United States.[11] It seems to have spread elsewhere in Europe during the Napoleonic Wars, when armies of diverse national origins fought in Spain and soldiers picked up a custom largely unknown in their own countries.[12] Cigars and cigarettes, with significant variations by country, posted constant gains until they eclipsed snuff, pipes, and chewing tobacco during the nineteenth century in most of Europe and early in the twentieth century in the United States.[13]

The tobacco trade of the Antilles was twofold: overseas manufacturers imported the leaf, or merchants brought the manufactured product. Accordingly, Hamburg and Bremen imported large amounts of Dominican leaf as early as the 1840s, and US and British merchants habitually bought Havana cigars from the onset of the century.[14] In Spain itself, the king instructed the directors of the royal factories in 1817 to "manufacture in imitation to those remitted from the Havana factory, improving, where possible, their manufacture."[15]

In 1830, the Spanish colonial government authorized private firms to export the cigars manufactured by the Philippine tobacco monopoly.[16] Manilas, as tobacconists and smokers identified them, became a sign of status among South Asian elites to the extent that manufacturers shipped some 230 million to Java alone in 1856–1864.[17] The archipelago's foreign exports increased to an average of four hundred thousand cigars annually during the 1866–1870 period.[18] Indeterminate quantities of Manilas made it to the British Isles and France, where they quickly became fashionable and gained something of a reputation as a distinct, quality smoke.[19] Despite their early promise, the royal monopoly in Spain did not promote the Manila trade name, although from 1839 and on, it manufactured cigars wholly or partially made from Philippine leaf that it sold under the name of "common cigars."[20]

Manila cigars were second to Havana cigars, which smokers considered truly exceptional. "How Havana tobacco embarked upon its conquest of the world"[21] is well known, and Fernando Ortiz recapitulated it concisely:

> As civil liberties triumphed and political constitutions were guaranteed, the cigar came into the ascendancy once more, coinciding with the advent of economic liberalism in Cuba, which threw the port of Havana open to all nations. And in this atmosphere of free industrial and commercial enterprise Havana tobacco, by the unanimous plebiscite of the world, was awarded the imperial scepter of the tobacco

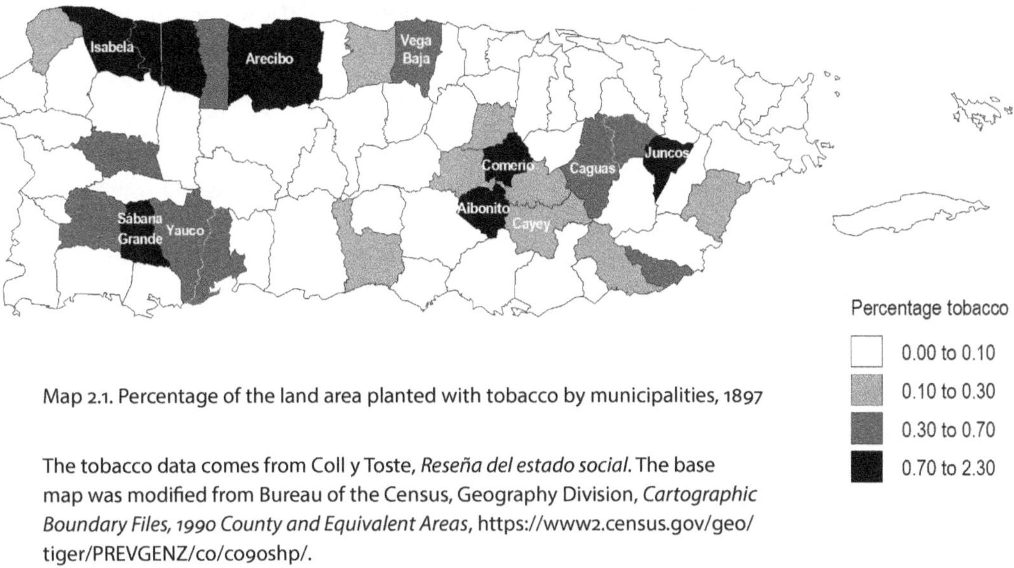

Map 2.1. Percentage of the land area planted with tobacco by municipalities, 1897

The tobacco data comes from Coll y Toste, *Reseña del estado social*. The base map was modified from Bureau of the Census, Geography Division, *Cartographic Boundary Files, 1990 County and Equivalent Areas*, https://www2.census.gov/geo/tiger/PREVGENZ/co/co90shp/.

> world. Havana tobacco from then on became the symbol of the triumphant capitalistic bourgeoisie. The nineteenth century was the era of the cigar.[22]

By the 1850s, Havana cigars and Vuelta Abajo leaves set the standard to judge other cigars and cigar filler in the Caribbean, the Americas, Asia, and Europe. Farmers, merchants, and manufacturers elsewhere oriented their production to the lucrative Cuban standard through several strategies. Many planted Cuban seed in soils with precipitation, sunlight, and drainage similar to those of Vuelta Abajo. Mexicans in Veracruz and the British in Jamaica stimulated it with Cuban hands during the 1860s.[23] During the 1870s, Canary Islanders used the Cuban model to improve their participation in the Spanish market.[24] Dutch planters were successful in Indonesia, particularly with the Sumatra cigar wrapper.[25]

EXPANSION AND TRANSFORMATION OF TOBACCO GROWING

At mid-century, the leading type of local tobacco was employed in the manufacture of roll-chewing tobacco for the domestic market.[26] Growers and merchants retained the best, while the lesser grades were exported.[27] Small amounts made their way to the Netherlands, where they already had something of a reputation as pipe tobacco that spread to nearby countries such as France.[28] Hamburg and other Hanseatic ports bought 52.8 percent of leaf exports between 1845 and 1849 while the British took 31.1 percent during the same period. The Hanseatic ports and the British remained the main destinations for domestic leaf during the next quarter century with Cuba and Spain gaining considerable ground after 1870.[29]

Map 2.1 identifies the three chief tobacco-growing regions in the prelude to the US invasion. The map represents the percentage of the total land area of each municipality planted with tobacco along four categories, reported in 1897. The main district was the northern coastal plain between Vega Baja and Aguadilla. The region along the western end of the northern littoral included the leading municipalities of Camuy and Quebradillas, with 1.62 and 2.27 percent of their respective land areas planted with tobacco. An age-old district encompassed the rolling hills of the southwest centering around Yauco and Sábana Grande. Yauco and its vicinity seem to have been the main tobacco area until sometime in the nineteenth century.[30] The better leaf from these two districts was suitable for roll-chewing tobacco, and the remnants, which were considerable, were exported mainly as scrap, *boliche*, for the manufacture of cigarettes, pipe tobacco, and short filler for cigars.[31] Finally, Map 2.1 identifies a developing tobacco region in the slopes and valleys of the eastern highlands between Juncos and Aibonito, the latter being the third leading tobacco municipality with 1.55 percent of its land area planted with the leaf.

Tobacco agriculture experienced three major changes during the second half of the nineteenth century. The first refers to the nature of the commodity produced in the mountainsides and the narrow river valleys of the eastern highlands identified in map 2.1. The leaf that slowly ascended and spread to the Cordillera Central was not the one consumed domestically as quids of tobacco with its inferior grades exported to inexpensive markets in Europe; it was a superior leaf, if employed, in the manufacture of cigars. For instance, a nineteenth-century observer considered the leaf from Cidra excellent, and as early as 1878, merchants and manufacturers identified the tobacco of the highland municipality of Sabana del Palmar, by the trade name of Comerío, and considered it the best in the island.[32]

Puerto Rican growers and merchants had long been aware of the reputation and exceptional characteristics of the leaf from Vuelta Abajo. They sought to produce a cigar filler patterned on this successful model and, accordingly, sowed new varieties and harvested on the Cuban system.

A case in point was the adoption of Cuban techniques to harvest tobacco, remove it from the field, and, finally, carry it to the curing barn. Traditionally, field hands would cut the fully mature plant by the stalk (hence the practice became known as *de mata*, or stalk cut), let it wilt under the basking sun in the field, and, finally, carry it to the curing barn. Men tied the stalks to sticks, which, in turn, hung from the ceiling of the structure.[33] This harvesting technique, dominant in the early nineteenth century, started to give way to what domestic growers, as well as those in other latitudes, called the Cuban method. When the plant started to mature, known when the lower leaves started to yellow, the grower or

Figure 2.2. Men carrying tobacco sticks into a curing barn near Cayey. Reprinted from US War Department, Military Government of Porto Rico, *Arrangement of Annual Reports of the War Department for the Year Ending June 30, 1900* (Washington, DC: GPO, 1901), 192.

his employees went on to cut the leaves from the top down in pairs, known as *mancuernas*, which they sorted immediately as wrapper or filler tobacco. Each plant went through two to four such cuttings. Field hands first hung the pairs of leaves across a man's arms and then slipped them off on tobacco sticks, known as *cujes* and more recently *varillas*, some three yards in length. Figure 2.2 shows several men carrying three *varillas* full of *mancuernas* about to hang in a very modest curing barn to dry by air.[34] The differences between the two harvesting techniques affected the distribution of space and the internal structure of the barns.

By 1888 the men and women from the highlands had gained considerable experience with different varieties and growing and harvesting methods so that their agricultural practices were clearly distinct from the traditional ones: "Havana seed has been taken to Puerto Rico several times, and it has not kept its superior qualities; on the other hand, an indigenous seed provides the exquisite tobacco of Cayey, Caguas, Comerío and Morovis."[35]

By 1895, merchants and smokers alike associated the tobacco of the highlands rather than that from the northern plain or the hills to the southeast with the best Cuban tobacco. For instance, La Flor de Cayey factory "established, as it is, in one municipality of the island that enjoys the most legitimate fame due to its extensive tobacco plantations, bordering Caguas and Aibonito . . . it has become the Vuelta Abajo of Puerto Rico, it uses superb leaf. In [the 1888 Universal Exposition of] Barcelona it summoned much attention and attained, in justice, a gold medal."[36]

The second change experienced by tobacco growers refers to its substitution of foreign leaf. As the quality of local cigar filler came closer to the Cuban model,

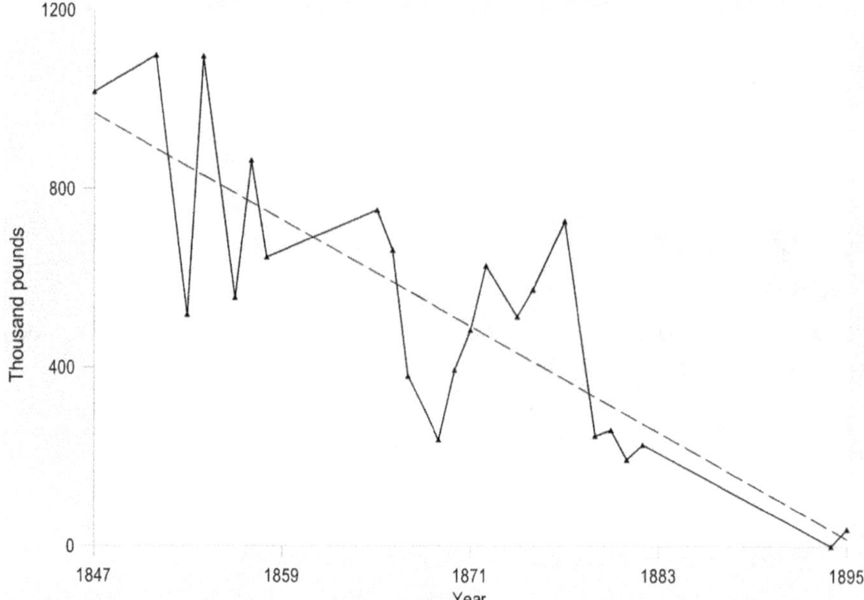

Figure 2.3. Tobacco leaf imports to Puerto Rico, 1847–1895.

Sources: Ricardo C. Aguayo, *Manual del cultivo de tabaco*, 2nd. ed. (Ponce: El Comercio, 1884), 19; Frank H. Hitchcock, *Trade of Puerto Rico* (Washington: GPO, 1898), 18.

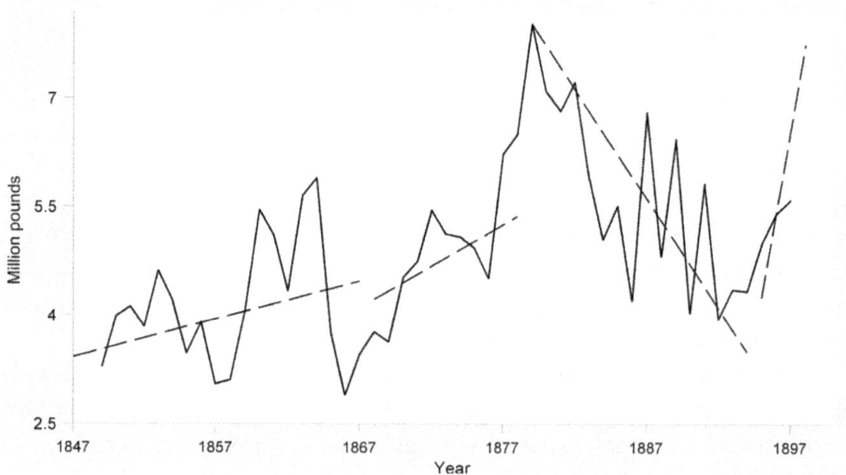

Figure 2.4. Puerto Rican tobacco leaf exports: Five-year moving averages and trends, 1847–1898.

Sources: Edmundo D. Colón, *Datos sobre la agricultura en Puerto Rico*, 289–291; Gaztambide Báez, "La historia del tabaco," 11.

fabricants had less need to import if from the sister island. "From that time [1860s] the intervention of some intelligent manufacturers and the increase of domestic demand, because of the shortage of Havana leaf, insured more attention on cultivation. Nowadays, the improvement is such that nobody seeks tobacco from Havana. The wrapper harvested summons prices ranging from $50 to $100 per hundredweight in their [Puerto Rican] factories."[37] Figure 2.3 presents leaf imports to Puerto Rico and the linear trend from the three major sources: Cuba, Virginia, and the Dominican Republic for selected years between 1847 and 1895. The figure clearly identifies a reduction to the point of self-sufficiency by the end of the century.[38] It suggests that local growers and merchants, albeit aided by a tariff, consolidated their position in the domestic cigar-filler market.[39] Needless to say, roll-chewing tobacco, the major product—with its own varieties, harvesting and curing methods, and consumption patterns—was always secure.

The third major agricultural transformation was the increase of tobacco leaf exports. During the second half of the century, expanding consumption of cigars and cigarettes in the United States and Europe stimulated Puerto Rican leaf exports. Figure 2.4 presents the five-year moving averages of Puerto Rican leaf exports, showing their long-term tendency to rise despite strong cyclical fluctuations.[40]

The tendency, however, did not show a clear-cut linear pattern because exports conformed to the ebb and flow of Cuban leaf markets. The Cuban wars for independence and the intervention of the United States in the second conflict disrupted planting, manufacturing, and commerce that resulted in benefits for Puerto Rican growers and exporters, markedly so during the second war. These fluctuations did not go unnoticed as Miguel Meléndez Muñoz, an essayist and acute observer, held that the local economy became a thriving beneficiary of the paralyzation and ruin of Cuban industry and agriculture.[41]

The cyclical fluctuations of Puerto Rican leaf exports, presented in figure 2.4, responded to the civil turmoil caused by the Cuban wars for independence. Four broken lines give the linear trends of Puerto Rican leaf exports during periods of war and peace in Cuba. The first broken line shows a slow rising trend for 1847–1867 that becomes steeper during the first Cuban war for independence (1868–1878). While the main leaf export markets during the early stages of the war remained German, with a 41.6 percent share, and British, with 24.8 percent, Cuba and Spain entered the market in force to corner 17.9 percent and 11.9 percent respectively between 1870 and 1874.[42] Three years into the war, in 1871, a contractor of the Spanish tobacco monopoly was unable to fulfill his obligation with Cuban leaf. José Domenech, after gaining authorization to buy without the customary auction, substituted Cuban leaf with nearly half a million kilograms of Puerto Rican *boliche*.[43] On the other hand, small Cuban shops or buckeyes, *chinchales*, relied on other leaf sources, Puerto Rican leaf being one, to substitute the lesser grades of Cuban leaf in the manufacture of cigars and cigarettes for the domestic market.[44]

As the war went on, Puerto Rican leaf imports reached a level that alarmed Cuban growers, who started to organize and articulate a concerted opposition. Finding resonance in sectors of the Cuban press such as *El Eco de Vuelta Abajo*, *Revista Económica*, and *La Voz de Cuba*, the emboldened growers successfully pressured their colonial government to ban Puerto Rican leaf.[45] On 16 October 1876, the Dirección General de Hacienda of Cuba banned such imports starting on 1 November. The stated reasons for the ban were that the duty-free introduction of Puerto Rican tobacco, which had been in force since 1863, had "prejudiced" Cuban production and that Dominican tobacco had been consistently imported as if it were from Puerto Rico.[46]

After the colonial authorities of both islands took the matter to the Spanish government, on 27 February and 7 March 1877, the crown issued two decrees favorable to the duty-free entry of Puerto Rican tobacco.[47] By June, the Cuban colonial government complied with the decrees. Puerto Rican leaf imports were to be limited solely to the port of Havana so that a commission could inspect the leaf in an attempt to control the smuggling of Dominican leaf.[48] Nevertheless, Vuelta Abajo growers kept the issue alive for some time.[49]

Furthermore, during the early phases of the war, the scarcity and high prices commanded by Cuban leaf induced the Spanish tobacco monopoly to forgo the mandatory auction required to procure Puerto Rican leaf. Later, starting in 1872, the purchases of inexpensive *boliche* for the manufacture of cigarettes went through regular auction mechanisms.[50]

Figure 2.4 also presents the linear trend for the years following the first Cuban war (1878–1895). While these were lean years for Puerto Rican leaf exports, Cuba experienced increases in leaf exports up to 1896, and cigar exports rose between 1882 and 1890, when the United States again protected its cigar manufacturing industry with another tariff.[51]

Once more, Puerto Rican leaf exports present a steep rise during the second Cuban war for independence (1895–1898). In 1896, the Spanish authorities determined that tobacco from western Cuba was to supply the Spanish monopoly and colonial manufacture.[52] However, as war continued to ravage the tobacco-growing areas, Cuban merchants and manufacturers increased their dependency on Puerto Rican imports to the extent that Cuba became its leading market.[53]

In summary, domestic growers expanded and transformed tobacco agriculture along three dimensions by the end of the century. First, highland farmers shifted to a leaf that fitted the model of the Havana cigar. Second, such leaf began to substitute imports from Cuba and Virginia to the extent that domestic production supplied local demand. Lastly, domestic leaf exports increased across the board, but, significantly, Cuba itself became a major recipient of wrapper and filler for Havana cigars.

THE FACTORY SYSTEM

No tobacco factories appear before the 1870s because manufacture was either a cottage industry, as in roll-chewing tobacco, or the work of independent artisans rolling cigars and cigarettes by hand.[54] While the relations of production in the manufacture of roll-chewing tobacco remained much the same, the social relations between the men and women who crafted cigars and cigarettes and stemmed tobacco experienced sizable modifications during the following decades. Domestic cigar and cigarette manufacturing experienced four important economic changes and two social ones.

First, the beginnings of the Puerto Rican factory system formed part of the diffusion of Cuban cigar making to other lands as manufacturers attempted to participate in the bonanza of the Havana cigar by imitating its production. Cuban cigar makers and manufacturers established and operated factories in New York City, Key West, and, later, Tampa that handmade cigars with the same techniques employed in Havana and relied exclusively on Cuban leaf.[55] In due time, this type of cigar earned a good reputation and a distinct character of its own under the name of "Clear Havana."[56] Likewise, Cuban migrants planted tobacco and manufactured cigars in Jamaica; Veracruz, Mexico; and elsewhere in developments that coincided or antedated the first documented instance of a cigar factory in Puerto Rico.

José Rodríguez Fuentes, a Spaniard who learned the craft in Cuba, is a case in point. He went on to establish Las Dos Antillas, a buckeye, or *chinchal*, in San Juan in 1870. Six years later, it employed some thirty rollers.[57] Migrants like him carried the craft of the Havana cigar to other lands as under his "shadow commenced the development of the new industry in that country [Puerto Rico]."[58] The most common cigar shape, the *breva*, ceded space to additional shapes, *vitolas* in tobacco parlance, such as *regalías británicas* and others that consciously imitated Cuban *vitolas*, particularly in the larger manufactories.[59] By the end of the century, the Havana model dominated the domestic cigar industry.[60] Some manufactories, such as Las Dos Antillas, La Ultramarina, and La Flor de Cayey, gained sufficient acceptance for their imitations to become providers for the royal Spanish house.[61]

Although the diffusion of the Havana craft stimulated the Puerto Rican cigar industry, it was not enough by itself because indigenous circumstances had to be favorable. The second economic change refers to domestic conditions propitious for the establishment of the factory system. A reexamination of the tobacco leaf exports presented in figure 2.4 allows a partial explanation of these conditions. Figure 2.4 shows that the 1880s and early 1890s were years of contracting or slowly expanding tobacco leaf exports. That is, the growth of domestic manufacture coincided with the period of declining leaf exports (1880–1894). It is likely that growers, merchants, and exporters sought to balance the loss of foreign markets with import substitution in both cigars and cigarettes as they sought manufacture to balance their weakness in the foreign markets.

The 1880s were ripe for the development of the factory system in another sense. As indicated above, domestic growers had improved leaf quality by the 1880s so that local manufacturers had ready access to a choice binder and filler from the highlands that resembled more than ever the coveted Cuban model. Manufacturers and cigar makers embarked themselves in their pursuit of Cuban *vitolas* and by the 1890s had gained some mastery rolling leaf in the style of Havana. A similar downturn in leaf exports earlier might have had a different result.

The third economic change is the transition from artisanal shops to the factory. Workshops remained small during the 1870s. For instance, San Juan had six cigar establishments in 1879, but most of these seem to have been short-lived.[62] In 1883, the capital still had six, but the businesses failed to exhibit a stable nature because only José Rodríguez Fuentes appears twice; his factory, Las Dos Antillas, employed one hundred cigar makers and manufactured cigarettes.[63] Factories such as Portela and Lomba's renowned La Ultramarina appeared for the first time. By 1885 San Juan boasted nine manufactories with names that started to repeat themselves in the press and literature.[64]

The promotion of the trade began to assume more characteristics of a factory setting than the artisanal shop it was replacing. For instance, Las Dos Antillas traveled far to participate in the Universal Exposition of Barcelona in 1888, where it obtained a gold medal.[65] While mechanization was still rudimentary, Fructuoso Bustamante's La India Occidental in Ponce seems to have outstripped others in the introduction of machines by preparing the filler for its cigarettes with a US-made shredder.[66]

The factory system posted significant gains during the 1890s. Las Dos Antillas hired more than 100 rollers in 1892, and La Ultramarina employed some 160 cigar makers by 1897.[67] Rucabado and Company and Sánchez y Hermano, among others, established factories in Cayey and Comerío respectively, thus continuing the defensive strategies of tobacco merchants and growers.[68] Figure 2.5 presents a group of men, with a few youngsters, hand rolling cigars at their benches, possibly at Rucabado's La Flor de Cayey, which claimed to employ some sixty-eight rollers and produce thirty thousand cigars weekly.[69] In 1890, Mamerto Infanzón established La Habanera, a large cigar and cigarette factory, in Mayagüez.[70] During the last quarter of the century, the factory system employing wage labor began to displace the independent artisan and the buckeye. By the turn of the century, several factories had been in existence for years as capitalist production was becoming the dominant mode of crafting cigars and cigarettes.

As cigar-making grew in scale, the manufacturer lost direct contact with the consumer. The tobacconist began to mediate between them in specialty shops,

Figure 2.5. Cigar makers at the largest factory in Cayey. Reprinted from Dinwiddie, *Puerto Rico, Its Conditions and Possibilities*, 124.

already existing in Europe, that seem to have spread to the larger urban areas of the island. Elsewhere the tobacconist, and his Puerto Rican counterpart, most likely provided "both the material and symbolic link between production and consumption (that is, he both handed over the product and advised the customer as to its quality and meaning)."[71] El Escudo Español, one such shop, catered its genteel clientele with both domestic and Havana cigars, cigarettes, and cut tobaccos by the Ponce main square as early as 1892.[72]

Domestic production displaced Cuban imports from the local cigar market save for the small luxury sector that remained dependent on Havana workshops.[73] Import substitution began in the 1870s and accelerated with the expansion of the factory system during the following years. The same, however, does not hold for cigarettes as Cuban imports outproduced local manufacture. During the early 1880s, the value of Cuban cigarettes imported exceeded that of Puerto Rican leaf exports to Cuba.[74] Despite efforts from Las Dos Antillas, La India Occidental, and others, the cigarette market remained firmly in Cuban hands during most of the 1890s.[75] Besides, large Cuban firms promoted their cigarettes actively; for instance, each cigarette pack often included a single colorful and striking engraving, *marquilla*, depicting series of religious themes, sugar mills, royalty, "mulattas," military uniforms, and the like that were intended to be collected.[76] Additionally, Cabañas and Carvajal and La Corona presented tall and elaborate showcases to display their products during the 1893 exposition held in San Juan in observance of the fourth centenary of Columbus's landing in Puerto Rico.[77]

Figure 2.6. A machine-driven cigarette factory in Ponce. Reprinted from Bryan, *Our Islands and Their People*, 1:394.

The fourth economic change refers to the transformation of cigarette manufacture. Whereas cigars remained hand rolled, cigarette manufacturing experienced a mechanization process that started with shredding machines used to prepare the filler. Mechanical devices, such as the Dubrul employed by La India Occidental, shredded, sifted, sieved, and separated the resultant tobacco by size but left the rolling of the cigarettes in the hands of skilled craftspeople.[78] The Emery, Allison, and Bonsack mechanical rollers used shredded tobacco and paper as inputs to produce a finished cigarette in what has come to be known as continuous process production. These machines, the Bonsack in particular, squarely placed the control of production in the hands of factory owners as operatives did "little more than feed materials in the machines, keep an eye of their operations, and in some cases, when it was not yet done automatically, package the final product."[79] In consequence, mechanical rollers effectively signaled the disappearance of hand rollers after the 1880s in the United States and elsewhere somewhat later.[80] Figure 2.6 illustrates the reorganization of the factory as benches, hand rollers, and knives gave way to machines handled by operatives. The figure shows several mechanical rollers, aligned against the wall, powered by a hidden steam engine through a driveshaft that ran along the ceiling that was, in turn, connected to several belt-driven pulleys attached to each device. The output from a single machine was impressive: by 1884 the Bonsack produced between 200 and 220 cigarettes per minute, equivalent to the work of forty-eight craftspeople but manned by three operatives.[81]

Mechanical rollers became dear to entrepreneurs because they produced cheaper cigarettes than hand rollers, reduced labor needs, and employed readily trained operatives rather than craftspeople. However, the large output of the mechanical rollers entailed a change in the scale of the enterprise that most shop owners lacked the means to assume. Cigarette manufacturers had to secure steady supplies of leaf; invest in steam engines; pay the rental of the machines as they were rarely sold; and distribute, advertise, and market the large output of cigarettes over wide areas.[82] Additionally the domestic market was small—roll-chewing and cigars were more popular—and already cornered by Cuban cigarettes. Understandably, no domestic manufacturer crossed the threshold into the machine-made commodity until the end of the century.

Rucabado y Portela, a joint venture of two preexisting partnerships and appropriately named La Colectiva, was the only domestic firm to cross the threshold. While the cigar business remained in the hands of the original partnerships, La Colectiva was a vertically integrated firm dedicated exclusively to the manufacture of cigarettes. The firm operated a steam-driven factory employing eight Bonsack and several Comas mechanical rollers with a monthly output that ranged from one to twelve million cigarettes that represented but a fraction of the Bonsack's capacity.[83]

The Cuban colonial government enacted a high tariff on imported tobacco leaf that became effective in January 1898. After repeated attempts to have the tariff repealed, the local government responded with a tariff on Cuban tobacco manufactures, effectively reducing imported cigars and cigarettes, in particular, during the last months of Spanish rule.[84] The probable opening of the domestic cigarette market offered tempting possibilities to make the transition to mechanical rollers because their large output had, for years, discouraged their introduction.

Rucabado y Portela established La Colectiva in San Juan most likely at the end of 1897 to benefit from the anticipated effects of the retaliatory measure.[85]

La Colectiva sought to overcome another difficulty associated with the scale of mechanized cigarette factories by relying on the original partnerships for a steady supply of filler and advertised their role in these partnerships to capitalize on their goodwill. Besides, Rucabado and Company, one of the original partnerships, were growers themselves with considerable experience in financing tobacco production.[86]

As the artisanal shop gave way to the capitalist factory, the relations between those that stemmed tobacco leaf and crafted cigars and cigarettes experienced a profound transformation. The ways in which they worked and perceived themselves and each other experienced deep modifications during the last quarter of the century. Two significant social changes took place during the establishment and early expansion of the factory system.

First, a group consciousness began to emerge among entrepreneurs when they started to articulate their shared economic interests. Their first documented activity as a group was the tobacco pavilion within the fair-exposition held in 1882 in the southern municipality of Ponce where several tobacco factories, merchants, and growers exhibited their products.[87] In 1883 several entrepreneurs obtained the aid of both the colonial government and the Ponce city council for an exposition that included a competition of cigar and cigarette hand rollers with elaborate exhibitions from several enterprises. Conscious of foreign markets, the directors sought but failed to take the exposition abroad.[88]

The collective promotion and defense of the trade remained forceful in years to come. In 1885 the colonial government planned to employ inmates to run a cigar factory in La Princesa jail in San Juan. Tobacco manufacturers mounted a strong opposition, and the factory never got off the ground.[89] A few years later, around 1888, the Spanish parliament, the Cortes, considered a customs duty on Puerto Rican tobacco leaf exported to Cuba. Opposition by those who identified as taxpayers helped stop the proposed legislation. Again, in 1892, a draft of the Cuban colonial budget considered a duty on Puerto Rican leaf imports. As on previous occasions, growers and entrepreneurs from the eastern highlands—not from the other tobacco-growing areas—manifested a strong opposition.[90] A last attempt by the Cuban government to increase duties on imported leaf provoked a vigorous expression of solidarity among entrepreneurs in the tobacco sector at the end of the decade. In 1898, the Cuban government enacted a high tariff on tobacco leaf that effectively shut Puerto Rico off from its major market. Colonial government officials appealed the decision to the crown, and a commission, dominated by tobacco men, went to Havana to seek the repeal of the tariff. When both failed, merchants, growers, and manufacturers, in retaliation, sought and gained approval of high duties against Cuban-manufactured tobacco to stimulate the domestic industry.[91]

The second social change posits that the class struggle could not be reduced to the categories of factories and wage labor. Tobacco fabricants and cigar makers were identities that developed and acquired distinct meanings through the daily toil of men and women in the factories. Labor history amply documents how capitalists and workers in the tobacco trade began to view themselves in terms of this opposition.

In 1892, José Rodríguez Fuentes, owner of Las Dos Antillas, could not subdue his chanting and rowdy workers and went on to shut down the factory, effectively locking out more than one hundred workers.[92] Cigar makers went on strike at Sánchez y Hermanos' La Comerieña and a San Juan factory in 1895.[93] One hundred strikers paralyzed La Ultramarina for a week in 1897, and strikes affected La Colectiva and La Ultramarina in 1898.[94] Public condemnation became another weapon launched against factory owners. For instance, a group of cigar makers from Cayey wrote to Henry Carroll, the US commissioner who surveyed the island in 1898–1899:

> We belong to the working classes, who, up to the present time, have been ill treated by our eternal oppressors and the exploitation of our labor. The cigar-making industry in this country has dragged out a miserable existence, and the owners of factories have had no other end in view than the oppression of the artisan . . . That the whole world may know what means have been employed for this oppression, we have written you this letter, in which we state the plain truth.[95]

Tobacco manufacture experienced a profound transformation during the last quarter of the century. In summary, the trade sustained four economic changes and two social ones. The first economic change was the diffusion of the Havana style of cigar manufactures to other localities. Second, local conditions became favorable as domestic leaf gained in quality and its export markets weakened. Third, the artisanal shop started to give way to the factory system employing wage labor. Fourth, cigarette rolling became completely mechanized. The social changes were a rising consciousness among manufacturers to promote and defend their shared economic interests and the beginnings of class conflict between workers and manufacturers.

THE AMERICANIZATION OF TOBACCO MANUFACTURE[96]

The cigar makers also informed Commissioner Carroll: "This industry was started in the island by persons of capital who saw a profitable field of investment. It is needless to say that they were Spaniards."[97] Among them, some were migrants like Rodríguez Fuentes and the Rucabado brothers, who married into local families and became permanent residents.[98]

A different situation arose when manufacturing enterprises or merchant houses with substantial operations or financial resources in the developed world established or gained control of industrial operations elsewhere. Among expanding European foreign enterprises, a German firm, whose investments spanned three continents, got the head start in the establishment of tobacco-manufacturing facilities in Puerto Rico. Leopold Engelhardt and Company was a Bremen-based partnership with cigarette outlets in Egypt, a participation in a leaf-buying partnership in Colombia, and operations in Cuba. In May 1898, Engelhardt joined Fritze, Lundt and Company, a Puerto Rican–based partnership of German subjects, to become sleeping partners to Toro and Company, which set up a factory aptly named La Internacional. Luis Toro, whose sister married one of the German partners, managed the firm without contributing any capital.[99]

La Internacional employed more than five hundred laborers in a cigar plant in Ponce itself and a combined cigar and cigarette factory close to the harbor. Facing the same marketing problems as Rucabado y Portela, Toro contracted the same agents, Graham and Sánchez, to market its cigars and cigarettes in the United States soon after the invasion in 1898.[100] The partnership employed steam engines to run its Comas and Bonsack mechanical rollers and other devices at the combined cigar and cigarette plant.[101] Instead of using local printers, such as El Boletín Mercantil, they relied on German lithographers to make labels for their trademarks, Toro & Cª, La Internacional, and El Toro.[102]

The development of the factory system came to a halt in 1899 when the US tobacco trust, the ATC, made purchases consonant with its long-standing policy of growth and expansion in the cigarette business.[103] Puerto Rico became first ATC investment in the Caribbean when it secured both La Colectiva and La Internacional. The latter also manufactured cigars.[104] So to speak, ATC's first investment in the cigar business, save for cheroots, was accidental. Chapters 4 and 5 follow the tobacco trust and its local subsidiaries from their incorporation to the bankruptcy of the last in the 1930s.

Despite the trust's fast expansion and seemingly inexhaustible resources, independent manufacturers vigorously defended the local market and mounted an aggressive pursuit of the US cigar market. After the invasion, several US residents and businesses became an important force in the local tobacco industry. A few bought tobacco land in Cayey, Caguas, and elsewhere; they established cigar factories and stemmeries, and some became leaf merchants. As discussed in the following chapter, Rucabado and Portela established a cigar factory in Providence, Rhode Island, in 1900 that employed Puerto Rican leaf.

The Solá family, often with others, formed several partnerships over the years that stood up to the trust when it attempted to monopolize the cigar industry but collaborated with it in other ways. For instance, in 1893, Solá y Compañía appeared as tobacco farmers in Borinquen, a barrio in the rolling hills of Caguas.[105] The 1898 Cuban leaf tariff had a deep effect on tobacco exports that Modesto

Solá shipped to Cuba. Once the Foraker Act, enacted in 1900, substantially reduced the tariff followed by a quick sunset provision, the Solás joined other manufacturers, the tobacco trust among them, in crafting cigars to reach the US market.[106] However, lacking experience and knowledge of the aromas, styles, and shapes—*vitolas*—appreciated by the US smoker, Marcelino Solá, who by this time had become the head of the family business, established in 1901 a partnership with Magín Argüelles, a Spaniard who had learned the business in Cuba and was knowledgeable of the US market.[107] Solá, Argüelles and Co. rolled cigars in the style of Havana for export and led a continuous existence up to at least 1910.[108] Around 1900, Solá formed a short-lived partnership for the manufacture of cigars with Quintiliano Cádiz who, like Argüelles, knew the tastes and markets of the North from the vantage point of Cuba.[109] At the end of the partnership in 1902, Cádiz went into business by himself.[110] As the Solá business interests oriented themselves to the US market, one of their partnerships gained, as early as 1902, a lasting presence on Pearl Street, in the heart of the New York tobacco district.[111]

M. Solá e Hijos maintained a branch, in the jargon of the times, to handle cigar exports and the US end of the business separate from its manufacturing division.[112] Relatives and associates traveled routinely to New York to confer with jobbers, sales agents, and importers in downtown Manhattan. Just to take an early year, Marcelino set sail for New York to tend business with his brother Mauricio in April 1903, and Magín Argüelles, a business partner, joined a Solá brother that June.[113] While the Solá partnerships competed with the trust for a share of the cigar market, although a minuscule one, they did not refrain from a long chain of collaboration that ranged from selling it tobacco that they grew to serving as their leaf buyers in the Caguas area.[114]

Other local factories followed the same path and opened offices and established depots in New York to be closer to their clients. Portela's La Ultramarina survived the presence of the trust's PRATCO as a "principal factory" and tended its export business in Manhattan's tobacco district as early as 1900.[115] After the closing of the Providence manufactory, Mateo Rucabado maintained for years an office for La Flor de Cayey on Pearl Street in Manhattan.[116] Other useful marketing strategies proved to be the booths and medals obtained in exhibitions held in Buffalo, Chicago, and Saint Louis by Infanzón and Rodríguez's La Habanera between 1902 and 1905.[117] In summary, over half the cigar business remained outside the orbit of the trust as independents exported 57 percent of all cigars to the United States in 1906.[118]

CONCLUSION

This chapter has examined the transformation of Puerto Rican tobacco planting, manufacture, and trade from the mid-nineteenth century to the early years of the twentieth. It examined the introduction of a model of tobacco growing patterned on Cuban leaf and cigar manufacture on the styles of Havana that gained the upper hand against the older standard based principally on tobacco suitable for roll-chewing tobacco and secondarily on exports for cheap cigar filler and pipe tobacco in Europe. The deep changes that affected the local tobacco industry were part and parcel of a large-scale transformation of the habits of tobacco consumption in Europe and the Americas during the nineteenth and early twentieth centuries. Focusing on two aspects of Cuban culture that dispersed throughout the globe, whether the taste for the cigars crafted in Havana or the diffusion of Cuban tobacco (Vuelta Abajo leaf), accompanied with its distinct methods of cultivation, this chapter has identified the pains and toils of growers, merchants, and manufacturers of diverse means to provide their commodities, whether leaf or cigars, the same identity as those originating in Cuba.

What happened in Puerto Rico bears striking similarities to the general identity of the cigar industry in the Caribbean, the United States, Europe, and lands as far away as the Philippines and Sumatra with respect to Cuban tobacco so that "Havana" and "Vuelta Abajo" started to signify a style and not a place of origin. Wars, turmoil, and civil strife in Cuba and US tariffs to protect its own cigar manufacturing industry—whether in the nineteenth century or even, much later, because of the 1959 revolution—provided a fertile ground for the diffusion of the art and culture of crafting cigars and leaf growing.[119] Migrant craftspeople, growers, and manufacturers—mostly anonymous, as well as the likes of José Rodríguez Fuentes, Magín Argüelles, and Quintiliano Cádiz—became themselves an efficient mechanism of diffusion.

This chapter explored the metamorphosis of the tobacco industry along three dimensions. The first dimension refers to three major changes in the character of tobacco agriculture during the second half of the nineteenth century. One, local growers sought to participate in the bonanza obtained by the leaf from the Vuelta Abajo district of Cuba and started to follow closely the Cuban paradigm. Two, as local cigar filler gained in quality, leaf imports from Cuba and Virginia became substituted with domestic leaf from the eastern Cordillera. Three, tobacco leaf exports exhibited a general tendency to increase.

The second dimension refers to the transformation of cigar and cigarette manufacture. The craft of Havana cigars diffused over many locations, Puerto Rico included, which had good domestic markets and access to superior leaf. Several merchants and growers picked up the craft and started the passage from the artisanal shop to the factory system. As the transition advanced, capitalists and workers began to develop and gain consciousness of their opposition to each other. Despite considerable success, most domestic producers faced difficulties with the mechanization of cigarette manufacture in their path to the modern factory system. Nevertheless, one colonial firm crossed the threshold together with a German firm. This industrial capacity was not export oriented but was destined almost exclusively to the domestic market and contributed to the substitution of Havana cigars and Cuban cigarettes with domestic ones.

Finally, the chapter documents how the sudden entrance of the ATC, the trust, stymied the growing yet fragile bourgeois impulse in tobacco manufacture. While the ATC gained control of cigarette manufacture and entered other sectors of the industry, production of cigars for domestic consumption and a considerable part of its exports remained in the hands of local residents for years to come. However, after the ATC, the configuration of the tobacco industry precluded the large capitalist enterprise such as Rucabado y Portela, particularly in the cigarette sector, but allowed for a prosperous leaf-growing and a short-lived independent cigar manufacturing sector. At times, the participation of the Rucabado brothers and associates as minority shareholders of the trust or that of Marcelino Solá as one of its buying agents, though both managed cigar manufactories of a certain scale, blurred a clear-cut distinction between the ATC and the independents.

CHAPTER THREE

The Development of the "Porto Rico" Cigar and the Independent Manufacturers, 1899–1929

By the mid-twentieth century, an excellent cigar most likely meant a cigar crafted in Havana. Perhaps with some hyperbole, Fernando Ortiz claimed that "Havana tobacco, by the unanimous plebiscite of the world, was awarded the imperial scepter of the tobacco world."[1]

However, a closer view of the fin de siècle cigar world reveals a more complicated pattern. If Havanas held the "imperial scepter," other incarnations held lesser regalia and, at times, struggled for the imperial one. While Rudyard Kipling, the celebrated poet of empire, praised "peace in a Larranaga [*sic*], there's calm in a Henry Clay," which were two iconic Havanas, he showered praise on the mildness of the fine cigars handcrafted in Manila.[2]

Well before Kipling, George Sand's weakness for the Manila cigar is well documented.[3] She "held a cane in her hand and smoked a Manila with a very graceful aplomb" in Parisian streets, promenades, and boulevards alike, well before it was commonplace for women.[4] Sand did not smoke cigars but Manilas. Around the same time, *The Count of Monte Cristo* described a small tobacco salon in the home of a wealthy nobleman. Dumas gave a detailed account of the room well stocked with "every species of tobacco" that identified the Manilas in cedar boxes beside the Havanas.[5]

Across the Atlantic, noted Boston Brahmin and Pulitzer-winning poet Amy Lowell was extremely partial to the Manilas.[6] She reputedly bought some ten thousand in 1915 to carry her through shortages anticipated because of World War I. Manilas kept "her creative fires kindled."[7] Consummate smokers, bearing no relation to the tobacco trade, could identify the Manila with a distinct flavor, aroma, and burning qualities that differed from the Havana.

Along the same line of thought, the Porto Rico cigar, handcrafted from local leaf, gained a devoted following in the United States that privileged it over the Havana or the Manila. For instance, Brooks, who "repeated without change" his passion for "Porto Rico cigars," bored Vuyning, another character, to such an extent that he cursed as he left the men's club in a 1908 short story.[8] By 1913, Louis Massen, a longtime Broadway-based actor and producer and a lifelong member of the Lambs, a Manhattan men's club, was a case in point. Interviewed at the club, he reasserted his loyalty to the Porto Rico cigar by boasting a "through and through" preference for the Savarona.[9] Conrad Aiken's "Impulse" short story begins with Michael's biweekly escape from the wife and children to play bridge in a hotel room with three other friends. A warm room, gin, and some Porto Rico cigars lent the appropriate atmosphere to the evening.[10]

Porto Ricos, Havanas, and Manilas gained loyal followers who smoked in public and private spaces. Cigars such as these were part and parcel of the space that clubs—like the Lambs—billiard halls, and saloons provided for social networking and served men as a refuge from work, home, and family.[11]

THE BEGINNINGS

By the fin de siècle, local leaf, cigars, and cigarettes had no presence in US market. That absence began to change when, in 1897, Morris J. Levi was buying leaf in Havana for his Manhattan-based partnership. By a stroke of luck, he came upon Puerto Rican leaf in a warehouse. He found that, despite the shoddiness of the sorting and curing of the leaf, "its merits were easily discernable." The cigars he commissioned from that leaf amounted to a "revelation."[12]

While he remained in Havana, his business partner, Alexander Blumenstiel, sailed to Ponce via Santo Domingo aboard the *Julia*, a steamship of the Herrera Line. Then he traveled in a horse-drawn carriage along the Carretera Central, the central road, where he bought some twenty-five packs of leaf in the highlands and had them shipped from San Juan to New York. With doubts of the quality of the leaf, Levi asked a reputable fabricant, under an oath of secrecy, to inspect the leaf at the Acker-bonded warehouse and to manufacture some cigars at his Third Avenue factory. The unnamed manufacturer considered "the basic quality was there for good cigars" but complained about the improper sorting and curing of the leaf.[13]

Blumenstiel's second trip proved to be satisfactory. He boarded a San Juan–bound steamer in New York; hired Félix Pardo, a tobacco man, as his firm's local representative; and bought about four hundred packs of leaf. Subsequently, Levi Blumenstiel cabled Pardo with instructions to buy tobacco.[14] Their first recorded shipments after the invasion consisted of thirty-one bales of leaf tobacco received in New York on 18 April 1899 and thirty-seven leaf packages on 22 May 1899.[15]

As local leaf made its forays in US tobacco factories, it did so anonymously because cigars made from local leaf did not identify their place of origin. Levi recalls how a respected Key West manufacturer would "creep" into his firm's Water Street warehouse like a "burglar" because he did not want others to see him in the building. Another fabricant covered the brown burlap over Puerto Rican leaf packs with empty cloths removed from Havana bales.[16]

The anonymity of Puerto Rican tobacco continued when the Levi Blumenstiel partnership set up the American West Indies Trading Company (AWITCO) to manage its local cigar and leaf operations. On 2 March 1900, Levi Blumenstiel's Manhattan warehouse received one package of cigars from Puerto Rico, which was a first for the firm.[17] It started to export in a "small way" El Falco cigars.[18] The 1901 registration of the label with the patent office did not allude to Puerto Rico but identified the local subsidiary as the owner, which, given its name, might implicitly suggest Cuban origin.[19] Years later, none of the thirty-one advertisements that the University Smoke Shop ran in the *Cornell Daily Sun*, from December 1908 to October 1916, identified this cigar's place of origin.[20] However, the Lewis Bear Company, which distributed the cigar in the Pensacola area, showed no reservations about identity when it ran fifteen advertisements in the general press that clearly marketed it as a Porto Rican cigar.[21]

Levi Blumenstiel's reticence to identify El Falco as a Porto Rico cigar perhaps resulted from their assessment of domestic production. Morris J. Levi considered "these primitive Porto Rico cigars," where "the leaves used for wrappers were rather rough looking, but of very decent smoking quality, invariably very dark in color, but of good combustion and with a white ash."[22]

Cigar shipments were very limited in the aftermath of the invasion. The sale of local cigars in the United States was so small that, during 1899 alone, they amounted to some ten shipments, none of which exceeded half a dozen cases or packages of cigars.[23] Table 3.1 shows that the largest importers were G. W. Sheldon and Jerónimo Menéndez, followed by a tie between Levi Blumenstiel, Ames Pearson, De Ford & Co., and others.[24] Save for Levi Blumenstiel, this research has been unable to identify the manufacturers or their marketing strategies for cigars in the United States before 1900.

G. W. Sheldon, the largest shipper, and De Ford, which tied for third place, left no other discernable tracks in the tobacco world. Seemingly both sought gains in the unsettled and uncertain waters that after the invasion brought to an end to long-standing leaf sales to Cuban firms and the Spanish tobacco monopoly. G. W. Sheldon, which served as "receivers and forwarders of imports and exports, general shipping and customs agents," had a representative in San Juan, and De Ford & Co. was a banking firm and major investor in the large Aguirre sugar mill.[25]

Contrary to Levi Blumenstiel's cautious approach, many smokers and some fabricants found enticement in the cigars from the new colony. According to the

Table 3.1. Shares of cigar and cigarette exports from the three largest independent shippers, 1899–1907

	1899–1900	1901–02	1907
Share	7.1	6.9	11.2
3rd shipper	*	DB	WI
cases	1	326	781
Share	14.3	10.1	12.5
2nd shipper	JM	GS	CC
cases	2	478	874
Share	57.1	14.2	24.0
1st shipper	GS	LB	LB
cases	8	671	1,674
Total cases	14	4,726	6,978
Shipments	(8)	(424)	(416)

Sources: Data for 848 shipments to New York as reported in US Congress, House, *Importers of Goods from Porto Rico*, 56th Cong., 1st sess., H. Doc. 589 (Washington, DC: GPO, 1900) and forty-seven issues of *Tobacco* and the *United States Tobacco Journal*.

Notes: The table excludes the tobacco trust. * a tie for third largest shipper.

CC	Cayey-Caguas Tobacco Co.	JM	J. Menéndez & Co.
DB	Durlach Bros.	LB	Levi Blumenstiel & Co.
GS	G. W. Sheldon & Co.	WI	West Indies Cigar Co.

Table 3.2. Independents' shipments to the United States and output of the tobacco trust, 1901–1906

Year	Trust percentage	Trust cigars	Independents' cigars	Total cigars
1900		133,147		
1901	10.2	2,955,431	26,108,569	29,064,000
1902	16.8	14,916,447	73,927,553	88,844,000
1903	42.7	23,044,293	30,865,707	53,910,000
1904	33.2	25,100,772	48,909,228	74,010,000
1905	39.5	44,489,868	59,883,132	104,373,000
1906	43.0	61,364,075	66,105,925	127,470,000

Source: Data adapted from Bureau of Corporations, *Position of the Tobacco Combination*, 429.

journal *Tobacco*, several tobacco interests "anticipated an easy and speedy capture of the United States, to use the racing term, in dash."[26] Having no qualms with the Porto Rico label, in 1898, New York lithographer Schmidt & Co. copyrighted a label for the "New Porto Rico" cigar that, despite the initiative, had no known takers.[27] In 1900, T. C. Brooks and two others established the Porto Rico Cigar Company in Red Lion, Pennsylvania.[28]

Jerónimo Menéndez, the second largest fin de siècle importer shown in table 3.1, was a Manhattan-based distributor. His firm was an early importer from unidentified manufacturers that made a point to identify the cigars' place of origin as attractive. A trade journal considered that some of these cigars were

> so superior to the ordinary cigars hitherto imported from Porto Rico, as to put them practically into another class . . . these cigars were well made, and quite a good imitation of the fancy styles of Spanish or Cuban works, produced in such perfection that one might believe them made in Havana. And then the wrapper! Perhaps nothing so fine on cigars from Porto Rico had ever been seen in the United States; free from coarse veins, soft and silky in appearance, and light in color.[29]

Substantial exports followed when the Foraker Act allowed them, at 15 percent of the Dingley tariff, in May 1900, and custom free after July 1901.[30] The 1899 trickle reached some twenty-nine million cigars exported in 1901, as shown in table 3.2. In September 1900, Rucabado, Portela & Co. established operations in Providence, Rhode Island, to distribute leaf and manufacture cigars.[31] For the occasion, they introduced the Máximo cigar, whose label displayed its origins by pinpointing, over a map, the municipalities where the firm had operations.[32] The Máximo used its geographic roots as a significant marketing strategy. Its Salt Lake City distributor reinforced the appeal by placing newspaper advertisements that prominently displayed its point of origin in large bold letters.[33]

Portela's La Ultramarina and Rucabado's La Flor de Cayey, although not owned by their combined partnership, were two long-standing firms that, by 1900, advertised in New York trade journals. La Ultramarina maintained an office in New York and La Flor de Cayey had an office in Providence, Rhode Island.[34] In consistency with the Máximo identity and, perhaps in anticipation of exports to the US market, La Ultramarina exhibited the island's name in the inner and outer labels and in the seal of every cigar box, as shown in figure 3.1.[35] Some manufacturers found a venue away from the jobber and sold directly to the tobacconist shop and the drugstore. Macy's advertised La Flor de Cayey as a "Porto Rican cigar," at its flagship location in Herald Square, New York.[36] Kauffman's, a large downtown Pittsburgh department store, also advertised this cigar by stressing the virtues of its place of origin.[37]

Figure 3.1. La Ultramarina, outer label, 1899. La Ultramarina de Portela y Cª, 17 May 1899, AGPR, Colecciones Particulares, Junghanns, caja 27, expediente 1100.

PRATCO, the main local subsidiary of the tobacco trust, participated in the enthusiasm that US smokers showed for local cigars. The inner label of their El Toro cigar box prominently depicted a woman blowing a horn while sitting over a golden globe of the world, with a disproportionately large arch of the Greater Antilles, that identified the island of Porto Rico with its name. It also pointed out the location of their factory in "San Juan, P. R." and fully spelled out the PRATCO name.[38] Despite the popular misconception that the trust dominated the cigar trade from its founding, table 3.2 shows that it exported 133,147 cigars in 1900 and a modest 2,955,431, for a 10.2 percent market share, in 1901.

Knowledgeable jobbers and tobacconists considered the first New York–bound cigar batches to range from primitive and promising but not well-made smokes. Consequently, several manufacturers sought Cuban master cigar makers and packers to train local hands.[39] As discussed in chapter 2, some partnerships, organized by the Caguas-based Solá family, hired experienced men in the manufacture of Havana cigars and the tastes of US smokers, among them Quintiliano Cádiz and Magín Argüelles. In time, one Solá partnership established an office on Water Street, in the midst of the Lower Manhattan tobacco district.[40] Their Aguey-Naba, marketed in Philadelphia, Boston, San Francisco, and other cities, stood out among the firm's brands.[41] The Solá interests also manufactured the Tantos and the El Resumen cigars, whose advertisements identified both with the place of origin.[42]

AWITCO, familiar with the current limitations and possibilities of local cigars, also hired Cuban-trained tobacco men. Gregorio López Falcó was, in some ways, representative of the concerted efforts that sought to attune local production to the tastes and standards of the smokers in the North. He left Spain in his youth for Cuba, where he learned the insides of tobacco manufacturing and marketing.[43] He seems to have left Cuba, in the aftermath of the second Cuban war for independence, for Caguas, with his Cuban-born wife.[44] As early as 1898 he was an officer and board member of AWITCO.[45] He also became the superintendent of the company and lent his mother's surname to the El Falco cigar that provoked a long and acrimonious suit from El Falcon cigars in 1902.[46] The manager maintained his position in the firm until 1906.[47] In his character as local representative and superintendent, he welcomed Samuel Gompers, the president of the American Federation of Labor, at La Turina factory in Caguas during 1904.[48]

Under his management, the firm registered La Turina, in 1900, for export to the United States. La Turina's embossed label displayed the brand name across the top in simulated gold leaf. It showed an aristocratic looking woman, dressed in nineteenth-century fashion, that contrasted with the woman on La Ultramarina label, presented in figure 3.1, who wore robes reminiscent of classical antiquity. La Turina's dress exhibits considerable embroidery laced with golden ribbons and an in-vogue décolletage. The blond woman, with rosy cheeks and a small mouth, wore a large, deep-red hat with gray feathers. Other than the cigar name, the remaining lettering is limited to the identification of the manufacturer, at the bottom of the label, in unusually small black print, when compared with the equivalent in figure 3.1.[49] The label does not include the place of origin that served others as an enticement for the smoker, thus following the same marketing strategy employed with El Falco.

After the Foraker Act came into effect in 1900, AWITCO, which was Levi Blumenstiel's local subsidiary, garnered 14.2 percent of all cigar and cigarette exports to New York City. As shown in table 3.1, it comfortably displaced G. W. Sheldon's 10.1 percent to become the largest shipper during 1901–1902.

Some retailers followed the company's policy about place of origin by advertising it with other cigars. For instance, Gardner & Hudgins, a store in Newport News, Virginia, offered a "pointer" on "something tempting" for clients to consider La Turina, alongside the Duke of Warsaw, with no reference to the origins of either.[50] However, other retailers highlighted precisely La Turina's place of origin. The District of Columbia store of G. G. Cornwell & Son provides a good illustration of the latter.[51]

In 1899, the Durlach Brothers partnership expanded its business interests beyond diamonds into the tobacco trade.[52] At least one brother embarked for San Juan, in 1900, to explore the tobacco market and other venues of profit in the unsettled local milieu. For instance, this brother opened an office in San Juan, in association with a Springer, to claim, in the local press, their great expertise as shipping agents, while also giving the Maiden Lane address of the tobacco partnership.[53] Soon the shipping venture gave way to a decades-long business activity with tobacco. Late in 1901, Milton Durlach shipped to New York fifteen cigar cases and twelve bales of tobacco leaf.[54] In the post–Foraker Act period of 1901–1902, the partnership became the third largest shipper with a 6.7 percent share of cigar exports, as presented in table 3.1. The partnership opened factories in Caguas and San Lorenzo and had plantations in the former.[55]

Durlach Brothers promoted El Rigodon and El Bogador more than any of the other brands it manufactured.[56] However, the partnership did not follow Levi Blumenstiel's strategy of concealing the point of origin of its products. In fact, the Durlachs claimed that their cigars "have made Porto Rico cigars famous in the United States" and that Porto Ricos were "an established and staple factor in the retail cigar business."[57] When retail outlets relied on newspaper advertisements, they generally identified the point of origin to bolster the allure of the Durlach Brothers cigar.[58]

In 1899, the Porto Rico cigar, from manufacturers independent of the trust, reached the US market in negligible amounts, followed by a phenomenal increase that almost tripled the twenty-six million cigars of 1901 to some seventy-four million in 1902, as presented in table 3.2. Smokers seemingly developed an insatiable appetite—they were "hungry"—for these cigars, although many fell short on quality.[59] The demand was such that, for a time, the Porto Rico seemed poised to displace a popular cigar crafted with Havana filler and Connecticut wrapper.[60] Local factories proved incapable of fully satisfying the increased demand.[61] The growth resulted in cigars of uneven quality, where some manufacturers maintained the quality that had attracted a devoted following for their brands while others "flooded" the market with the "poorest kind of trash."[62]

A "TEMPORARY SETBACK"

While tobacco men generally agreed on the uneven quality of cigars and the increasing proportion of rank and trashy ones, they offered different explanations. One stressed that the warm reception led to the multiplication of local factories, the tobacco trust included, and to an increase in the output of existing firms. A corollary of the account might be that the inordinate expansion of production became associated with a decay in quality.

In consistency with the account, the Solá, Cádiz and Co. factory in Caguas moved to a larger location to make space for more cigar makers.[63] Las Riberas del Plata, a nineteenth-century operation held by Heraclio Mendoza, added the export trade to its domestic market. In 1901 it committed itself to ship ten thousand cigars per month to F. Bonilla, a New York import company held by a Spaniard.[64] Some four factories, hiring about six hundred cigar makers in total, were to open in San Juan around 1902.[65]

In 1902, a group of Chicago men incorporated the Porto Rico Export Company to enter the cigar business.[66] Almost concurrently, they introduced the Exporto brand and bought Marcial Suárez & Company's La Industrial factory with its tobacco-growing farmland.[67] In keeping with the marketing strategy of other brands, La Industrial and Exporto labels sought the benefits that derived from the identification of their place of origin.[68]

Henry W. Dooley provides another instance of the expansion. After participating in the invasion, he returned immediately after the armistice seeking benefits from the redirection of the colony's trade to the United States.[69] He became a partner of Dooley, Smith and Company, an exporting firm, and established a retail store and a tobacco and cigar business in San Juan.[70]

Another account of the increase in poor-quality cigars placed responsibility on the leaf but not on the handiwork. In 1901, *La Democracia* became one of the earliest voices of alarm over the use of *boliche*, a cheap grade of leaf tobacco, from Cuban and Philippine origin in the manufacture of faux Porto Ricos. Blaming inferior foreign leaf, the article feared for the survival of manufacturers employing local leaf.[71] Another defense singled out unscrupulous firms that employed US leaf in locally manufactured cigars that were then shipped to New York. The counterfeits would bring discredit to the "genuine" product.[72]

The notable increases in the number and scope of cigar manufactures taxed severely the pool of skilled cigar makers, leaf sorters, cigar packers, and others. Just considering one craft, the apprenticeship period to roll, by hand, the more demanding shapes, *vitolas*, lasted for at least three years.[73] Consequently, the increased shipments came at the expense of placing the burden on lesser-skilled hands that did not result in "a corresponding increase in the quality. Indeed, many of the Porto Rico cigars shipped to this country during the past six months have been of decidedly rank and trashy quality."[74] Reputable fabricants had created a niche for the Porto Rico cigar while "others are the poorest kind of trash."[75] The resulting contraction of exports led to a reduction in the number of cigar makers to the extent that a Bureau of Labor report took notice of the "temporary setback" during 1903 and 1904.[76]

A third explanation is that the extraordinary expansion referred to previously not only taxed the capacity of local manufacturers to maintain the quality but enticed some US-based manufacturers to partake in the bonanza by selling their products as manufactured on the island. According to a cigar dealer interviewed by the *New York Times*, the rising demand led to the proliferation of buckeyes, small factories, in the east side of Manhattan to manufacture inferior imitations of the real products but reaping economic benefits because they sold at regular prices.[77] The phenomenon did not go unnoticed among manufacturers and leaf dealers because, for instance, Durlach Brothers denounced the "factories which have sprung up like toad stools, almost in a night, and which are turning out cigars made from anything but genuine Porto Rican leaf."[78]

Consequently, local cigars began to sell at a slow pace, and both jobbers and retailers began to accumulate large inventories.[79] Table 3.2 shows that local exports among independents slumped to thirty-one million units in 1903. The reduced demand seems to have been greater within the cheaper cigars. The more expensive nickel or dime cigars apparently maintained their ground in 1902 and 1903 and contributed to the beginnings of the recovery in 1904.[80] The table also shows that independents shipped some twenty-three million cigars in 1903 that increased to sixty-six million units by 1906, for a remarkable 114 percent expansion.

CAYEY-CAGUAS TOBACCO COMPANY

In a context of oversupply and quality crisis, a new large firm helped to recover the lost ground and pick up the growth of the Porto Rico cigar. Sometime in 1903, a group of investors with limited knowledge of the tobacco industry sought to profit from the trade. Among them, Murray M. Coggeshall, about to become president of the board of directors of the Cayey-Caguas Tobacco Company, established Coggeshall & Hicks, a firm dedicated, from 1906 and on, to banking and the stock market.[81] T. Ludlow Chrystie, a longtime board member, was a well-reputed and an experienced estate tax lawyer from New York.[82] An early board member, Rutger B. Jewett, was soon to become a manager with the Appleton publishing house.[83]

A fourth investor, Frederick R. Hoisington, who became a lifelong board member in 1904, had already provided some economic assistance to Harrison

Johnson when the latter was trying his fortune in Caguas. Johnson became, by 1900 or 1901, a leaf dealer and a cigar manufacturer in association with a member of the Solá family. The factory crafted a common style of a cigar, a *breva*, named McKinley.[84] Johnson's expertise in the field, although limited, earned him the vice presidency of the board of the newly established firm.[85]

Hoisington kept relying on expatriates who, having arrived earlier, had already gained some experience in the field. Brooklyn-born Henry W. Dooley was another early contact who proved useful. In December 1903, his brother William Dooley served as an incorporator of the Cayey-Caguas Tobacco Company in New York and as a signatory that authorized $30,000 in capital stock during March 1904.[86] Henry became the company's first treasurer and local agent while William assumed the post of secretary.[87] Coming full circle, early in 1904 the company bought Henry's tobacco business in San Juan.[88]

The Cayey-Caguas Tobacco Company expanded operations by buying the old La Industrial factory in Cayey and accompanying farmland from the Porto Rico Export Company.[89] At the end of 1904, the new firm had factories in Cayey and Caguas and a head office on Wall Street.[90]

During December 1904, the newly founded firm participated actively in the independent tobacco exposition held in Philadelphia, where all exhibitors had to uphold their opposition to the ATC, the trust. It presented a booth alongside nearly fifty other installations.[91] Maintaining the same antitrust lines, Cayey-Caguas Tobacco sponsored and installed a booth in the 1905, 1906, and 1907 tobacco expositions held in New York's Grand Central Palace or Madison Square Garden.[92] Its antitrust stance went beyond the exhibitions when it strongly opposed the trust's request to build a railroad between Caguas and Río Piedras, discussed in chapter 4.

According to table 3.1, Cayey-Caguas Tobacco accounted for about 12.5 percent of cigar shipments to become by 1907 the second-largest exporter among independents. By 1910, it was second only to the trust.[93] In consonance with the growth in exports, the shareholders authorized the duplication of its capital stock to $60,000, with $50,000 paid in money, shown in table 3.3, to finance its expanding operations. The notable growth of the company's capital reflects a substantial expansion up to 1912, if not later, when the capital stock paid in money reached nearly a quarter of a million dollars.

Substantial parts of the increase in capital provided for the expansion of the workforce in already-established structures and plantations and the rent, purchase, and construction of new ones. By 1905 it employed three hundred cigar makers in Caguas alone.[94] In 1906 it built a large concrete building to house the factory, followed the next year by a concrete warehouse, both in Caguas. Cayey came after with a new concrete cigar factory, a warehouse, and tobacco sheds for the Rincón plantation.[95] Then came the purchase of a concrete building to house its growing workforce and warehousing needs in San Lorenzo.[96] In 1906,

Table 3.3. Capitalization of the Cayey-Caguas Tobacco Company

Year	Authorized capital stock	Capital stock paid in money
1904	30,000	n.a.
1905	60,000	50,000
1906	120,000	80,550
1907	240,000	125,800
1912	360,000	240,075

Sources: "Herbert S. Michael et al. v. Cayey-Caguas Tobacco Company," *Supreme Court of New York, Appellate Division, First Department* 190 (1920): 620–22; Cayey-Caguas Tobacco Company, "Informe anual," 1905–1912, AGPR, Estado, Corporaciones foráneas con fines de lucro, caja 5, expediente 86.

the company moved its offices and depot to a larger structure on Front Street, followed by a 1908 relocation to Water Street, also in Manhattan.[97]

Cayey-Caguas Tobacco quickly integrated vertically to become an agribusiness. As stated, it purchased some farmland in Cayey when it bought La Industrial factory, but when the need arose, it rented additional farmland. As the manufacture of cigars kept growing, it expanded on the initial farmland by buying additional acreage that, by 1906, included 200 acres planted with tobacco.[98] Franklin H. Bunker, another expatriate, joined the firm in 1906 to head the planting department, where he was responsible for the purchase and cultivation of two plantations, a 167-cuerdas one in barrio Borinquen of Caguas and another, with 380 cuerdas, in barrio Rincón of Cayey.[99] Like other large agribusinesses, such as PRATCO, it established the Johnson Development Company to manage the agricultural side of the enterprise.[100] Sometime later, the company purchased 211 cuerdas in barrio Arenas of Cidra.[101] By 1912, the firm held 1,047 acres dispersed in several municipalities.[102]

The firm seems to have been profitable up to 1911. Dividends for 1908–1911 averaged 8 percent and 9 percent in its preferred and common stock respectively.[103] Shareholders reaped large benefits comparable to those of local subsidiaries of the tobacco trust, discussed in the following chapter. To cap it all, in 1911, the firm paid an enormous stock dividend of 100 percent that derived from accumulated earnings. Possibly stimulated by the hefty returns from their investments in local tobacco and cigars, three board members, Coggeshall, Chrystie, and Hoisington, chartered the Imported Cigar Company in New York in 1910.[104]

However, a closer look at the financial data shows a consistent reduction in net profits from $54,334.87 in 1909 and $44,183.11 in 1910 to $18,819.25 in 1911.[105] As its well-being deteriorated, by 1912 it had ceased paying dividends. In a civil suit, the company successfully claimed that it had no surplus or net profits and its assets after 1912 did not cover the debts and the value of its outstanding stock.[106]

During 1904–1907, the company had vigorously assumed an antitrust position, but by 1913, possibly due to lower cigar production, it was in business with its former adversaries. The reversal serves as a useful indicator of the company's difficulties. During the 1913 and 1914 seasons, Cayey-Caguas Tobacco partly financed its leaf growing through a $20,000 crop lien, *refacción*, with PRATCO. It committed to plant seventy-five cuerdas of shade-grown tobacco in its Borinquen and Rincón plantations.[107] In 1916, Franklin H. Bunker left the company's plantations to manage those of PRLTC, another former trust company.[108]

Cayey-Caguas Tobacco and its related enterprises, the Johnson Development, and the Endorso Cigar companies began to sell their assets in a process that ended with their dissolution by 1918.[109] In that same year, Mateo Rucabado bought the barrio Arenas farm, which had already abandoned tobacco for growing sugarcane financed with a crop lien from the Cayey Sugar Company. Rucabado also purchased the Rincón plantation then held by the Johnson Development Company.[110] H. Duys and Company, a large Manhattan leaf firm, diversified into the local leaf market by taking over the Caguas warehouses that Harrison Johnson started to manage in 1919.[111] The trademarks of Cayey-Caguas Tobacco left no known records after the firm's end save for the Savarona brand, which survived in the hands of other manufacturers at least until 1921.[112]

In 1905, Cayey-Caguas Tobacco introduced a cigar style under the name of Savarona that became its leading brand.[113] Following a common practice among larger manufacturers, the firm provided materials to retailers that displayed the brands in a shop window.[114] One such display was in a Schulte chain store, at the impressive Penn Station in New York.[115] The Fay Lewis & Brother Company often dedicated a shop window to the Savarona cigar at its Pabst Building store, in what was Milwaukee's first skyscraper. At times the displays also featured views of the company's factories and plantations.[116] Other less-upscale stores like Baltimore's Lilly, Duncan & Company, displayed the cigar in their shop windows.[117] Some retailers followed another common promotion of the times by promoting their goods with tokens. One of these was "Good for one Savarona 10¢ Porto Rican cigar."[118]

The company promoted itself and its products often in the tobacco trade journals. For instance, between October 1910 and February 1911 it posted nine nearly identical advertisements in a preordained sequence in the *United States Tobacco Journal* and *Tobacco World*. This campaign identified eight reasons for smoking Savaronas, where the first three factors drew on the benefits of association the cigar with its geographical origins.[119]

However, Hoisington, by then the firm's president, went on record to state that it advertised sparingly in newspapers read by the general public. He followed a policy "to put the value into the goods rather than into advertising."[120] Nevertheless, some retailers posted a few ads pointing out that Savaronas were the "nearest approach in taste to real Havana cigars," but carefully stressed their national origin because they were "strictly high grade 10c Porto Rican cigars and not Havana."[121]

THE IMPLOSION

Following the invasion, many independent manufacturers developed the "Porto Rico," a type of cigar that briefly had a space of its own. However, this world experienced a notable collapse during the 1910s. The collapse entailed the closing of factories in several locations that included Cayey, Caguas, Utuado, Arecibo, and other municipalities within a brief spate of time. These factories changed the structure of several urban centers by giving them their "first large secular buildings."[122] They altered town life by spawning a large working class that challenged the domination of traditional elites. What is another explanation for the anarchist Centro de Estudios Sociales in Caguas and its profound antagonism that led to the murder of Adrián Pérez, who managed an AWITCO factory?[123] As reviewed previously, where would Samuel Gompers have stopped by, in 1904, had AWITCO's factory, known as La Turina, not been in operation? Gompers's trip took place at a time when, according to table 3.2, independents produced two cigars for each that PRATCO manufactured.[124]

As the chapter's early section documented the organization and expansion of these manufacturers, what follows presents the implosion of AWITCO. Two partners of Levi Blumenstiel, AWITCO's parent company, engaged in a legal dispute in 1907 that left it in the hands of receivers.[125] Aside from the lawsuit in the parent company, in 1908 the subsidiary maintained its expansion by increasing its authorized capital from $250,000 to $500,000.[126] Again, the assets of the corporation increased to $710,478.83 in 1909.[127] The subsidiary retained a constant presence in the export market to at least January 1912.[128]

Whether related to the legal proceedings or not, in 1908, the American and West Indies Sales Company, a New York corporation, intended to take over the sales department of AWITCO.[129] Presided by Morris J. Levi, it also served for some time as sales agent to some Havana factories and in time started to manufacture cigars in Pennsylvania.[130] It also had an $8,000 participation in two New Orleans tobacco companies, Valloft & Dreux and the Independent Cigar Stores.[131] Its radius of action extended well beyond AWITCO's specialization in Puerto Rico to include manufacture and distribution in the United States and a participation in the Havana trade. Despite their separate corporate structures, both firms maintained close economic relations for years to come.[132]

Investments that went sour—like the New Orleans venture that ended in a 1912 bankruptcy—bad decisions, and the changing tobacco trade led the interrelated companies to severe economic difficulties that became public in 1915. For instance, the American and West Indies Sales Company owed the Girard National Bank in Philadelphia more than $104,000, not including costs and interests. This tobacco company had repaid some $38,000 in cash and about $19,000 in accounts collectable, leaving an unpaid balance of $52,000. The tobacco company transferred the note to the American West Indies Cigar Company [*sic*], which, in turn, endorsed it to the Plantation Company, with the latter turning it over to Girard. The bank, unable to recover the balance, sued to gain possession of $15,000 worth of Puerto Rican tobacco belonging to the Plantation Company, American and West Indies Sales Company, and AWITCO. Earlier, the Philadelphia Warehouse Company had, in custody of the court, additional unspecified quantities of tobacco to cover unpaid debts.[133] These court cases left AWITCO and its related companies "sadly crippled."[134]

In 1916 another interrelated company, identified as the American West Indies Company, transferred several cigar brands, including the well-known La Turina, to the Cien Porciento Company.[135] While Gregorio López Falcó notified the Puerto Rican treasurer of the dissolution of AWITCO in 1916, it was most likely that the affiliated companies also ceased operations.[136] By 1918, Cien Porciento had its main office on Liberty Street in Lower Manhattan, with factories, warehouses, and plantations in Caguas, Gurabo, and Aguas Buenas. Spreading across three municipalities and being vertically integrated, the corporation itself employed some 250 workers. This Delaware corporation's capitalization, at $50,000, was much lower than the comparable figures for AWITCO, reviewed previously.[137]

While AWITCO's failure was unique in many ways, it followed a pattern where all large independent cigar manufacturers went out of business in a short period during the mid-1910s. Among these stood out the Cayey-Caguas Tobacco Company and Infanzón y Rodríguez, which sold La Habanera to PRATCO in 1916.[138] The West Indies Cigar Company ceased operations in 1917, and Durlach Brothers closed its factories sometime in 1914 or soon afterward but remained a significant leaf dealer and lien merchant for years to come.[139] By 1918, all the major independent cigar manufacturers (with shares for 1901–1902 and 1907 presented in table 3.1) had ceased all tobacco operations or, at least, shuttered their cigar manufacturing venues.[140] Their failure was unrelated to the onslaught of the cigarette that came after World War I or to technological developments like the mechanical cigar maker, whose introduction dates from 1919.

Chapter 5 discusses the factors that affected PRATCO and its subsidiaries and that most likely hastened the collapse of the more fragile independent manufacturers. Consequently, as time went on, PRATCO manufactured an ever-increasing proportion of local cigars. Although no systematic production statistics are available after 1906, data from Reavis Cox allows an estimate of 77.5 percent in 1921.[141]

A few old factories, like La Flor de Cayey, maintained a presence into the twenties, and new ones like Bosch Brothers entered the field and maintained offices in the Manhattan tobacco district.[142] Beyond a handful, what remained was a plethora of buckeyes with scant advertising resources in the press and magazines, virtually no displays in cigar stores, and few if any sales representatives canvassing their territory.[143] Consequently, it is very likely that PRATCO manufactured the Porto Ricos smoked in the hotel room, described at the beginning of this chapter, from Conrad Aiken's 1934 short story.

CHAPTER FOUR

The Tobacco Trust in Puerto Rico, 1899–1911

In 1910, all 1,979 residents of barrio Toíta of Cayey were native born save for three Spaniards and two US citizens. All five men worked in agriculture, as did most who were gainfully employed. While the Spaniards worked on diversified farms, the other two worked on tobacco farms where a subsidiary of the ATC, the trust, had extensive plantations that specialized in shade-grown tobacco. George T. Bullock was a farm foreman who lived alongside the Carretera Central in La Plata Valley in living quarters he shared with George N. Lewis, who was the sole farm manager living in the barrio. Both were married but unaccompanied.[1] By 1917, Bullock had been promoted to Cayey representative of the same tobacco firm.[2]

George and his brother Walter, both born in Williamsboro, North Carolina, started attending the North Carolina College of Agriculture and Mechanic Arts in 1891, with the latter earning an agricultural degree in 1895 and the former dropping out due to an extended illness. Upon graduation, Walter worked for a big farming concern in Decatur County, Georgia, where shade tobacco growing was expanding.[3] George worked in a tobacco test farm in Rocky Mount, North Carolina, before joining Walter at Decatur in 1906 to plant tobacco on their own, but they had to sell for lack of working capital. Both then worked for the trust from 1909 to 1917, with Walter residing in Aibonito and George in Cayey.[4] Seemingly, the college training in a major tobacco-growing state served them well in southwestern Georgia, where the brothers must have picked the techniques of shade growing that they subsequently carried to La Plata.[5]

When researchers refer to the ATC, they typically have in mind the cigarette manufacturing colossus that expanded its monopoly to plug tobacco in the United States and cigarettes in the United Kingdom. With so powerful a reach, the US Supreme Court dissolved the trust in a landmark decision. This chapter, however, connects the microcosm of Lewis, the Bullock brothers, and the anonymous men and women toiling in distant tobacco plantations back to 111 Fifth Avenue in New York City. It traces the development of three subsidiaries whose range went from large tobacco plantations in Puerto Rico to cigar marketing in the

United States. The chapter documents ATC's beginnings in San Juan, follows its diversification into cigars and the development of an agribusiness, and ends with the court-mandated partition in 1911.

When the representatives of the trust arrived in the aftermath of the invasion, the partnership of Rucabado y Portela manufactured cigarettes in a steam-driven plant in San Juan. Within the factory, leaf sorters and graders manually classified the dark tobacco grown in the plantations of Rucabado and Company, which had an economic interest in the partnership. A group of tobacco cutters fed the leaves to, most likely, Dubrul shredders that cut and granulated the filler to desired shapes and lengths such as *hebra brea* or *pectoral*.[6] Then, eight leased Bonsack machines and several Comas manufactured the shredded tobacco into various types of cigarettes depending on the characteristics of the cut tobacco.[7] Finally, the packers fitted the loose cigarettes into paper boxes printed at the *Boletín Mercantil*. La Colectiva, as the plant was known, had a daily production of some four hundred thousand cigarettes.[8]

THE BEGINNINGS OF THE PORTO RICAN–AMERICAN TOBACCO COMPANY

In 1899 John Blackwell Cobb, a Tar Heel tobacco man and a major figure in the ATC, traveled to Puerto Rico to take advantage of the window of opportunity opened by the invasion. Together with a group of men connected to his employer, he incorporated PRATCO in Newark on 22 September 1899.[9] Cobb attended personally the negotiations where the company bought, on 9 October, La Colectiva from Rucabado y Portela. The October acquisition was retroactive to mid-August, perhaps delayed by the slow recuperation from the massive hurricane named for San Ciriaco that made landfall on 8 August. At the end of 1899, ATC held $99,100 of the $166,000 worth of PRATCO while Rucabado y Portela owned the balance.[10] The deal did not amount to sailing in clear waters for an important third party, the machine operatives, who had claims of their own. In October 1899, they drafted a flyer and went on the first of many strikes while denouncing changes in factory personnel and Rucabado y Portela for a lucrative deal that denied them a piece rate increase.[11]

Within months, in May 1900, PRATCO brought La Internacional, which included the factories of Toro y Cía. in Ponce, for $153,716.40 on terms similar to those for Rucabado y Portela. Toro employed some five hundred workers in its single cigar manufactory in Ponce proper and in its combined cigar and cigarette factory by the Playa de Ponce. The firm had a yearly production of six million cigars and seventy-five million cigarettes.[12]

The addition of the two firms to the newly organized PRATCO followed the ATC's well-traveled path of acquisitions. The board of directors and the incorporators included John Blackwell Cobb, who was a high-profile trust man with a presence on the island. George M. Gales, another Tar Heel tobacco man with ample experience in the tobacco trade, was also an incorporator and member of the first board of directors.[13] However, the "rich financial people," in the words of James B. Duke, were nearly absent from the board of directors of the local company but were all board members of the ATC, the primary trust company, in 1904. Duke was the only member of the six men in control of the trust to join the board of both companies. These men need not be present in any subsidiary because the ownership structure allowed them full control of the parent company and, through it, of all others.[14] From 1899 to 1901, only two ATC directors, Duke and Cobb, appeared as directors of the local company.[15]

Four men, bearing a property relation to the acquired plants and a junior participation in the new one, became directors between 1899 and 1901. José Portela, Fausto Rucabado, and Mateo Rucabado were partners of Rucabado y Portela. Additionally, Fausto and José worked for the company for a year, with Fausto serving as second vice president. Luis Toro had been the managing partner of Toro y Cía., which owned La Internacional, and then in 1901 he assumed the presidency of PRATCO for more than thirty years.[16]

The ATC did not integrate the new company fully into its management structure, possibly because it could not procure the subsidiary's leaf input from its own buying department, nor could its marketing department sell locally manufactured cigarettes such as Colectiva and Toro. PRATCO employed dark tobacco from the island's highlands, whereas the ATC relied on flue-cured bright leaf from the tobacco belt of Virginia and the Carolinas, and the former's market was the island itself whereas the ATC's was the United States.[17] The result was that the ATC provided the legal and organizational structure to control a cigarette manufacturing firm that could not be merged with the US-based cigarette manufacturing plants.

During its first three years, PRATCO significantly increased its shipments of cigars to the United States through channels independent of the trust. The cigar output for 1899 is unavailable, but it must have been negligible because its manufacturing capacity rested in cigarettes. Once the Organic Act of 1900 (known as the Foraker Act) allowed the duty-free entrance of Puerto Rican cigars and the firm had acquired La Internacional, both in 1900, the firm contracted Julius Becker to distribute El Toro cigars from the Ponce plant.[18] The trust still lacked an adequate sales structure to market cigars. In 1900, it shipped 133,147 cigars to New York in time for the Christmas season. A year later, it manufactured 2,955,481 units, all of them exported to the United States. The 1901 shipments amounted to 10.2 percent of the 29,064,000 cigars exported.[19]

The local subsidiary maintained a formidable presence in the manufacture of cigarettes for the domestic market. Its cigarette output for 1899 is unavailable, but it was sizable because its main competition came from La Internacional and the much smaller La Habanera in Mayagüez. Its cigarette output for 1900 was 117,455,950, and for 1901 it amounted to 143,454,415.[20]

In 1900, PRATCO announced the construction of a three-story cement, brick, and mortar plant with an approximate area of 22,500 square feet to match its projected growth. During the same year, the company increased its outstanding capital from $166,000 to $300,000 by issuing more shares to finance the new plant.[21] Opened in 1901, La Marina factory, in Old San Juan, accommodated between 400 and 500 workers, but by 1903, it employed close to 1,200 in several departments that included the old stemming and cigarette departments from Rucabado y Portela and a new cigar-making one.[22]

The return rate on the value of the $166,000 par value of stocks for 1899 is unavailable. However, PRATCO had profits in the order of 6 percent of the $300,000 par value of its stock for both 1900 and 1901. The comparable earnings of the American Cigar Company, the main trust's cigar division, were a paltry 0.9 percent in 1901 in comparison with the three major trust companies, which had earnings of 12.6 percent over total investment for 1900.[23] The local subsidiary was more profitable than the American Cigar Company but fared well below the major trust companies.

When organized in 1890 through the merger of five cigarette manufacturing companies, the ATC manufactured 88.1 percent of the US cigarette production, which subsequently increased to 93.0 percent in 1899.[24] Consequently, its specialty in cigarettes dictated its manufacturing policy abroad. Up to 1901 it had either bought or established fourteen cigarette enterprises outside the United States. With factories in Australia by 1894, in New Zealand and Canada by 1895, in Japan by 1899, and in Germany and Britain by 1901, it entered a price-slashing war and business takeovers against British interests over worldwide control of cigarette markets in 1901. The "Tobacco War," settled advantageously to the ATC in 1902, granted it more benefits from the British American Tobacco Company, the joint venture that brought the conflict to an end.[25] The buyouts of La Colectiva and La Internacional were trendsetting in the Caribbean but were part and parcel of the expansion of the ATC's cigarette business to the four corners of the world.[26]

THE CIGAR TRADE

By 1899, the trust had achieved extraordinary market shares over nearly all major tobacco products that included cigarettes, snuff, and smoking tobacco in the United Sates. It had just emerged with 60.6 percent of chewing tobacco production after the "Plug War" of 1895–1898 against Liggett and Myers and the Union Tobacco Company.[27]

However, the ATC was a minor player in the most important tobacco business in the United States, the cigar. In 1904, the value of cigars was more than 50 percent greater than the combined value of all other tobacco manufactures. In 1891, the ATC gained a limited participation in the cigar business with the purchase of P. Whitlock with branches in Richmond and Baltimore and in 1899 with Banner from Lancaster, Pennsylvania, and M. S. Pacholder & Co. also from Baltimore; two of these manufactured a native cigar known as cheroot. The trust also purchased the United States Cigar Machine and Manufacturing Company in 1899. These purchases gained the trust 4.0 percent of all cigars in 1899 and 4.8 percent in 1900.[28] Three factories, a cigar machine company, and the purchase of La Internacional, with its cigar-making department, were the beginnings of the trust's attempt to control the manufacture and market for cigars.

Preparations continued with increased cigar production in established plants, a new factory in Cincinnati, and experimental work in a small New York workshop. In late 1899, the trust attempted but failed to buy the recently consolidated Kerbs, Wertheim & Schiffer and Straiton & Storm Company, one of the largest cigar manufacturers in the United States with some four thousand employees in 1897 and accounting for approximately 2.5 percent of cigars manufactured in 1896.[29] Cigar manufacturing in the United States, in contrast to cigarettes and plug before the trust, was highly fragmented into countless firms. When the trust incorporated the American Cigar Company in January 1901, it did not face a Liggett and Myers or an Imperial Tobacco Company, large rivals that led to the competitive wars that preceded the formation of the Continental Tobacco in plug and the British American Tobacco in cigarettes.

The primary trust companies transferred the brands and factories of most of their cigar businesses to the new subsidiary, the American Cigar Company. The companies that organized the ATC in 1890 lost their idiosyncrasies and separate legal structures soon after. In this sense, the ATC followed the known path after the founding of the trust. At the inception of American Cigar, to present an example from the cigar trade, what remained of the P. Whitlock company was a plant with the firm's name, a valuable brand, and the owner converted to an employee, Philip Whitlock, who joined the board of directors. The cigar company lost its commercial and legal identity very much the same way the original companies of the trust had lost theirs.

Rucabado y Portela and La Internacional lost their legal personae to PRATCO. Other than the brand names of their cigarettes, what remained of Rucabado y Portela was the name La Colectiva, which the public transferred to the new company. However, the ATC did not merge PRATCO into the American Cigar Company. PRATCO retained a separate corporate structure with its own directors and stockholders that seems to have corresponded with the types of cigars that then characterized the US market. By 1906, the ATC organized stogies, usually manufactured in West Virginia and Pennsylvania with short (chopped) filler, into the (1) American Stogie Company; (2) the American Cigar manufactured inexpensive cigars named cheroots, nickel cigars from US tobacco, and the blended "Seed and Havana" from Cuban and US tobacco; the (3) Havana-American Company handcrafted "Clear Havanas" manufactured in the United States from imported Cuban leaf; the (4) Havana Tobacco Company for those crafted in Cuba itself; and finally (5) the PRATCO for the cigars known as "Porto Rico."[30] The American Cigar Company controlled the four companies where, in turn, many of these firms had their own specialized subsidiaries. The result was that the ATC "provided the legal form to maintain tighter control over a federation" of cigar-related manufacturing companies.[31]

EXPANSION OF CIGAR MANUFACTURES

When the ATC sold half its stock in PRATCO to American Cigar in 1904, the local subsidiary had already started a two-prong expansion. It expanded the cigar-making department that came with La Internacional and developed a new one with the 1901 opening of La Marina factory in the capital, where the combined output of the two plants amounted to 2,955,431 units a year. Within five years, exports grew quickly to 61,364,075 cigars for a 43.0 percent market share in 1906, to 117,500,000 units for a 41.7 percent share by 1912.[32]

PRATCO's expansion carefully considered that the ATC's monopolistic practices provoked strong public, trade union, and legal opposition in the United States that eventually led to a court-ordered dissolution. In response, the trust created several seemingly independent firms to cater to the tastes of its enemies. In 1903, a group of men close to the trust and PRATCO organized and managed the Industrial Company.[33] It was much smaller than PRATCO. The former's capital stock in 1907 was $83,000, whereas the outstanding stock of the latter stood at $1,999,400.[34] In 1906, PRATCO's output of cigars added to 54.8 million, whereas the Industrial Company manufactured 6.6 million.[35] Given its Ponce location, its assets were most likely those of La Internacional.

Managers and officials probably sought to convey an image of independence from the trust.[36] The subsidiary manufactured "El Timonel," whose lithograph, in the inner lid of the cigar box, identified the Compañía Industrial as its current owner and the previous one as Sucesores de Mayol Hermanos with no reference to the PRATCO.[37] As another sign of independence, in 1903, the Industrial Company had storage and marketing facilities at 135 Front Street in Lower Manhattan close to many independent cigar firms and away from PRATCO's offices.[38] Julius Becker, perhaps too identified with the trust, ceased managing La Internacional's cigar exports.

In 1902, *Tobacco*, a US-based trade journal, stated that "one of the marked developments in the cigar trade during the past few months has been the steadily

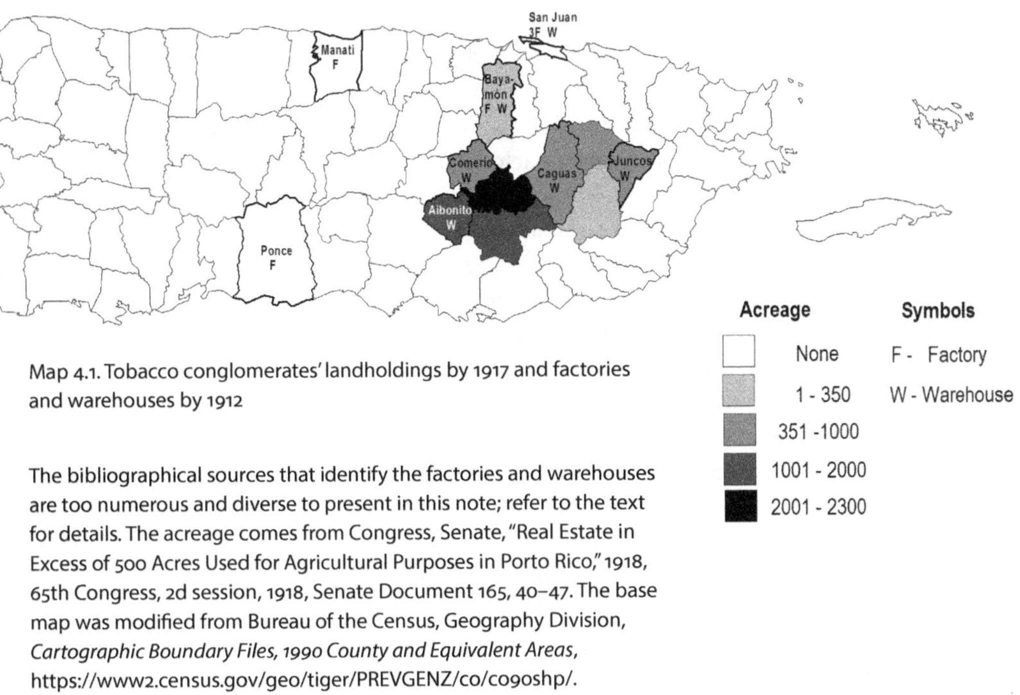

Map 4.1. Tobacco conglomerates' landholdings by 1917 and factories and warehouses by 1912

The bibliographical sources that identify the factories and warehouses are too numerous and diverse to present in this note; refer to the text for details. The acreage comes from Congress, Senate, "Real Estate in Excess of 500 Acres Used for Agricultural Purposes in Porto Rico," 1918, 65th Congress, 2d session, 1918, Senate Document 165, 40–47. The base map was modified from Bureau of the Census, Geography Division, *Cartographic Boundary Files, 1990 County and Equivalent Areas*, https://www2.census.gov/geo/tiger/PREVGENZ/co/co90shp/.

growing demand for Porto Rico cigars. At the present time, the demand is far in excess of the supply, and it seems likely to continue so for some time to come."[39] La Marina and the Ponce factories evidently failed to satisfy the growing appetite for "Porto Rico" cigars. Around 1903, the trust established a branch in a rented two-story house by Bayamón's town square that, within a few years, it moved to a new four-story brick-and-mortar plant in the same town. By 1906, La Marina and Bayamón branches employed 1,726 workers.[40] Map 4.1 shows the geographical spread of the trust from its initial factories in San Juan and Ponce.

As the market for "Porto Rico" cigars kept expanding, the trust responded by increasing production. Following the Bayamón factory, PRATCO established a new branch when, in 1906, it bought from the city of San Juan the building that had housed the provincial jail.[41] As on earlier occasions, the board of directors partially financed the expansion by a large increase in the capital stock to $2,000,000. Soon after, the Puerta de Tierra factory opened to become the largest cigar factory on the island for decades to come, with its vicinity becoming the home to thousands. Together with the Bayamón branch, the working-class culture that developed around, in, and out of the factories became a hotbed for socialist and anarchist ideas and organizations.[42]

The PRLTC, another subsidiary, opened the fifth trust plant with steam-driven machinery to manufacture cigar boxes and shipping cartons. Beside the

Miramar suburb of San Juan, the factory was conveniently located by the tracks of the American Railroad Company that connected it to the Puerta de Tierra factory and, farther down the line, to the docks. Nevertheless, the subsidiary sought government authorization to build a road through the mangroves to the San Juan estuary.[43] The factory started operation sometime between 1907, when the PRLTC bought the land parcel, and 1916, when it first appears reported.[44]

PRATCO experienced an unabated expansion from inception to soon after 1906. During the following years, expansion continued at a slower pace. The company established no more branches until 1911, seemingly satisfied with increasing production from the five in operation. In 1912, it started the construction of a branch in Manatí and an overhaul of the Ponce plant.[45]

Increasing cigar production needed a swift articulation to a wide-ranging distribution and marketing network. Julius Becker, an independent jobber who briefly distributed PRATCO's cigars and cigarettes, had a small radius of operations that did not extend far beyond Manhattan. In 1901, as the trust attempted to monopolize the cigar trade with Havanas, Porto Ricos, cheroots, and the like, it incorporated the United Cigar Stores Company to distribute mainly its own cigars and other tobacco products in retail outlets throughout the United States.

Within six years, the chain had opened 392 stores, giving priority to large cities with 178 outlets in New York City alone, 38 in Chicago, 31 in San Francisco and 12 in Boston. The outlets had elaborate window displays, and some were appealing enough not only to entice the passerby but also to become newsworthy. For instance, the *Tobacco* journal reported that PRATCO's "Porto Ricans are this week displayed in attractive fashion at the Flatiron store of the United Cigar Stores Co." on the corner of Twenty-Third Street and Broadway in Manhattan.[46]

The trust supplemented the retail outlet strategy with a less expensive concept that assured a deeper market penetration. The National Cigar Stands Company, founded in 1905, sold its products to participating pharmacies at a discount and provided specially designed cases to exhibit the merchandise. By 1907, it had contracts with 2,062 pharmacies.[47]

BACKWARD INTEGRATION INTO AGRICULTURE: THE PORTO RICAN LEAF TOBACCO COMPANY

When the trust purchased leaf for cigarettes, snuff, smoking tobacco, and plug in the United Sates, it did not acquire tobacco land suitable for these products. The ATC participated in the hogshead and loose-leaf auctions and, in time, developed its own purchasing department. Its expansion into the cigar trade required a large and stable leaf supply. It typically bought binder and filler leaf in Ohio, Pennsylvania, Wisconsin, and New York under the country sales system in which the farmer contracted his crop with the buyer during the growing or curing season. Wrapper marketing showed a variation by the fact that the buyer, usually a packer or dealer, partnered with the farmer to further process the leaf.[48] Many US dealers and large manufacturers also bought Sumatra and Java wrapper at yearly auctions held in Rotterdam and at Frascati in Amsterdam.[49]

However, the policy changed when it came to leaf for Havana and Porto Rico cigars. This chapter holds that the reversal was intimately related to a change in the ways that cigars appealed to the smoker during the last third of the nineteenth century. Smokers began associating mildness with light-colored wrappers that led to enormous demand for a leaf in short supply.[50] The development and diffusion of light-colored wrappers offer an explanation for the ATC's policy shift. From about 1863 until the Second World War, the Dutch organized and managed a system of plantations in some sectors of Sumatra that set the standard for light-colored wrappers. The sun-grown leaf was thin, elastic, light in color, and finely veined with excellent combustibility and a pleasing aroma.[51] While cigar manufacturers paid premium prices for the commodity, growers elsewhere experimented with different leaf strains, planting, cultivating, and harvesting methods to imitate, if not surpass, the coveted wrapper.[52]

During the 1880s, Francisco B. Cruz, a Cuban agronomist, noticed that, during a rainy winter, tobacco leaves approximated the Sumatra standard. Consequently, planters started to irrigate the crops destined for wrappers. Irrigation became, in time, a powerful complement to cheesecloth-shaded tobacco because the latter reduced evaporation. Luis Marx was the first Cuban to plant tobacco under cheesecloth in 1901 on his farms in Alquízar. He was followed by Calixto López in 1902 in Vuelta Abajo.[53] When F. A. Schroeder traveled to Cuba, he saw wrapper leaf intercropped with trees to benefit from the shade. Back in Gadsden County, Florida, in 1896 he had half an acre planted with tobacco shaded by evenly placed slats that soon gave in to "cloth tenting" by the Owl Commercial Company. In 1901, growers planted a thousand acres of shaded tobacco that was the beginning of a commercial success.[54] The ATC's incursion in the manufacture of cigars took place when "cloth tenting" from Georgia and Florida had already reached Cuba and the Connecticut Valley.[55] Had the trust purchased Kerbs, Wertheim & Schiffer and Straiton & Storm Company, as indicated previously, it would have entered the shade tobacco business as early as 1899 because the latter owned the Owl Commercial Company.[56]

The establishment of the American Cigar Company in 1901 took place in the midst of the diffusion of shade-grown tobacco. Hoping to bring the price down by growing its own wrapper leaf, in March 1902 the ATC expressed an interest in 150 acres of shade tobacco in Suffield, Connecticut, but seemingly lost it when the media described the 1902 and 1903 crops as the "Sumatra fiasco."[57] As of 1902, the trust had been unable to plant its own sources of light-colored wrappers, whereas the Kerbs, Wertheim & Schiffer, and Straiton & Storm Company, its main competitor, had them.[58]

In 1902, the American Cigar Company, possibly encouraged by the ongoing ventures with shade tobacco, incorporated the wholly owned Cuban Land and Leaf Tobacco Company in New Jersey to grow, buy, and handle leaf principally to supply its manufacturing branches. By 1906, it claimed to control 210,000 acres, much of it forested, in western Cuba and had some eight thousand employees.[59]

Also in 1902, American Cigar and PRATCO organized the PRLTC with the same goals and an authorized capital stock of $150,000. However, the trust's incursion into shade tobacco growing in Puerto Rico was not as sure footed as the Cuban one. In 1901, a tobacco planter, most likely Rafael María González, offered the Department of Agriculture suitable land in La Plata Valley with labor, gear, and implements for experimental purposes.[60] Months later, under González's supervision, workers prepared seedbeds and transplanted the seedlings to a cheesecloth-covered field that yielded, early in 1902, large and bug-free leaves deemed satisfactory for wrappers.[61] Then, Johannes van Leenhoff, a Dutch tobacco expert with a position at the Agricultural Experiment Station in Mayagüez, evaluated the benefits of several growing and cultivating methods in the local context during 1903–1904. These experiments—carried out in various locations, among them Jayuya and Aibonito—led to the conclusion that "it may safely be said that shading increases the yield, quality, and percentage of wrappers sufficiently to make shading a profitable business."[62] The trust harvested the first fruits because its employees carried the Aibonito experiments.[63] Luis Toro, the PRLTC's president, announced that as of 1904 the shade tobacco "experiment" covered 115 acres between Cayey and Aibonito, with plans to extend it to Juncos.[64]

During those years, several southerners, like the Bullock brothers and George N. Lewis, joined the company to manage and supervise the shade tobacco plantations. They must have diffused the wiring and covering tobacco with cheesecloth techniques from the Georgia and Florida border and the appropriate harvesting methods. Priming, which consists of removing individual leaves as they ripen without affecting the stalk, was common in the harvesting of Sumatra wrappers, dominant in flue-cured tobacco for cigarettes, and indispensable for shade-grown tobacco.[65]

Large expenses in wooden posts, wire, and cheesecloth to cover the field and heavier use of fertilizers, which in La Plata ranged from seven hundred to one thousand pounds per acre, discouraged small and medium farmers from planting shade tobacco.[66] Labor became more intensive as a result of priming instead of stalk cutting and additional care in the drying barns. Consequently, locally as elsewhere, shade tobacco became the province of corporations such as the PRLTC and the Cayey-Caguas Tobacco Company or large growers like Baltasar Mendoza.[67]

As of 1906, PRATCO held 11.9 percent of the common stock of the PRLTC, while American Cigar owned 50.7 percent, with the balance in other hands. As in earlier expansions, PRATCO partially financed its participation in the PRLTC by increasing its outstanding capital in 1902 to $400,000 by issuing additional stock.[68] The composition of the PRLTC's directors and officers followed the model that the ATC had used with other subsidiaries. James Buchanan Duke was the only member of the group of the six largest shareholders of the trust to appear as a director. Duke and Cobb were the only members of the primary trust companies to sit on the board of the local company.[69] However, three men with knowledge of the tobacco trade, who once had a property relation to La Internacional and Rucabado y Portela and holding a junior participation in the new one, became directors. Luis Toro assumed the presidency for years to come. H. C. Fritze was a principal in a partnership with a strong economic participation in Toro y Cía. Manuel Otero Varela had been a partner to Rucabado y Portela and complemented his commercial and banking activities with tobacco growing.[70]

When the trust entered tobacco growing, it did not buy established firms with formidable market shares as happened with PRATCO's purchase of La Colectiva and La Internacional. In comparison, the development of a large tobacco-growing and financial structure proved more difficult. The PRLTC started from a base where thousands of farmers grew tobacco, but few had achieved any vertical integration. It developed an infrastructure to prepare seedbeds and plant, cultivate, harvest, and cure tobacco. It also built a network to finance tobacco growing among independent farmers. The company also built warehouses and stemmeries and contracted thousands to stem, classify, ferment, and transport leaf.

The PRLTC secured leaf for PRATCO and American Cigar through diverse mechanisms. It bought, administered, rented, mortgaged land, and financed crops. One such transaction presents the painful and complicated process of building up a large estate and a web of business relations.

In 1893, Sobrinos de Ezquiaga owned two wooden houses in Cayey, one of which housed a coffee mill with a steam-driven engine to dry, shell, and fan the beans. This firm opened a 25,000 pesos credit line and lent the properties to Modesto Munitiz Aguirre, a Spaniard, to run the mill on a profit-sharing arrangement. However, Sobrinos de Ezquiaga took Munitiz to court in 1904 for breach of contract and claimed an accumulated debt of US$80,199.40 to be satisfied by an embargo of the defendant's properties. On appeal, the Puerto Rico Supreme Court lifted the embargo until the plaintiff practiced a balance on the account.[71] Munitiz gained time to salvage his dire financial situation.

In his predicament, he reached several economic arrangements with John Blackwell Cobb, who acted on behalf of the PRLTC. In 1906, on the very same day that court lifted the embargo, Munitiz mortgaged twenty-five properties for $29,900. He also sold several mortgages in his favor for $5,000. Munitiz con-

Figure 4.1. A. Moscioni, 396 Porto Rican American Tobacco Company, La Plata, 1907–1915, UPR, Colección Puertorriqueña, Fotografías de A. Moscioni, foto 9.

tracted to plant sixty-five cuerdas of tobacco on his property named Lucía and sell the leaf to the company. He also sold his ox teams and their respective carts for $10,000, with the repurchase agreement, while contracting the transport to the company's leaf from Aibonito to San Juan for additional fees. Munitiz, given more felicitous circumstances, could have made a preferable deal. He doubtless got a reprieve from his down-spiraling situation where Cobb negotiated from a position of strength.

He seems to have survived his financial straits. The Treasury Department identified him as the owner of six properties in Cayey—excluding Cidra, where he also had real estate—for the 1910–1911 tax year. One was the old 222-cuerda hacienda Lucía, presumably then a tobacco plantation. A second property was a 71-cuerda farm in barrio Montellano assessed at $3,990, with three or more houses valued at $6,000 and an unidentified movable property at $5,770 that could well have been the coffee mill that led to the business relation with Sobrinos de Ezquiaga.[72]

The trust's investment in tobacco agriculture was a work in progress. By 1906, it had some 250 acres of shade-grown tobacco (as shown in figure 4.1) in La Plata Valley. The PRLTC reported a workforce of two thousand men and women and was busy establishing a network of growers to supply the trust's factories with farmers like Munitiz.[73] As the company expanded its radius of action and gained a deeper penetration in the tobacco-growing areas of the eastern highlands (as presented in map 4.1), the board of directors felt compelled to increase its capitalization. In April 1906, it authorized a capital increase from $300,000 to $2 million, of which half a million dollars was actually paid for by 1907.[74]

Cobb and others continued laying the groundwork for the PRLTC with seemingly simpler transactions. In 1880, Bartolomé Borrás owned the Santa Catalina, a 1,400-cuerda sugar estate with an installed steam engine. As of 1901, Celestino Solá leased the hacienda, located in Caguas, from the heirs of Borrás. However, by 1905, the Santa Catalina had run its course as a sugar manufacturer due to the partition of the hacienda and the lack of capital to modernize it. Subsequently, in 1907 Francisco Ramis Borrás, a grandson, sold his part of the estate (174 cuerdas) to Cobb and Luis Toro Passarell to grow tobacco.[75]

Most of the individuals who had business with the PRLTC were not wealthy, nor did they have the social and legal resources available to Ramis or Munitiz. One such case was Cecilia Toledo Vicente, a single and childless thirty-year-old white woman who, in 1910, lived in a straw hut, probably similar to the ones in figure 4.1, on a nineteen-cuerda farm planted with mixed crops in barrio Toíta of Cayey. The Department of the Treasury assessed the hut at $10 and the farm at $1,490. Ceferina Vicente Díaz, who was Toledo Vicente's eighty-year-old widowed mother, and Práxedes Santos González, a forty-year-old single white man, also lived in the hut. According to the census, Ceferina farmed the property, Cecilia tended the house, and Práxedes worked as a farm laborer. All were illiterate. The two closest neighbors were probably relatives because they were widows of men with the Vicente surname.[76]

In 1911, Toledo sold thirteen cuerdas to PRATCO for $1,344. Ten years later, the Treasury Department did not identify any property under her name in Toíta, but she owned a house assessed at $140 on a forty-square-meter lot valued at $40 on Nicolás Jiménez Street of Cayey.[77]

The crop lien, locally known as *refacción*, is an often overlooked but, nevertheless, major mechanism to procure leaf. The PRLTC extended credit to a grower on a specified acreage, where the tobacco itself served as collateral to the loan. Accordingly, the company provided the credit in steps depending on the state of the crop.[78] For instance, Juan Ortiz and his children contracted the firm, represented by Luis Toro, to prepare, plant, and cultivate sixty cuerdas of tobacco on their 136-cuerda farm. Ortiz gave the company a lien on the crop and obliged himself and his children to deliver the tobacco exclusively to the company.[79]

While tobacco growing on its own farms allowed the PRLTC a greater control over several qualities of the leaf such as combustibility, aroma, and color, the importance of crop liens cannot be overstated. It was an effective method to manage leaf production in three ways. The lien helped bring down fixed costs in leaf growing and processing. The trust did not have to buy land, construct and maintain curing barns, and keep yokes of oxen, plant seedbeds, and the like. Second, Miguel Meléndez Muñoz, a keen observer from the cordillera, argued that corporations used the crop lien as a strategy to saturate the market to bring down leaf prices.[80] Third, the PRLTC directors who were southerners, such as Cobb, the Bullock brothers, and Patrick H. Gorman, should have been conversant with the lien since it was a standard and well-known practice in their region of origin.[81] Locally, the *refacción* was a long-standing practice.[82]

Independently of tobacco-growing arrangements—be it on its own plantations, on leased land, or through crop liens—air-cured tobacco in barns on the farms underwent several steps before being ready for manufacture. Company employees packed leaf in bales and moved them to warehouses where graders unpacked them to classify the leaf according to quality and intended use as *pie*, *medio*, *corona*, *picadura*, *salcochado*, and other categories. Operatives then carefully placed the leaf in stacks to ferment under controlled conditions and readied it for shipment in barrels or bales tied in burlap.[83] The company had its own stemming operations, but frequently PRATCO or American Cigar did their own.

While the PRLTC was acquiring land and financing tobacco growers, it started to establish the infrastructure to handle leaf. The company built warehouses and other installations close to the tobacco-growing centers as clearly shown in map 4.1. A few years after the construction of the Bayamón cigar factory, the company built two concrete buildings to grade and store leaf. In time, more than a thousand women worked at the facilities.[84] By 1907, the firm also had warehouses in Comerío and La Plata.[85]

The remaining warehouses left almost no paper trail. However, a good indicator of their early presence is the company's phone system. The PRLTC built an infrastructure with the greatest number of phones and the longest line length of all private systems having a switchboard, with ten phones in Juncos, another switchboard with six phones in Caguas, and one with seven phones in La Plata. The Juncos and Caguas warehouses must have been in operation by 1907.[86] Finally, the firm might have built a warehouse beside the cigar-box factory in the Miramar district of San Juan sometime after 1907.[87]

Trust activities extended from San Juan in the north to Cayey in the south, from Juncos in the east, and as far as Ponce and Manatí in the west. Although the excellent macadam road traversing the island provided an outlet for much of the trust's leaf, cigars, and cigarettes, its hinterland, nevertheless, comprised a wide area, over which an effective combination of roads and vehicles was necessary. Oxcarts, like those bought from Munitiz, and pack trains over terrain unsuitable for carts were not efficient means of transportation. Figure 4.2 presents two pack trains with their respective muleteers over a trail about to cross a mountain brook. The trust embarked on the expansion of an interconnected transportation network.

Figure 4.2. A. Moscioni, Carrying Tobacco to the Factory, 1907–1915, UPR, Colección Puertorriqueña, Tarjetas Postales, PRDH013PC00370.

With large plantations in La Plata Valley, the trust built a three-kilometer road to connect them to the Carretera Central in 1907. Additionally, the government appropriated funds to connect the public road to the trust's private one in the municipality of Comerío.[88]

The trust launched an ambitious project to construct a railway from Caguas through Carolina and Río Piedras to a point adjoining a station of the American Railroad Company in San Juan.[89] PRATCO sought to transport leaf from its hinterland in Juncos, Cayey, and Aibonito to a central location in Caguas and thence by rail to reach the Bayamón, Miramar, and San Juan factories and the piers. In 1906, it incorporated the San Juan and Caguas Railway Company in New Jersey with $300,000 in capital. After negotiations with the American Railroad Company, it withdrew the franchise application. Nevertheless, it committed itself to assist the railroad company in raising funds in exchange for tobacco transportation on satisfactory terms.[90] Despite the efforts, the deal fizzled out, and a competitor, the Porto Rico Railways Company, constructed the line from Caguas to Río Piedras.[91]

The reaction of independent tobacco firms was consonant to widely held opinions of the trust's tactics. These firms, notably the Cayey-Caguas Tobacco Company, reacted to the incursion with dread while the *Tobacco* journal reported that the project "alarmed" the independents because it "would have been used to crush out competitors." Unaware of the negotiations between the trust and the latter, independents became "jubilant" when two companies—Porto Rico Railways and American Railroad—won franchises. Nevertheless, *Tobacco*, which did not accept trust advertising, called for continual vigilance because it might still arrive at an understanding with the rail company.[92]

THE PARTITION OF THE TRUST AND ITS EFFECTS ON PRATCO

The widespread media exposure to the government's upcoming antitrust case against the ATC, its subsidiaries, and large shareholders provided the context for the expressions of the Cayey-Caguas Tobacco Company, the *Tobacco* journal, and others. In 1905, a grand jury of the circuit court for the Southern District of New York started a behind-closed-doors investigation of the ATC for possible violation of the Sherman Act.[93] With considerable publicity, in June 1906 the grand jury indicted two trust subsidiaries and their presidents for engaging in the restraint of the trade of licorice, which was a crucial component of tobacco plug.[94] The jury selection began at the criminal branch of the US Circuit Court in December 1906 and the trial itself in the following July.[95] Six years later, the adversaries must have felt gratified when the government prevailed in the Supreme Court decision of 1911.

The Supreme Court directed the circuit court to devise a plan to dissolve the monopoly and eliminate the restraints to trade.[96] The lower court partitioned the trust into fourteen independent corporations, where three of the successor companies manufactured cigars other than stogies. The P. Lorillard Company took over the factories, brands, and other assets of the Federal Cigar Company. The ATC retained the American Cigar Company, including all Cuban operations, which were considerable. While sharing the PRLTC with American Cigar, PRATCO became the smallest of the successor companies. Lastly, the United Cigar Stores that did not engage in manufacture, since it was the trust's chain store, also became an independent firm.[97]

While PRATCO and its subsidiaries remained untouched, its position within the United States suffered a major reorientation. Since PRATCO's cigar output was exported to the United States, the company entered uncharted waters in a highly competitive environment.

About the time of the court-mandated dissolution, the trust was the largest firm in the highly fragmented US cigar market with a 13.36 percent market share by 1910. In sharp contrast, the local operations of the trust were, by far, the largest in a way that approached the degree of industrial concentration the trust had achieved in several other tobacco sectors. PRATCO garnered 69.5 percent of the local cigar exports in 1912, which, however, contrasted poorly with its 1.67 percent share of the US market.[98] When compared with all US manufacturers, it ranked sixth, following Siedenberg & Co., well below the leading manufacturer, the Federal Cigar Company, which controlled 5.2 percent of the market.[99] It was a comedown that, perhaps, went unnoticed on the island but cast the company in a completely different light in the United States.

Besides the downsizing, two factors affected PRATCO in the post-partition era. Although the cigar was the most common way to consume tobacco, it was not the major source of the ATC's earnings. From its founding in 1899, PRATCO benefitted financially from the inordinate profits of the trust's cigarette and plug divisions. Another important loss was the unfettered access to the United Cigar Stores chain. In the new era, PRATCO had to and did negotiate the terms under which the store chain carried the Portina and Ricoro brands.

However, the partition had its benefits. From the inception of the American Cigar Company, the trust's manufacture of cigars in the United States had been its province. Upon the dissolution, such restraint disappeared, with PRATCO establishing factories in Florida and New Jersey within the next few years. US-based manufactures allowed the firm to diversify its production beyond the Porto Rico cigars and into the Clear Havana and Seed and Havana types.[100] Furthermore, labor management relations had been tense from the moment the trust ventured into the island and were about to turn more so as tobacco workers' unions agitated for a general strike to uniform pay scales across the island. Chapter 8 discusses how manufacturing facilities in the United States provided a getaway from local labor.[101]

By 1917, the former trust subsidiaries had amassed 6,879 acres of land for agricultural purposes. The PRLTC remained PRATCO's major leaf provider and a significant one for the ATC. PRATCO did not enter the post-partition period solely as a cigarette manufacturer but as the largest local tobacco agribusiness. It was the dominant tobacco enterprise and rivaled, in scope and wealth, some important sugar firms. Although not as profitable as during its first few years, it entered the post-partition era paying dividends with a 14 percent return on capital in 1911 and 16 percent the following year.[102]

CHAPTER FIVE

"Sailing Close to the Wind": The Porto Rican–American Tobacco Company, 1912–1939

This chapter examines PRATCO and its subsidiaries from the court-mandated partition until 1939. It addresses the major challenges facing the company, which included the shift in overall consumption from plug and cigars to cigarettes, the mechanization of cigar crafting, and then the concentration of manufacture in a handful of firms with marketing emphasis in one or two brands in aggressive campaigns in newspapers and, later, radio shows. It also examines the adjustments upon partition of the trust and the strategies to conjure low profits and deficits, the difficulties of wrapper leaf production, and the ATC's depredation during the twenties.

COMPETITION BETWEEN CIGAR MANUFACTURERS IN A CONTRACTING MARKET

At the fin de siècle, skilled hands crafted tobacco leaves into cigars in labor-intensive buckeyes (*chinchales*), tenements, or in large plants like those of the La Internacional locally, the Henry Clay & Bock & Co., in Havana, and the Kerbs, Wertheim & Schiffer and Straiton & Storm Company in New York.[1] Managers and owners responded to a highly competitive market by focusing on bringing down the price of labor. However, lowering or even maintaining the cost of labor proved to be difficult, locally and elsewhere, because cigar makers had a long tradition of unionization and labor militancy.[2]

Frequently, large firms established branches away from the centers of intense labor militancy and close to areas of limited economic activity and specially so during strikes.[3] In the midst of a companywide and protracted strike during 1914, PRATCO outsourced the manufacture of El Pordella brand to the already established firm of Pavón Álvarez and Co. in Ciales and opened factories in Cayey, Coamo, and Toa Alta.[4] In the heat of the strike, Luis Toro, president of the three former trust subsidiaries, threatened to transfer manufacture to the United States, a feat partially accomplished in 1918.[5] Even after the limited transfer to Tampa and Perth Amboy, discussed below, PRATCO kept establishing and reopening local branches when the intensity of the conflict merited it. In 1917 the liquidation of the West Indies Cigar Company offered the company a target of opportunity that led to the acquisition of the former's Utuado factory and other buildings.[6]

Originating in Germany and diffusing across the Atlantic to the United States first and thence to Cuba, Puerto Rico, and elsewhere in the Americas, the two-part wooden mold with cigar-shaped grooves proved successful at lowering the cost of labor. The mold allowed the decomposition of the cigar-making craft into a team made up of a buncher and two wrapper rollers, each with a different skill.[7] The fragmentation of the craft shortened the apprenticeship period that allowed manufacturers to contract women, who earned less than men. Despite initial opposition from cigar makers' unions, PRATCO introduced the mold and teamwork in two factories. One of those, La Marina branch, employed 504 workers.

However, the philosopher's stone did not lie in strong responses to counter demands from labor, branching out, decomposing the cigar-making craft, or the incorporation of labor-saving devices like suction machines. Inasmuch as these measures helped bring down the price of labor, manufacturing firms still had to employ men and women crafting cigars with their militant labor unions. The alchemist's substance laid in a machine that would make a complete cigar in one continuous series of operations, beginning with the bunching of filler leaf and ending with the wrappers rolled over the finished bunches. Machine operatives would completely do away with cigar makers and teamwork, consequently dealing a powerful blow to trade unions and, most significantly, considerably bringing down the cost of production. The American Machine and Foundry, a former trust subsidiary, spent some $7 million to develop and market, by 1919, a fully operational cigar-making machine.[8] PRATCO started buying them in 1921, and by 1931, 75 percent of its local production was machine made.[9]

FROM THE INVISIBLE TO THE VERY VISIBLE HAND OF OLIGOPOLY

The old ATC management was well aware that the Bonsack cigarette-making machine eased the way for the decrease of manufacturing enterprises and the eventual formation of the trust. In 1900, ATC officials sought to replicate the same feat with cigars that were then far more important than cigarettes. The diffusion of the cigar machine accelerated changes far beyond the labor-saving mechanisms that had been accumulating in the industry, the most remarkable being the fast pace of industrial concentration.

The mechanization of cigar manufacture, unlike that of cigarettes earlier, has a limited literature where Reavis Cox, for instance, highlighted the "concentration of manufacture and alteration of merchandising policies resulting from the adoption of machine methods."[10] Wilmoth D. Evans noticed that small firms lacked the resources to install the usual batteries of six or more machines.[11] Generalizing far beyond the cigar industry, Alfred P. Chandler stated, "Their new processes of production were so capital-intensive . . . that production for the national and global market became concentrated in just a few plants."[12] Mechanization has received credit for easing the concentration of production in large firms and the decimation of small ones.

While the mechanical cigar maker raised entry-level costs, the beginnings of concentration of manufacture predated their use; witness the size of a handful of firms, including the American Cigar Company, well before the cigar-making machine. In 1903, at the firm's zenith, it accounted for 16.4 percent of US cigar output. Almost a quarter of a century later, in 1930, General Cigar's share was 13.7 percent—close but still below the mark.[13] In the words of William G. Roy, American Cigar's size responded to "financial transfusions ATC gave it until it could stand on its own."[14] PRATCO and other cigar manufacturing subsidiaries benefitted enormously from the trust's attempt to control cigar manufacture.

The American Cigar Company and PRATCO did not follow the anticipated path of the mechanical cigar maker as the harbinger of concentration of manufacture because their large sizes antedated the machine. Nevertheless, mechanization gave a notable boost to concentration. The top ten manufacturers accounted for 22.6 percent of all cigars in 1912, increasing to 55.1 percent in 1930.[15]

PRATCO joined other large firms and installed cigar-making machines sometime in 1921. Later, in 1930, it announced plans to mechanize completely save for the small niche covered by La Habanera, formerly a competitor and then a subsidiary.[16] As stated, by 1931, 75 percent of its local manufacture was machine made. However, mechanization did not lead to greater market shares or increases in output. Whereas PRATCO's 117.5 million cigars manufactured in 1912 garnered a 1.67 market share, the 1930 figures stand for a production of 105 million for a 1.78 percent share.[17] United States and Puerto Rican cigar manufactures declined over the period under consideration.

A MANUFACTURING BASE IN THE UNITED STATES

The trust developed PRATCO into the major manufacturer of cigarettes for local consumption and only one type of cigar known as Porto Rico for export.

As partition did away with the constraint, it diversified by manufacturing the Seed and Havana and other types to compensate for lagging sales of its mainline cigars and strong labor conflict. For that purpose, the company incorporated the M. Alvarez & Co. in Delaware in 1918 to take over the Tampa manufacturer of the same name. The subsidiary became intertwined with the main firm's operations as it received tobacco leaf from several sources that most likely included PRATCO's Puerto Rican plantations.[18]

Additionally, the firm absorbed, in 1917, the old Industrial Company of Porto Rico, which had operations in the Ponce area, and incorporated a company with same name in 1918 in Delaware. The new company operated factories in Perth Amboy, New Jersey.[19]

The expansion led in 1919 to a major corporate change, with the incorporation of a locally based company of the same name to own and manage its operations on the island.[20] Puerto Rican operations became legally distinct from US-based manufactures, and the old PRATCO, a New Jersey firm, became a holding company.

In 1921, the New York–Tampa Cigar Company, a newly incorporated and wholly owned subsidiary, took over the assets of M. Alvarez and the Industrial Company. The directors of the primary company had ambitious plans for the subsidiary when they authorized a capital stock of $2,000,000.[21] During the same year, PRATCO issued ten-year 8 percent bonds for $2,841,600 "to fund floating debt and to increase working capital," where they must have invested some in the new subsidiary.[22]

When established, the New York–Tampa Cigar already manufactured Seed and Havana and other types of cigars under the Personality and Recollection brands.[23] Luis Toro assumed the presidency of the subsidiary, whereas Fred J. Davis became a vice president.[24] Davis was an experienced tobacco man who had been a partner in Samuel I. Davis & Company and worked for the Consolidated Cigar Corporation after the latter bought the former.[25] While Percival R. Lowe, following the lead of large cigar manufacturers, became the company's leaf broker, the firm entrusted the Recollection cigar to the United Cigar Stores, which was the largest cigar chain in the country.[26]

The subsidiary expanded in the aftermath of a prolonged and crippling tobacco workers' strike in Tampa that ended in 1921. For instance, it bought Francisco Arango & Co., which had gone bankrupt due to the strike.[27] In 1922, the subsidiary moved the M. Alvarez factory from its West Tampa location to the brick building bought from Arango, where it could provide space for a thousand workers.[28]

Francisco Arango & Co. was an established firm with a market for its fifty to sixty thousand "Pancho Arango" daily production. This was PRATCO's first inroad into the high-end trade that manufactured Clear Havana cigars in the United States solely from imported Cuban leaf.[29] When Francisco Arango left the firm, the New York–Tampa Cigar Company contracted Jaime M. Pendás,

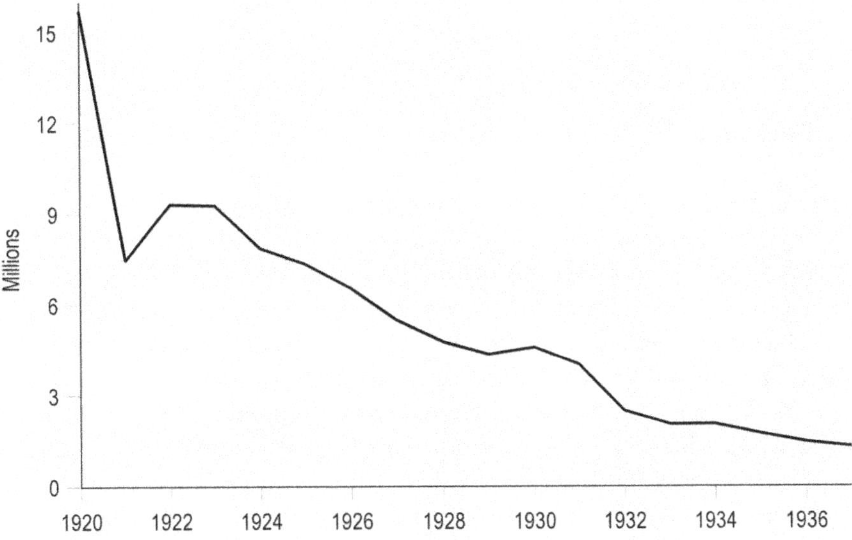

Figure 5.1. Net sales of the Porto Rican–American Tobacco Co., 1920–1937

Source: FTC, *Investigation of Concentration of Economic Power*, 17716–17717.

from the Pendás y Álvarez family firm that had considerable experience in the Clear Havana trade.[30]

By 1922, PRATCO had diversified into cigars beyond its staple Porto Ricos with Clear Havana and Seed and Havana types. Also, it spread geographically to manufacture in Perth Amboy and Tampa, far beyond the reach of local trade unions. However, after 1923, the expansion of the New York–Tampa Cigar Company failed to satisfy the expectations of the directors of the parent company. Investments ceased, and Jaime Pendás returned to the Puerto Rican subsidiary in 1923.[31] In 1924, Fred Davis resigned as head of the firm's manufacturing department while retaining his position as a member of the board of directors.[32] Between 1922 and 1925, the New York–Tampa Cigar Company chugged along, making few ripples that reached the journals of the tobacco trade. Finally, in 1925, president Luis Toro traveled to Tampa and sold the factories, buildings, and trademarks, save for the Recollection brand, to a new firm called Schwab, Davis and Company whose principals were Fred I. Davis and Leon Schwab. Estimates of the deal's price were in the region of $250,000, which was far below the authorized capital.[33]

US cigar manufacturers failed to reverse the 21.3 percent drop in cigar sales between 1922 and 1925 shown in figure 5.1. The Pancho Arango, Recollection, and Personality cigars left a thin trail in the trade journals and in the more mainstream media. None of them seem to have gained a following similar to the staples of El Toro, Portina, or Ricoro.

FROM DARK TO VIRGINIA TOBACCO CIGARETTES IN A PREDATORY MILIEU

From its beginnings, PRATCO employed locally grown dark tobacco leaf in its cigarette division. It manufactured Colectivas, Violetas, and Casinos from scraps left from cigar manufacture and *boliche* that consisted of the lower leaves that were unsuitable for cigars.[34] So to speak, cigarettes were byproducts from cigar manufacture. La Marina factory in San Juan, a newly built building in 1901, produced the company's machine-made cigarettes for over a quarter of a century.[35]

Dark-tobacco cigarettes were clearly distinct from early twentieth-century *tabaco rubio*, which relied mainly on flue-cured bright leaf from the Virginia and Carolinas belt and was known as "straight Virginia." Some added burley from Tennessee and Kentucky and/or Turkish leaf to form the "blended" cigarette, while straight Turkish cigarettes were in a class by themselves.[36] Since dark-tobacco cigarettes did not conform to the tastes of the US smoker, the firm, consequently, marketed them domestically with only a small fraction destined for export.

Industrial concentration of the cigarette inched forward when Infanzón y Rodríguez's La Habanera became a wholly owned subsidiary in May 1915.[37] During the twenties, the Universal Leaf Tobacco Company, a major leaf-purchasing concern in the United States, ventured into the manufacture of dark-tobacco cigarettes a few years after it had gained a local foothold in La Plata Tobacco Company.[38] Universal, through another subsidiary, La Regional Sales Corporation, sold an average of eight million cigarettes per annum during the years preceding 1925, when sales dropped to two million cigarettes. La Regional lost its competitive edge, quit the manufacture of cigarettes, and sold its machinery to PRATCO.[39]

Given PRATCO's near monopoly of cigarette production, local cigarette statistics serve as an indicator of its production. Figure 5.2 presents the firm's declining shares of the local market. Manufactures experienced variations up to 1920 before suffering a gradual decline during the next few years. Starting in 1929, the number of imported cigarettes surpassed local manufactures that started a free fall until 1937, when they stabilized.[40] As local production declined, imports gained momentum from a minimum of 249 million units in 1924, to a maximum of 823 million in 1940. The local smoker had effectively undergone a transition from dark- to blended-tobacco cigarettes, from PRATCO's cigarettes to US imports.

The sharp downturn in PRATCO's manufactures after 1929 did not respond exclusively to the operation of market forces. The old ATC had an earned reputation for strong predatory practices of price slashing to force competitors out

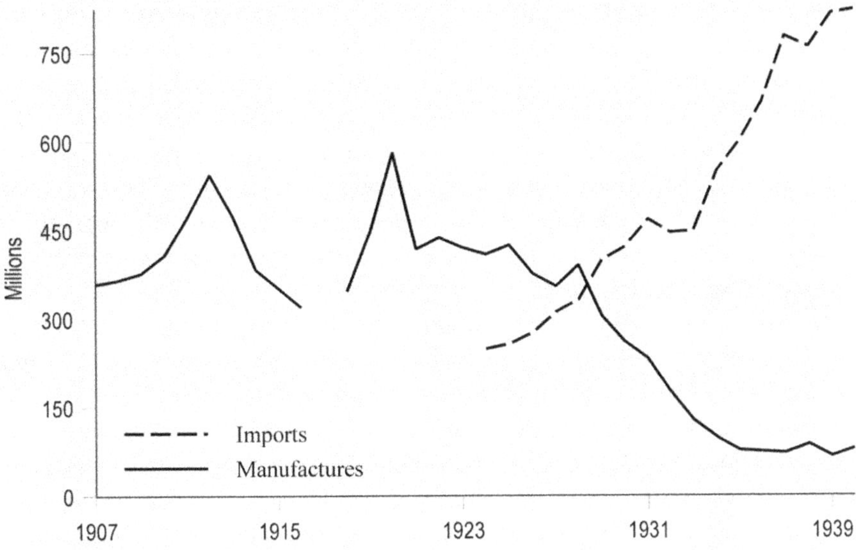

Figure 5.2. Cigarette manufactures and imports to Puerto Rico, 1907–1940

Sources: Department of Agriculture, *Annual Book on Statistics of Puerto Rico, 1934–35*, 147; Department of Agriculture, *Annual Book on Statistics of Puerto Rico, 1940–41*, 228; Economic Development Administration and Department of Agriculture, *Annual Book on Statistics of Puerto Rico, 1949–50* ([San Juan]: n.p., 1950) 99–100, 371.

of the business. These practices, among others, led the Supreme Court to order its partition in 1911. The only documented post-partition case is that of the ATC against PRATCO, which makes it even more unusual because some fifteen years earlier both had been in the trust. Furthermore, their bonds were more current than historical since both owned the same subsidiary, the PRLTC.

In May 1927, the colonial legislature held hearings on a bill to increase the tax on cigarettes selling wholesale above $2.00 per thousand. While representatives of the ATC challenged the projected tax increase, PRATCO's officials halfheartedly opposed it.[41] ATC officials claimed that Luis Toro had agreed to oppose it.[42] When the law came into effect on 30 June, ATC raised Lucky Strikes from its long-standing $0.15 to $0.18 per pack of twenty.[43] Not affected by the revenue tax, PRATCO's Casino cigarettes kept retailing at $0.12 per pack of twenty and its Colectivas at $0.06 for half a pack.

However, ATC officials summoned J. D. Woodward, the president of Gillies & Woodward and its sole local representative.[44] While in New York, Woodward accepted a $20,000 guarantee in profits a year to cover the difficulties of a price war. Within two weeks of the increase, ATC started selling Lucky Strikes at a substantial discount so that Gillies & Woodward could lower the price, not to its pretax level of $0.15, but to $0.12.[45] The ATC backed the discount with an aggressive newspaper campaign and large-scale use of billboards explicitly designed to harm if not ruin its competitor. As the war unfolded and the local representative accrued $18,200 in losses for August and September alone, the ATC expressed a disposition to absorb them at the rate of $175,000 per annum.[46] The conflict reduced the ATC's profits marginally because Puerto Rico was but a small segment of a market that was truly global. Nevertheless, with the island as its single market, it devastated the smaller firm's cigarette division, which claimed a $300,000 loss within a year.[47]

In September 1927, PRATCO petitioned the US District Court for an injunction to revert the price reduction, which the court overruled in October.[48] After some months of duress and uncertainty, the court determined that PRATCO had proven the charges of unfair competition and proceeded with the injunction. The suit claimed that the ATC had violated the Clayton Act, which forbade price discrimination across interstate commerce.[49] In January 1929, the circuit court of appeals sustained the injunction.[50] Despite the setbacks, the ATC appealed to the Supreme Court for a reversal that, however, fell on deaf ears.[51]

PRATCO sued at the district court in Newark, in June 1928, for $300,000 in damages, which the Clayton Act specifically allowed to be tripled to $900,000.[52] The parties settled the case out of court for a then undisclosed sum of $508,193.62, in November 1929.[53]

The ATC's price slash and unusually aggressive advertising campaign probably accelerated the steep market loss that PRATCO endured after 1929. Cheap Lucky Strikes briefly widened the circle of consumers who whetted the appetite for blended-tobacco cigarettes—a habit that, once fired, most likely left a craving for more after the court ordered price rollback.[54] This exposure, in combination with the gradual contraction of dark-tobacco cigarettes from 1920 to 1929, must have hastened the switch from PRATCO's to blended-tobacco cigarettes, as presented in figure 5.2.

THE COLLAPSE OF THE PORTO RICAN LEAF TOBACCO COMPANY

As documented in the previous chapter, the trust bought large expanses of land from big and small farmers alike. The PRLTC kept adding farmland to its tobacco plantations until at least 1915.[55] By 1917, the former trust subsidiaries (PRLTC, American Cigar Company, Industrial Company, and PRATCO) held 6,879 acres in the highlands.[56] Luis Toro, as president of all the firms except American Cigar, managed the plantations that procured wrapper and filler tobacco for the primary companies. The PRLTC also cured, stemmed, classified, fermented, and transported the leaf to local cigar factories or to US-bound ships.

During several years the shade-grown tobacco proved satisfactory, but in time it "degenerated," presenting difficulties to maintain its commercial significance.[57] Despite the inconveniences, the firms still planted some 3,500 acres of shaded tobacco up to the 1920s, while carrying on more experiments with imported and local leaf.[58] One source went as far as to report on experiments with flues, mandatory for bright leaf, that, however, failed to produce suitable light wrappers.[59]

The 1927 price war between the ATC and PRATCO worsened the difficulties facing shade tobacco in several ways. Experimentation ceased and commercial planting ended but for cigar-filler tobacco.[60] The PRLTC explicitly stated, in late 1927 or early 1928, its intention to dispose of its plantations.[61] Deeds followed the words when, as of 1932, thirteen growers made $21,935.25 in payments for land mortgaged to the firm.[62] Furthermore, the firm ceased to pay some property taxes and accumulated a debt of $4,198.67 between 1926 and 1929. Finally, PRATCO, which then owned one-half of the PRLTC, sold its participation to the ATC, which incorporated a wholly owned subsidiary with the same name. The ATC's commitment to local shade tobacco was, perhaps, weak because it already had secure sources in Cuba.[63] The new PRLTC subsidiary assumed the assets and liabilities of the old one, which disappeared in November 1929.[64] About 1935, the new firm lost its legal persona, having its assets and liabilities transferred to American Suppliers.[65]

Before its dissolution, the PRLTC faced another setback, this time from a movement of tobacco growers.[66] After the company prepared seedbeds, arsonists destroyed one of its barns in Cayey and four in Cidra on 20 August.[67] During October 1931, about a dozen armed men broke the peace of the night in a firm's seedbed in Cayey by attacking the two guards, leaving one wounded, and in effect destroying the nursery.[68] The following day, a group of men destroyed another seedbed and burned down a barn in Cidra after an exchange of gunfire that left nobody wounded. The authorities identified close to twenty men and arrested a dozen; the court system later found none guilty.[69] In December six masked horseback riders failed to burn a company barn in Cidra.[70] In summary, the company had decided enemies that destroyed six curing barns and two seedbeds; consequently, it planted little if any tobacco for the 1932 season.

In spite of its declining fortune, the PRLTC still had some five to six thousand employees in activities that ranged from planting and cultivation to more industrial operations such as stemming and fermenting leaf in warehouses.[71] By 1935, its landholdings still amounted to 4,530 cuerdas for agricultural purposes, and it had several lots with buildings worth more than $10,000 each, which suggest stemmeries and warehouses in Bayamón, Caguas, Cayey, Comerío, and Gurabo.[72] The ATC's complete divestiture from local tobacco planting came in the same year when American Suppliers sold 4,322 cuerdas to the Puerto Rico Reconstruction Administration, a New Deal agency.[73] From a much-celebrated success a quarter of a century earlier, the degeneration of shaded tobacco transformed the subsidiary into a burden to be disposed of.

"SAILING CLOSE TO THE WIND"

As discussed, PRATCO undertook a significant step to reverse the declining trend in its net sales by a considerable investment in the New York–Tampa Cigar Company. The expected absorption by the Tobacco Products Corporation that would have been a lifesaver by providing "unlimited capital for still further expansion" failed in 1923.[74] After selling New York–Tampa Cigar in 1925, the firm's net sales continued their downward march that, as shown in figure 5.1, amounted to a 10.8 percent decline between 1925 and 1926. Save for losses in 1921, 1922, and 1924, the primary firm remained profitable but well below pre-1920 levels.[75]

By 1926, PRATCO officials were again actively seeking ways to gain a more secure footing to its weakened status. Consequently, the company entered conversations over control of the Congress Cigar Company, which had 350,000 shares outstanding. PRATCO bought 200,000 shares held by members of the Philadelphia-based Paley family for some $12,750,000 payable in a combination of stock and cash obtained from an $8 million issue of fifteen-year 6 percent bonds dated January 1927.[76] With a cigar output estimated at 250 million units, it was larger than the parent company, whose manufactures included nearly all the 214 million cigars exported from Puerto Rico.[77] As usual in this type of purchase, Samuel and Jacob Paley retained their positions as president and vice president respectively when both brothers entered the service of the subsidiary as employees until 1931.[78]

Profitable control over the Congress Cigar Company led PRATCO to repeat the feat in July 1929. Waitt & Bond specialized in the Blackstone, a medium-priced, machine-made cigar manufactured in Newark. It became the smallest firm in the combination with a capacity between 125 and 150 million cigars, where actual production was likely to be lower.[79] PRATCO purchased 150,000 Class B shares from a total of 200,000 in an exchange of stock and cash worth nearly $3 million that the buying firm most likely financed in part by a $1,360,000 increase of the gold bonds due in 1942.[80] As the Waterman family relinquished control, Luis Toro became the chair of the board, but William E. Waterman and James M. Porter retained their positions as president and vice president respectively.[81]

A knowledgeable analyst held that the Congress Cigar Company became the "principal factor" or the "chief source" of earnings for the primary PRATCO between 1927 and 1931.[82] To take one significant year, in 1931 the company posted a net loss of $238,200.[83] This deficit would have been greater, most likely around $570,000, had it not been for the addition of the dividends accrued from Waitt & Bond and the Congress Cigar Company that amounted to $336,000.[84]

At the time of the takeover, the expected economies of scale with Congress Cigar were estimated to result in savings exceeding $1 million.[85] However, control did not include dismantling the subsidiary or its integration into the structure of the parent company. La Palina, which was Congress Cigar's leading brand, combined Java wrappers with Havana and Puerto Rican filler. In 1924, the firm established a leaf-buying department with its main office in Philadelphia and a local one in Caguas, by the acquisition of Max Gans' Sons, which specialized in Puerto Rican leaf.[86] The companies did not consolidate their leaf-buying department or shared packing, warehousing, or stemming functions in their local operations.[87]

The consolidation of the sales departments took place in 1931, when Philip M. Forristall became the sole director of the three firms in an integration that implied a single advertising office, the closing of earlier offices, and the conversion of the old Congress Cigar factory in Philadelphia into a storage facility and home of the retail department.[88] The sales department contracted the same jobbers to handle the cigars of the combined manufacturers.[89]

However, some brands remained outside the scope of the new sales department. As stated above, the United Cigar Stores Company had marketed several of PRATCO's brands, among them the Ricoro cigar, since the times when both were subsidiary to the trust. Nonetheless, the cigar chain stores had been facing economic difficulties since 1928 that led to filing for bankruptcy in 1932.[90] Net sales, as shown in figure 5.1, declined 38.3 percent from 1931 to 1932 alone. The reorganization of the chain store worsened PRATCO's predicament by reducing newspaper advertising and the window displays of merchandise as retail outlets declined from 2,850 in 1925 to 500 by 1934.[91]

The shortcomings of the United Cigar Stores affected the distribution and sales of the mid-priced Ricoro, thus propelling El Toro, an inexpensive nickel cigar, as PRATCO's leading brand in sales.[92] Gone were the elaborate displays in the upscale store at the Flatiron Building's prow in Manhattan and the Ricoro advertisements at *Harvard Illustrated Magazine*.[93] The shift from Ricoro to El Toro showed the changing winds of fortune, from the classy to the pedestrian.

PRATCO claimed to have promoted El Toro aggressively on the NBC radio network and through newspaper advertisements that went as far as to include Theodore Roosevelt Jr., the colonial governor.[94] However, the efforts failed to reverse the sales decline (as shown in figure 5.1), most likely because advertising was not comparable to the revenue that firms, like the General Cigar Company, invested in brands such as the White Owl cigar.[95]

As the Puerto Rican subsidiary reduced manufactures, the primary firm's solvency started to depend on dividends from its other controlled corporations. By 1932, the primary firm was "sailing close to the wind": its 6 percent bonds dropped to 32 percent of their face value with a rebound to 50 percent in 1935 because finances were "none too strong."[96] In fact, much of the primary company's weakness stemmed from the subsidiary on the island, whose net profits from sales were negative from 1931 until 1937, the last year with available data.[97]

While US cigar manufactures experienced a 34.5 percent drop from the all-time high of 8,097 million cigars in 1920 to 5,303 million in 1937, the local PRATCO subsidiary suffered a 91.7 percent fall in sales, presented in figure 5.1.[98] Its collapse outpaced the general contraction of the cigar market. While declining net sales showed the crisis facing the local PRATCO, the overall picture for the primary PRATCO was also critical. The primary company posted net losses from 1931 to 1938 save for 1935.[99]

The local subsidiary's frailty, in contrast to the more robust performance of the other two subordinate companies, must have weighed considerably in changes to management that were even more significant than those experienced with the partition of the trust. The transformation started when, in June 1931, James M. Porter, instead of Luis Toro or someone from the PRATCO camp, assumed the presidency of Congress Cigar upon the resignation of Samuel and Jacob Paley, who had been president and vice president respectively.[100] Porter was not a major stockholder in Congress as the Paleys had been, and, in fact, his experience had been with Waitt & Bond, where he had been a vice president.[101]

A few months later, in October, Luis Toro, PRATCO's president for more than thirty years, resigned from all positions in the combination.[102] By the end of 1932, William E. Waterman, who was a major stockholder at Waitt & Bond, was chair of the board of the local subsidiary and Congress Cigar. James M. Porter went on to succeed Toro as president of the local subsidiary. C. H. Knapp, who had been a director at Waitt & Bond, joined the boards of Congress and the local subsidiary.[103] In a matter of months, the combination fell under the leadership of men from the Waitt & Bond subsidiary.

Board members and upper-level managers from the Waitt & Bond firm lacked familiarity and commitment to Puerto Rican operations. In consonance with figure 5.1, by August 1937, PRATCO suspended the wetting of wrapper leaves for immediate manufacture and the blending of filler leaves in its large Puerta de Tierra branch. Nine hundred jobs were in jeopardy because the company had already sent to the United States thirty cigar-making machines in three different ships, leaving thirty-four in Puerta de Tierra.[104] A month later, Charles J. Charles, a company vice president, explained that the firm had ceased all cigar manufactures save for the niche of handmade ones because of the loss of market and local labor difficulties. He held that the company had not made a final decision as to the fate of the factory.[105] Accordingly, company personnel moved the remaining cigar-making machines to storage facilities in La Marina branch and either readied or shipped the single cigar-tin machine, eleven cigar-banding machines, and thirty-six stemming machines. The firm laid off most workers, including office workers, except those of the leaf-buying department, some fifteen men and women who kept operating the cigarette-making machines, and ten men crafting cigars by hand all in La Marina branch, thus vacating the Puerta de Tierra building.[106]

The sudden surge of unemployment proved devastating to Puerta de Tierra, where most stemmers and operatives lived. The firm employed about a thousand workers ranging from those recently employed to the likes of Ángel Gorbea, who had thirty years of experience in the packing department. Employees had included some three hundred men and women who sorted cigars, placed bands, and wrapped them in cellophane paper and some four hundred stemmers, mostly women.[107]

Cigar exports, its mainstay for decades, vanished, leaving but a buckeye, a collapsing cigarette market, and heavy debts incurred in gaining control of other manufacturers. Probably sensing the coming debacle, William E. Waterman and James M. Porter, chair and president respectively of the companies in the combination, presented and gained approval for a resolution to separate Waitt & Bond from the other firms. In 1938, Waterman purchased 151,300 shares of Waitt & Bond from PRATCO, regaining control of the company.[108] T. C. Breen, a long-standing board member of all the firms, assumed the presidencies of PRATCO and Congress Cigar.[109] As the situation became untenable, the primary PRATCO filed a petition to reorganize at the bankruptcy court in July 1939.[110] In 1940, the firm emerged as the Rican Corporation, basically a firm holding the bonds that the Consolidated Cigar Company issued to purchase all the assets of Congress Cigar.[111]

CONCLUSION

PRATCO employed several strategies to adapt to the fiercely competitive environment among cigar manufacturers. Ahead of many firms, it successfully mechanized the manufacture of cigars that effectively reduced the challenges posed by labor unions. It diversified beyond its original colonial confines, from its specialty Porto Rico cigars to dwell into the Clear Havana and Seed and Havana types by buying small firms in the United States and nurturing them within the Industrial Company first and later the New York–Tampa Cigar Company. When the venture proved unsatisfactory, it disposed of its investments in 1925.

With the benefit of hindsight, one can state that PRATCO faced a history of unremitting decline in sales after 1920, as presented in figure 5.1. It halfheartedly promoted El Portina in newspapers, an innovative marketing strategy that proved very successful for El Producto and to a lesser extent for White Owl. Deferring to tradition, PRATCO attempted to create and maintain demand for its products through the active promotion that regional merchants, known as jobbers, offered.

Finally, the firm granted the United Cigar Stores chain exclusive contracts for the Ricoro and other brands.

The context of the decline is important, as cigar consumption in the United States, to which the island's exports were pegged, also faced steep decreases. The firm's dark-tobacco cigarettes, for the local market, were ceding ground to blended-tobacco cigarettes that led to a price war with the more powerful ATC. In the midst of these difficulties, PRATCO's management encouraged a purchase from the better capitalized Tobacco Products Corporation that failed before it was consummated. Later, PRATCO embarked on a diversification and aggressive expansion model by takeovers of large and well-established companies, such as Congress Cigar and Waitt & Bond, in an attempt to avert its own economic weakness. In spite of these ventures, the failure of the United Cigar Stores, to which it had entrusted some of its bestselling brands, severely reduced sales. In the end, PRATCO's own weaknesses led to the suspension of cigar manufactures in the Puerta de Tierra factory that signified the end of the Porto Rico cigar as an export product.

PRATCO experienced a veritable transformation between independence from the trust in 1911 to bankruptcy in 1939 as it morphed from a significant tobacco grower and large manufacturer to become a holding company at the time of going under. It moved operations from the colony to become domiciled in the United States.

CHAPTER SIX

Tobacco Leaf Dealers, Stemmers, and Merchants after the Invasion

Most research has concentrated on working-class activism in tobacco manufacture and the characteristics of leaf growing. Very little research has focused on the intermediaries who bought leaf from the growers to process it for sale to the manufacturers. This chapter attempts to overcome this deficit by examining the changing nature of these middlemen after the US invasion in 1898. It ends with the formidable concentration of leaf commerce into few firms and the growers' response during the 1920s.

During the nineteenth century, these leaf buyers ranged from a side activity of the large landed estate, shopkeepers, general export merchants, and the contractors to the Spanish tobacco monopoly.[1] This chapter holds that US rule fostered a dealer whose sole or primary specialty was the leaf trade. They accompanied their ventures with leaf stemmeries and packing plants, with the larger ones maintaining offices and warehouses in the tobacco district of Lower Manhattan. These intermediaries also included the intervention of the occasional bank, the cigar manufacturers themselves, and ultimately the growers' cooperatives with liens on their members' crops.

After the invasion, Puerto Rico lost the Cuban and Spanish leaf markets and experienced a complete reorientation of exports to the new colonial power. The loss led to the end of the general export merchant that dealt with different types of merchandise. In fact, none of these merchants of Spanish colonial times survived the invasion as leaf dealers.[2] The few who weathered the invasion specialized solely in tobacco in anticipation of the coming trend. For instance, José Portela, who appears as a manufacturer elsewhere in this volume, exported five cigar cases to Saint Thomas and another two to Hamburg in January 1892.[3] In 1899, he exported, as a partner to Rucabado y Portela, 444 packs of tobacco to Hamburg, and in 1902 he exported under his name alone 19 cigar cases to New

York.[4] Portela gained a direct presence in the United States soon after the invasion. In 1900, he opened a warehouse on Front Street.[5]

AFTER THE US INVASION

Levi Blumenstiel & Co., a New York–based firm that specialized in Cuban leaf, got a modest head start in the export business with its 1897 arrival in Puerto Rico.[6] It started to buy *pacas*, through a local representative, from unidentified growers or dealers from Caguas and Cayey and shipped them to New York aboard steamers like the *Arcadia*. Thus, the firm began complementing the Cuban leaf sold to its Canadian customers with leaf from Caguas and Cayey, being reticent about selling it in the more exacting New York market.[7] Its prewar experience eased the way for the 9 September 1898 incorporation of the American West Indies Trading Company (AWITCO) with an authorized capital of $250,000 and a charter that allowed it to delve into a wide range of tobacco-related undertakings.[8]

The firm shipped 1,585 bales of leaf, 851 packages of leaf, and one package of cigars to become, as table 6.1 shows, the largest leaf exporter with a grand 43.7 percent share between Februray 1899 and April 1900.[9] The same table shows that Levi Blumenstiel maintained its dominant position, from November 1901 to May 1902, with 44.5 percent of leaf exports to New York. Its prewar arrival in conjunction to its expertise in the Havana trade must have contributed to its early domination of the export market.

John H. Goetze & Co., the second-largest exporter during 1899–1900, was a well-established firm, specializing in Sumatra leaf, that ventured briefly into local leaf soon after the invasion up to approximately 1902.[10] Between February 1899 and April 1900, the firm shipped to New York 861 packages and 77 bales for a 16.5 percent market share.[11]

Lewis Sylvester was a New York dealer who specialized in Cuban tobacco. His son Allie became a dealer under his father's guidance and turned into a partner well before 1901, when Lewis retired.[12] Between February 1899 and April 1900, Lewis Sylvester & Son shipped one package and 506 bales to become, as table 6.1 shows, the third-largest exporter with a 9.2 percent market share. Upon the retirement of the elder Sylvester, the son abandoned the Puerto Rico trade until he joined the leaf department of the American Cigar Company in 1909 and became a director of the PRLTC in 1912.[13]

The three largest exporters were long-standing dealers with offices and depots in the midst of the main tobacco district, in Lower Manhattan.[14] US-based dealers alleviated the pressing needs of growers, who had recently lost their two major markets.

Table 6.1. Shares of leaf exports from the three largest independent shippers, 1899–1933

	1899–1900	1901–02	1907	1920	1933
Share	9.2	11.7	10.5	8.0	10.0
3rd shipper	LS	GS	ML	JL	DB
pounds	60,836	16,320	49,680	136,958	58,245
Share	16.5	17.5	11.7	9.6	23.4
2nd shipper	JG	MA	CC	IP	GG
pounds	109,116	24,360	55,320	165,125	136,200
Share	43.7	44.5	15.1	13.4	32.7
1st shipper	LB	LB	JC	SM	GC
pounds	288,916	62,040	71,460	229,135	190,200
Total					
pounds	660,665	139,440	472,320	1,715,698	581,622
Shipments	(82)	(29)	(121)	(211)	(71)

Sources: Data for 514 shipments to New York as reported in US Congress, House, *Importers of Goods from Porto Rico*, 56th Cong., 1st sess., H. Doc. 589 (Washington, DC: GPO, 1900) and sixty issues of *Tobacco* and the *United States Tobacco Journal*.

Note: The table excludes the tobacco trust.

CC	Cayey-Caguas Tobacco Co.	JG	J. H. Goetze
DB	Durlach Bros.	JL	J. B. Lichtenstein & Co.
GC	General Cigar Co.	LB	Levi Blumenstiel & Co.
GG	García Grande Cigars, Inc.	LS	Lewis Sylvester & Son
GS	G. W. Sheldon & Co.	MA	Melchior, Armstrong & Dessan
IP	International Planters Corp.	ML	Morris J. Levi
JC	J. Cohn & Co.	SM	Stern-Mendelsohn Co.

Most leaf growers and local leaf dealers either consigned or sold their leaf to US-based export dealers to dispose of it.[15] In addition to José Portela, a handful of other local dealers opened and maintained an office and a depot in the United States, typically in Manhattan. For instance, Marcelino Solá e Hijos, which had a participation in several Caguas-based tobacco partnerships, had an office on Pearl Street by 1902.[16]

Concomitant with Levi Blumenstiel's specialty as dealers, the firm's local subsidiary AWITCO bought a warehouse, later known as La Turina, by the Caguas town square in 1899. Within a year, the firm started to integrate vertically through a cigar factory and the purchase of the 460-cuerda La Esperanza plantation in the same municipality.[17] The local operations of the firm benefitted from the acquired knowledge and resources of the Havana trade from its Cuban subsidiary, the National Cuba Company.[18] AWITCO repeated its dominant position among leaf exporters during 1901–1902 with a 44.5 percent share, which is the maximum in table 6.1.

Levi Blumenstiel's exports for 1907 were much lower from those of earlier years shown in table 6.1. Morris J. Levi, a major shareholder, appeared as the third force in the local export market with a 10.5 percent market share. While AWITCO continued to submit the annual reports to the local State Department, ship manifests shifted from Levi Blumenstiel to Morris J. Levi. The firm's decline might have resulted from a strong "disagreement" that, perhaps, started in 1907 or earlier. The conflict led Alexander Blumenstiel to sue Morris J. Levi in a case that made it to the *New York Times* and resulted in the court's appointment of two receivers.[19] Another plausible explanation is that the firm might have been facing economic straits that the hiring of experienced managers brought in from Cuba in 1906 failed to correct.[20] During the following years, the firm endured a "checkered career," in the words of Levi, accompanied by name changes already discussed in chapter 3.[21] At any rate, the remarkable degrees of market concentration of the 1899–1900 and 1901–1902 data garnered by the three largest exporters ranged between 69.5 and 73.7 percent respectively, reflected Levi Blumenstiel's dominance more than anything else.

REDEFINITION OF THE LEAF EXPORTER

A few years after the invasion, the leaf exporter experienced a significant change. Up to the waning decades of the nineteenth century and the early years of the twentieth, tobacco exports consisted mostly of unstemmed leaf because the leading practice among manufacturers was to stem their own leaf. Around 1912, the practice started to change, and exporters began to shift their preference for bales or barrels packed with stemmed leaf.[22]

Consequently, several large leaf exporters developed or expanded stemming operations. H. Duys and Company, a large firm in Lower Manhattan with a specialty in Sumatra leaf, is a case in point. In 1919, the firm entered the local market with the explicit purpose to "specialize in stripped Porto Rican fillers of the finest types only." Duys brought Harrison Johnson's warehouses and stemmery in Caguas and employed him in what became the nucleus of its local expansion.[23]

New operations short on capital or exporters with lesser operations required already-stemmed leaf from local packers.[24] Lucien Francois Theyskens and William B. Shaw provide an illustration. Both had been in the employ of the International Planters Corporation, with the first specializing in Europe and the latter in Puerto Rico.[25] Upon the collapse of the corporation in 1922, they established Theyskens & Shaw on Front Street in Manhattan to serve as dealers in the same markets where they had worked before.[26] The firm represented Aragunde y Ca., a local partnership with a considerable tobacco business whose activities ranged from growing to packing stemmed and fermented leaf for shippers to export. In 1917, the society, with Ángel Aragunde, Cesáreo Echevarría, and Manuel Otero Varela as partners, owned 1,337 cuerdas and rented another twenty-six in Aibonito, Cayey, Cidra, and Salinas that it dedicated to tobacco, coffee, and grazing animals.[27] In 1921, it owned a business assessed at $27,570, three motor vehicles at $3,000, and tobacco curing barns at $2,500.[28]

Robustiniano A. Echevarría, Cesáreo's brother, joined Theyskens & Shaw as secretary, further cementing the articulation with Aragunde y Ca.[29] Aragunde owned La Judía in Cayey, where innumerable women stemmed leaf.[30] Francisco Echevarría, another brother, had a depot that served to prepare and pack its own leaf and possibly that of others.[31]

Theyskens & Shaw was short-lived; established in 1922, it left no paper trail after 1925. Ángel Aragunde exported leaf through this firm as he had recently done with others like the Independent Tobacco Growers Corporation, where he was a small-time shareholder.[32] Cesáreo Echevarría, while represented by Theyskens & Shaw, simultaneously carried on business with Durlach Brothers, one of the largest and lasting leaf dealers of the time.[33] Aragunde y Ca.'s business ranged from planting to stemming and packing with very limited, if any, participation in the export business, thus complementing the limitations facing Theyskens & Shaw.

Most tobacco growers were not well off like Aragunde or the Echevarría brothers. One such case was the married couple Monserrate Almedina and Matilde Martínez de Jesús, who were fifty-five and sixty years old respectively in 1920. They lived with two sons, a daughter, and a young lodger, ranging in age from eight to thirty-five, in Cayey's barrio Cercadillo. The census identified the two elder sons as hands in cattle grazing, while the remaining youngster stayed at home, most likely providing labor in and around the house with fowl, livestock, and garden vegetables. Education does not seem to have been a priority because none of the school age children attended school and the whole family, except the father, was illiterate.[34]

In 1911, this white family owned a mixed-crop farm of sixty-four cuerdas in barrio Pasto Viejo and a second thirteen-cuerda farm in Cercadillo, neither mortgaged. By 1921, as the family fortunes declined, only the smaller farm remained in the family. The Department of the Treasury assessed the land at $570 and the adjoining house and barn at a paltry $60.[35] Like countless farmers, in 1922 Almedina pledged to prepare, plant, cultivate, and harvest ten cuerdas of tobacco, perhaps on his own land. Galo Rivera Malavé would provide $300 divided in several advances until the end of the harvest. In return, Almedina gave Rivera a lien on the crop and obliged himself to deliver the leaf to the creditor.

Forty-four-year-old Galo Rivera Malavé identified himself as a tobacco farmer who had recently married his second wife, Carmen, aged nineteen. In 1920, the

Rivera household occupied a plot by the Carretera Central in barrio Toíta of Cayey. It included Aurora Rivera Guiot, a twenty-two-year-old daughter from an earlier marriage, and eight-month-old Lidia Rivera Rivera. Like the Almedinas, all were white, but in sharp contrast all the adults were literate.[36]

Rivera owned properties in barrio Rincón and Toíta and in the urban area of Cayey. His properties, assessed close to $5,000, consisted of two farms adding up to twenty-five cuerdas, a 641-square-meter plot, a few houses, two barns, two motor vehicles, and $260 in profits.[37] While the motor vehicles are consonant with the transportation needs of a lien merchant, the Treasury Department failed to identify warehousing facilities appropriate for this type of leaf dealer. Rivera trucked the procured leaf in his own vehicles to a dealer with warehouses and a stemmery.[38]

The lien on Almedina's crop was but a fragment of Galo Rivera Malavé's network of growers that covered Aibonito, Barranquitas, Cayey, and Cidra in the highlands. Rivera held liens on the crops of more than sixty growers. Most rarely exceeded ten cuerdas and on occasion covered as little as one and a half cuerdas for $50.[39] Occasionally, the land itself served as guarantee to the loan, as was the case of Higinio Santiago Quiñones and his wife, Micaela Rivera, who received $400 to plant eight cuerdas at an interest rate of 12 percent.[40] When Rivera proved lacking in capital in January 1922, Durlach Brothers extended him a $20,000 loan destined for crop liens and direct purchases of leaf. The loan itself, with a 9 percent interest rate, was a lien on the leaf that Rivera contracted over the year.[41] A year later, in 1923, Rivera acknowledged funding nearly eight hundred cuerdas of tobacco on behalf of Durlach Brothers.[42]

The business relations between Rivera and the Durlach Brothers grew closer when the corporation employed Galo Rivera Jr. at the main office in Manhattan in 1923.[43] In anticipation of such eventualities, the son had already attended the Bryant & Stratton School in Boston in 1920, where he polished his English and learned bookkeeping to complement his knowledge of the local tobacco market.[44]

In 1899, three US-born sons of German immigrants Isaac and Hannah Durlach enlarged the scope of their Manhattan-based partnership to include tobacco growing, manufacture, and distribution in the United States.[45] Soon after, partners Milton, Nathaniel, and Henry established operations in Puerto Rico, where Durlach Brothers would employ dozens to manufacture cigars in the ostentatiously christened Sociedad Internacional Cigar Factory. However, they ceased manufacturing in the mid 1910s but maintained their enduring specialty as leaf dealers and lien merchants.[46] Accordingly, the firm integrated vertically into agriculture, and for fourteen years, it planted both filler and shade-grown wrapper tobacco seemingly in its own Fortuna and Colón plantations in Caguas.[47]

The firm's performance through time was uneven because it closed its cigar factory, and at times, it seems to have assumed a relation of dependency on more powerful interests in the leaf trade. For instance, during 1915, PRATCO financed Durlach Brothers liens and purchases up to $150,000, and the firm committed to turn over to the lender all the leaf bought in Puerto Rico and the United States.[48] Durlach Brothers assumed the same role that Galo Rivera would undertake a few years later. The capitalization and resources of the three firms were remarkably different. PRATCO stood at the top of the scale while Rivera struggled at the bottom.

After the PRATCO deal, the firm entered an extended upturn. A few years later, in 1919, it ceased to be a partnership to become a corporation wholly owned by Milton and Henry, since Nathan had died in 1910.[49] During the 1920s, Durlach Brothers ventured outside the tobacco industry with an urban development plan for Caguas.[50] After navigating the changing realms of the tobacco world, including the Great Depression, by 1933, the firm went on to become the third-largest leaf exporter with a 10 percent share of the market, as shown in table 6.1.

THE CONCENTRATION OF THE LEAF TRADE

Soon after the invasion, Levi Blumenstiel became the largest leaf exporter due to its early entrance in the local market. After it collapsed, the market shares of the leading firms reflected the highly fragmented nature of leaf dealers overall and more specifically of leaf exporters. Table 6.1 consequently shows that during 1907 and 1920, the three largest exporters failed to surpass 37.4 percent shares of exports. Their combined share was well below what Levi Blumenstiel alone had accumulated at earlier dates. With the passing of time, this highly competitive state of affairs started to give way to a remarkable concentration of trade among a few firms. The reduction of trading firms developed along three innovations as follows.

Corporate Leaf Dealers

After the court-mandated dissolution of the ATC in 1911, a few large corporate leaf dealers sought to occupy the space left by the trust in the procurement of leaf for the newly independent cigarette manufacturing companies. In 1921, the FTC stated that "the most important change that has taken place in the industry since the dissolution of the combination has been the formation of the Universal Leaf Tobacco Co."[51] Despite an outsize share of the US leaf market, Universal's local presence was limited to a participation in the middling La Regional Sales and La Plata Tobacco corporations.[52]

The FTC identified the International Planters Corporation as the second most important leaf dealer. Organized in 1916, it grew to become a more significant local presence than Universal (as shown in table 6.1) when it became the second-largest leaf exporter with a 9.6 market share in 1920. Its presence, however, was ephemeral because, as already indicated, it collapsed by 1922. While the forces leading to the concentration of leaf trading were already playing themselves out, it would take a few more years before the local pattern of leaf dealers showed the trend.[53]

Possibly influenced by the sheer size of the Universal and International companies, an important consolidation that plied the more upscale niche of the cigar market took place in 1920. When Maximilian Stern Inc. merged with Mendelsohn, Bornemann & Company into the Stern Mendelsohn Company, it had $1 million in capital.[54] Maximilian Stern was already a significant factor in Cuban leaf in its own right or when presiding over the Cuban Land and Leaf Tobacco Company and Henry Clay & Bock & Co., which were two important subsidiaries of the ATC.[55] On the other hand, Mendelsohn, Bornemann & Company had distributed both Havana and Puerto Rico leaf from their office and warehouse in Lower Manhattan since 1906.[56]

Before the merger, Cullman Brothers, which at the time was a large leaf-trading partnership, already had a participation in the Stern firm and had just bought Louis Bornemann's share in the Mendelsohn business. Having a participation in both, Cullman Brothers stimulated its consolidation, leaving Stern as chair of the board, Joseph F. Cullman Jr. as president, and Mendelsohn as vice president. The new company became domiciled in the Lower Manhattan tobacco district.[57] Table 6.1 shows that Stern Mendelsohn became the largest exporter of leaf in 1920. Fernando Álvarez was the resident manager in charge of stemming and packing operations in Cataño.[58] Probably representing Stern Mendelsohn, Álvarez served as lien merchant for several tobacco growers. In 1923, for instance, he advanced $30,000 to Baltasar Mendoza for six thousand hundredweights of leaf.[59]

The Leaf Department

Besides the large expansion of the Universal and International companies and the consolidation of leaf merchants, the world of the cigar leaf dealers experienced a second transformation. The cigar manufacturing sector faced deep changes—resulting from a combination of the mechanization of cigar making and the aggressive marketing of a few brands—that became two important factors leading to the concentration of production.[60] Consequently, thousands of small cigar manufacturing enterprises ceased operations because they lacked the financial resources to install the usual batteries of six or more machines in a single establishment and the marketing resources to distribute the expanded production.[61]

Max Gans's fortunes manifest the consolidation of cigar manufacture from the perspective of a long-standing leaf merchant. He got a start with several small-scale enterprises that included a stint as a Philadelphia cigar manufacturer before dealing in Connecticut leaf. A few years later, in 1905, Max Gans & Son entered the local leaf market, joining the likes of Levi Blumenstiel. The partners closely supervised local operations, at times staying for months at a time and, in their absence, relying on Frank Becerra, who attended the business from their warehouses in Caguas.[62] As of 1912, Gans still complemented local operations with imported Havana leaf and dealt in seed leaf from its Water Street offices in Manhattan.[63]

Undercapitalized, the partnership underwent profound changes to expand operations. In 1919, it ceased to be a partnership to become a corporation capitalized at $500,000, with Elias Bach and Son subscribing a "large block" of stock. Sons Robert and Charles Gans became president and secretary of the newly founded Max Gans & Son corporation that would deal exclusively in Puerto Rican leaf, shedding previous leaf interests.[64] The arrangement, however, proved short-lived; within two years, Elias Bach sold their stock in the corporation.[65]

Soon after, in 1922, H. Duys and Company became large stockholders in the Gans company, perhaps buying Elias Bach & Son's participation.[66] The close articulation of both firms led to moving Gans's offices to the same Water Street building that housed Duys's.[67] The association was consonant with Duys's earlier expansion policy with Harrison Johnson, discussed previously. In 1924, Duys relinquished its shares of the Gans corporation, most likely to Congress Cigar, which transformed it into a leaf department under the stewardship of the Gans brothers, Robert and Charles, with Frank Becerra.[68]

Congress Cigar's absorption of the Gans company conformed to a strikingly different pattern than Duys's employment of Harrison Johnson; the Theyskens & Shaw association with the Aragunde partnership; or the merger that resulted in the Stern Mendelsohn company. It was also different from Elias Bach's and H. Duys's large stock purchases in Max Gans. Congress was not a leaf dealer in any sense of the word. Established in 1896 as a Chicago buckeye, the Congress Cigar Company had grown quickly to become, by 1930, the seventh-largest US cigar manufacturer. By then, it had already shed its dependency on leaf dealers, as its own leaf department attested.[69]

The purchase was trend setting and uncommon since the times of the tobacco trust's development of the PRLTC and the Cuban Land and Leaf Tobacco Company two decades earlier. For instance, the Consolidated Cigar Corporation, the third-largest manufacturer in 1930, grew some of its wrapper tobacco but relied on leaf merchants, like Cullman Brothers, for additional wrapper and binder leaf.[70] As late as 1924, Consolidated relied on leaf merchants like Percival R. Lowe for its local leaf.[71] Perhaps following Congress Cigar's lead, the General Cigar Company, which was the largest US cigar manufacturer, started its own leaf procurement department.[72]

Charles Gans severed his relation with Congress Cigar to become General Cigar's main local representative from at least 1928 to well into the 1930s.[73] The 1933 leaf shipments to New York, presented in table 6.1, reveal General Cigar's hold of the market as it shipped 32.7 percent of all local leaf to New York. Its market share was only comparable to that reached by Levi Blumenstiel soon after the invasion. Additionally, General Cigar's leaf department was active in other regions, such as the Connecticut River Valley.[74]

Around 1933, General Cigar had seven large warehouses with a combined storage capacity of eleven million pounds in Caguas, San Lorenzo, Juncos, Manatí, and other tobacco-growing municipalities. Three to four thousand workers, mostly women, stemmed, fermented, and packed leaf while a sizable contingent of men made regular rounds of visits to supervise the firm's liens on the tobacco of innumerable growers.[75]

Independent leaf exporters, such as Durlach Brothers, reached a pinnacle in 1933 but became less salient afterward.[76] Since the 1910s, independent leaf dealers first started to yield primacy to consolidated firms like Stern Mendelsohn and International Planters and, later, to the cigar departments of large cigar manufacturers like General Cigar and García Grande, as presented in table 6.1. Aside from the latter manufacturers, the Consolidated Cigar Corporation secured a greater share of the local market that reached to about one-fourth of leaf exports at the end of the decade.[77]

The Growers' Cooperatives

The 1920s gave birth to a third type of leaf dealer: the growers' cooperative. During the first two decades of the century, frictions over the terms of crop liens and leaf price settlements facilitated the coalescence of two groups around this antagonism. Responding to differences in their shared interest in tobacco, growers, large and small, began to view themselves as distinct and with economic interests opposing those of the new types of leaf dealers. The rift became public with the Asociación de Cosecheros de Tabaco in 1921, followed by the establishment of cooperatives in several municipalities to manage crop liens and market the leaf of its members that started in 1925. This estrangement between the dealers and the alliance of a new national and the older municipal cooperatives, the Asociación de Cosecheros, and the powerful Asociación de Agricultores escalated so much that they organized a strong campaign for growers to sell the 1930–1931 crop at "reasonable" prices. Upon the failure of the sale, the organizations called for a no-planting campaign in 1931 to raise the leaf price. The open and very public aspects of the campaign included some forty meetings, marches, and the like that intermixed with more than 192 events that ranged from scattered episodes of violence and considerable attempts and actual destruction of seedbeds, patches, curing barns, and warehouses.[78]

In 1923 the US Congress established the Federal Intermediate Credit Banks to finance credit corporations that included cooperatives, which could extend loans to finance the production and marketing of agricultural goods. Two years later, the enabling act suffered modifications that extended its operations to Puerto Rico. The colonial legislature, in turn, regulated the cooperatives, allowing them to market crops and to finance production, which included "advances" that proved attractive to members.[79]

The advances helped the growth of the cooperatives by allowing the widely practiced crop liens and enabling them the capacity to market the financed leaf. In effect, the cooperatives became a new type of leaf dealer in a changing market that was becoming less and less competitive.

The cooperatives became a significant factor in the leaf market by putting up for sale a large pool of tobacco at the end of each season. In this limited sense, the cooperatives displaced some leaf dealers—in particular, small-time ones with liens on the growers' crops. These organizations came into being in the moment of the concentration of cigar manufacture and leaf exporters. During the twenties, these associations did not attempt to gain a presence in New York, like medium- to large-sized dealers such as Durlach Brothers had done previously, but chose to sell to leaf exporters that, as their relations soured, became derided as hoarders, *acaparadores*.[80] Early on, the cooperatives sought to sell directly to the leaf departments of major manufacturers. Such was the case of the G. H. P. Cigar Company that bought the tobacco pools of some cooperatives during their first season in the market.[81] After the 1931–1932 no-planting campaign, the cooperatives maintained sales with large leaf exporters and manufacturing behemoths such as General Cigar and Consolidated Cigar.[82]

CONCLUSION

The changing characters of tobacco dealers, stemmers, and merchants offer remarkable continuities and ruptures between the end of Spanish colonial rule and the depression of the 1930s. As continuities go, the lien on the growers' tobacco crop remained the powerful link that tied growers to the middlemen.

For a leaf that resembled the Cuban, few US leaf dealers had made it to the local trade before the invasion. After 1898, US merchants with an interest in local leaf first trickled and then cascaded onto the island after the Foraker Act. In what amounted to a rupture, dealers, who specialized in tobacco leaf, substituted the general-purpose merchants of the nineteenth century. Commission merchants and overseas consignees disappeared as distinct figures in the leaf trade. The US leaf dealer embodied all.[83]

The concentration of leaf companies that served as go-between growers and manufacturers took place much later than in the well-known case of cigarette and plug intimately associated with the ATC. Starting in the 1910s, formerly independent dealers became embedded in the corporate structures of large leaf companies first and then in the leaf departments of large cigar manufacturers. Finally, the 1920s saw the emergence of leaf growers that sought to face the dealers on a more equal base. Dealers grudgingly surrendered a fair share of their space to growers' cooperatives that had liens on the tobacco of their members.

CHAPTER SEVEN

The Social Organization of Tobacco Growing, 1899–1950

In 1918, Víctor Sosa, a tobacco merchant, bought twenty-three rolls of *tabaco hilado*, chewing tobacco, from his brother-in-law Alberto Gutiérrez. The latter declared having bought the rolls in Isabela, receiving them by the train tracks, and sending the merchandise by way of the American Railroad Company to Río Piedras, where Sosa received the shipment.[1]

However, José Cardona Piquet attested ownership of the rolls, claiming a theft from his establishment in Isabela. He had them confiscated and deposited in Aguadilla as evidence in a criminal case, where the district attorney accused Gutiérrez of stealing the twenty-three rolls in Sosa's possession and several additional ones in the hands of others.[2]

"WHICH ONE POORER": CHEWING FROM TOBACCO ROLLS[3]

Although common at the time of this event, chewing from tobacco rolls has practically disappeared. Rolls, *tabaco hilado*, consisted of tobacco leaves twisted in the shape and length of a rope and later wound into a cylinder sweetened with molasses. Well before the invasion, tobacco rolls were the primary medium of tobacco consumption and remained so until sometime in the twentieth century.[4]

Despite the trust's control of US plug manufactures, discussed in chapter 4, the ATC never tried to enter the local tobacco roll market. Perhaps the market differences between the rolls and plug were insurmountable. Left outside the sphere of the trust and other large corporations, it always remained oriented to the domestic market.

Neither local roll manufacturers nor growers with a specialty in this type of leaf achieved the concentration that affected the growing of leaf for cigars and their manufacture. Benefitting from proximity to the sea and other factors, it

Figure 7.1. Retailing chewing tobacco at an open market in San Sebastián, 1962. Photograph by Luis de Casenave, UPR, Biblioteca General, Colección de *El Mundo*, photo UI 5007

remained the province of small farming families that grew tobacco with short and thick leaves employing the best in the manufacture of rolls.[5] Independent artisans purchased the leaf for women to twist in home shops.[6]

Tobacco rolls, as an industry, shared the stigma associated with its consumers in the peasantry and the working poor, in contrast to the cigarette and cigar that gained the favor of the more upscale elements of society.[7] "In the big house, cigars and cigarettes. In the footpaths, pipes, *cachimbos*, and quids, *mascaduras*."[8] By the mid-twentieth century, hucksters still retailed the rolls by the inch, in quids or chaws that consumers chewed for the enjoyment of their juices. Some peddlers sold the quids at small stores, stalls, or from just open tables along the streets, crossroads, or by the town squares or marketplaces as illustrated in figure 7.1. Others, who left their homes at dawn after a small cup of black coffee and bread for breakfast, would load the ubiquitous tobacco roll along with other wares typically on their shoulders or less frequently on horseback. Peddlers would spend the day visiting sporadic clients, "which one poorer" along well-traveled paths and little-known shortcuts that traversed brooks, plains, and hills. They would return home under the gaze of the stars.[9]

Map 2.1 shows that at the fin de siècle, the main region extended from Barceloneta to Aguadilla along the northern littoral, with Quebradillas and Camuy having the most intensive tobacco agriculture in the country. By 1929, Isabela and Quebradillas had the largest proportion of farmland in this region dedicated to the leaf, with 6.33 percent and 5.73 percent respectively.[10]

A smaller chewing tobacco district extended from Guayanilla to Lajas along the southwestern coast and extending inland into San Germán and Sábana Grande, where the latter had the most intensive use of tobacco with 0.88 percent of its farmland dedicated to the leaf.[11] By 1929, Yauco and Sábana Grande had the largest proportion of farmland dedicated to this leaf, with 1.52 percent and 1.13 percent respectively.[12] Yauco's tobacco area sprawled across the plains and rolling hills that occupied the barrios closest to the Caribbean, away from the highlands that were planted with coffee.[13]

During the first decades of the century, tobacco farmland increased notably, benefitting enormously from the opening of the nearly insatiable US tobacco market. By 1918, tobacco leaf displaced the once-dominant coffee industry, only trailing sugar, to become the second export commodity.[14] The 4,264 cuerdas planted in 1897 increased slightly to 5,963 in 1899, eventually reaching 52,947 acres in 1929.[15]

COFFEE AND TOBACCO

However, the increases in the two chewing areas paled in comparison to the vertiginous expansion of the cigar leaf districts. Whereas in 1897 52.6 percent of all tobacco farmland corresponded to land usage in chewing type municipalities and 32.3 percent to the cigar type, years later the pattern had more than reversed to the benefit of leaf for cigars. In 1929, 81.8 percent of all tobacco farmland corresponded to cigar type municipalities to 12.0 percent to the chewing type.[16] In brief, the cultivation of leaf appropriate for chewing tobacco started to cede primacy during the waning of the nineteenth century to lose it during the early decades of the twentieth. The island entered the "Tobacco Era" with three distinct regions whose relative importance was about to change as leaf exports shifted away from the Cuban and Spanish markets to the United States.[17]

At the end of the Spanish regime, the main region oriented to cigar leaf occupied many mountain slopes and valleys of the Cordillera Central between Juncos and Aibonito. By then, the latter municipality had become the third major tobacco municipality with 1.55 percent of its farmland planted with the leaf. During the next decades, the region extended farther west along the highlands through Orocovis to reach Utuado. The former municipality's growth ranged from some 6 cuerdas in 1897 to 1,802 acres in 1929 that represented 4.60 percent of its farmland.[18]

The uneven expansion of the cigar leaf district along the Cordillera assumed two forms that need to be placed in context. The fin de siècle inflicted strong blows on the coffee industry. San Ciriaco, the 1899 hurricane, leveled perhaps as much as 60 percent of the coffee and shade trees needed for successful harvests.[19] Lacking the tariff protection enjoyed by the sugar and tobacco industries in the United States, coffee growing would have only short recoveries, amid considerable fluctuations, until the devastation brought forth by San Felipe, a major hurricane in September 1928.[20]

The first type of expansion refers to tobacco becoming an indispensable supplementary income to coffee farmers. In the aftermath of the invasion, many haciendas maintained coffee as their main staple but to remain profitable diversified into tobacco, which became their "indispensable crutch" with minor fruits and other subsidiary activities. Fernando Picó for Utuado and Eric Wolf for Ciales hold that tobacco did not displace coffee but supplemented it.[21] A powerful indicator of the crutch effect is that, during the first half of the century, the coffee-growing areas of Utuado and Jayuya that introduced either tobacco or sugarcane experienced "great population gains" in contrast to rural areas that did not.[22]

In effect, the proportion of land planted with tobacco in Utuado and Ciales between 1897 and 1930 experienced a net increase of 3.69 and 2.13 percent respectively. However, table 7.1 suggests that the increase did not entail a clearance of coffee trees. On the contrary, both municipalities experienced net increases of 3.40 and 6.57 percent respectively in coffee farmland during the same period. Utuado and Ciales, the municipalities with a modest increase in tobacco cultivation, are associated with the expansion of coffee, suggesting a symbiotic relation between the two.[23]

The second form of tobacco expansion refers to a more extreme reaction to the coffee crisis where the crutch replaced the ailing patient. Overall, Meléndez Muñoz described the frenzy that led many to plant tobacco. He explains why Portalatín Aponte decided to clear the coffee and shade trees from his seventeen cuerdas to replace them with tobacco. A friend convinced Portalatín "that thaumaturgical tobacco improvised wealth and transformed any good-for-nothing into a millionaire within a six-month period."[24]

In 1897, Aibonito, as indicated above, planted 331 cuerdas—that is, 1.55 percent of its land area—with tobacco, being the major cigar leaf planting district in

Table 7.1. Net change in the proportion of land planted in tobacco and coffee farms in the Cordillera, 1897–1930

Municipality	**Tobacco**	**Coffee**
Aibonito	14.94	-9.63
Barranquitas	10.57	-5.33
Cayey	11.19	-9.41
Cidra	17.46	-4.66
Comerío	19.42	-4.96
San Lorenzo	19.05	-2.24
Ciales	2.13	6.57
Utuado	3.69	3.40

Sources: Coll y Toste, *Reseña del estado social*; Bureau of the Census, *Fifteenth Census*, 232–37.
Note: The 1897 statistics of Utuado included Jayuya. The 1930 statistics maintain Jayuya within Utuado to make the data comparable.

absolute and relative terms. Despite the saliency of its tobacco, coffee was much more important when its 2,118 cuerdas represented 9.94 percent of the land area. Table 7.1 shows that in 1897 to 1929, the tobacco land area increased by 14.94 percent and coffee decreased by 9.63 percent. By 1929 the tobacco frenzy had inverted the relation to 3,441 acres or 16.50 percent for tobacco and 65 acres or 0.31 percent of the farmland with coffee trees.[25]

During the nineteenth century, growers from Sabana del Palmer cultivated a well-reputed tobacco that went by the trade name of Comerío.[26] In 1894, the town assembly requested the Ministerio de Ultramar to change its name to Comerío, to that of the leaf "most esteemed in the island," because "nobody thinks highly of tobacco from Sabana del Palmar, it is known everywhere as 'Comerío.'"[27] Despite tobacco's prestige, coffee remained the mainstay of the town's economy. In 1897, tobacco's 142 cuerdas represented 0.77 percent of total farmland to coffee's 1,064 cuerdas accounting for 5.77 percent. Table 7.1 documents the profound transformation as the proportion of tobacco farmland increased by 19.42 percent and coffee decreased by 4.96 percent between 1897 and 1929. As of 1929, tobacco's 3,418 acres represented 20.19 percent of all farmland to coffee's 136 acres that represented 0.80 percent of all farmland.[28] Comerío also became a tobacco town.

In summary, Barranquitas, Cayey, Cidra, and the other selected municipalities who experienced a 10 percent increase or more in tobacco cultivation suffered the clearance or abandonment of coffee. It was an expansion that lacked parallels in the chewing tobacco regions, where the increases were far more modest.

The fast expansion of tobacco in the eastern highlands provoked significant changes in the social organization of agriculture that merit additional examination. In many ways, the life of Baltasar Mendoza represented the fortunes of the cigar leaf districts of the eastern Cordillera Central. Sidney Mintz's characterization of Taso, in general terms, applies to Mendoza: "What happened to him happened in the broadest terms to" tobacco cultivation in the highlands.[29] Relevant aspects of Mendoza's life mirrored the expansion and eclipse of the cultivation of leaf during the early decades of the century.

BALTASAR MENDOZA AND HIS PEERS

At the fin de siècle, Baltasar Mendoza had an affair with Inocencia Coto when she was around fifteen or a few years older. Subsequently, she gave birth to Ofelia, Felia Coto in the records, around 1898. Felia carried a single surname, her mother's, because Don Balta, as he was known, legally acknowledged his paternity only decades later. The relationship seems to have been brief so that she did not become a kept woman, a *querida*, because in 1901 she gave birth to Hipólito from a relationship with another man.[30]

Inocencia, who was born around 1875 or maybe as late as 1884, probably became estranged from her family after her relationship with Mendoza.[31] According to the 1910 census, she did not live with either of her parents or siblings. Instead, she headed a household solely composed of three of her four children, in a barrio with plenty of farmworkers and a few cigar makers. Felia, the eldest, lived elsewhere. Interestingly, Inocencia did not hold an income-earning occupation.

By 1920, she was still head of a household composed of four of her children, an elder brother, and a roomer. The brother's presence likely signified a mending of family relations. The four men in the house joined Inocencia as field hands in tobacco farms in barrio Toíta of Cayey. Her six- and ten-year-old daughters were completely illiterate, did not attend school, and must have been in charge of housework, the kitchen garden, and the fowl, fed more for the eggs than for the meat.[32] Felia did not live with her mother and siblings because she was already residing elsewhere with her legal husband.[33]

As in other latitudes, some men of power and wealth acted on their attraction and satisfied their passion with young peasant women. Such relations were common in the tobacco-growing areas as elsewhere in the Caribbean, usually between people of unequal rank, social class, and race that consequently "brought additional benefits to the girl's family."[34] Probably due to the briefness of the relationship, few benefits seem to have accrued to the daughter, less to her family. For instance, Felia remained illiterate like her sisters.[35] The palpable benefits seem to have been her father's legal recognition, the right to bear his surname, and a $500 bequest in his will.[36]

The affair and the *querida* system exhibited strong regional variations. According to Sidney Mintz, "The *querida*, or mistress pattern, which assumes the proportions of an institution in the more privileged classes, is missing [in the communities of rural proletarians in the sugar producing regions] . . . Such an arrangement lies beyond the economic means of the working people."[37]

Simply put, the affair and the mistress relation were common in regions with significant class and gender stratification where it reinforced the subordination of the weak, here a peasant and a woman, by the powerful, here an hacendado and a man. A knowledgeable observer from the tobacco highlands did not describe these relations in the sober economic analysis, just cited, but emphasized the exercise of power and satisfaction of lust that they entailed.[38] "The unhappiness of the peasant's wife or daughter for being beautiful ('Oh, the misfortune of being born beautiful!' said the poet) was an abundant and easy delicacy for the sexual appetite of the landlord, father of the *agrego*, etc., who satisfied it with the same abandon as the ancient feudal lord." Mendoza's relation with Inocencia was not an isolated incident but responded to the pattern identified by Manners and Meléndez Muñoz. He had other out-of-wedlock children.[39]

Baltasar Mendoza was around twenty-nine years old at Felia's birth.[40] His mother, Magdalena, raised him after his father died in 1871, when he was two years old. His father's private will suggests the presence of some properties that probably allowed Baltasar and other siblings to attend school, helped them to avoid joining the ranks of the peonage, and, maybe, lasted long enough to provide a head start in their adult lives.[41] At twenty-five years of age, he married Irene Carattini in the Aibonito Catholic church.[42]

By 1910, he owned 195 cuerdas in barrio Toíta, where Inocencia lived, for a total of 235 in Cayey alone.[43] One of his main landholdings, appropriately named El Banco, the Bank, helped bankroll Don Balta's expansion and growth as an hacendado. The estate appears under his name in 1913 and at least until 1926, if not until his death. El Banco, in barrio Rabanal of neighboring Cidra, was a 676¼-cuerda holding with tobacco as its main staple. It serves as an important indicator of tobacco in his economic activities. He gave the PRLTC crop liens, *refacción*, worth $35,000 in 1913 and again in 1914, on El Banco and two additional farms.[44]

A few years later, in 1917, Don Balta's agricultural holdings included 1,185 and 873 cuerdas in Cayey and Cidra respectively, with an additional 253 leased in Cayey, which were dedicated to tobacco, sugarcane, and pasture.[45] As the extent of his tobacco farming increased, so did the crop liens. For instance, he financed the 1925–1926 season from three different sources. The PRLTC advanced $52,000 in exchange for liens on the leaf to be planted in 500 cuerdas, the Banco de Ponce lent $7,000 for liens of leaf planted in 65 cuerdas, and a third creditor lent $16,000 for 120 cuerdas. In total, Mendoza encumbered the leaf to be planted in 685 cuerdas for $75,000 with annual interests that ranged from 7.5 to 10.0 percent.[46]

During the 1920s his accumulation of land continued unabated. By 1931, a year before his death, Mendoza owned 188 cuerdas in Aibonito, 258 in Caguas, 1,492 in Cidra, and 4,605 in Cayey, amounting to 6,543 cuerdas.[47]

Don Balta's economic ascendancy extended well beyond his agricultural endeavors. His success in electoral politics dates from 1906, upon becoming a councilor in Cayey on the Union Party ticket.[48] As his party maintained a majority in the municipality until 1932, he retained the position almost uninterruptedly until elected mayor in 1928.[49] In effect, Mendoza became a powerful contender in local politics in a close association with his brother Heraclio, who was a longtime mayor, and a political ally, Benigno Fernández García, who served as councilor, mayor, and representative to the colonial Assembly of Delegates.[50]

Don Balta's ascendancy grew to such an extent that Fernández García's eulogy described him as follows:

> He was our town's captain, he was the guide, he was the counselor, he was the man who would not be daunted by the most difficult of situations. He had the amazing gift to make out the light in the dark. When dejection spread, when we failed to see the trail that led to safety, Baltasar Mendoza with this eminent intelligence, with his dazzling criterion, would identify the rescuing formula, the remedy to evil, and all of us would follow, because we learnt to trust his indisputable gifts to conduct the affairs of men.[51]

Baltasar Mendoza was not the lone hacendado in the tobacco-growing areas. He formed part of a social class that was often intertwined with kinship relations. His brother Heraclio is a case in point. In 1917, he held 265 cuerdas in Cayey, 720 in Cidra, and 51 in Aguas Buenas for a total of 1,036 cuerdas dedicated to tobacco, sugarcane, and grazing animals.[52]

Lending credence to the proverb that "money begets money," in 1917 Tomás Rodríguez Rivera, a wealthy farmer in his own right, married Angelina, one of Heraclio Mendoza's daughters.[53] That same year the tax rolls identified him as owning 476 cuerdas and leasing another 389 in Cayey, where he grew tobacco and sugarcane and grazed animals.[54] His activities on behalf of tobacco farmers led to his election as the founding president of the Cayey leaf growers' cooperative in 1925, where he remained an active member for years to come.[55]

Large tobacco landholdings were not unique to Cayey but were common in the tobacco districts of the eastern highlands. For instance, Modesto Cobián Rivera and Rafael Solares joined the ranks of merchants and identified themselves as such late in the nineteenth century.[56] However, during the first decades of the twentieth century, their economic activities gravitated more to agriculture so that by 1930 they had assumed the identity of tobacco farmers.[57] By 1917, their partnership, Cobián Solares & Co., grew tobacco and grazed livestock on 849 cuerdas in

Comerío and Naranjito and on 830 leased in Coamo.[58] The importance of their leaf activities was such that Cobián took a leading role in the organization of the growers' cooperative in Comerío. Becoming its founding president in 1925, he held the position for the next few years, whereas Solares joined the organization as a regular member.[59] Like the Mendozas, kinship was a significant bonding factor when both partners married Josefa and Manuela, two Espina Rivera sisters.[60]

THE HACIENDA AND THE SMALLHOLDING DURING THE TOBACCO ERA

Where did the Don Balta and his peers fit in the wider social and economic space of the tobacco-growing region of the eastern Cordillera? The closest characterization stems from Charles Rogler's sociological study of Comerío during the mid-1930s. Tax assessments allowed the identification of the twenty-five largest farmers as the same individuals that owned about half the land in barrios Vega Redonda, Piñas, Río Hondo, and Palomas, the four tobacco-growing barrios. Some 4,000 people lived on the farms of these landowners that Rogler called "tobacco planters." Each estate had an average of 160 residents on farms that averaged 223 acres in extension.[61]

Although the tobacco hacienda had long embarked on the route to capitalism, several forms of labor associated with serfdom—mainly sharecroppers and those locally known as *agregados* or *arrimados*—provided labor to the propertied.[62] While most Comerío hacendados paid their workers wages, a small number added mechanisms, more prevalent during earlier days, that assured them a stable labor force. These included rent-free housing, authorization to raise pigs and chickens, or granting a plot to grow vegetables.[63] In Barranquitas, a neighboring tobacco municipality, they also benefitted from occasional free milk, firewood, and, in earlier times, rice grown on the farm.[64]

While Rogler's twenty-five "tobacco planters" earned their sustenance from the land, nineteen did not live on their farms but in the urban area, where they had their "social interests" and raised their children.[65] For instance, Modesto Cobián lived on Georgetti Street and Rafael Solares on de Diego Street. Plácido Longo, however, lived in the countryside but on the outskirts of town, in the junction of barrios Naranjo with Palomas and Vega Redonda.[66] In the interest to prepare their children for a world beyond the narrow confines of the highlands, Modesto embarked for New York City with daughter Josefa and son Ángel in 1920. Soon after, his son and namesake went to college in the United States.[67]

This research holds that the social and economic organization of tobacco production during the first half of the twentieth century was far from homogeneous. Leaving aside the extensive farmland of the tobacco trust, land, labor, and capital for tobacco growing coalesced around three distinct arrangements that their participants also recognized as meaningful: first, large farms owned by hacendados and worked by *agregados*; second, small independent peasants; and finally, sharecroppers.

However, many influential scholars have consistently stressed that tobacco growing had been the domain of the small farm. For instance, Robert A. Manners did an ethnography of Barranquitas, a tobacco and minor crop's municipality, as part of *The People of Puerto Rico* project, under the direction of Julian H. Steward. After addressing the nuances of tobacco agriculture with considerable subtlety, he identified the leaf as the "poor man's cash crop" in contrast to coffee and sugarcane.[68] Both Manners and Steward held that tobacco was a "cash crop requiring little acreage," which in combination with subsistence farming made the "survival on smallholdings more feasible."[69] Another scholar, John P. Augelli, carried a geographic investigation of a river basin nested in the eastern highlands that roughly corresponded to the tobacco-growing town of San Lorenzo.[70] Although acknowledging an earlier period that he called the Tobacco Era (1898–1932), Augelli still associated tobacco farming with "small farms where slopes are steep and soils have a low fertility rating."[71] An important recent study by César Ayala and Laird Bergad holds that mostly "very small-scale producers" were responsible for the tobacco crop between 1899 and 1935.[72] At the other end, Miguel Meléndez Muñoz pointed out a clear difference between the small farm and what he called the *fundo*, the country estate.[73]

The association of tobacco farming with smallholdings was typical of pre-invasion Puerto Rico. In the late nineteenth century, tobacco was "the appropriate crop to preserve and support the nucleus of small farming proprietors."[74] Nevertheless, nineteenth-century smallholders had in their midst not only the Rucabado brothers, who had sizable leaf-growing operations, but also others such as Modesto Solá, Caguas's largest tobacco grower, who, with 926 cuerdas of farmland, has not been the subject of research.[75]

During Augelli's Tobacco Era, the small farmer coexisted with a vigorous hacienda system. The interregnum proved consistent with Rogler's "tobacco planters" and Meléndez Muñoz's *fundos*, the Mendozas, the Cobiáns, and others.

COLLAPSE OF THE HACIENDA

Shortly after the invasion, the insatiable appetite for tobacco employed in US cigars absorbed an ever-increasing local production until the mid-1920s. The rising demand for local leaf led to the reorientation to tobacco production in the Cordillera that eased the way for the development of a small but significant hacendado class. What had been a veritable expansion ended during the second half of the 1920s and led to a 50 percent collapse of leaf prices that, in turn, translated into a considerable reduction in exports during the following years.[76]

An economic study of 270 tobacco farms in 1936–1937 showed that commercial banks had crop liens on twelve landholdings that their owners had relinquished because of excessive encumbrances. Each of these "very large farms" averaged 194 cuerdas and represented 4 percent of the farms but accounted for 17 percent of leaf production.[77] Meléndez Muñoz identified a vulnerability to economic downturns, as the Great Depression, that led to a greater weakness and fragility of the large landed tobacco estate, the *fundo*, in contrast to the sturdiness and greater efficiency of the small farm. The latter benefitted from family labor, who earned no wages, and could substantially rely on the produce obtained from crop rotation on their farms after the end of the leaf harvest.[78] In summary, the crisis of production had a stronger effect on the hacendados than over the small independent peasants.

A bit over a decade later, Manners identified the "abandonment of large tobacco farms by most of the bigger producers." At the time of his research, only two recipients of government-issued quotas had "a fraction over one hundred cuerdas."[79] Gone was the extensive farmland that Baltasar Mendoza planted with tobacco and that of others, such as the 150 cuerdas that Julio Esteves Solá from Caguas planted with tobacco on his 286 cuerdas of farmland in 1928.[80]

Consequently, the hacendados initially held their ground firmly during the twenties but began to wither away during and after the depression of the thirties. In 1932, an essayist, newspaper editor, and senator personified their collapse when he declared that "Baltasar Mendoza, the most important of all, our fraternal and dear friend, who ought to and became a millionaire, then in the inclined plane of life, facing the perspective of the ruin he passed on to his children, died of deep moral prostration."[81]

However, they did "not go gently into that good night" but raged "against the dying of the light."[82] Several hacendados like Baltasar Mendoza, Tomás Rodríguez, Modesto Cobián Rivera, and Plácido Longo Solares became strong supporters and provided a substantial part of the leadership of a social movement built around the cooperatives and other organizations such as the Tobacco Growers Association. The leadership attempted to replace lien merchants with marketing cooperatives in an attempt to control the financing and distribution of the leaf. Begun during the late twenties, the hacendado-directed movement organized a no-planting season, the "Año de la no siembra," to raise leaf prices during the 1931–1932 season.[83]

WOMEN IN TOBACCO FARMING

During the Tobacco Era, the corporate landed estate, the hacienda, and the smallholding became the main forms of organizing production. *Agregados*, farm

Table 7.2. Number and proportion of women in tobacco agriculture, 1910–1950

	Number	Percent	Total
1910	842	13.6	6,188
1920	6,807	22.3	30,489
1940	1,617	8.9	18,171
1950	1,337	8.8	15,217

Sources: Bureau of the Census, *Thirteenth Census, Occupation Statistics*, 4:295; Bureau of the Census, *Fourteenth Census, Population 1920 Occupation*, chapter 8, 4:88; Bureau of the Census, *Sixteenth Census, Characteristics of the Population*, 2:48; Bureau of the Census, *Census of Population: 1950*, vol. 2. *Characteristics of the Population*, part 53, Puerto Rico, chapter 7 (Washington, DC: GPO, 1953), 186.
Note: Data unavailable for the 1930 and 1935 censuses.

managers, hacendados, sharecroppers, and smallholders entered different kinds of social relations to grow and cultivate the commodity. However, class divisions did not exhaust stratification because gender added a powerful dimension to social class in the tobacco fields.

The labor force participation rates of women in farm work varied considerably depending on the agricultural sector in which they labored. Nonetheless, women in tobacco farms had participation rates that surpassed those of other agricultural products during the late nineteenth century, if not earlier.[84] Possibly intended as hyperbole, a noted essayist went as far as to claim that women made up half of those working in tobacco agriculture.[85]

Their strong participation extended well into the twentieth century. For instance, in 1940, women's 8.9 percent of the labor force in tobacco agriculture clearly surpassed their proportion in sugarcane fields at 1.0 percent, in coffee farms at 2.9 percent, and other farming at 4.5 percent.[86] Table 7.2 shows that the proportion in tobacco farming during the period hovered from a low of just beneath 9.0 percent in 1940 and 1950 to a high of 22.3 percent in 1920. The rate of participation during the first quarter of the century was markedly higher than during the second, perhaps suggesting that nineteenth-century proportions might have been higher.

The fair proportion of women in tobacco agriculture did not imply that most worked the fields beside the men. Overall, local women, such as Inocencia Coto, typically weeded the seedbeds by hand; transplanted seedlings to the fields; wormed the leaves of the growing plant, stringed harvested leaves on cords, and then tied them to sticks that men hung to dry in the sheds; and only occasionally worked the fields in the company of men. Hoe cultivation and harvesting remained mostly reserved for men.[87]

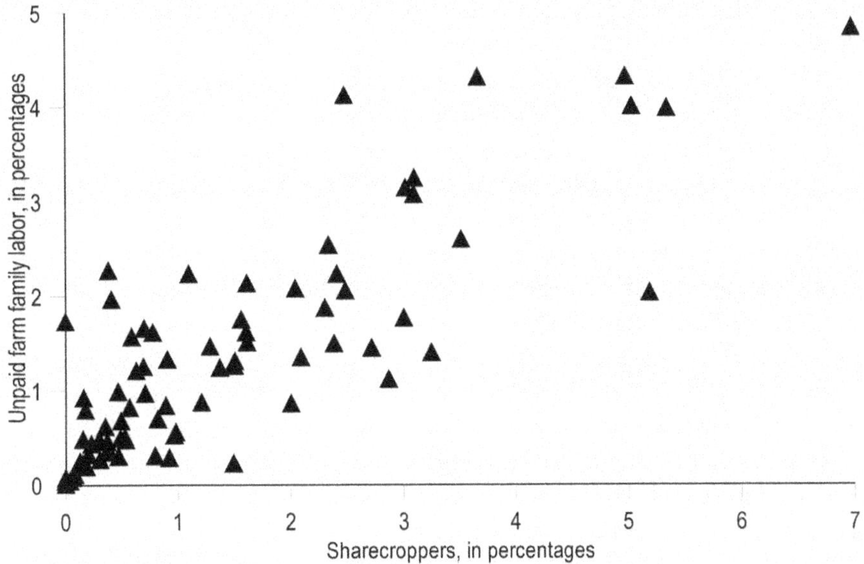

Figure 7.2. Unpaid farm family labor by sharecroppers, 1950

Sources: Bureau of the Census, *Census of Population: 1950*, vol. 2. *Characteristics of the Population*, part 53, Puerto Rico, chapter 6 (Washington, D.C.: GPO, 1953), 84–93; Bureau of the Census, *Census of Agriculture: 1950*, vol. 1. *Counties and State Economic Areas*, part 34, Territories and Possessions, chapter 5 (Washington, D.C.: GPO, 1952), 164.

A 1928 study of tobacco farms documented that the gender-based division of labor was more widespread in small family farms as members of the growers' households actively participated in planting and cultivation in farms with less than six acres planted with the crop.[88] Those with larger farms incorporated wage labor and sharecroppers, where the latter in turn depended on their families, notably women and children, to cultivate tobacco.[89] Haciendas and plantations relied on both, to which they added *agregados*.[90] Besides enduring occupational segregation, women were not usually independent wage earners on par with men.

The pairing of small-scale farming and sharecropping with unpaid family labor helps to explain this variant of the subordination of women. Their articulation with unpaid family work represented an arrangement of the labor force whereby all able-bodied members of a household would partake in the production of agricultural goods for the market. The centrality of the male breadwinner in tobacco planting broadened to include the wife and children. However, the man of the house retained "full authority" over family members in tobacco agriculture and acted publicly on their behalf.[91]

Census data allow a statistical look at the relation between family labor and sharecropping. Their distribution was uneven across the land, but figure 7.2 shows that municipalities with an above-average proportion of sharecroppers were likely to be the same towns with above-average proportion of the unpaid family farm labor.[92] In 1950, Naranjito, a significant tobacco-growing municipality, had the highest percentage of unpaid family farm labor, at 4.84 percent, and simultaneously the highest percentage of sharecroppers, at 6.97 percent of the total population of the municipality. San Lorenzo, with the third-highest proportion of tobacco farmworkers, had the second-highest percentage of unpaid farm family workers, at 4.33 percent, and was the fifth in the concentration of sharecroppers, at 4.97 percent. The strong relation observed in figure 7.2 yields a remarkably high Pearson correlation of 0.828, with data for all seventy-seven municipalities, between the percentage of sharecroppers and that of the unpaid farm workers.

The quantitative look also allows restating that sharecropping with unpaid farm family labor became inextricably associated with tobacco growing. With information available for all seventy-seven municipalities, the Pearson correlations of both variables with the proportion of women employed in tobacco agriculture amounted to 0.498 and 0.587 respectively.

Only the 1950 census includes information on sharecroppers at the municipality level during the period under study. It must be kept in mind that by mid-century, tobacco agriculture had experienced considerable change. Corporate plantations, such as those run by the PRLTC and the Cayey-Caguas Tobacco companies, and most tobacco haciendas had disappeared by the 1930s. By 1950, large farms were no longer a significant factor. Consequently, the nature and extent of women's participation in large-scale tobacco agriculture are hard to estimate.

The very limited evidence on large landholdings derives from the November 1918 strike that affected farmworkers in several Comerío plantations during the heyday of the PRLTC. Starting in the Buena Vista plantation, it spread to the Río Hondo, Sabana Buena Vista, and Siembra Limón farms. Seedbed workers, who were mostly women, were the only type of worker identified in the conflict. Furthermore, both police reports and newspaper articles stressed the saliency of women strikers when they referred at times to "over one-hundred women, men, and children" at one point and to "some forty peons of both sexes" at another. The available information, however, does not offer additional details about the proportion of women.[93]

While women on tobacco farms had labor participation rates that surpassed those of other agricultural products, they experienced strong occupational segregation. Women seem to have had a strong presence on small independent farms and among sharecroppers that guaranteed the supervision of the women to the male head of their household. Besides, they must have been a significant, if undetermined, proportion of workers on tobacco plantations; it remains to be found if women were straight wage workers or their insertion into salaried work experienced a mediation by the presence of male relatives, as among sharecroppers.

CONCLUSION

This chapter has examined tobacco agriculture from its expansion and transformation to its crisis during the first half of the twentieth century. It has followed the social organization of tobacco farming along several dimensions including type of tobacco harvested, nature of the expansion in the hinterland, the displacement of coffee, the development of an hacendado class, and finally the strong participation of women.

At the turn of the century, tobacco leaf had already earned a reputation in the manufacture of cigars. Contrary to commonly held beliefs, the bulk of tobacco leaf then planted was destined for the manufacture of tobacco rolls and not into cigars. In fact, the largest agricultural district, located around Isabela in and along the northwest littoral, grew a leaf mainly employed in the manufacture of chewing tobacco.

The tobacco-growing region that expanded in the valleys and mountain slopes of the eastern Cordillera differed significantly from that of the northwest littoral because its leaf became cigars and cigarettes. This region experienced an enormous expansion during the early decades of the twentieth century to become the largest and most reputed district.

The veritable expansion of tobacco in the eastern highlands did not reclaim much fallow or virgin land for agriculture but entailed the near complete displacement of coffee, with the noticeable exceptions in Utuado and Ciales, duly noted in the literature. Notable researchers generally considered tobacco growing as the domain of the smallholding. Contrary to most of the literature, the expansion eased the way for large farmers or smaller ones that accumulated land to join the ranks of a small but vibrant class of hacendados that lasted until the end of the Tobacco Era during the 1930s.

While several researchers have noted the participation of women in cigar manufacture, their presence in tobacco agriculture has attracted little attention. In contrast to women in manufacturing, their work in small independent farms and within sharecropping families kept most under the close supervision of the male heads of their households. Nevertheless, women in tobacco farms had the highest participation rates of all agricultural sectors.

CHAPTER EIGHT

Strikes and the Institutionalization of Trade Unions in Tobacco Manufacture, 1892–1927

Well into his nineties, Demetrio Guzmán reminisced about his apprenticeship at the shoemaking shop of an uncle, recalling his craft with pride while emphatically denying he was ever a cobbler. He also remembered his years in buckeyes and those in the employ of the trust, where his limited cigar-making skills forced him to craft the cheaper styles. This young man became immersed in the militant working-class culture of Cayey and went on to become a reader in tobacco factories and a socialist agitator one hundred years ago.

As an agitator he appeared, for instance, as a speaker at a Socialist Party meeting in 1920.[1] Sometime later, in 1922, he lamented the incapacity of labor unions from his municipality to celebrate Labor Day in due form and had to settle for a mass meeting.[2] He became a labor organizer for the Federación Libre de Trabajadores, an AFL affiliate, in his spare time up to the point where he became an officer in a provisional union of agricultural workers in 1923.[3]

When speaking of the role of trade unions, this agitator, however, held that the most important working-class organizations of his youth were churches and social clubs, known as *casinos*, for dancing and where the more-educated workers held poetry readings, conferences, and other cultural activities. He stressed that labor unions were clearly of lesser saliency than *casinos* and churches. In his words, "there were no organizations but those *casinos* and churches, those for praying and those for dancing. What else was there?"[4]

The current conception of strikes evokes powerful images of unions gaining certification to represent workers and in calling, leading, and bringing walkouts to an end. Guzmán's recollections pose a sharp contrast to this imagery. In the virtual absence or profound weakness of trade unions, after a strike arose the workers

> would meet and had to nominate someone to deal with the businesses taking place, were they cigars or whatever they may be. They had to meet, and at the meeting they needed somebody to deal with the matters at hand, and if there were four or five people, well, one became the leader. And that leader had their respect and to that one they talked . . . They knew you were the most active in those matters. Go, look for and talk to so and so and he will tell you: one should do this.[5]

Guzmán's memories resemble, in many ways, the experiences of countless workers and agitators for the simple reason that his crafts and political consciousness parallel many of those with similar trades. The subservience of unions to strikes was the way things were in his municipality, and probably in the country, and among, perhaps, craftspeople, if not workers, in general. This chapter explores the earliest relation between unions and strikes, passing over to that depicted by Guzmán, to end when it assumed a form recognizable to a current observer or participant.

Modern-day strikes are generally large, peaceful, short, and, of course, union led while a century ago the reverse was the norm. In the industrial world, the transition from one model to the other seems to have occurred during the 1930s and 1940s. According to Edward Shorter and Charles Tilly, French strikes "modernized" and found "new sophistication" after the Popular Front of the 1930s. Recent strikes have many participants but are brief when compared with pre-1930 ones. The growth of national unions that could mobilize their membership was important for the transition to take hold.[6] According to David Snyder, strikes over "union organization," as opposed to those over work and economic conditions, were more frequent in the United States before World War II.[7] Both articles suggest that management in early twentieth-century France and the United States had not yet accepted the fact of unions and strikes. Seemingly, such acceptance came only after the Second World War.

If management had a hard time adjusting to strikes and unions, so did workers, although for different reasons. Labor and socialist agitators developed, reflected on, and propagated strikes and trade unions. They struggled intensely for their ideas to take hold among workers. The very idea of membership in unions and holding strikes—so intertwined with working-class culture today—provoked resistance from many workers because they were used to other forms of expressing grievances against their foes and solidarity with friends. The acceptance of strikes and unions among workers needs a clear conceptual distinction between mass and leadership, between the articulate and the silent, between mass and agitator. Barrington Moore documented the cleavage when he stated:

> Once a critical mass of potentially discontented people has come into existence through the working out of large-scale institutional forces the stage is set for the

appearance of "outside agitators." It is important to recognize the crucial significance of their role because social critics are inclined to minimize it for fear of carrying water to the mills of conservatism and reaction. Since the time of the Apostles, and perhaps earlier, no social movement has been without its army of preachers and militants to spread the good tidings of escape from the pains and evils of this world. It is always an activist minority that promotes and promulgates new standards of condemnation.[8]

For strikes and unions to be effective, they needed acceptance by capital and labor alike. This chapter examines both, focusing primarily on their articulation. Typically, strikes antedated unions. Speaking for the German case, Moore described early stoppages as "the brief flare-up in the form of a strike over some apparent injustice by the employer: the sudden announcement of a wage cut or the firing of a fellow worker."[9] Trade unions arrived later only after many failed attempts to bring the strike under union control. Michelle Perrot examined the relation between strike and union in late nineteenth-century France and documented the complete autonomy of the strike with respect to the unions.[10]

Labor agitators spread the word about the advantages of trade unions as the locus of the strike by stressing that success against the employer entailed a strong sense of discipline and considerable advance planning. They presented the trade union as the organization to initiate, lead, and end strikes. Union officials sought the institutionalization of the strike by removing its organization from strikers and putting it in trade unions, thus implying the subordination of the mass to leadership in their common conflict against capital. Nineteenth-century French and German trade unions, in due time, gained control of the strike, in effect bureaucratizing it. Union recognition was not only a matter for capital to recognize, as Snyder rightly documented, but also for workers to accept.

The loss of spontaneity among the represented, unforeseen by labor agitators, became an important consequence of the institutionalization of strikes. This fact has not gone unnoticed by researchers. For instance, Perrot expresses sadness over union control of strikes:

> Union action did not, as certain economists and politicians expected, reduce the number of strikes, but it did undoubtedly transform strike procedure and rationalise the opening stages. It remains for us to discover, however—and this is a great problem and which still concerns us today—whether it is possible to harness the energy of spontaneity without the source running dry. Does taming a wild animal necessarily mean domesticating it?[11]

When union officials came to represent workers, they sought to demobilize initiatives that could thwart success in a strike. The locus of struggle for better labor conditions and higher wages moved from the workers to their leadership.

Barrington Moore calls it the appropriation of outrage by the labor organizations for they offer space only for rational calculus, none for anger. Moore identified sadness with institutionalization and the loss of the joy of spontaneity. Trade unions expropriated the strike in much the same way that the articulate subordinated or, perhaps, silenced the inarticulate.[12]

This chapter examines the articulation of union and strike in a colonial situation very different from the industrial world. Nevertheless, this colonial experience followed the industrial one in its early stages and, with important qualifications, during the later ones. The subordination of strikes to unions was fragile and short-lived when referring to the tenacity of workers in staging strikes and the helplessness of union officials to control them.

In addition, it documents the differentiation of strikes from other forms of collective conflict and the changes they underwent from the earliest workers' organizations to the growth of large and powerful trade unions. These modifications and transformations in local tobacco manufacture between the 1890s and the mid-1920s range from the very first strikes to the last major one in the industry. The choice of this sector obeys the fact that the tobacco industry became a well-developed industrial sector where cigar makers had a head start in the establishment of guilds, strikes, trade unions, and the development of a nationwide federation of unions. Women in the industry, mostly stemmers, were among the first to join unions, and their strike record was unparalleled during the period under scrutiny.[13]

This chapter is a case study followed in detail for some thirty-five years that allows an in-depth examination of the process of articulation between the strike and trade unions in a single industrial sector. This approach permits the identification of continuities and breaks in the relation. Concentration on a single case goes beyond statistical series and into collective agreements, the statutes of guilds and unions, police records, propaganda leaflets, and a press that are rich expressions of a vibrant working-class culture.

This analysis surveys the strike and its articulation with unions in local tobacco manufacture along five phases. First the strike emerged as a grievance mechanism distinct from others as the food riot and the march. It is only after the strike had already gained social recognition for addressing capital and labor relations that trade unions started to emerge. Second, early relations between strikes and unions developed when unions were short-lived and lent strikes support instead of leadership. Third, initial union attempts to control strikes proved unsuccessful, but unions began to have an important role not in the opening stages but in their settlement. Unions gained a social space by providing other services and benefits to the workers. Fourth, with powerful assistance from US trade unions, local unions representing cigar makers at the largest manufacturing firm effectively subordinated the strike. Cigar makers' unions deliberately excluded women, mostly leaf sorters and stemmers, even if employed by the same firm.[14] Women struck, bargained, and reached collective agreements through intimately related but gender-segregated trade unions. Lastly, the subordination of the strike by trade unions, contrary to the European experience, proved short-lived. The strike regained its autonomy from unions although retaining some traits developed by the cigar makers' unions.

THE EMERGING FORM OF THE STRIKE (1892–1900)

Changes in tobacco manufacture provided the material foundation for early labor disputes and strikes. Late nineteenth-century manufactures included three products: roll-chewing tobacco, cigars, and cigarettes. Before 1870, cigar and cigarette manufacture were in the hands of independent artisans and growers who twisted chewing tobacco, *tabaco hilado*, into rope and rolled it in their own homes. Mechanization and factories were nonexistent.

As discussed in chapter 2, cigar and cigarette production began a transition to wage labor in a factory setting after 1870. By the early 1890s the urban landscape became dotted with factories where a handful employed more than a hundred workers. They stood alongside artisanal shops, *chinchales*, while roll-chewing tobacco remained a cottage industry.

A dictionary definition considers the strike as a "refusal to work organized by a body of employees as a form of protest, typically in an attempt to gain a concession or concessions from their employer."[15] However, it misses fundamental social considerations such as its cultural character and its historically changing character. Take notice that while strikers were wage laborers not all laborers did strike. Neither did the strike spring out in contemporary form. Men (women were few) created and re-created the strike, and capital and labor invented each other. Early labor strife contained elements from earlier relations of production and from previous forms of collective conflict.[16] Extant forms of conflict started to give way to the strike as people assumed and interpreted new wage labor and factories in different terms. The contemporary form of the strike developed only gradually among pieceworkers, mainly cigar makers, employed in factories. Consequently, strikes bore no relation to manufacture among independent producers, family labor, or those paid in kind.

A sequential examination of nine early labor disputes in cigar and cigarette manufacture provides the background to examine the emergence and modifications to the primitive forms of the strike. These labor conflicts, occurring between 1892 and 1900, exhibit a wider range of variation that started to coalesce around a more standard form by 1900.

"Unruly" actions, as a social mechanism to challenge authority in the workplace, started to give way to strikes. While early strikers improvised much on the expression of grievances, they shared several characteristics: (1) They were sudden. (2) Strikers milled about the factory without pickets, slogans or rallies. (3) If management received written demands, it was after the strike had begun. (4) Strikers developed an early interest in winning over public opinion. They relied on propaganda leaflets and newspapers. (5) Strikers attempted to gain support from organizations with other functions. (6) They sought binding arbitration.

An early labor dispute in tobacco manufacture took place in Las Dos Antillas, which was then the oldest and largest factory in the colony. In operation since 1870, the factory employed more than thirty cigar makers by 1876 and by 1883 more than one hundred.[17] The factory also had had a cigarette-making department since the 1880s.[18] For nearly a quarter of a century the relation between capital and labor had been in the making until it went sour openly in 1892. Chanting and rowdy cigar makers did not respond to authority at the workplace on more than one occasion.[19] The owner of the establishment understood the action only as ungratefulness and disrespect because he had nurtured the workers into the craft.[20] He locked more than a hundred out of the factory, possibly responding to a European cultural practice already in use by tobacco fabricants in Havana and about to spread to their Philippine counterparts.[21]

These repeated challenges to authority within the cigar shop itself suggested a new identity for the workers in their opposition to capital. While chanting and rowdiness were part of the cultural resources to defy authority in other settings, they proved useful in the workplace. Chanting and disorderly behavior were, probably, more in consonance with contemporary collective contention as the contemporary march in coastal Humacao, where hundreds demanded bread from the mayor. Catcalls, yells, and chants also typified the common people who marched by city hall, the court of justice, and the governor's palace to condemn a raise in tariffs on ordinary consumption articles.[22] The strike—in the sense of a work stoppage manned from outside the workplace—was an acknowledged possibility that had powerful and vocal opponents in the working-class press as late as the year of this lockout.[23] Not surprisingly, the cigar makers did not strike, but they disrupted work within the confines of the factory while, disoriented, the owner shut down the factory, only to reopen later. The strike was not yet part of the repertoire, of the cultural modules, to vent up grievances. The incident was seemingly a first in the industry.[24]

Two years later working-class reaction was markedly different when colonial authorities in Madrid imposed heavy taxes on the local monopolies of matches and petroleum, forcing a noticeable rise of their retail prices. The situation worsened in the face of a monetary crisis when merchants accepted small change, the money of the common people, at half its value.[25] Late 1894 and early 1895 saw the urban riot and a large wave of strikes.[26]

In 1895, cigar makers abandoned La Ultramarina, in San Juan, expecting a pay raise, while those in the Sánchez y Hermanos factory in Comerío won a raise after a one-day strike.[27] *La Democracia* newspaper was at pains to show the "deferent" behavior and "familial affection" of the proprietor for the workers as strike and stoppage awed owner and journalist alike.[28] Cigar makers were beginning a new relation with manufacturers, a relation of opposition. Whereas the riot and noisy crowds were dominant as forms of contention in 1892, the strike gained ground in 1894–1895. After 1895, the strike became a common resource of cigar makers in their conflict with capital.

One hundred sixty cigar makers struck La Ultramarina for six days during 1897 over wage reductions and their refusal to stem tobacco. The strike was a combination of past forms of contention and the new. It began spontaneously; strikers milled about the factory, held no pickets, and did not shout slogans. Management received written demands, not on the first day, but on the third.

An important dimension of early strikes was to summon old organizations for new purposes. The Ultramarina strikers lacked a formal organization as a trade union, but many were members of the cigar makers' guild. They attempted, unsuccessfully, to involve the guild as its president refused because the statutes did not cover strikes. Strikers called for an extraordinary assembly of the guild to oust the president.[29] Expected support must have been loans or outright payment of economic benefits that guilds usually paid members in case of illness or incapacity.[30]

Despite their larger size and longer duration, turn-of-the-century strikes failed to elicit the amazement and awe of the first stoppages. Both workers and manufacturers had developed means to deal with each other in situations where nobody reminisced on lost nurture, deference, and familial affection. While the strike became an important element in the cultural repertoire to address the relation between labor and capital, it did not crystallize into an unchanging form because workers kept innovating on its pattern. For example, strikers developed an interest in winning over public opinion with propaganda leaflets and sought, where possible, favorable newspaper coverage.

Soon after the invasion, cigarette machine operatives struck La Colectiva over wages and personnel changes. Workers were said to be preparing a leaflet, and a delegation visited the newsroom of a San Juan newspaper.[31] La Ultramarina experienced a three-month strike by some ninety cigar makers that was settled early in 1899.[32] The strikes seem to have lacked coordination despite the fact that both firms were in San Juan and affected two Portela y Cía. enterprises (wholly owned La Ultramarina and partly owned La Colectiva). However, the form of the strike continued to develop new dimensions when both parties submitted the wage disagreements to binding arbitration and management agreed to publish the settlement.[33]

After the ATC's purchase, La Colectiva continued to face powerful labor demands. In 1899, women making cigarette cases seemingly had friction with management over working conditions in a section of the factory that was to be remodeled.[34] Cigarette machine operatives struck twice in 1900 over work conditions, higher wages, and the adjustment of wages after the US dollar substituted the Puerto Rican peso.[35]

During the same year, cigar makers joined other San Juan workers in a large strike that labor leader Santiago Iglesias went as far as identifying as a general strike.[36] Conscious of the value of propaganda and public opinion, they published a newspaper appropriately called *La Huelga*, the strike.[37]

The strike is a relation between people, not the mechanical consequence of wage labor and factory management. Early strikes, as the ones reviewed, clearly show the cultural character of the practice. Tobacco workers were becoming strikers by improvising on knowledge from strikes in other lands, in other industries, and from their own experiences. The strike developed from known and tried traditions of dissidence and opposition, as the riot and the march, within the context of existing forms of associations like the guilds that served independent artisans and wage earners. By 1900, cigar makers had developed general rules for strikes and could modify them to meet the particularities of the situation.[38]

Early strikers tried to adapt long-standing practices to new uses. Guilds and mutual aid societies changed and, probably, assumed new functions, as in the 1895 strike planned in the artisans' clubhouse, a *casino de artesanos*, or the attempt of strikers to gain support from the Gremio de Torcedores in 1897.

TRADE UNIONS SERVE THE STRIKE (1901–1906)

Nineteenth-century strikes in tobacco manufacture were neither trade union led nor supported. This does not point to anomie because they followed other lines of organization. As strikes predated the union, the strike itself was the articulation of worker protest. The pairing of union and strike, so indissoluble today, was long and tortuous. Formal organizations, with the strike as one of its tenets, appear only after 1901.

The relation between early labor organizations and strikes can be summarized along three points. First, strike committees and delegations became the earliest form of organization. They were as ephemeral as the strike itself. While they seem to have been important in Europe and other lands, the local record is weak. Second, enduring cigar makers' organizations included dispositions regarding strikes while maintaining guild-like functions. Agitators from the main labor federation, the FLT, were crucial in the organization of the first unions. Despite a strong initial rejection, eventually, some affiliated with the US-based Cigar Makers International Union (CMIU). The third point refers to the weak bond between union and strike. Most unions were paper institutions or organizations brought to life by the strike itself rather than the other way around.

In Europe the unmediated and spontaneous strike gave way to an elementary structure: the election, or perhaps better, the selection of delegates and the constitution of strike committees to present grievances to the employer.[39] The domestic record for tobacco manufacture on this matter is poor because strike committees did not appear as the elementary structure of the strike but as an arm of a trade union or guild. A plausible explanation might be that craftspeople, such as cigar makers, had a long-standing tradition of organization in guilds that facilitated the transition to the trade union. Another explanation might be that while workers in industrial countries were articulating the strike itself, local cigar makers found a ready-made cultural form that they could import from other lands.

The second point refers to the link between strike and labor organizations. Cigar makers developed three forms of organizations with a bearing on strikes: guilds, trade unions, and social studies centers. Early trade unions combined the strike with guild-like functions.[40] At other times the guilds themselves incorporated the strike into their repertoire. The centers, while more concerned with education and ideology, involved themselves in strikes. Most early labor organizations bore testimony to what was passing away and what was still to come. A case in point is the Gremio de Torcedores, the cigar makers' guild, from Comerío. Despite its name, the bylaws stipulated the organization of shop commissions and required cigar makers to submit strike plans to the board.[41] Often the organization bears both tendencies, such as the Gremio de Rezagadores in San Juan, which identified itself as a trade union.[42] Occasionally, other organizations, like the social studies centers, lent their support to strikes; however, the centers gained more stature later.

Propriety and moralism, characteristics that Michelle Perrot identified in early French trade unions, appeared among local cigar makers.[43] For instance, the bylaws of a cigar makers' union required union officials to urge parents to educate illiterate apprentices.[44] The sense of propriety is recurrent. In 1902 cigar makers from highland Cayey went on strike to oppose the employment of illiterate apprentices. Cigar makers wore suits to and from the factories.[45] Shop commissions guaranteed order in the factory, prevented fights, and guarded against foul language.[46]

Cigar makers' organizations began to consider the strike only at the turn of the century. For instance, the Comerío guild recognized strikes but avoided a specific role for itself either in the strikes' opening or closing stages.[47] By 1902 the bylaws of trade unions from Caguas, Cayey, and San Juan, in clear distinction from current practices, placed the control of the strike squarely in the hands of shop commissions. Nevertheless, the rules required the commissions to notify the union board of strike plans to ease coordination with other shops.[48]

Around 1901 and 1902, FLT agitators began to organize cigar makers and leaf sorters into trade unions.[49] It is likely that the organizations just mentioned were FLT affiliates as their bylaws bear a likeness that suggests a common origin.[50] These unions, however, proved short-lived. Despite organizing efforts in several locations, by 1903 the FLT identified only a cigar makers' affiliate in Caguas and another in San Juan.[51] Although apparently affiliated with the FLT, cigar makers at the time rejected the ties with the CMIU that Santiago Iglesias and Samuel Gompers cherished.[52] As of 1903, Iglesias felt the environment was more favorable to the CMIU.[53] Union building among cigar makers continued, and leaf sorters established a union in 1903.[54] Cigar makers in and of themselves did not seem to organize trade unions as strikes also failed to evolve into trade unions. At some point the so-called outside agitators, activists, and organizers, mostly from the FLT, came in.[55] In this sense, outsiders from various locations helped reorganize the cigar makers' guild in Utuado in 1902 and another one in Ponce that bore the FLT mark.[56]

Late nineteenth-century workers developed social studies centers in a milieu where several displayed anarchist orientations. They supported strikes but did not attempt to displace unions or create their own.[57] While the centers left no surviving constitutions or bylaws to examine their vision and role in strikes, this research documents their active participation in, at least, a large one.[58] Some held trade unionist views, but others had stronger anarchist inclinations. For instance, Caguas cigar makers organized a social studies center in 1902.[59] While José Ferrer, a founding member, headed an FLT cigar makers' union and organized sugarcane workers for the FLT, another founding member, Juan Vilar, held "pure radical ideas."[60] The center, as with most early labor organizations, was short-lived, and in 1906 it reorganized itself as the Solidaridad group around the weekly *Voz Humana*.[61]

The third and last point refers to the hold that the organizations of cigar makers—guilds, trade unions, and social studies centers—had over workers in tobacco manufacture and their strikes. This research maintains that their hold was tenuous, at best, until about 1913. Repeated failures to control strikes are eloquent testimony of their fragility. Rather than lead, organizations followed the strike.

As documented above, during 1901 and 1902 labor organizers started trade unions in the most important manufacturing centers. The spate of strikes of 1902 and 1903 allow an assessment of the organizations. Union and strike maintained a weak link as accounts of the strikes seem to state the supporting, not leading, role of the organizations.

In April 1902, cigar makers from three Bayamón factories went on strike when management refused a petition to increase piece rates to the levels of San Juan and other better-paid locations.[62] April witnessed two strikes when shop heads ordered coats to be put away in a place with no hangers. Cigar makers at

La Ultramarina became offended, and those at the PRATCO factory took it as an expression of mistrust. The stemmers in the latter establishment joined the walkout in solidarity.[63] At the end of November, Cayey cigar makers staged a march after striking two factories over piecework reductions.[64] The press coverage does not identify a union behind these five strikes.

Sometime in late June or early July, the cigar makers at La Internacional went on strike over a decrease in piece rates. Other factories joined the walkout in a situation where many were returning to their towns while workers and management attempted to reach a settlement.[65] The first mention of a San Juan cigar maker's union appears at the end of July, when the union was holding a meeting to end a conflict. In view of the "unsustainable" situation, the union suspended the rule that prohibited its members to work while on strike, thus allowing the workers to seek gainful employment in other shops even if they paid less.[66] The aftermath of the strike left a bitter taste that raised issues about the legitimacy and hold of the union over its constituents.[67] A disaffected worker blamed the union for the strike's failure by singling out the leadership's "supine ignorance," lack of "good judgement," and inexperience.[68]

Early in September, disaffected cigar makers struck La Internacional, a PRATCO factory, over responsibility for spoiled wrapper leaves. A worker "put on his hat and coat and walked out" after refusing management's attempt to charge him for several unaccounted leaves. All the other workers joined, staged a march in San Juan to end the day with an assembly. The San Juan trade union organized the following stages of the conflict, which included a successful plea for Caguas and Aguadilla cigar makers to join the strike, which now demanded a raise in piece rates.[69] Weeks into the dispute, PRATCO in San Juan and the union brought the strike to an end with pay raises extended to strikers in other factories and localities such as Caguas, whose union celebrated a victory meeting.[70]

Workers elected union officials, strike committees, and instruments of propaganda in the heat of the strike. Labor organizations did not plan and put stoppages into effect because the strike led the way. For instance, in the midst of the strike at La Internacional, a commission from Caguas, Ponce, Bayamón, and San Juan in representation of several cigar makers' unions reorganized the corresponding strike in Utuado.[71] While organizational efforts predated the strike, the San Juan union presented its bylaws to the state just before the beginning of the walkout.[72] At the start of the struggle the union launched *Unión y Trabajo*, a freely distributed weekly.[73] While the historical record identifies very few guilds or unions with a leading role in strikes, labor organizers were busy incorporating such organizations in San Juan, Cayey, and Caguas that date from this spate of strikes.[74]

In November 1903, cigar makers struck La Internacional over the number of daily cigars crafted. They met immediately after in the union's headquarters to develop a plan of action that included a list of demands to Luis Toro, the company president. An active union prepared a propaganda leaflet, and strikers established a negotiating committee. The strike spread from San Juan to several factories in the highlands.[75]

The next few years saw few walkouts but continued the weak link between union and strike. None of these, as reported, had a strong union link, despite more aggressive actions by the employers as the hiring of strikebreakers.[76]

The social studies centers also had a weak hold over the strike. Soon after cigar makers struck the Caguas factory of the Cayey-Caguas Tobacco Company, in August 1906, the long-dormant center became reactivated with the Solidaridad name.[77] The strikers resorted to several tools they had developed during the last few years that included a strike commission, an arbitration committee, and the center. The latter became deeply embroiled in the dispute with the preparation of propaganda leaflets and supported the stoppage from the weekly *Voz Humana*.[78] The walkout spread to other shops in Caguas and late in September to neighboring Cayey.[79] Following the same pattern of unions and guilds, Solidaridad became inactive after the strike.

Perrot's findings for late nineteenth-century France serve to describe the strikes in the domestic tobacco industry at the onset of the century: "The strike could be said to have dominated the organization, generating its own forms. The union itself was often merely its creature, born through and for it, living off its success and being killed off by its failure."[80]

UNIONS OUTLAST THE STRIKE (1907–1913)

FLT agitators, which by this time included many cigar makers, met little success in the "general" strikes in the sugar industry during 1905 and failure in 1906.[81] As a partial response to these shortcomings, the FLT launched the *Cruzada del Ideal* in 1906 to organize and rebuild unions and strengthen working-class organizations such as the social studies centers.[82] Agitators and organizers singled out the union as the mechanism that could maximize the possibilities of success because organizations guaranteed a permanent leadership and provided mechanisms to accumulate savings that would carry workers through stoppages. In addition, the union could enhance the chance of success by planning the timing of a shutdown and ensuring it had enough support among workers. This process of rationalization amounted to shifting the control of the strike away from the workers by placing it in union officials.

Stronger trade unions brought to the fore tendencies overshadowed by the earlier FLT policies of the general strike and participation in local electoral politics. After the invasion the newly created FLT sought close relations with US labor and socialist organizations to gain domestic political leverage and some measure of economic well-being from US comrades. It affiliated with the Socialist Labor Party in 1899 and with the Social Democratic Party in 1900.[83] It began a lasting relation with the AFL in 1901, and soon after, the AFL hired FLT president Santiago Iglesias as a paid labor organizer for years to come.[84] While, as indicated previously, FLT agitators affiliated only one of the nascent unions of 1902 and 1903 with the CMIU, the *Cruzada del Ideal* proved more successful as agitators organized enduring trade unions and affiliated them with their US counterparts, including the CMIU.[85]

The FLT sponsored a national assembly of tobacco workers with representatives from twenty-five municipalities to stimulate union building and affiliation with the CMIU.[86] Commissioned by the assembly to organize cigar makers, Eugenio Sánchez López claimed nine unions for the international by mid-1907 and soon after became its paid organizer.[87] Other agitators, such as Esteban Padilla, helped Sánchez organize CMIU locals.[88]

However, the growth of unions among tobacco workers was uneven because stemmers and leaf sorters, mainly women, had fewer unions than cigar makers and cigar packers, who were mostly men.[89] At the beginning of the *Cruzada del Ideal*, FLT agitators organized new cigar makers' unions and reorganized others during 1907 in Cayey, Cidra, Puerta de Tierra, Caguas, Gurabo, and Utuado.[90] They dissolved the San Juan union of 1902 to reorganize it in 1906.[91] In 1906, Bayamón cigar makers organized a second union, which admitted stemmers and leaf sorters, but it failed immediately, having to reorganize a year later.[92] The organization drive proved particularly successful among cigar makers. By 1907 the FLT claimed to represent 977 cigar makers, compared favorably to the paltry 63 affiliated in 1904.[93] FLT unions kept posting gains to claim 1807 members in 1910.[94] Furthermore, the AFL required FLT cigar makers to join the CMIU.[95]

Save for cigar packers, FLT unions dominated all branches of tobacco manufacturing, effectively preempting the organization of independent unions.[96] Packers established the Sociedad de Escogedores, which consistently rejected the overtures for affiliation with the CMIU and the FLT.[97] Efforts to organize packers into rival unions proved short-lived and gained little support.[98]

After the *Cruzada del Ideal*, unions generally outlasted any particular strike. While they proliferated and came to represent more workers, agitators and organizers struggled to make them part and parcel of the daily lives of cigar makers. Union officials complained continually of spontaneous strikes and of workers unaccustomed to long-term planning. A tradition of spontaneous solidarity placed control of the strike squarely in the mass of the workers. It ran head on against attempts to bureaucratize it—that is, put it under the control of union officials. This research maintains that unions had a feeble hold over their constituents and a weaker one over the strike.[99] A probe of the proposition looks at two extremes of the union movement: at one end, near the mass of workers and, at the other, close to the topmost layer of the trade union leadership.

The community level, where the union was close to the mass of workers, allows an examination of sympathizers and rank-and-file members in their interaction with the union officials that composed the first layer of organization. It has a drawback in the fact that the historical record bears the mark of the more articulate, who were generally union officials and journalists. I selected a municipality with a long tradition of manufacture and distant enough from San Juan, the headquarters of higher-level CMIU and FLT organizations.

In April 1907, Cayey cigar makers reorganized the 1902 union, elected a new board of directors, and applied for and obtained CMIU recognition a few months later.[100] The union managed internal affairs smoothly by electing new officials to cover vacancies. When union officials sought to represent the workers in community matters, they helped organize a meeting and marched to denounce health problems in the municipality.[101] Cigar makers struck and shut down Las Riberas del Plata briefly in mid-June over a pay raise, and when the strike failed, the local union correspondent summoned unaffiliated strikers to join the trade union.[102] When a one-day strike against the Cayey-Caguas Tobacco Company failed in late June, union officials were quick to blame the failure on lack of organization.[103] A long strike against the same corporation started in late July. Soon after, it spread to neighboring Caguas and San Lorenzo with strikers demanding a pay raise and better tobacco leaf.[104] The Cayey union was active in the strike: union officials formed part of the strike commission, and the union prepared two propaganda leaflets.[105] When San Lorenzo strikers suspended the strike late in August, union officials dutifully identified the lack of a union and economic weakness as cause for the failure.[106] Workers at the Cayey factory returned to work in early September.[107]

All three strikes were spontaneous and union supported but not union led. Despite three consecutive failures, the union outlasted them all, not a small achievement. However, turnover of officials was high, attesting to union fragility. It elected new officials in October, the third time in six months.[108] Notwithstanding, the union gained a wider constituency during its early years. From 28 members in 1907, it went to 105 by 1910—that is, 31 percent of all cigar makers in town.[109] Slowly, the union built a presence in the daily life of its constituents. When it decided that a meeting place was essential, the union pooled resources with the carpenters' union to share common quarters. When the carpenters dropped out, the cigar makers paid the complete rental.[110] Three years later the union added a library for worker education.[111] It also provided benefits beyond strike funds that agitators used to publicize the organization.[112] It disbursed small amounts, running close to $500 between 1907 and 1910 in sick leave, loans, and unemployment benefits.[113] Lastly, the union-appointed correspondent had a regular column in the working-class daily *Unión Obrera*.[114]

Years later, the strike still dominated the union. In August 1910, it supported a strike against La Flor de Cayey that was not union led and failed.[115] Stemmers, with a combination of union and nonunion members, struck in December 1910 the factory that Antonio León Candelas managed, and the cigar makers' union joined in solidarity.[116] Strikebreakers defeated a walkout at the Cayey-Caguas Tobacco Company during the summer of 1911.[117] Despite failures, the union became an enduring fixture, although a frail one, in the life of cigar makers and in the town itself. It lacked control over strikes other than supporting them, but it provided a meeting place, a rallying point against perceived injustices, a library, a newspaper column, and economic benefits to its membership.

The second way to examine the hold of unions over the strike is through the highest level of union organization, the Joint Advisory Board of local cigar makers' unions. The board, established in 1907 by representatives from trade unions, included top union officials and full-time CMIU organizers Eugenio Sánchez López until his death and Prudencio Rivera Martínez afterward. It was the point of contact between local unions and the CMIU in the United States.[118]

When the FLT sponsored an assembly of cigar makers in 1907, it sought to reorganize, establish, and make cigar makers' unions powerful by affiliation with itself domestically and the AFL and the CMIU in the United States. FLT officials resolved that the strike was to be union controlled, and in agreement, the assembly sharply denounced spontaneous strikes. An approved strike resolution required a unanimous vote taken in a union assembly and notification to the Puerto Rican labor movement.[119] This complied partially with the CMIU requirement that local unions petition the home office for strike funds and remain open to negotiations for a month before beginning the actual strike. In effect, CMIU rules transferred the locus of the strike from the workers to union officials. As indicated previously, older trade unions required shop commissions only to notify the union board of strike plans.

Such changes seemed to herald a new era for labor in tobacco manufacture. However, the praxis of cigar makers would prove it mistaken when, two months after the assembly, cigar makers infringed the resolution. They struck large PRATCO factories in March 1907 in the usual way with a worker-led and union-supported spontaneous strike. Sánchez López, then an FLT organizer, suspended the organization drive to aid the strikers.[120] The walkout failed despite the support of three CMIU locals from San Juan and Bayamón that paid lip service to the resolution by vowing that never ever would they support spontaneous strikes.[121]

While the strike did not follow CMIU regulations, the Joint Advisory Board managed to get funds.[122] Although the three union locals survived the strike, it still forced the unions into a supporting role.

Sánchez López, board president, criticized spontaneity at the 1908 cigar makers' assembly. To wrath and spontaneity, he opposed rational action: "A few strike attempts have emerged, some quite serious, but they involved only the protest of the moment instead of deliberate action for a just cause . . . We must clarify and support the principle that a successful strike, when it does not seek the complete revolution of the craft in the country or nation, is a mathematical question, daughter of calculation and strength, fully empirical."[123] He might have stated the same three years later when the Joint Advisory Board intervened in two well-documented strikes. Early in March 1911, Caguas cigar makers struck the Cayey-Caguas Tobacco Company, La Turina, and West India Commercial Company, bringing tobacco manufacture to a standstill.[124] Workers from neighboring San Lorenzo also struck the local Cayey-Caguas Tobacco factory, possibly in solidarity.[125] Soon, they established a strike committee that included local union members and some anarchists. The FLT supported the strike, and the *Unión Obrera* daily provided sympathetic coverage. Two fatal shootings and many arrests, summarized later, marred the walkout.[126]

On 9 March, Ventura Grillo, publicly considered mentally deranged, killed a factory manager of La Turina (an AWITCO factory) and a merchant who came to his rescue. Grillo, a cigar maker, was a member of a social studies center with anarchist orientations.[127] The propertied felt threatened by the possible ideological connection. For instance, on the day before the arrests, Alexander Blumenstiel, whose firm employed the manager, mailed the police chief fifty dollars "for the suppression of any anarchistic movement that might arise."[128] After 20 March the state conducted several searches, including two social studies centers, and arrested nearly three dozen men, the complete strike committee and many center members, on conspiracy charges. Since many were not union members and some did not even work in tobacco factories, the arrests touched other organizations such as the Federación de Espiritistas. In the end, all were eventually acquitted except Juan Vilar, who was convicted of another crime. Excessive deployment of force and extensive arrests caused apprehension in Caguas. The material resources of the social studies centers were negligible like those of most other working-class organizations. While the spiritualists provided for the defense of their brethren, others could not. What remains important is the ubiquity of the unions. As in other situations, the local union and the FLT—the CMIU refused to foot legal costs—assumed the defense of most of the arrested, including Vilar.

In September 1911, San Lorenzo cigar makers from Cayey-Caguas Tobacco and Alvarez y Cía. went on strike while cigar packers and cigar makers from Caguas and cigar makers from Cidra joined the strike in solidarity. After the strike had begun, the local CMIU union requested strike funds that the home office denied, leading many workers to resign from the union.[129] In another petition, the approval of strike funds came in late because the CMIU packers' union had already returned to work. The Cidra union received unemployment benefits from the home office. The Sociedad de Escogedores also joined and offered economic support to other strikers.[130] In October, cigar makers from Cayey joined but returned to work without ever requesting assistance from the home office.[131] These unions persisted as strikes failed and frustration with an unresponsive home office took their toll.[132] Membership in cigar makers' unions from Caguas, Cayey, and San Lorenzo declined from 303, 105, and 71 in 1910 to 261, 62, and 45 respectively in 1912. Only Cidra fared better: membership increased from 40 to 55.[133]

The shop movement, *movimiento de taller*, defied the discourse of rationality and the attempts to bureaucratize the strike.[134] Unions, however, made important strides between 1907 and 1913—that is, from the first permanent CMIU local to the eve of the general strike against PRATCO. The FLT came to represent organized tobacco workers; it occupied the field. All cigar makers' unions and a few cigar packers' unions were CMIU, AFL, and FLT affiliates. Stemmers' and leaf-sorters' unions belonged to both the AFL and FLT. Only the Sociedad de Escogedores remained independent. Union penetration continued unevenly in tobacco manufacturing occupations. It was considerably higher among cigar makers and cigar packers, mostly men, than among women stemmers and leaf sorters.

By 1913, on the eve of the general strike, unions showed signs of retrenchment from the advances made since affiliation with the CMIU. Dues-paying members reached 1,805 in 1910 but declined to 1,318 two years later.[135] Despite their inability to subordinate the strike, tobacco workers' unions managed sizable strike funds. While workers continued to initiate strikes following the norms of anger and outrage, they enlisted union support more frequently. The CMIU alone disbursed nearly $17,000 between 1907 and 1912. On other grounds, the unions became a fixture of working-class life among cigar makers. Union locals were places of camaraderie, discussion, and relaxation that bred solidarity, and a few had libraries. CMIU locals paid more than $30,000 in sick aid and close to $7,000 in unemployment benefits. These unions managed $92,000 between 1907 and 1912.[136] *Unión Obrera*, the daily published by the FLT, clearly outmatched *Voz Humana* and other periodicals put up by independent working-class organizations. The unions were not the sole voice of tobacco workers—they shared the ideological spectrum with other organizations such as the anarchist animated social studies centers—but they became the dominant force.

THE UNIONS TAKE OVER CIGAR MAKERS' STRIKES IN TRUST FACTORIES: THE CMIU (1914–1920)

The general strike, with distinct meanings to the libertarian, syndicalist, anarchist, and socialist, became a powerful, if not the ultimate, method to address capital work relations in diverse lands. Charles Tilly described its attraction: "The idea that workers could liberate themselves through one great effort resonated with daily experience."[137] It gained currency among French and US workers during the late 1880s.[138] It spread soon after to Catalonian and Andalusian anarchists, and, closer to Puerto Rico, anarcho-syndicalist agitators espoused its merits to Cuban workers in the island itself and among cigar makers in Key West during the 1890s.[139] In Puerto Rico, the idea antedated craft unions as the large wave of strikes in 1895, triggered by currency devaluation, raised its specter.[140]

During 1902, and markedly so in 1903, tobacco workers, with either guild or union support, struck factories in several municipalities in what nearly became an industry-wide strike. Sugarcane workers staged two industry-wide strikes in 1905 that FLT officials called a "general strike" due to their ample diffusion through the island and the powerful implication of emancipation the phrase evoked. The first covered north coast sugar mills and plantations and ended with modest economic benefits for the strikers. Immediately, the second one started on the south coast, where it counted strong FLT support. The workers obtained small wage hikes, but the FLT failed to gain recognition as the representative of the workers. These strikes assumed their wide character by diffusion, through spontaneous solidarity and the hard work of strike committees. Both "general strikes" partook in the tradition of spontaneity and solidarity, similar to that of tobacco workers of the same period. In consonance, sugarcane workers lacked previous plans to negotiate work conditions on an industry-wide basis, although the south coast strike was more of a planned matter.[141]

Limited success in the sugar strikes led the third FLT assembly in 1905 to propose another general strike for the coming year. It affected only the north coast and, ultimately, failed. In response, the FLT launched the *Cruzada del Ideal* and held intense debates on the benefits and nature of a general strike. FLT president and AFL organizer Santiago Iglesias favored an all-encompassing general strike while FLT secretary and CMIU organizer Eugenio Sánchez López proposed a limited general strike for crafts with a 50 percent unionization rate. Sánchez López had his way at the fifth FLT assembly in 1908.[142]

By 1911, the assembly of CMIU unions raised the unionization rate to 60 percent of cigar makers, excluding sorters and stemmers, at PRATCO's factories in San Juan. While it could hardly be called a general strike, the strong imagery of freedom evoked was probably instrumental in maintaining the designation. Plans called for a two-stage industry-wide strike. Cigar makers were to strike independent factories first, and upon settlement, they would hit PRATCO and the Industrial Company, the two cigar-making subsidiaries of the trust. Union funds and material assistance from those who remained at work were to finance the strike. In 1913, the cigar makers' Joint Advisory Board considered an $80,000 war chest adequate. By this time the general strike lacked any revolutionary purpose since it was aimed at leveling wages and gaining more benefits for cigar makers.[143]

Union members, following CMIU conventions, conceived the general strike to be craft based by limiting it to trust factories that manufactured cigars despite the fact that other subsidiaries counted with sizable stemming departments. Thus, the anticipated general strike excluded the PRLTC, a major corporation held by the trust. In doing so, the planned strike excluded thousands of leaf sorters and stemmers, mostly women, and the field hands who tilled extensive plantations in the highlands.

The strike envisioned by cigar makers followed the CMIU in other respects. It demanded a shift from extant relations between strike and union. At last, CMIU officials believed, the strike would submit to organization. The proposed policy of rationalization offered no space to sudden denunciations of perceived abuse, indignation, or anger.

Despite years of planning, the general strike did not open under the foreseen scheme of rationality nor even in a cigar factory. On 16 February 1914, a foreman suspended a woman from a PRATCO stemmery for a week because she was not doing her job properly. Four hundred workers struck the San Juan stemmery in solidarity.[144] Nine hundred cigar makers from a close-by PRATCO factory joined the day after. Within days the strike spread to most PRATCO and Industrial Company factories and several PRLTC leaf-classifying establishments. Workers at the trust cigarette factory in San Juan were the notable exception; they never joined.[145] Stemmers, sorters, cigar makers, and other strikers numbered more than five thousand.[146] By 20 February, an assembly of strikers presented a series of demands to PRATCO.[147] Strikers held countless, often well-attended, meetings, pickets, and marches.

Groups of cigar makers, sorters, and stemmers from Gurabo, Juncos, Manatí, San Lorenzo, and other locations offered strong resistance to the strike. Union officials, strike committee members and militants traveled frequently to these sites to organize meetings, marches, and pickets.[148] In the heat of the strike, Luis Toro, president of the three corporations affected, threatened to transfer manufacture to the United States and actually established cigar factories or outsourced manufacture in Cayey, Ciales, Coamo, and Toa Alta.[149] Cayey factory workers strongly resisted the walkout and the overtures of the San Juan strike committee members.[150] Recurrent violence, frequent arrests, and prison sentences marred the four-month strike.[151]

Trade unions played a central role in the strike. Samuel Gompers and George W. Perkins, AFL and CMIU presidents respectively, and other high-level US union officials traveled to Puerto Rico in late March. They met the colonial governor and participated in strike-related activities.[152] Prudencio Rivera Martínez, CMIU organizer and president of its local Joint Advisory Board, presided over the island-wide strike committee that included non-union members.[153] By the end of April, CMIU locals alone had disbursed $22,000.[154] In the end, they contributed close to $37,000 of the $50,000 estimated cost of the strike.[155] While the strike began spontaneously and propagated in the tradition of solidarity, it ended in the discipline and rationality long demanded by union officials from both workers and employers.

While union officials conceived the strike as a cigar makers' strike, it did not develop in that fashion. It started in a San Juan stemming department and spread to PRLTC factories not anticipated in the original plan. However, the strike committee settled it as planned, by the principle of rationality embodied in a binding contract with each corporation. Leaf sorters, mostly women, negotiated a separate collective agreement with the PRLTC early in May. More than 1,500 returned to work in Caguas, Gurabo, and Juncos.[156] The strike committee negotiated with PRATCO and the Industrial Company and agreed on work and pay conditions for cigar makers and other employees. They signed a second collective agreement ratified by worker assemblies in several municipalities and more than 2,000 returned to work in mid-June.[157] Tobacco workers obtained economic benefits while the unions gained in legitimacy and, at last, controlled a major dispute. The unions emerged with enlarged membership.[158] Dues-paying CMIU members reached 1,805 in 1910, declined to 1,318 in 1912, and posted a large increase to 2,079 members by 1915.[159] Negotiators obtained union recognition from the trust and the right of workers to elect their own shop commissions. Workers earned the right to decide, at the shop level, the nature and amount of dues the firm deducted from wage earners, union members or not, through majority votes. Shop commissions became an important mechanism for the material well-being of the trade unions. PRATCO collected dues from all workers for union officials to manage.[160]

In practice the general strike became one against trust-owned corporations (except cigarette manufacturing and tobacco growing) rather than an industry-wide one against all cigar manufacturers. It had two distinct settlements, one with the PRLTC and another for the cigar subsidiaries. Only the second phase of the original plan went into effect as the independents remained untouched. The CMIU, in maintaining its organization by craft, chose not to become an industry-wide union in tobacco manufacturing despite the strong participation of PRLTC stemmers and leaf sorters in the strike and the role of cigar makers in gaining a settlement. However, it was a dispute with the largest corporation in the industry that assured control, if an uneasy one, over the strike. Cooperation between AFL, CMIU, and FLT continued for years to come.

The sequel of the strike against the trust was not quiet. The Bureau of Labor intervened in a strike of 38 cigarette machine operatives and another of 30 cigar box makers against PRATCO in San Juan, five strikes involving 980 stemmers, 24 leaf sorters in a Ponce walkout, and six more involving 3,525 cigar makers. Two of the strikes spread to factories in adjacent municipalities. This added up to 13 strikes and 4,597 strikers just in 1916.[161]

The largest resembled that of 1914, while the smallest displayed spontaneous solidarity. An example of the latter occurred during March 1916 when seventy to eighty workers struck Tomás Rodríguez's manufactory over the reduction of the piece rate for a *vitola*, a cigar style.[162] Cigar makers at Rucabado's Flor de Cayey and Isidro Vázquez's shop contributed materially and petitioned those at the nearby PRATCO branch for assistance. Cornelio Negrón, local CMIU president, collected the funds.[163] As before, the strike was not union led but supported and depended on the solidarity of cigar makers within the community.

In a different case, about three thousand cigar makers struck PRATCO factories in San Juan and Bayamón on 8 August 1916. Its initial stages seem to have been a mixture of the old and the new. It does not seem to have been the spontaneous reaction to shop grievances but opposition to piece rate reductions and recognition of shop commissions contained in the 1914 collective agreement. The unions did not declare the strike as CMIU rules required, but the workers elected a strike committee, called the strike, and proceeded to gain support from other PRATCO branches. Several members of the committee were union officials, and the CMIU Joint Advisory Board soon assumed a leading role. Despite some strike activity in Cidra, Manatí, and San Lorenzo, it remained localized.[164] At Cayey, the commissioners called an assembly of company employees in the spirit of rational solidarity espoused by union officials. They presented and defended their case, and upon joining the strike, the assembly elected a strike committee headed by Cornelio Negrón.[165] Upon settlement, the strikers gained better piece rates for some *vitolas*.[166]

The large 1914 and 1916 strikes against PRATCO started a sequence in which the unions began to have more control over the strike. The tradition of spontaneous solidarity ceased to run the massive strike. Union officials, the likes of Prudencio Rivera Martínez and Esteban Padilla, started to lead strikes in the name of rationality, displacing the spontaneous solidarity that drew its strength from shop workers. However, spontaneous solidarity kept the unions at bay in smaller but decidedly spirited walkouts.

A 1917 strike against the Cayey branch of the PRLTC started to approximate the latter model.[167] About three hundred women, mostly leaf sorters, and thirty men abandoned the factory, demanding higher piece rates. They staged a meeting at the factory entrance followed by an assembly at the town cinema to elect the strike committee. The day ended with an evening meeting in the town square. The next day, some three hundred cigar makers at the nearby PRATCO factory joined in solidarity for a one-day strike and demanded better binder for their cigars. The combined strikers held an afternoon and evening meeting at the town square. The PRLTC factory remained closed on the third day of the strike. Two commissions of strikers left for Caguas and Aibonito to petition strikes in solidarity, and PRATCO cigar makers from Aibonito joined. While police records do not identify union support or leadership, the newly founded Socialist Party became the organizational vehicle for the leaf sorters.

Summing up, the strikers developed a pattern of daytime picketing, sometimes reaching two hundred participants, followed by an early evening march through working-class neighborhoods, often to the strains of the Marseillaise, to rally supporters for the coming meeting. They held an additional twelve meetings between 8 June and 11 July at the town square, in working-class districts, and by the factory. Despite the frenzy of activity and deep militancy, it experienced few incidents of violence. Some strikers and sympathizers blamed the police when the walkout petered out.

Although it manifested a strong undercurrent of spontaneous solidarity, the 1917 companywide strike against PRATCO and its sister, the Industrial Company, came close to the ideal supported by the CMIU and the local union leadership. The conflict went through two phases marked by the workers' acceptance of two collective agreements. The first phase ended in October and the latter in December with the ratification of the second agreement. The stoppage affected stemmers, cigar makers, and all other occupations in several factories. According to some accounts, the strike included as many as fifteen or up to twenty thousand workers.[168]

Eighty-eight delegates assembled in August 1917 to demand better piece rates, shorter working hours, and a leveling of piece rates across all factories. They entrusted their representation to the Joint Advisory Board of the cigar makers.[169] However, on 18 September, as the board had just finished the preparation of the demands to be presented to both firms, Bayamón cigar makers walked out due to the poor quality of the tobacco to be elaborated.[170] Next day, as union officials presented the list of demands to the manufacturers, the Bayamón strikers were actively spreading the news of their walkout, and soon workers from five factories across the island joined them.[171]

Nonetheless, the workers at the large Puerta de Tierra factory remained in the shop as they hesitated for a few days out of respect and fidelity to the agreements reached at the assembly of tobacco workers. They felt torn between the "principles and discipline [concomitant] with the granting of powers to a representative body, as the Joint Advisory Board," and "the solidarity and unity of the trade needed against the policies of the trust."[172] In joining the strike, the Puerta de Tierra officials expressed that the forces of struggle and combat could not be exclusively at the mercy of the "mandate of reason."[173] As on earlier occasions, the leadership of the unions failed to demobilize the shop movement. The Joint Advisory Board held that the workers "paralyzed more than ten thousand persons working in the tobacco industry, who were not in strike-mood, but waiting for the final decisions of the Joint Advisory Board."[174] The unfolding and early stages of the first phase of the strike suggest that the rationality of the assembly on the one hand and spontaneity and fraternal solidarity on the other were each following their own script.

This first phase of the 1917 strike, however, included two significant events that distinguished it from earlier ones. An assembly took place well before the Bayamón workers euphemistically decided to "wait" for the outcome of the negotiations in the streets. Despite the presence of the shop movement, the Joint Advisory Board remained the sole negotiating organism throughout the conflict. Up to this conflict, it must be underscored, strike committees often included non-union members. In due time, by early October, the Joint Advisory Board negotiated an agreement with management that the workers ratified by a close vote of 1,291 in favor and 1,195 opposed.[175]

The second phase of the 1917 strike started probably before the ink of the collective agreement had dried. Upon ratification of the collective agreement, the workers were to resume their trades, starting with tobacco sprayers, followed by the leaf sorters, and others in stages to start the production process.[176] However, the Joint Advisory Board questioned management's decision to delay the dates of reentry of leaf sorters and therefore of all who depended on their output. Then "local difficulties" slowed the pace of work for stemmers.[177] Soon after, the advisory board added the refusal to honor pay raises among certain categories of stemmers and decried that the trust denied some rights of shop commissions to mediate between management and workers. Finally, upon their return to work at the Ponce factory, the cigar makers intoned the Marseillaise to find the factory closed on the following day. Consequently, the advisory board gave the trust an ultimatum to honor the collective agreement, to its satisfaction, or face a strike.[178] On that Friday afternoon, the workers took to the streets and an assembly formally decreed the strike on the following day.[179] So the formal strike, in distinction from the earlier phase of waiting in the streets, followed the rational script long espoused by union officials.

While the main issues of the strike involved the price of labor, some matters dealt with the recognition and functions of shop commissions to intervene between labor and capital in the routines of the workday. These commissions strengthened the presence of the union in the shop floor itself. The cigar makers' unions gained further strength and legitimacy as the CMIU home office granted strike and unemployment funds to cigar makers, but unfortunately, the stemmers' union requests to the AFL were unsuccessful.[180] On 22 December, the strike ended with another one-year collective agreement ratified when Bayamón and San Juan workers accepted a compromise to one section of the collective agreement.[181] Besides the extension of union benefits obtained in 1914, such as dues for diverse causes—deducted by the employer and managed by union officials—and control of shop commissions, the 1917 contract increased piece rates and granted sick leave.[182]

Union control over strikes advanced considerably after the 1914 and 1917 strikes. However, the shop movement and spontaneity among cigar makers prevented a strike-less year at PRATCO in spite of a collective agreement in force. As early as February 1918 cigar makers at the Cayey factory denounced the quality of drinking water, due to a broken filter, and the accumulation of water and human waste on the ground floor of the factory. When Marcial Bosch, who was the factory manager, failed to remedy the situation, they went on strike for a week in August over the health hazard and demanded the removal of the manager. The walkout ended only after the cigar makers entrusted their representative to negotiate with Bosch, who ultimately agreed to solve the problem.[183]

Negotiations started as the collective agreement of 1917 neared its end. On 11 December 1918, days before its expiration, the union representatives presented their demands, which included the leveling of piece rates to those of San Juan factories, the reopening of recently closed branches, and piece rate increases for all *vitolas*.[184] On 20 December, the firm's president, Luis Toro, offered to share 15 percent of PRATCO's net profits with operatives and employees instead of pay raises.[185] President Toro also anticipated that the firm would close on 31 December to reopen on 10 January to make the annual balance. As negotiations continued, the general manager, Florentino Miranda, informed the union leadership that the factories might reopen in early February and announced, among other things, more branch shutdowns. In response, the Joint Advisory Board of the cigar makers' unions called for an extraordinary assembly on the very same day that factories were to reopen. The assembly denounced the factory closings, rejected the profit-sharing plan, approved a strike, and voted to "resist" what they termed a lockout.[186]

After the January 1919 assembly and following instructions from the Joint Advisory Board, the trade unions met and ratified the resolutions of the assembly. In the spirit of rationality, the notification of the meetings generally mentioned the AFL requirements to grant strike funds.[187] During the large trust-wide strikes of 1914, 1916, and 1917, the opening events of the walkout had resisted their subordination to union strictures much more than the closing sequences. The beginning of the 1919 strike, however, strictly followed the guidelines long proposed by union leaders, starting with the early negotiations to the sequence of assemblies that formally endorsed it. In fact, a satisfied advisory board proudly stated: "We have always used the strike as the medium of last recourse; and we have always preferred conciliation, mediation, and discussion of our issues before the strike, whose consequences we know, by experience, better than anyone."[188]

During the stoppage, the enactment on 9 June 1919 of a minimum wage for women weakened the position of the employer. José María González, who at the time was vice president of PRATCO, wrote about his firm's actions opposing the law and worried that the minimum wage was, in fact, the maximum wage that women earned in the industry. In fact, Fernando Álvarez, who was an important tobacco packer and owned and managed stemmeries, carried his opposition all the way to the Supreme Court and lost.[189] Besides a more receptive legislative assembly, the strikers probably received CMIU funds, as on earlier occasions. Yet, in contrast to the 1917 general strike, the AFL disbursed funds, but in minute amounts, to sixty-four stemmers from union number 12722 in Bayamón and to twenty-four tobacco sprayers and drying room attendants from union number 15206 in San Juan.[190] Some six months in duration, the strike ended early in the summer of 1919 with the ratification of a collective agreement that maintained deductions for dues and sick leave, worker control of shop commissions, and increased piece rates.[191]

Again, the unions gained legitimacy by achieving victory through their management of the conflict. Wage deductions paid to shop commissions and trade unions were substantial: they amounted to $167,532.59 for a nearly eighteen-month period around 1920. They amounted to a bit more than 3 percent of PRATCO payroll.[192] However, the shop movement retained a presence manifested when PRATCO cigar makers went on strike in spite of the collective agreement in force. Nearly three hundred cigar makers abandoned the Aguas Buenas branch over faulty tobacco in December 1919.[193]

Rational and calculated strikes, although punctuated by smaller stoppages to the chagrin of union officials and firm alike, started to give way to a businesslike and rational relation between the CMIU and PRATCO. Both parties negotiated in earnest to avoid walkouts. This was a significant departure from the general strike for the complete revolution of the craft espoused by some labor leaders at the turn of the century or for that matter from the earlier tradition of spontaneous solidarity. In this spirit, the Joint Advisory Board of CMIU unions and company officials signed a one-year collective agreement on 29 March 1920 effective on 31 July.[194] It was similar to previous ones save for provisions in case of a downward swing of the business cycle. If demand for cigars declined, the firm would distribute work equally among workers, considering partial closure of some shops.[195]

By the end of the decade, the subordination of the strike to unions in PRATCO had advanced considerably. CMIU unions played an important role in the large strikes against the firm in 1914 and 1916, and a leading one in two companywide strikes in 1917 and 1919. On the other hand, the tradition of spontaneous solidarity ruled over independent cigar manufacturers, leaf-classifying establishments, and stemmeries—some large, such as PRLTC. Thus, outside PRATCO factories, the strike seems to have been dominant, tenaciously independent of union leadership particularly in its opening stages.

This articulation of strikes and union had no parallel among leaf sorters and stemmers. Despite large strikes against PRLTC, the unfolding of disputes never approached a companywide pattern with unions representing stemmers, leaf

Table 8.1. Occupation of strikers in tobacco manufacture, 1916–1920

	Percentage of strikes by			
Year	**Stemmers**	**Cigar makers**	**Others**	**Total**
1916	33.3	50.0	16.7	(12)
1917–18	43.5	41.9	14.5	(62)
1919–20	79.5	12.8	7.7	(39)

Sources: Computed from Negociado del Trabajo, *Quinto informe anual*, 33; Governor of Porto Rico, "Annual Report, 1917," 3:552–53; Bureau of Labor, *Special Bulletin*, 34–36; Governor of Porto Rico, *Annual Report, 1920*, 557–59.

sorters, and others. Two PRLTC strikes in 1920 conformed to the pattern of the previous years. Two hundred fifty leaf sorters struck PRLTC at Cayey briefly in March and then for about two weeks in April.[196] Independent stemmeries experienced the same fate. Settlement of disputes occurred factory by factory, but with frequent solidarity strikes by workers in nearby plants. For example, a dozen Caguas stemmers went on strike in September 1919 in "sympathy" with fired workers; stemmers from Corozal staged another for the same motive in February 1920.[197] The same pattern held for independent cigar factories. For instance, thirty-five cigar makers went on strike at Lanza's La Flor de Cayey in March 1920 over piece rates.[198] No trade union appears in any of these labor disputes.

Table 8.1 supports the proposition that the unions failed to gain control of the strike in firms other than PRATCO. In 1916, only two years after the historic settlement with PRATCO, cigar makers still represented half the strikes in the industry to one-third by stemmers while those in other tobacco related occupations accounted for the remaining 16.7 percent. However, it shows a significant decline of strikes among cigar makers, due in part to companywide settlements. Despite the large number of participants in many walkouts carried out by stemmers and leaf sorters, which even included an early collective agreement in 1914, and the fact that the PRLTC was a long-standing firm and a major factor in the tobacco industry, union officials proved incapable of submitting strikes to union control, particularly in their opening stages. When stemmers went on strike, they did not do so on a companywide basis but in a factory-by-factory pattern with frequent solidarity strikes from nearby shops. Thus, table 8.1 shows that, by 1919–1920, stemmers represented 79.5 percent of strikes against 12.8 percent for cigar makers.

The articulation of union and strike in PRATCO factories follows the classical model depicted for France and Germany by Perrot and Moore with a single, yet important, exception. The role of the US-based CMIU in the molding and strengthening of local unions bears no parallel with the European cases. Strong

CMIU locals among cigar makers at PRATCO factories might have precluded other forms of capital labor relations. For instance, Cuban cigar makers failed to develop powerful unions early in the century, and many practiced a strain of syndicalism close to anarchist lines.[199] Without the CMIU, local cigar makers might have followed a course closer to the Cuban experience and the tradition of spontaneous solidarity might have retained its hegemony.

UNION AND STRIKE PART COMPANY, 1921–1927

The string of success came to an abrupt end only months after the 1920 agreement. Decomposition of the cigar-making craft and the ultimate mechanization of cigar manufacture amounted to deep structural changes within the industry itself.[200] Furthermore, cigar consumption experienced a profound modification. It ceased to expand; it leveled, soon to decrease, while cigarettes experienced a seemingly unending surge.[201] Such changes destroyed the material bases on which unions, strikes, and particularly cigar makers depended. These medium-term tendencies in the industry hastened on the short term in 1920. The handcrafted cigar market peaked in 1920, never to recover its previous saliency. Lastly, by 1926 a very large proportion of cigars were machine made instead of hand rolled.[202]

Union officials claimed that the firm violated the 1920 agreement, specifically the provisions in case of business contraction. Workers struck over breach of contract on 30 December.[203] Company accountants ceased making deductions for the unions within the first two weeks of 1921. In April the firm declared the collective agreement to be invalid. Florentino Miranda and Arthur H. Noble, company directors, declared in court that the firm had ceased to make payroll deductions because it lacked union representation.[204] PRATCO mounted an aggressive campaign against the union in newspapers and other mediums.[205] By April the firm reopened several shops manned by strikebreakers.[206] As in previous strikes, the company opened factories in areas with little union organization, such as Sábana Grande, Yauco, Las Piedras, Ciales and Aguadilla. The walkout ended in mid-October after an assembly of strikers voted, by a small majority, to return to work under existing conditions. The institutionalization and legitimacy of the unions were such that, even in defeat, they controlled the strike. A month later the firm imposed, with no opposition from labor, a substantial reduction in piece rates.[207]

In July 1922, the firm decreed another large reduction in piece rates. Neither the FLT nor the CMIU Joint Advisory Board responded, save for its president, Prudencio Rivera Martínez, who offered "counsel and cooperation to defend the craft." Cigar makers from individual factories, as in Cayey, Cidra, and Las Piedras, held local assemblies to decry the reduction.[208] Upon application of the reduction, Caguas cigar makers took to the streets, held an assembly on 10 July, and called for a companywide convention of the craft on 13 July. A tobacco workers' assembly in Caguas, in the spirit of rationality espoused by union officials, petitioned PRATCO to withdraw the cut and allow cigar makers to hire readers, *lectores*, at their own expense. Both were denied.[209] Workers struck briefly eleven of the fourteen factories owned by the firm, mainly in the districts where the company had established operations in the midst of the previous strike or recently, in towns such as Caguas, Utuado, Las Piedras, Aguadilla, Yauco and Gurabo.[210] Representatives of the strikers blamed the absence of cohesion for its failure. San Juan cigar makers refused to participate, in contrast to their previous disproportionate share of leadership in unions and strikes.[211]

The 1922 strike against PRATCO began and ended in the tradition of spontaneous solidarity when cigar makers resumed work, accepting cuts in piece rates. It was the first companywide strike in a decade without union leadership and thus indicative of their failure to bring the firm to the negotiating table. It also broke, temporarily, the union's control over strikes. However, its failure left cigar makers with no other recourse but weakened unions.

The unions of stemmers and leaf sorters, mostly composed of women, were decidedly more fragile than those of men, whether CMIU unions or the Sociedad de Escogedores. As a result, stemmers and sorters relied throughout this period on the tradition of spontaneous solidarity more so than did cigar makers. Two stoppages in 1922 show the lesser scale of the strike and the anger and spontaneity of the disputes. Stemmers in Juncos and San Lorenzo sustained two different strikes over the dismissal of workers, the first by 191 women and the latter with 23 women.[212]

Contraction of employment in cigar manufacturing due to decreased consumption and mechanization also affected cigar packers. When PRATCO also pared their wages, they staged a month-long strike during 1924. Midway through the strike, they scaled down their petition to what they had earned previously. Many returned to work under wages and rules dictated by the firm.[213] They lost badly, as had cigar makers working for the same firm a few years before. While the cigar makers' unions survived, in a weakened state and with less legitimacy, the Sociedad de Escogedores dissolved itself in the aftermath of the failure.[214] It had been the only important union in the industry that remained independent from the FLT.

While changes in the industry led to many business failures, the surviving independent firms continued to experience labor strife in the tradition of spontaneity, but adding some elements of the project to subordinate the strike to the judgement of union officials. A well-documented instance of this situation was the 1926 strike of one hundred cigar makers against Bosch Brothers, manufacturers of Ribosch cigars, in Cayey.[215] On 28 October, the firm introduced an expensive style of cigars, but its workers rejected the proposed piece rates that, in turn, provoked a partner in the firm to threaten to dismiss half the workforce. In the tradition of spontaneous solidarity, the workers took to the street. Yet in the spirit of rationality, they held an assembly, called a strike, and elected a strike committee and carried over the stoppage to the neighboring Bosch factory in Coamo.[216] It received friendly coverage in the working-class press. A few days later the strikers distributed a propaganda leaflet denouncing the firm and requesting cooperation and understanding from the community.[217] As in early strikes, no union led or lent support. The factory reopened in mid-November after granting a small raise in piece rates and allowing a reader and an elected shop commission.[218]

By the mid-twenties, the contraction of employment among cigar makers continued unabated. The last companywide strike against PRATCO began like innumerable ones before. It was the instantaneous expression of solidarity with fired fellow workers in the Utuado factory. From its 28 July 1926 origin it spread to the remaining factories, resulting in a formal strike declaration on 3 August.[219] The strikers included not only cigar makers working by hand but also the operatives of semi-mechanized and fully automatic cigar-making machines. Quickly, the cigar makers elected a central strike committee and several local ones. This and the 1922 strike were the only companywide strikes without CMIU economic assistance in over a decade. However, it had support from the FLT, local unions, US unions (particularly those working the Clear Havana industry in Tampa), and sympathetic coverage from *Unión Obrera*. While worker demands changed somewhat during the dispute, they always included shop commissions, factory readers, 1920 piece rates and the defense of the collective agreement.[220]

After months of negotiation and after the strikers had rejected more than one preliminary accord, they rejected one that was acceptable to their representatives on 24 March 1927. The strike committee petitioned strikers to reconsider the 531–390 rejection. Immediately, the committee embarked on a powerful propaganda campaign to overturn the vote.[221] The committee prevailed, but worker dissatisfaction with the agreement ran high. After eight months PRATCO reopened operations on 8 April.[222] Strikers did not gain much; neither shop commission nor factory readers appeared in the agreement, while piece rates increased modestly.[223]

Workers and labor agitators developed mechanisms and strategies such as walkouts, trade unions, shop and strike committees, collective agreements, picketing, and a powerful necessity to subordinate the strike to unions in their struggle against capital. Among domestic workers, only a sector of cigar makers' unions and to a lesser extent the Sociedad de Escogedores, all composed primarily of men, gained considerable control over the strike. Leaf sorters and stemmers also developed trade unions, but union officials in these organizations proved incapable of controlling strike activities, particularly during its early stages. Nevertheless, they adapted and modified many traits developed by cigar makers. Large failed strikes led to the collapse of the cigar packers' union and weakened those of the cigar makers, if not more so, than those of stemmers and leaf sorters. In this new state of affairs, however, a return to previous forms of conflict between labor and capital was impossible, and cultural practices cherished by union officials during the first years of the century were in dire jeopardy. Cigar makers' unions relinquished the field to the shop movement. Nevertheless, many cultural practices, strategies, and mechanisms developed by agitators and union officials to subordinate the strike became inseparable from stoppages even in situations in which unions only played a supportive role.

CONCLUSION

This chapter follows Snyder, Shorter, and Tilly in considering the strike as a form of contention, always in the making between labor and capital. They stressed the historical character of the strike as for duration, frequency, and size. Snyder attributed additional emphasis to the historical decline of strikes over "union organization"—that is, strikes to pressure capital to recognize unions as a mechanism in the management and settlement of labor disputes. This research builds on these works but places its emphasis on the other side of the coin, which was the resistance of labor to accept trade unions as the main vehicle to attend disputes with capital.

Following Moore, the chapter makes a distinction between union leaders and rank-and-file workers, between representatives and the represented. This dichotomy is the crux of understanding the relation between strike and union. The defense of unions and the attempts to bring the strike under union control sought to transfer control of labor disputes from the strikers to the leadership of an organization.

This research examined strikes and trade unions in tobacco manufacture with emphasis on the articulation of both. It starts with the earliest strikes during the 1890s and ends with the last major strike staged by cigar makers in 1927. The discussion followed five stages in the articulation of strike and union. First, early strikes among tobacco workers ran independently of trade unions or guilds. Second, the first unions, as Perrot pointed out for France, were creatures of the strike as their existence depended on the strike.

Third, while union officials and labor agitators pleaded for the rationalization of worker outrage against the employer, union efforts to control the strike failed. They called for a strong sense of discipline and, consequently, distrusted spontaneity and mass enthusiasm. The rise of unions implied a rift between officials' interest in subordinating the strike and the tradition of spontaneity and sudden strikes. In practice the rift assumed two forms. On one hand are the CMIU locals with their officials; on the other, the *movimiento del taller*, the shop movement. While the union officials disapproved of the shop movement, the participants in the latter did not feel any conflict between the two models. Within the tradition of spontaneous solidarity, workers on strike viewed trade unions and the CMIU as useful for some matters such as the provision of material support and expertise in achieving a beneficial settlement, and the shop movement as a mechanism of flexibility and, yes, useful for the immediate expression of anger and outrage.

Fourth, from a union perspective two types of strikes began to coexist, the union led and the shop movement. Walkouts led by trade unions responded to CMIU practices, and the shop movement followed older traditions. Worker culture apart, these two types of strikes bear a powerful relation to firm size, occupation, and, through the latter, gender. Cigar makers' unions, composed mostly of men, subordinated only large strikes at the major firm in the country. Union officials at all other cigar factories, some with hundreds of workers, failed to bring the strike under union control. Despite the organization of unions and militant strikes, leaf sorters and stemmers, principally women, continued to strike in the tradition of spontaneity. On another note, some stemmeries and leaf-selection establishments hired workers by the hundreds and one by the thousands. Successful control of the strike became associated with cigar makers working for trust factories. All others remained within the tradition of spontaneity.

Fifth, the subordination of the strike to trade unions, contrary to the experience of the industrial world, proved to be brief and unique. Trade unions in industries other than tobacco were unable to control the strike but provided material support, negotiating skill, and direction to the course of events and particularly so to the ending sequence. This situation prevailed for small-scale walkouts as well as in the massive strikes of the sugar industry during the early decades of the century. The downturn in cigar consumption first and the mechanization of manufacture later severely weakened the material bases of the cigar-making craft. As the economic position of cigar makers waned, the largest manufacturers launched an aggressive policy to free themselves from their ascendancy. During the 1920s cigar makers at PRATCO posted small victories and large failures that ultimately broke the subordination of the strike to the union. The strike regained its autonomy from the unions, although the experience with union discipline had a lasting impact on the character of subsequent strikes that retained traits developed by the cigar makers' unions such as strike and shop commissions and contract-like collective agreements between management and union.

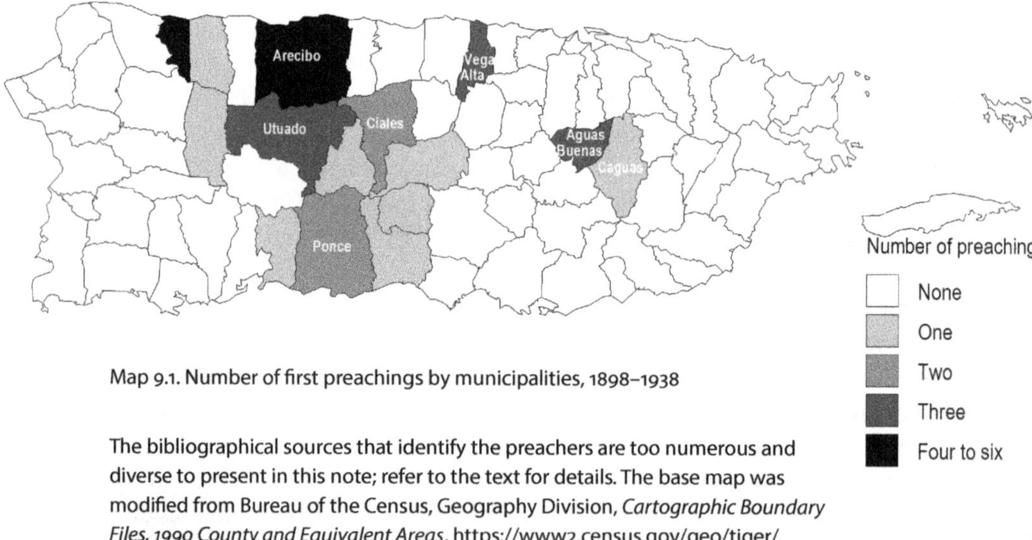

Map 9.1. Number of first preachings by municipalities, 1898–1938

The bibliographical sources that identify the preachers are too numerous and diverse to present in this note; refer to the text for details. The base map was modified from Bureau of the Census, Geography Division, *Cartographic Boundary Files, 1990 County and Equivalent Areas*, https://www2.census.gov/geo/tiger/PREVGENZ/co/co90shp/.

CHAPTER NINE

The Hermanos Cheos: Religious Resistance to the Breakdown of Order and Market Forces, 1898–1938

In the summer of 1906, "Saint Francis of Siena" began to preach in Ponce: "From the heavenly homeland, I come extending my hand. Receive the blessing that we send: that of the Father, the Son, and the Holy Ghost. I come from the heavenly homeland, disappearing the five bodily senses from this being and penetrating it with the five spiritual senses."[1]

Upon the possession of the woman, he stated that seven years before God Almighty was about to devastate everything with the floods of the 1899 hurricane. Within fifteen minutes of the end, the Virgin Mary pleaded and begged her Son to stop the punishment and "pour the lights of the inspired" to give her worldly children an opportunity to amend their ways. Once detained, the flooding gave way to God-sent inspirations.

Dozens of men and women "inspired" by the Doctors of the Church, the Apostles, and other saintly preachers began to conduct missions in various regions of the island. In time, they merged into a distinct religious movement briefly known as *Los Ángeles*, the Angels, and later as los Hermanos Cheos.[2] Map 9.1 presents the number of preachers who began their missionary work in a given municipality.

This chapter explores the movement as a significant expression of smallholding peasants, sharecroppers, and peons to compensate the disruption provoked by the invasion in 1898, the 1899 hurricane, the dislocation of tobacco markets, and the phenomenal expansion of tobacco agriculture that followed. The rise of tobacco, at the expense of subsistence crops and coffee production, subjected thousands to a commercial agriculture that responded to US firms. These changes provided the space for new forms of belief that explained the turmoil and furnished mechanisms to deal with it; the Hermanos Cheos were one. These lay missionaries started preaching soon after the invasion. Identifying with the Catholic Church, their early preachings assumed an apocalyptical and eschatological character.[3]

A limited review of the literature raises four points of discussion and dissent among researchers. This chapter examines the Hermanos Cheos along these to shine some light on these religious movements.

Some scholars seek the causes of messianic movements in, above all, long-standing popular religious traditions explained and understood in religious terms. Cultural traits like devotion to the saints, fundamental to Latin Christianity, become central explanatory elements. Todd Diacon, for instance, considers the interplay of the religious with other elements in the Contestado rebellion in early twentieth-century Brazil, which emerged "when a society is suffering from spiritual as well material crisis."[4] Still others, such as Roger Bastide, regard religious culture as an indispensable component of messianic cults but do not yield it the centrality bestowed to other social strictures.[5]

Second, a powerful breach of the established order facilitated the surfacing of underlying religious beliefs. Large groups interpreted the rupture as a divine signal that the established order of things had ceased to be inevitable. Apocalyptic movements have blossomed after the occurrence of a major event perceived by the devout as premonitory of the end to come. For instance, Robert Levine writes about itinerant holy men and receptivity to messianic calls that were deeply intertwined with a major political event. Thus the 1889 establishment of the republic in Brazil appeared as an aggravation of long-standing conditions of deprivation associated to market forces, to violence due to weakening bonds of social control, and the like.[6] According to Michael Barkun, rupture and rift of the social fabric constitute the single mechanism that widens the appeal of prophecies of hellfire and brimstone. He holds that apocalyptical ideas spread only when disaster and rupture shatter the world people are accustomed to. A ruined way of life, nothing else, makes the doctrines of doom and imminent salvation palatable.[7]

Third, the development of capitalism appears as a crucial component to modern religious movements with apocalyptic components. However, no research explains these movements as solely deriving from capitalist relations. For instance, Eric J. Hobsbawm makes a strong argument for the primacy of capitalist relations, but only in combination with political processes. He considers the irruption of capitalism, abrupt rather than slow, as inevitably accompanied by sweeping political changes—often the result of conquest, revolution, and the like—in messianic movements.[8] In explaining the emergence of Olivorio Mateo, Jan Lundius and Mats Lundahl give the primacy to the stress that capitalism caused on Dominican life while considering the importance of the religious context within which he arose.[9]

Fourth, apocalyptic forms can become influential when major disruptions, such as the irruption of capitalism, dissolve, at least partially, the bonds that tied the poor to the propertied and the powerful. For instance, Patricia Pessar has argued that under circumstances of extreme duress the elites can prove incapable of fulfilling their traditional obligations to the peasantry.[10] These obligations often go beyond the economic sphere and into relations of servitude and protection. This incapacity opens a cultural space that religious beliefs can occupy by providing an alternative understanding of their vicissitudes in life. Todd Diacon's examination of the Contestado rebellion considered a variation of the theme. Here the propertied made common cause with the expanding railroad through the region and broke the patron-client relation, thus leaving the peasants to fend off by themselves.[11]

OF DOOMSDAY AND DAMNATION: THE CATHOLIC ROOTS OF THE HERMANOS CHEOS

A central doctrine of Christianity is the role of Jesus as the redeemer. Christians of all persuasions believe in the "active" intervention of a deity and its emissaries in the final destiny of humanity, in the midst of trials and tribulations, accompanied by prophecies of damnation. It is so central a belief that even a brief and fundamental statement of doctrine such as the Nicene Creed, for instance, contains it.

Church authorities—believers who became emissaries of God on earth, and more infrequently Jesus himself, the Virgin Mary, or the saints—reissued periodically this eschatology. Witness the church acknowledgment of the apparitions, prophecies, and healings—attributed to the Virgin Mary—at Lourdes in France after 1858 and Fátima in Portugal after 1917. They are eloquent testimony to this shift.[12] Although Spain lacked a modern supernatural phenomenon of major significance, pilgrimages to and healings at Lourdes and Fátima were common.[13]

By the early twentieth century, Puerto Rico had not witnessed a major apparition by a deity.[14] Nevertheless, devotion to the saints had powerful manifestations among the well-to-do and the rural poor alike. Note the well-known intervention of the Virgin of Montserrat, who saved a young Gerardo González as he pleaded to the Virgin for mercy from a charging wild bull. In gratitude for the miracle, he built and furnished a shrine in Hormigueros at the site of the miracle. The shrine became a popular place of worship, where countless pilgrims made votive offerings to the Virgin that hung from its walls and ceiling.[15] This veneration, associated with a creolized Catholic heritage, had its counterpart in the popular devotion to the saints in the form countless wooden figures, hand-carved by rural artisans, which then populated domestic altars.[16]

The Hermanos Cheos derived from a Latin Christianity that granted holy men and women, independent of the institutional Church, the authority to admonish the irresolute speaking for a deity that could cause great calamities, if not the end of the world. A powerful belief in coming trials and tribulations as the condemnation for sin was common among Cheo preachers. For instance, in 1907, Saint John the Evangelist became the "Holy Inspiration" that descended briefly from the moral world to take José de los Santos Morales, the leading Cheo preacher, to admonish the assembled congregation in these terms:

> Oh, dear brothers, thou are at the end of time, the day of the Antichrist is close, he will become incarnate in an old sorceress from Asia, will meet the Pope, the Pope will kill him, and [he] will resurrect within five days to kill the Pope and then thou shall say farewell to the physical world. St. Jerome's trumpet will resound God's voice through the whole universe and the souls will meet the bodies that the earth will deliver to all and sundry, the rooster from Christ's Passion will crow, the Holy Cross dressed in black and white will be seen from east to west. . . . See, dear brothers, that other lands are on fire, don't wait for the terrible days to repent, there will be an angel in the middle of the blue firmament holding a pointed sickle to throw it on the earth, and everything will be destroyed.[17]

The areas with Cheo preachers bear a modest relation with wooden saints for household cult. These artifacts, so common as to be found in all households in many barrios, had their heyday during the nineteenth century and the early decades of the twentieth.[18] Starting in the 1940s and extending through the following decades, collectors of folk art combed the urban shantytowns and the rural landscape for the previously scorned hand-carved saints. The municipalities that yielded the largest number of images were, at times, likely to coincide with those where the Cheo preachers began their missions. Thus, Arecibo to the north was both a cradle to the movement and rich quarry of wooden saints while Cayey, poised in the Cordillera, was neither. Aguada and San Germán were important foci of devotion to the saints but harbored no preachers while Juana Díaz was not salient for its devotion to the saints but had two preachers. A correlation coefficient of 0.213 confirms a positive, yet weak, relation.[19]

The Hermanos Cheos emerged in municipalities with a moderate devotion to household saints. This culture also had a belief in the active intervention of deities in worldly affairs and proved receptive to preachings of impending doom and damnation. These elements remained close to Hispanic Catholicism.

BREACHES OF ORDER: INVASION, CHURCH, AND HURRICANE

While the Last Judgement is central to Christian beliefs, the doctrine might lie dormant for extended periods as a ritual with little contemporary effect and, at other moments, it gains a large following of believers awaiting the impending end. The question is why these ideas fire up small cadres of militants and capture the imagination of a mass of supporters at a given time and, at other times, fail to elicit a powerful response. According to Barrington Moore, a significant reason for people to denounce and seek redress to human misery occurs when hardship increased rapidly enough to deprive people of opportunities to adjust to their new station in life. Additionally, people condemned and sought remedy for deprivation more often when the perceived causes of decay in their living conditions were felt to be new and clearly identified.[20]

Novel and identifiable causes of rising hardship abound as explanations of movements of doom and damnation. The invasion is the obvious analogy with the Cheos.[21] Some indicators suggest the precipitating effect of the invasion; for instance, more preachers became "inspired" in the years immediately following the war than at any other time. Twenty-four preachers, accounting for 77 percent of the thirty-one whose date of first preaching I could ascertain, began their missionary work before 1905. Eudosia, the first Angel and the immediate forerunner of the Cheo preachers, began her missionary work in Quebradillas just weeks after the invasion.[22]

However, direct references to the invasion are hard to come by. Eudosia's preaching might have been one. Nevertheless, Cheo missionaries did not construct a blissful and impeccable Hispanic past to challenge a dire and gloomy Anglo-Saxon present and future. Nonetheless, the retrenchment of the Catholic Church, an unavoidable consequence of the invasion, may have been a rupture that eased the way for countryside preachers to reject the inevitability of the social order and gain a large following.

While the Spanish regime severely limited Protestantism, the United States established at once the separation between church and state, consequently depriving the Catholic Church of substantial benefits. To wit, several US Protestant churches coordinated an aggressive campaign that penetrated most corners of the country by 1905.[23] The Catholic clergy experienced a notable reduction from a high of 183 in 1897, to 132 in 1898, and finally to a low of 110 in 1899.[24] Soon after the invasion, many priests had to attend two and even three parishes.[25] This visible and palpable weakening of the institutional Church represented a powerful breach of the established order that seemingly boosted the emerging Cheos. Figure 9.1 plots the number of Cheo-like preachers who began their missionary work between 1898 and 1930 in a given municipality by the number of priests per ten thousand inhabitants in 1899.[26]

Figure 9.1 shows that all preachers received their "inspiration" in municipalities with 1.5 or fewer priests per ten thousand inhabitants. The plot presents a clear pattern between the lack of the clergy and the number of new preachers. For instance, six men and women started preaching in north coast Quebradillas and Arecibo, municipalities with 1.35 and 0.54 priests respectively. Four preachers started their missions in the highland municipality of Utuado that had 0.23

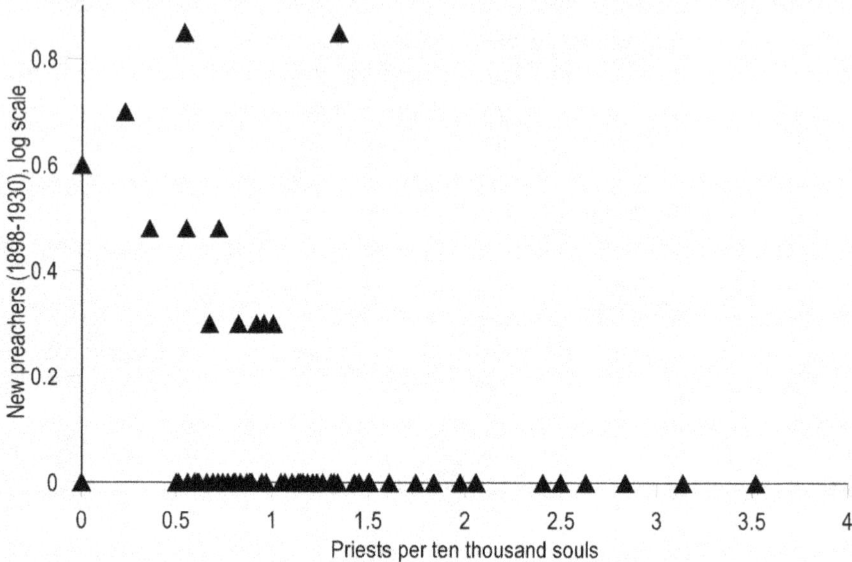

Figure 9.1. New Cheo preachers by presence of priests, 1899

Sources: The number of priests follows "Clero parroquial," *Boletín Eclesiástico* 29, no. 1 (20 Jan. 1899): 5–8. The population statistics come from Bureau of the Census, *Thirteenth Census of the United States, 1910*, vol. 3 *Population-Porto Rico/Report by Cities with Statistics for Counties, Cities and other Civil Divisions*, table 38 "Composition and Characteristics of the Population" (Washington, D.C.: GPO, 1913), 32–45. The references that identify the preachers are too numerous and diverse to present in this note; refer to the text for details.

priests per ten thousand persons. Neither Aguas Buenas nor Vega Alta, shown with a single triangular mark, had any priests, but three preachers started their missions in each. On the other extreme of the figure, Trujillo Alto and Guayama retained 3.54 and 3.14 priests respectively and were not cradles to preachers.[27]

Michael Barkun considers a "disaster-prone environment," rather than a single disaster, to be more conducive to apocalyptic movements because a series of ruptures are more likely to loosen existing allegiances, thus paving the way for the mass adoption of other commitments.[28] Late nineteenth-century Puerto Rico approached this cataclysmic environment with three major ruptures: the 1898 invasion, the Church's 1898–1900 crisis, and the 1899 hurricane.

The hurricane of 8 August, named San Ciriaco, provoked some 890 deaths attributable to the winds; subsequent flooding accounted for another 1,296; and many more perished from dysentery by drinking contaminated water during the following months.[29] A young army doctor stationed in Ponce described the aftermath of the disaster in the following terms: "When the water at last began to recede, municipal trash carts went about by day collecting the dead. Nights were made hideous by shots, screams, and indescribable crimes."[30]

Table 9.1. New Cheo preachers by mortality rate per 1,000 on account of San Ciriaco

Mortality rate	Average number of preachers logarithm	number	municipalities
No deaths	0.014	0.05	(21)
0.0 to 2.0	0.094	0.47	(30)
2.0 to 4.5	0.135	0.63	(8)
4.5 to 16.5	0.290	1.63	(8)

Sources: The deaths attributed to the hurricane follow G. G. Groff, "Apprendix D. Report on Hurricane," in *Appendices to the Report*, ed. Military Government of Porto Rico (Washington, DC: GPO, 1901), 141. The population statistics come from Bureau of the Census, *Thirteenth Census of the United States, 1910*, Statistics for Porto Rico (Washington, DC: GPO, 1913), table 38 "Composition and Characteristics of the Population" (Washington, DC: GPO, 1913), 32–45. The bibliographical references that identify the preachers are too numerous and diverse to present in this note. Suffice it to state that Santaella Rivera's *Historia de los Hermanos Cheos* is the best source.

Besides the preachings of Saint Francis of Siena, reviewed at the opening of this chapter, other references to the hurricane include Policarpo Rodríguez, a Cheo missionary who preached that Heaven granted the Virgin a limited time following San Ciriaco for people to amend their ways, attend mass, and receive the sacraments.[31] A major Cheo-like preacher, Elenita, started her missions in 1899 after, according to some believers, holding tightly to a piece of timber from a shipwreck as she struggled with the waves along the coast during San Ciriaco.[32]

San Ciriaco did not affect the country evenly. Fajardo, Vieques, and Cabo Rojo suffered less in sharp contrast to Arecibo, Utuado and Ponce. Hence, an examination of the relation between the hurricane's damage and the emergence of Cheo preachers is possible by comparing municipalities. Table 9.1 presents the number of Cheo-like preachers who began their missionary work between 1898 and 1930 in a given municipality by the mortality rate attributable to the hurricane.

According to table 9.1, the number of preachers increased noticeably in municipalities where the mortality rate also rose. Aguadilla, Camuy, Santa Isabel, Vega Baja, and others that went less affected by San Ciriaco, barely had preachers (0.05). On the other extreme, Arecibo with a 10.92 mortality rate had six preachers, and Utuado with 11.90 had four. All towns with rates above 4.5 had an average of 1.63 preachers.[33] The table suggests that one important link to new preachers lay in the path of death traced by San Ciriaco.

The institutional crisis of the Church, the invasion, and the hurricane were, in all likelihood, the awaited signals to fire up a small cadre of preachers to defend a Catholicity under siege and helped them gain a large following. Not one but several major destabilizing events reinforced each other to nurture a belief in the immediacy of the Day of Judgement.

THE DEVELOPMENT OF CAPITALISM AS A CRUCIAL COMPONENT TO CONTEMPORARY RELIGIOUS MOVEMENTS

While the previous sections of the chapter have elaborated on two salient characteristics of apocalyptical movements, research often considers that profound transformations of the economic fabric, particularly those that affect deeply embedded cultural practices, create favorable conditions for such movements. A powerful trend that includes researchers as diverse as Eric J. Hobsbawm, Robert M. Levine, Todd Diacon, and Jan Lundius and Mats Lundhal has privileged the transition to capitalism—be it in the private property of the land or the growth of a market for agricultural or pastoral commodities—as a major explanation of modern religious movements.[34]

This research does not consider the transition to capitalism, in the general sense stated above, to be at the root of the Hermanos Cheos but, nevertheless, understands that an intense dislocation of the economic relations offered a strong impulse to the movement. The region that saw the origin of the missionaries had already privately held farmland worked by independent peasants and sharecroppers who practiced crop rotation of subsistence goods with commercial production. Concretely speaking, the material causes for the Cheos seem to be found in the loss of the Cuban and Spanish tobacco markets, due to the invasion and the subsequent reorientation of the economy.

The US occupation compelled strong economic adjustments among both the propertied and dispossessed. The maintenance of US tariffs after the invasion, followed by a significant reduction in 1900 and, later by their elimination, opened the US market for Puerto Rican tropical exports.[35] Cuba protected its agriculture by enacting high tariffs just before the invasion, and Spain applied its customary customs duties after the conflict.[36]

The changes, experienced by exports, provide a rough indication of the deep modifications of the occupation and the hurricane on the local economy. Coffee, sugar, and tobacco, the three main exports in order of value, adjusted to the US economy in different ways. Sugar exports in 1897 amounted to 58,000 tons—there are no statistics for the intervening years. By 1901 they reached the low 60s, and by 1906 they exceeded 183,000 tons.[37] The adjustment of sugar exports to the new situation was a brief jolt followed by a powerful upturn in exports, production, and investments that transformed the colony into a sugar island.[38]

Coffee fared differently as San Ciriaco's destruction and the reorientation of the markets constricted but did not eliminate the bean's historical markets. In brief, coffee exporters struggled to maintain the Spanish and Cuban markets; they never gained access to the United States but, fortunately, retained German and French commerce.[39] Exports for 1901 suggest a bleak picture: they amounted to twelve million pounds from the fifty-one million pounds exported in 1897.

However, government relief for the ravages of the hurricane lessened the plight of the coffee industry more than that of other sectors of the economy. In fact, both policy and actual practice of the Charity Board, the agency that distributed the aid, favored the coffee region.[40] Additionally, the 1902 Commercial Reciprocity Treaty between the United States and Cuba substantially reduced the tariff on coffee exports to Cuba.[41] Recovery was under way by 1906 with exports of twenty-eight million pounds that amounted to 55 percent of prewar levels.[42]

US colonialism hit tobacco harder and longer than sugar or coffee. In fact, local tobacco endured a reorganization that changed the type of leaf exported, a geographical shift of producing areas, and the substitution of traditional markets for the United States. With more than 6.0 million pounds in 1897, exports dwindled to nearly 5.0 million in 1901 but slumped to some 1.5 million pounds in 1906, a scene of devastation that amounted to just 25 percent of prewar levels.[43] Afterward tobacco leaf gained a strong presence in US markets and became second only to sugar.

In order to examine the economic underpinnings of the movement, one must recall the tobacco-growing regions, starting with the major one stretching along Vega Baja and Aguadilla to the north and northwest. The oldest region had its center around Yauco and Sábana Grande in the southwest. Growers manufactured the better leaf from these two areas into tobacco rolls, having the remnants exported to Spain. The third was a fast developing one, in the eastern Cordillera. As discussed in chapter 2, this region grew tobacco suitable for cigars, with the better grades exported to Cuba or locally manufactured into cigars. As in other regions, the Spanish took in the *boliche*.

The worldwide expansion of cigar smoking first and later that of the cigarette—at the expense of snuff, plug, pipe, and other forms of tobacco consumption—during the nineteenth century was generally beneficial to local tobacco growers. The invasion and its aftermath ended the bonanza and for all practical purposes closed the foreign markets. Figure 9.2 presents the deep downturn of leaf exports in the wider time span of 1885 to 1907 to appreciate the profound effects of the invasion. After 1898, exports dropped to the lowest level since yearly records began to be kept in 1828.[44] The invasion shattered the foreign markets and tore asunder the roll-chewing tobacco area. However, the cigar tobacco region to the interior underwent a brief jolt that left it relatively unscathed.

The tobacco areas of the littoral retained only the roll-chewing market; the Spanish *boliche* market was lost for good, and it failed to gain a foothold on the expanding market for cigars in the United States. The distress was probably of such magnitude that leaf dealers, lien merchants, and large farmers failed to provide an independent peasantry and peons with economic security. The loss of markets, the disruption of economic relations, and probable loss of encumbered properties surely brought feelings of hopelessness to uncountable growers and their families.

Figure 9.2. Puerto Rican tobacco leaf exports, 1885–1906

Sources: Colón, *Datos sobre la agricultura de Puerto Rico*, 289–291; Descartes, *Basic Statistics on Puerto Rico*, 54; Gaztambide Báez, "La historia del tabaco," 11.

The collapse of tobacco exports, by itself, can hardly be considered a cause of the Cheo movement. However, the breakdown was another dimension favorable for Cheo development in addition to a devotion to the saints, the active intervention of deities in worldly affairs and apocalyptic beliefs common to Hispanic Christianity, and the breaches to the social order provided by the hurricane, the crisis of the Church, and the invasion reviewed earlier. For instance, after attending a Friday Via Crucis during the Lent of 1901, Juana, a young woman calling herself the Archangel Gabriel, asked the parish priest of Quebradillas for the church to give a mission. The clergyman directed her to the church porch that faced the town square and remained to listen. She addressed a multitude running into the thousands with deep religious fervor and admonished them for cursing, for the belief in spiritualism, and for their practice of civil marriage. The Archangel advised them to live by the sacraments, practice Marian devotion, attend Sunday mass, and recite the rosary. According to the priest, this woman and the other lay preachers were lacking in formal education and preached in a coarse and unrefined peasant-like fashion but achieved more than several Church-appointed missionaries. They "brought crime hardened hearts down to their knees in ways that only a supernatural force could."[45] Another case is José de los Santos Morales—a farmer with periods of landlessness, born to farmers in Arecibo—whose eschatological and moralistic preaching became so celebrated that many took him for a "man god."[46]

Table 9.2 presents the number of new Cheo preachers by tobacco cultivation in the roll-chewing areas. The table shows that as the tobacco acreage increased

Table 9.2. New Cheo preachers by chewing tobacco municipalities

Percentage of land planted with tobacco for chewing	Average number of preachers logarithm	number	municipalities
0 to 0.19	0.074	1.19	(55)
0.19 to 0.75	0.165	1.39	(8)
0.75 to 2.30	0.287	1.85	(4)

Sources: Tobacco data from Coll y Toste, *Reseña del estado social*. The identification of the chewing tobacco growing areas follows Abad, *La exposición agrícola e industrial*, 97; Abad, *La República Dominicana*, 353; Infiesta, *La exposición de Puerto Rico*, 214 and Gage, *Tobacco Industry*, 14. The bibliographical references that identify the preachers are too numerous and diverse to present in this note. Suffice it to state that Santaella Rivera's *Historia de los Hermanos Cheos* is the best source.

so did the number of Cheo preachers who started their mission in a given municipality. The municipalities with the highest concentrations of tobacco in the table averaged 1.85 preachers each. Quebradillas and Camuy, which were among the municipalities with the highest concentrations of tobacco, contributed respectively 6 and 1 preachers. On the second tier, the number of preachers averaged 1.39. Arecibo and Juana Díaz, which fell in the middle category of tobacco, contributed respectively 6 and 1 preachers. These four municipalities accounted for more than a third—from a total of 37—of the Cheo preachers starting their missionary work. The remaining preachers went public on their vocations in towns that grew no tobacco or with very little land tilled with tobacco to be twisted into rolls. In summary, the table suggests that Cheo preachers started their missions, more often than not, in these areas of an unremitting plight in the immediate aftermath of the invasion.[47]

The tobacco region of the eastern Cordillera, discussed in chapter 2, fared differently. In January 1898 the Cuban government imposed a tariff on Puerto Rican tobacco, which Havana manufacturers employed mainly in the manufacture of cigars, effectively closing the major market. However, a high Puerto Rican tariff on Havana cigars and Cuban cigarettes immediately balanced market loss by stimulating the domestic industry that processed leaf from the highlands. Soon after, in 1899, the ATC, known as the tobacco trust, expanded production on its newly acquired cigarette and cigar factories. In brief, the invasion dealt cigar tobacco a harsh but brief blow, comparable to that received by sugar, followed by a strong expansion. For instance, Aibonito and Comerío, the major producers in the cigar region, grew 331 and 142 cuerdas respectively in 1897 that expanded phenomenally to 1,182 and 1,322 in 1910.[48] These municipalities enjoyed a remark-

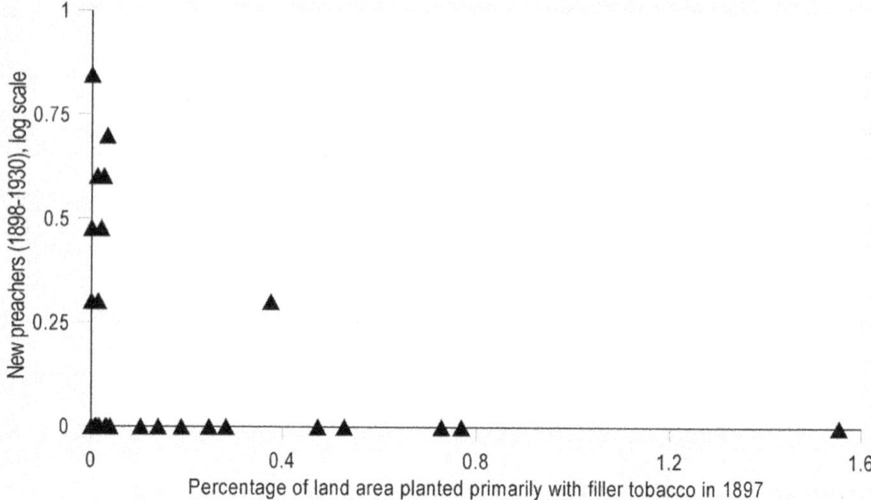

Figure 9.3. New Cheo preachers by filler tobacco in Puerto Rican municipalities

Sources: Tobacco data from Coll y Toste, *Reseña del estado social*. The identification of the filler tobacco growing areas follows Abad, *La exposición agrícola e industrial*, 97; Abad, La República Dominicana, 353; Infiesta, *La exposición de Puerto Rico*, 214; Gage, *Tobacco Industry*, 14. The references that identify the preachers are too numerous and diverse to present in this note; refer to the text for details.

able 529 percent expansion in tobacco land, overshadowing the change in the roll-chewing regions.

Since cigar tobacco, in the short run, withstood the reorientation to the US economy with relative ease, in comparison to other export regions, it did not provide the material bases to a soul-searching and a possible questioning of religious beliefs. This factor, with others examined previously, probably forestalled the immediate development of the Cheos in the region after the invasion. Figure 9.3 documents this line of thought, presenting the number of new Cheo preachers and the intensity of cultivation in the cigar tobacco areas in 1897. The relation is radically different from that of the roll-chewing areas; as the proportion of land tilled with tobacco for cigars in each municipality increased, the number of new preachers declined modestly. As presented in the figure, Caguas was the only municipality within the cigar tobacco areas to witness a new vocation, the mission of Madre Elenita.[49]

PEASANT SUBORDINATION

The blow to export agriculture in the roll-chewing tobacco areas probably allowed for a weakening of the relations that men and women established between themselves to secure their well-being. In this sense the blow could also mean the straining of the mechanisms that subordinated peasants' households to large landholders, dealers, credit merchants in town, and tobacco consignees in port cities. This might have had the effect of somewhat freeing the peasant from economic obligations but also from social ones as relations of servitude, the selection of godparents, and stimulated soul searching that led to the modification of religious beliefs. Invasion, reduction of priests, San Ciriaco, and plummeting exports followed one another as if the whole world might be coming to pieces.

Once the invasion had run its course; reconstruction from San Ciriaco finished; new priests ministered previously closed churches; and the loss of the scrap, *boliche*, markets a *fait accompli*; the people eking a living from the roll-chewing leaf areas began to rebuild their lives in a world that they no longer perceived to be catastrophic. The readjustment, carried out within a decade of the occupation, bred a new stability that seems to have been unfavorable to the Cheos, and the missions began to wither in the areas of origin. As the countryside returned to the farming cycles and routines of planting and harvesting and less to the extraordinary, many ardent Cheo preachers lost their inspiration or paid heed to husbands and parents to quit preaching. For instance, Juana, the young missionary inspired by the Archangel Gabriel, was active for just a few years in and around Quebradillas at the turn of the century.[50] Two young preachers, one inspired by Saint Gil and the other by Saint Joseph, who accompanied Juana in their 1901 petition to the parish priest, do not reappear in the literature.[51] Gumersinda Ríos, who as an eight-year-old girl inspired by Saint Dominic started her missions in her native Camuy, was close to retiring when she preached in highland Jayuya in 1910.[52] While the Cheos built long-standing, if frail, chapels in the areas where they gained a lasting following in later years, they built none in important roll-chewing towns like Quebradillas, Camuy, Isabela, or Arecibo.

As discussed in chapter 7, the cigar filler and wrapper region went through the invasion, suffered the hurricane, lost the Cuban market, and gained immediately the domestic market by the expansion of manufacture. Additionally, exports to the United States started to pick up after the tariff reduction of 1900, and its eventual abolition ended up transforming the rural landscape. The economic transformation also entailed a change in the social and economic relations of production. The advent of the new markets implied a displacement of peasant subordination from local merchants to the tobacco trust and other large US-based corporations and their representatives. Besides the large corporate plantations it also experienced a notable expansion of haciendas, which were dependent on a combination of day laborers, sharecroppers, and peons held in servitude, locally known as *agregados*.

Cheo missionaries carried apocalyptic prophecies, calls for a life according to the sacraments and Catholic devotions on their pilgrimages, to these areas whose economic fabric belatedly suffered profound transformations. The migration of preachers documents the transition to the eastern Cordillera. For instance, Eusebio Quiles, inspired by Saint Augustine, started his missions in Quebradillas and in nearby Arecibo. He then moved with his wife, Juana, the former missionary inspired by the Archangel Gabriel, to Juana Díaz first and Cidra later, where he established and attended Cheo chapels in the Cordillera for over a decade.[53] After preaching for some two years in Ponce under the inspiration of the apostle Saint James the Greater, Pedro Laboy followed other missionaries into the highlands. Laboy offered missions from two rural chapels, one in Juana Díaz and a second one in Barranquitas, above in the highlands, before returning to Ponce in 1933.[54]

José de los Santos Morales began his missions in north coast Arecibo and, soon, preached in Utuado in the highlands and in Ponce to the south. In 1907, he built and attended the main chapel, *El Trono*, the Throne of Saint John the Evangelist in the highlands of Jayuya, until he finally moved to Caguas in 1935. He stopped preaching in 1912 when "St. John ascended into heaven" but remained at the helm of the movement until his death in 1939.[55]

As the movement gained strength, new missionaries increased their presence in the expanding tobacco areas of the Cordillera. One of them, José Rodríguez Medina, who served as co-leader with José de los Santos Morales. Born to farmers from Adjuntas in 1880, he seems to have had a secular outlook, as suggested by his civil marriage in 1902.[56] Notwithstanding, he vowed to become a preacher upon recovery from a bout of jaundice and, soon after, in 1903, began preaching in Utuado. During his first years he built and held missions at Saint Anne's chapel in his native Adjuntas and later another in Ponce. After 1915, he carried missions to several towns in the highlands and held his ministry in Caguas from a chapel that he built and was dedicated to Our Lady of Mount Carmel. By 1930, he had left the highlands to manage a stall at the Ponce marketplace but remained preaching within the movement.[57]

Policarpo Rodríguez provides another illustration of the powerful presence of the Cheos in the Cordillera. Born in Juana Díaz, he moved over to Orocovis, in the central highlands, where around 1904 the preaching of the Hermano Che made him feel the "calling of the grace of God to join the congregation." He moved to San Lorenzo, where he started his ministry, and died in Caguas in 1932. Policarpo built a chapel in Aguas Buenas and preached widely over the area.[58] A Redemptorist priest from Caguas reported that the congregation believed him to be "inspired" by Saint Mark the Evangelist; his preaching reminded him of a "protestant revival," and he was impressed by the devotion of the people when "he gave the blessing to all twice, and I think all—men, women and children—knelt down in thick mud to receive it."[59]

When the movement got started along the northern littoral, its main foci were the individual preachers, who were itinerant, and the faithful and onlookers would congregate in the place of a particular mission. However, when the Cheos migrated to the Cordillera, the foci of the movement started to become fixed. More often than not, the place of prayer and worship started to become the home of a particular person, or better, a chapel. Hence Cheo missionaries built and tended a large number of chapels where one became its main place of worship. It was "the Throne" chapel, built with humble woods and not the more stately masonry, in rural Jayuya, and away from the plains of the littoral that gave it birth. It became, according to a knowledgeable insider, the Mecca or Vatican of the movement, a place where pilgrims congregated for days at a time during the major festivities of the movement. The believers assembled by the thousands to seek repentance, joy, peace, and tranquility in the preaching of the Hermano Che; his preacher wife, Micaela; and other missionaries, which reached their zenith on the feast of Saint John on 27 December.[60] The festivities did not deny, but stimulated, the joy of the Christmas liturgy that extended to the Epiphany on 6 January. However, the Cheo celebration attempted to restore the rightful place, in their view, to the proper religiosity of the period and avoided the excesses and profanity that had come to characterize much of it.

The least secularized holidays revolved around the liturgy of the Passion of Christ as throngs of penitents dressed in white crowded Catholic churches, their vestibules, and church yards on Palm Sunday and Good Friday.[61] During the nineteenth century, many penitents would "camp" in town with their provisions and beasts of burden in order seek atonement through the sacraments, confession in particular; to walk along in the procession where men carried the Mater Dolorosa, the *Virgen de Dolores*, on their shoulders; and witness the Holy Encounter with the procession of the dead Christ, the *Santo Entierro*.[62] The Cheos modified the liturgy so that the believers would congregate around the Throne chapel in Jayuya instead of going to their respective parish churches. The cult lasted for days at a time, reaching its peak on Good Friday, when the penitents would listen to the apocalyptic preachings of the missionaries, to the sermon of the Seven Words that Christ spoke from the cross. During the night they would lead a torch-lit procession, called the "Alboradas del Hermano Che," the dawn of brother Che, from the main Cheo chapel to the Catholic church by the town square.[63]

The chapel of Our Lady of Mount Carmel, the Virgin that inspired the Madre Elenita, became second only to the Throne in importance and was close to where she received hundreds of pilgrims.[64] Elenita seemingly started preaching in Caguas in 1899 to become the only preacher from the Cordillera to begin her missions about the same time as the earliest Cheo-like preachers. After carrying missions to the rural areas of Caguas, Cayey, and San Lorenzo, she moved in 1901, first to a cave and, later, to a hut in the Santa Montaña, between San Lorenzo and Patillas, that the faithful named after her.[65] Beyond the reports of assistance to her missions, she was effectively able to lead many to sacramental marriage. For instance, on 16 May 1902, five male sons of Luciano del Valle and Faustina Navarro got married

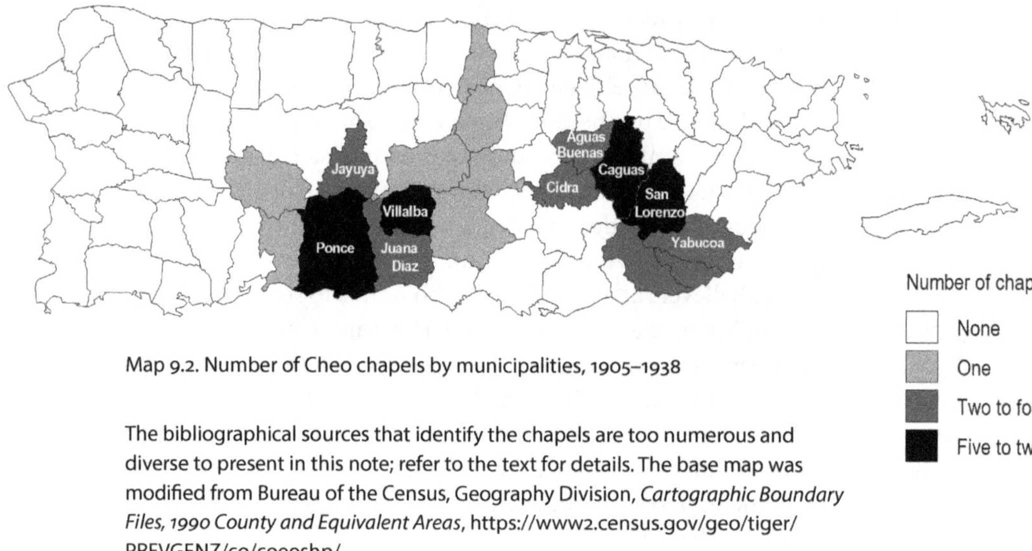

Map 9.2. Number of Cheo chapels by municipalities, 1905–1938

The bibliographical sources that identify the chapels are too numerous and diverse to present in this note; refer to the text for details. The base map was modified from Bureau of the Census, Geography Division, *Cartographic Boundary Files, 1990 County and Equivalent Areas*, https://www2.census.gov/geo/tiger/PREVGENZ/co/co90shp/.

in the Cayey parish church. One can presume that many other couples that got married on the same date were under the same influence. Marriage records for the same parish have another spike on 30 June 1902.[66]

Besides these two chapels of paramount significance, this research has identified fifty-four chapels built by the Hermanos Cheos during the first three decades of the twentieth century. While the chapels are far too numerous to identify individually, map 9.2 presents their distribution throughout the land. The map shows two clusters of chapels, the first in and around the Throne chapel in Jayuya and extending toward Ponce, Juana Díaz, Villalba, and Coamo.[67]

A second cluster, shown in map 9.2, spreads around the Santa Montaña, which lies at the boundary between San Lorenzo and Patillas. Elenita's charisma was such that, even after her death, the Cheos maintained a veneration to Our Lady of Mount Carmel to the extent that they dedicated some seven chapels in Caguas, Patillas, San Lorenzo, and Yabucoa to the Virgin.[68] Finally, a strip between the two clusters with municipalities shows few chapels, as in Barranquitas, Coamo, and Corozal, or none at all, as in Aibonito, Cayey, Comerío, and Naranjito. Also notice the complete absence of chapels along the northern littoral where the Cheos originated.[69]

The distribution of Cheo chapels in and around the two main chapels was uneven. For instance, chapels were numerous in some municipalities around the Santa Montaña like Caguas, Patillas, and Yabucoa but nonexistent in equally close towns such as Cayey and Juncos. The unevenness of the dispersion suggests that other factors were in operation besides the diffusion from the two most important chapels. The Cheo message of doomsday and damnation gained a foothold where major dislocations and the expansion of the market contributed to the dissolution, at least partially, of the bonds that subordinated the poor to the propertied and the powerful.

In a section of the tobacco-growing area of the Cordillera, the large landed estate, the hacienda, managed to subordinate not only its own sharecroppers, *agregados*, and day laborers but also the small parcel holders in its immediacy. Aibonito, Cayey, and Comerío had the largest average tobacco farms in 1930 where its growers, with those from Utuado and San Lorenzo, transformed the town halls into centers of their political power, the local farmers' organizations into vehicles to pursue their economic interests, and the social clubs, known as *casinos*, into showcases of their local hegemony. Farmers from Aibonito, Cayey, Comerío, and other nearby municipalities organized the Tobacco Growers Association in 1911 that, after 1914, included an elected board member to the Insular Experiment Station in Río Piedras.[70] A similar group of farmers established the Asociación de Cosecheros de Tabaco, a second organization, in 1921.[71] By the mid-twenties these growers had organized several local cooperatives, popularly known as *bancos tabacaleros*, to finance, stem, and market tobacco in an attempt to wrest control of the trade from US leaf dealers and manufacturers. By and large, the tobacco growers in this area embraced the *bancos tabacaleros* as a secular project of emancipation from the tobacco trust and other large leaf interests. A significant indicator of the relevance of the large growers in contrast to the Cheos is that, out of five municipalities with long-lasting cooperatives in 1932, only San Lorenzo had chapels.

On the other hand, the tobacco areas of the Cordillera lying outside the large growers' orbits showed a different type of social organization. Here, the rural landless, including the *agregados* and day laborers, worked on a more irregular basis than in the zone where the hacienda was the norm. These workers did not feel obliged to render services to the propertied. In contrast to areas in which the hacienda was dominant, where the landless subordinated themselves ritually to the landlords by asking the latter to become *compadres*—that is, godparents to their children—they sought instead *compadres* among their equals.[72] Sharecroppers in particular had real possibilities of becoming independent farmers if they had a highly profitable tobacco crop because farms were highly fragmented in most of these municipalities. Small farmers of the zone did not entrust the landlords, first, nor their cooperatives, later, with their tobacco for them to dispose because they contracted their leaf to dealers and credit merchants. Tobacco growers from Aguas Buenas, Barranquitas, Cidra, Jayuya, Orocovis, Yabucoa, and other municipalities seldom participated in the early growers' associations nor later in the cooperatives to finance, stem, and market the leaf. The Cheos, typically, did not establish roots near organized tobacco growers, but their missions flourished

Table 9.3. Cheo chapels by distance to the closest tobacco growers' cooperative

Distance categories	Percentage with Cheo chapels	Number of municipalities
1	20.0	(5)
2	60.0	(15)
3	28.6	(14)
4	19.0	(21)
5	0.0	(22)

Sources: Reyes, *La Santa Montaña de San Lorenzo* and Santaella Rivera, *Historia de los Hermanos Cheos* are the most comprehensive sources to identify the chapels. I estimated the distance between the town squares from the coordinates provided by the Departamento de Recursos Naturales, "Municipal civil divisions index," División de Inventarios, Sección de Recopilación y Ordenación de Datos, 1971.
Note: This is an updated version of Table 6 from Baldrich, *Sembraron la no siembra*, 147.

in those bereft of them. That is, they gained a presence where the independent tobacco farmer, the sharecropper, and day laborer were less subordinated to the landlords and the institutions of their local hegemony. In more concrete terms, the Cheo movement tended to thrive in areas where the rural population developed a culture independent of the organized landed interests in the financing, stemming, and marketing of tobacco and, therefore, remained relatively alien, among other things, to the cooperative project.[73]

One way to examine the saliency and domination of organized tobacco growers is to consider the physical distance to their cooperatives.[74] Those who toiled in the tobacco patch or plantation closest to the *bancos tabacaleros* were more likely to lead and follow this secular project to face leaf dealers and merchants. The farther away from a cooperative, the more tenuous their influence, if any at all. Conversely, tobacco people in the periphery of the cooperatives would not generally follow the secular project but opted for the Cheo eschatology. Table 9.3 presents the distance between the town squares of municipalities with Cheo chapels and those with tobacco marketing cooperatives. Twenty percent of the municipalities with *bancos tabacaleros* had Cheo chapels. The social and economic domination, suggested by the cooperatives nearly, preempted the Cheos from their midst. However, those municipalities that lay in the immediate periphery of the cooperatives had the highest proportion, 60 percent, of municipalities with chapels. As the distance from the cooperatives increased, the number of chapels showed a tendency to diminish.[75]

In summary, tobacco in the Cordillera developed two zones: one under the aegis of powerful tobacco growers that, in time, organized growers' associations and marketing cooperatives, and another with the predominance of small farmers in their relation with leaf merchants and credit merchants. The differences in methods of production, financing, and marketing became a cleavage, a line of division and contention, along which two groups of tobacco growers developed different visions of themselves, their friends, and their adversaries. Men and women from the areas outside the hegemony of the associations and cooperatives—such as Aguas Buenas, Barranquitas, Cidra, Jayuya, Orocovis, and Yabucoa—interpreted and reacted differently to the penetration of market relations. These men and women sought a better world in a religiosity that already formed part of their culture. If some growers took their chances on the associations and cooperatives to overcome leaf merchants, others looked for salvation in Cheo eschatology.

While the well-to-do tobacco growers and hacendados of the eastern highlands led, more often than not, amiable relations with their neighbors, they had some clashes over the Cheos. One such incident unfolded when the parish priest of San Lorenzo, Padre Puras, wrote to the bishop of San Juan in response to accusations that he supported the unorthodox practices of a Cheo preacher, Francisco Núñez. The priest denounced José Sergio Mangual and Juan Cruz Mangual as enemies of the Church. Padre Puras added that José and Juan did not give alms, had never set foot in the church, were Republican Party members, and had even bailed an anarchist and confessed atheist out of jail.[76] Both had strong interests in tobacco growing, and in time, one became a pillar of the tobacco cooperatives. Juan Cruz Mangual was to become the treasurer of the San Lorenzo cooperative in 1926 and its president from 1927 to 1933, while José Sergio Mangual owned some 689 acres of tobacco, sugarcane, and pasture in San Lorenzo in 1917.[77] On another occasion, an armed Freemason showed up at one mission given by the Madre Elenita with the intention of shooting her. She detected the ploy, publicly identified the gun and the number of bullets the man had in his pockets, and weakened him until he fell to the ground. At the end of her preaching, she called on him to leave at once because several hundredweights of his tobacco were burning and his home was in danger.[78] Lastly, Francisco M. Zeno, a learned man from the Cordillera, politician, and president of the Asociación de Cosecheros de Tabaco from 1921 to 1925, declared the Cheos to be a "morbid form" of religion incompatible with Catholic dogma.[79]

However, the early 1930s witnessed an open and acrimonious conflict between the cooperatives and leaf merchants. While the clash had several dimensions that are outside the scope of this chapter, a significant part of it pitted grower against grower, sharecropper against sharecropper, and peon against peon. When the tobacco leaf amassed by the cooperatives found no buyers in late spring and early summer of 1931, the discord erupted into open conflict. The cooperatives and their allies promoted the abstention of planting. To bolster their position, they sought the solidarity not only of its members but from all growers who planted filler tobacco.

Strong and widespread publicity accompanied the boycott with passionate resolutions at assemblies of growers, angry denunciations at meetings in town squares, a supportive colonial government, and a friendly press, but where eloquence failed, it gave way to the hoeing of seedbeds, the destruction of plantations, and the torching of the curing sheds and warehouses of dissidents. This research holds that growers who were members of the cooperative were more inclined to the boycott while those who were not would feel little solidarity and would plant tobacco. In this sense, the areas under the hegemony of the cooperatives would be expected to pay heed to the boycott, but the areas not subordinated to the growers' association would pay little attention to, if not refuse, the call for solidarity. Latent orientations and visions of the world that had been in the making during the previous decades gave way to clashes among tobacco growers when the *bancos tabacaleros* attempted to impose their will over a sector of tobacco growing in the Cordillera where they had scant following that, in turn, coincided with the areas with a strong presence of Cheo chapels as indicated in table 9.4.

The table examines the relation between the areas that had experienced strong Cheo proselytizing in the recent past and the property destruction phase of the boycott against those who prepared seedbeds and planted tobacco.[80] It presents the average number of Cheo chapels by the number of incidents involving property destruction in each municipality. The towns that experienced the most damage were also the ones that had the largest number of chapels.[81] In summary, that table suggests that the areas with greater resistance to the boycott coincided with the areas where those who sowed the land had sought consolation to the duress provoked by the tobacco market in the apocalyptic missions of the Cheos. Although their heyday had passed by the early 1930s, those same areas of former effervescence were the ones to oppose and withstand the anger of the secular project.

While the Cheo tobacco region of the highlands suffered the brunt of the hoe and the arsonist's torch, the boycott failed to elicit a response in fiery preachings and powerful eschatology. By then, José Rodríguez and Pedro Laboy were the only preachers of reputation who were somewhat active while others such as Eugenia Torres, José Morales, and María Lamberty were not preaching at all and new vocations had nearly ceased.[82] As the belief in the immediacy of the Day of Reckoning faded into memory, the movement lost much of its momentum. The charisma of the preachers slowly gave way to more traditional expressions of religiosity as the movement suffered a transformation.[83] However, the devout religiosity it aroused never faded completely, and the lack of subordination to the landed gentry remained a feature of a decayed movement as the conflict with the marketing cooperatives clearly showed.

The depression of the thirties, deep as it was, to which the intense conflict generated by the tobacco boycott must be added, did not jolt the world of the

Table 9.4. Average number of Cheo chapels by property damage during the tobacco boycott

Damage categories	Number of Cheo chapels	Number of municipalities
1	0.59	(56)
2	0.43	(7)
3	0.83	(6)
4	1.63	(8)

Sources: Reyes, *La Santa Montaña de San Lorenzo* and Santaella Rivera, *Historia de los Hermanos Cheos* are the most comprehensive sources to identify the chapels. The damages and destruction of tobacco warehouses, sheds, and plantations come from a daily examination of four major newspapers and the Querellas and Novedades series of the Puerto Rican Police corresponding to the tobacco-growing municipalities between July 1931 and February 1932.

agregados, small parcel holders, and sharecroppers to the extent that the invasion, hurricane, reduction of priests, commercial agriculture, and Protestants had at the turn of the century. Nevertheless, the boycott provoked several peasant marches, of a secular nature, to the town squares in search of food, land, and work. However, a subdued religious response did arise in penitent processions of supplicants within the countryside that occasionally reached the parish church by the town square. The "poor, the long-suffering of the Lord" organized these marches of men, women, and children to pray for deliverance from the hardship imposed by the boycott. Local Cheo preachers like Vicente Rosas and other small farmers led them in municipalities such as Aguas Buenas.[84]

Perhaps the farmers and laborers of the 1930s were more integrated and attuned to the fluctuations of commercial agriculture than those of the previous generation. Furthermore, the Economic Relief Administration, the Puerto Rico Reconstruction Administration, and other agencies of an expanding welfare state attenuated and mitigated the devastation of the disasters after 1932. For instance, in 1935 government agencies bought some 4,322 cuerdas in La Plata Valley, from an ATC subsidiary, to distribute in homesteads that ranged from 5 to 10 cuerdas a piece among the landless.[85] The Agricultural Adjustment Administration started to control acreage and guaranteed tobacco prices starting in the mid-thirties.[86]

The brisk expansion of tobacco cultivation in the Cordillera in the aftermath of the invasion weakened old social relations. The new ones were congenial, with the trust, leaf buyers, stemmeries, and manufactories on the one hand and, on the other hand, with dealers who sold the leaf that they had financed in the Water Street district of Lower Manhattan. This convulsion freed many peasants from traditional economic obligations and weakened, if not turned asunder, social ones such as relations of servitude and, as this research holds, stimulated soul searching that led to the modification of religious beliefs. These changes, however, did not affect the tobacco areas of the Cordillera in the same fashion. Sharecroppers, *agregados*, and day laborers in areas lacking large growers and their organizations eschewed subordination and refrained from its ritual variation through *compadrazgo*, coparenthood among persons of unequal rank. They financed their crops through credit merchants and leaf dealers, thus rejecting large landowners and their marketing cooperatives. The "religious" provided the cultural forms for the rural dispossessed to understand and act without the landed classes.[87] A popular Catholicism served as a "vehicle" for peasant disgust. Thus the peasant hands that joined the Cheo movement seem to have not been subordinated to the hacendados and their institutions.

CHAPTER TEN

The Unraveling of an Industry

By 1930, uncountable buckeyes and all large cigar factories but PRATCO had shuttered. The lone survivor introduced the cigar mold and then full mechanization but eventually went bankrupt. These changes brought large-scale mechanical cigar making, thus depriving men of a most desirable craft, the manufacturing sector of one its major occupations, the trade unions of one its most formidable mainstays, and the socialist tradition of one its bulwarks.

NO COMEBACK FOR THE PORTO RICO CIGAR

Chapter 3 dealt extensively with the development of the Porto Rico cigar in contrast to the famed Havana and the lesser-known Manila. As discussed in chapter 5, PRATCO's closing of its Puerta de Tierra factory in 1937 led to its disappearance from the US market. By the end of the year, its remaining manufacturing activities were some ten men rolling cigars by hand and about fifteen men and women operating the cigarette-making machinery, all in La Marina branch in San Juan.[1]

This small operation survived PRATCO's shuttering and bankruptcy as the Puerto Rico Tobacco Corporation. Within a year, the corporation moved to Bayamón and marketed the old trust cigarette brands of Colectiva, Toro, Casino, and Violetas.[2] The Colectiva and Toro cigarettes used to belong to the Rucabado y Portela and Toro partnerships respectively some forty years earlier. Nathaniel Pasarell was vice president of Puerto Rico Tobacco sometime between 1939 and 1941, which suggests that the firm had and maintained close connections with PRATCO.[3] A small firm concentrating in the local market, this corporation left a thin paper trail. In 1954, it turned out cigars valued at $323,000 to export a paltry 7.6 percent.[4] From its inception, the firm was the single cigarette manufacturer left.[5] When it closed the cigarette factory in 1955, its manufactures were so limited that a single operator manned the machines.[6]

Infanzón y Rodríguez's La Habanera had a long history that started in 1890 when Mamerto Infanzón established it in Mayagüez. It initially sought to substitute Havana cigars and Cuban cigarettes with its own hand-rolled cigars and cigarettes manufactured with steam-driven machines.[7] It promoted its cigars in the United States soon after 1898 through its participation in several exhibitions.[8] Like other manufacturers, it held its ground against the trust until the collapse of the independents, around 1915. Then PRATCO bought the cigar and cigarette factory, machinery, and brands for close to $50,000.[9]

This subsidiary maintained a facade of independence by keeping its own management, marketing, and manufacturing operations apart from those of the parent company. For instance, as late as 1935, Infanzón y Rodríguez maintained its manufactures in Mayagüez; it had Manhattan offices on Water Street and advertising that it did not share with PRATCO.[10] The subsidiary not only kept its brands but increased its portfolio by buying, in 1931, the Tantos cigar and cigarette brands from the Cien Porciento Company.[11] However, the cigarette-making division left no discernable trail suggesting its disappearance. Nevertheless, by 1934 Infanzón y Rodríguez had added a leaf-importing division in Mayagüez.[12]

Until the end of its relationship with PRATCO, around 1937, Infanzón y Rodríguez maintained offices at 128 Water Street in Lower Manhattan and had kept its operations in Mayagüez since 1890.[13] Harrison Johnson, who had been a long-serving vice president of the Cayey-Caguas Tobacco Company, managed the Water Street office during the 1930s but fails to reappear in the record after 1937.[14] In effect, the firm gave up the US market to concentrate locally.

Sometime in the 1940s, Infanzón y Rodríguez left Mayagüez for Caguas. Having ceased cigarette manufacturing, it became a distributor of the Penn Tobacco Company's Longfellow, a fancy cigarette with a wooden cigarette holder.[15] By 1950, it had added a stemmery in Aguas Buenas.[16] In consonance with its emphasis on local marketing, in 1954, it shipped only about 5 percent of its cigars to the United States.[17]

Table 10.1 permits a comparison of the importance, through time, of exports and local consumption of cigars. The early 1910s stand out for the highest local consumption and exports when the latter outnumbered those for local consumption. The data for the mid-1930s correspond to the last three years that PRATCO was manufacturing. Both exports and local consumption had declined, but exports still outnumbered local consumption.

The table shows the nearly complete collapse of exports during the late 1940s. The local market, in a reversal, became decidedly larger than the export one. When PRATCO collapsed, Infanzón y Rodríguez, the Puerto Rico Tobacco Corporation, and a plethora of buckeyes proved incapable of sustaining previous export levels. The island ceased to be an important cigar manufacturing center and became instead a leaf provider for US-based producers.

Table 10.1. Cigar manufactures in millions, 1910–1950

Year	Consumption	Exports	Production
1910–11	101.1	174.7	275.8
1911–12	111.7	169.8	281.5
1912–13	119.0	165.8	284.8
1934–35	28.5	63.2	91.7
1935–36	28.9	52.4	81.3
1936–37	50.0	51.2	101.2
1947–48	57.3	3.9	61.2
1948–49	63.1	4.2	67.3
1949–50	68.1	1.4	69.5

Sources: Department of Agriculture, *Annual Book*, 142; Economic Development Administration and Department of Agriculture, *Annual Book*, 100.

In view of the incapacity of the private sector to maintain a viable export market, the colonial government initiated its own manufacturing operation in an attempt to add a venue to channel tobacco agriculture and, simultaneously, create employment. In 1945, the government established a state-owned enterprise, the Puerto Rico Agricultural Company (PRACO), to pursue a few goals, among them "the expansion of commercial processing and manufacturing of the agricultural products of the Island."[18] The company invested $1.25 million to build and equip a modern cigar factory on El Troche farm of Caguas. The sixteen-thousand-square-foot structure included thirty-two stemming devices and six mechanical cigar rollers, making hand stemmers and hand rollers unnecessary. With no information about the type of cigar manufactured, whether it employed short or long filler, it installed a cigar band machine that would also wrap each cigar in cellophane. The factory had a capacity to manufacture between eight and ten million cigars yearly. Being a mechanized operation, it had only sixty employees.[19]

Harold Blum, the factory manager, claimed that the enterprise started production early in 1948 and that the first one hundred thousand cigars shipped had found acceptance in several cities in the United States.[20] PRACO contracted US jobbers and Lynn Baker to distribute and advertise the cigars in Washington and Philadelphia. The mechanical rollers produced a cigar shape called "perfectos" that retailed at ten cents each.[21] El Praco brand employed local tobacco filler, US wrapper, and Wisconsin binder in distinction to the Puerto Rico Tobacco Corporation, which employed "pectoral cigar paper" binders, possibly an early attempt of reconstituted tobacco, at least on the less-expensive styles.[22]

During its short life, PRACO had little impact on cigar exports. Table 10.1 shows only a modest increase from 3.9 million cigars exported in 1947–1948 to 4.2 during the following year. Upon failing to establish itself in a market that, more than ever, was the domain of a few immense corporations depicted in chapter 5, the factory closed in 1949 and liquidated its assets, leaving the colonial government with the same predicament it had before.[23]

Consolidated Cigar Corporation

Established in 1942 "to avoid the evils of absentee ownership of large scale capital," the Compañía de Fomento Industrial, a decade later, became the government agency to find a solution to the vacuum left by PRATCO's collapse.[24] During its first phase, it organized four state-owned enterprises that relied on local materials to substitute imported goods. When, under intense criticism, Fomento struggled to earn profits from its wholly owned factories, it reversed strategy. In 1945, it opened a New York office to induce private entrepreneurs to establish export-oriented factories with the Aid to Industrial Development program, which offered manufacturers a rental subsidy and a workforce earning much lower wages than those obtained in the United States. Later, in 1947, it added tax exemption to its incentives.[25]

After three years of negotiations with Fomento, the Consolidated Cigar Corporation opened its first factory in 1953. The contract obliged Fomento to build, at no cost to the manufacturer, a 130,000-square-foot, fully air-conditioned building in a seventeen-cuerda lot in Caguas. Fomento invested $1.6 million in real estate, and Consolidated invested $1.4 million in machinery.[26] The government lent the Escuela Vocacional Metropolitana during months before opening the factory to train many would-be employees under the supervision of Erick Johnson whom the firm brought in for the occasion.[27] As another incentive, Fomento contributed $35,000 and Consolidated $15,000 in a rotating fund to lend for state-of-the-art tobacco curing barns in a small-scale attempt to "modernize" the preparation of the leaf on the farm.[28] The factory started operations with one hundred cigar-making machines.[29] True to Fomento's pitch to induce the relocation of manufacture, between 1961 and 1965 the firm paid local wages at half the going rate in the United States for similar work.[30]

Consolidated probably secured more generous incentives than it would have obtained otherwise because its directors were acutely aware of what their factory meant for Fomento. Thus, the speech of Samuel Silberman as company president, at the laying of the foundation stone in 1952, drew attention to the fact that his firm was to be the first Fomento factory operated by a leading tobacco manufacturer.[31]

With a local presence dating from the purchase of the G. H. P. Cigar Company in 1926, Consolidated immediately became a significant leaf buyer that maintained hand stemmeries during the next few years without establishing cigar manufacturing operations until 1953.[32] The corporation maintained its position as a leading leaf buyer during the following decades.[33] In 1953, it bought approximately 60 percent of the tobacco crop while expressing an interest in manufacturing the leaf in the new Caguas factory and in the United States.[34]

By 1955, the firm claimed to employ 868 workers, who were overwhelmingly women. These manufactured some seventy-eight million machine-made cigars, which it exported to the United States.[35] The fast expansion of production led to the addition of a 38,000-square-foot, fully air-conditioned building in Caguas.[36]

In 1958, a commission of Comerío residents led by Mayor Eliseo Guerrero conferred with Stanley Keyser and Francisco Verdiales, two vice presidents of the firm, and Rafael Fábregas from Fomento over the course of several days. The commission supported the construction of a bridge that Consolidated needed to guarantee its expansion to Comerío.[37]

In October 1960, Consolidated opened a "threshing plant" in Comerío.[38] Fomento constructed a 132,000-square-foot building, valued at $838,000, to house the factory while the manufacturer committed itself to invest $250,000 in machinery and equipment. The factory's output would feed the Caguas operations. The manufacturer estimated a workforce of 150 to 200 workers, mostly men.[39]

Seeking to emulate the successful Caguas operations, a commission that included Mayor José Juan Meléndez and Representative Liberto Ramos met, in 1957, with Acting Governor Roberto Sánchez Vilella to request the speeding up of a second Consolidated factory in a thirty-cuerda lot in Cayey. Fomento had already done a feasibility study of the project, and the firm had shown an interest in the suggested location of the plant.[40] The factory started operations in 1961 in two buildings covering 540,000 square feet and designed by Lockwood Green Engineers. The Cayey factory had an estimated production of 200 million cigars from 140 machines whereas the Caguas operation manufactured, also using machinery, close to 150 million. With 500 machines to stem wrapper leaf from Connecticut, hand workers would stem local tobacco employed as filler. The firm announced, with pride, that the Cayey buildings and land would be wholly owned and not rented from Fomento, as the earlier structures had been.[41]

Consolidated's continual expansion led Keyser to rent a 23,000-square-foot building from Fomento in the Villa Blanca sector of Caguas in 1959. The firm started to install machinery worth $100,000 and announced the future employment of four hundred in the stemming and leaf-sorting departments. This plant would stem wrapper leaf, from the Connecticut River Valley, for use in its other Caguas establishment and the manufacturing plants the company operated in the United States. Francisco Verdiales, a company vice president, would manage the new facilities.[42]

By 1959, the investment was "paying off handsomely," with two operating factories in Caguas and others under construction in Cayey and Comerío. Overall, the two Caguas factories had reached 1,300 employees. By the end of the 1950s, its machine-made cigar output hovered around 150 million, and the firm bought 80 percent of local leaf in 1957.[43]

Cigar shipments from local manufacturers to the United States increased from 124 million units in 1957, when the Caguas factory was fully operational, to 483 million in 1962, after the Cayey factory started production.[44] Consolidated, being the only major manufacturer during the period, accounted for most of the shipments. Exports during the era of Consolidated were noticeably higher than those of the first decades of the century, presented in table 10.1.

According to the Census, 1950 opened with 97 women cigar makers, a number that ballooned to 1,063 women in 1960.[45] Most of these operatives worked for Consolidated Cigar, lending support to the large number of employees about whom Fomento and the manufacturer flaunted. This firm had effectively filled the vacuum left by PRATCO's cigar division with women operating cigar-making machines as the latter had during the 1930s.

General Cigar Company

In 1928 or thereabouts, General Cigar became a direct leaf buyer from local dealers, marketing cooperatives, and growers alike with (as presented in chapter 6) its own stemming, fermenting, and packing facilities. It became, then, the second-largest buyer of local leaf tobacco behind the former subsidiaries of the ATC.

During the 1950s, the company entered a new line of business by employing a chemist over several years to supervise hydroponically grown tobacco, possibly on "Hydroponics," a Cayey farm that already used the technology.[46] If viable, it would be a return to commercially grown wrapper leaf that ATC subsidiaries started early in the century to abandon during the 1920s. While the water-grown technology lessened the impact from several diseases, the project proved unfeasible due to the leaf's quality. In 1962, General Cigar, the local Department of Agriculture, and the Agricultural Experiment Station, which had joined the project, brought it to an end.[47]

In 1953, the firm's plantations in the Connecticut Valley began shipping shade-grown leaf to its Caguas facilities to sort by quality and size, ferment, dry, and pack for manufacture in its Pennsylvania factories. Satisfied with the results, the firm incorporated the Tobacco Products Manufacturing Corporation to take over these operations in 1954. Initially, it had some 250 employees who were mostly women.[48] Fomento reduced the processing expenses through generous tax exemptions and incentives for personnel training. As a result, the subsidiary moved, in 1960, to a new fifteen-thousand-square-foot annex of the already-existing facilities in Caguas.[49] In 1963, the year before General Cigar closed the subsidiary, its assets surpassed $1.3 million.[50] Alfonso Mayer managed all Caguas operations from 1957 to 1968, when David Levis assumed the position.[51] In 1964, other subsidiaries of General Cigar laid the foundation stone for a wholly owned, two-story building designed by Toro y Ferrer that expanded its Caguas leaf-processing area with an approximately $1.3 million investment. The extra sixty thousand square feet allowed additional sorting and packing of imported wrapper leaf for several brands—like Robert Burns, White Owl, and William Penn, manufactured in the company's US factories—and a labor force increase from 850 to 1,200 in Caguas alone.[52]

A later but, nevertheless, major expansion of the company needs examination in the context of the Cuban Revolution. The revolutionary government undertook several measures that provoked a series of reactions from the United States, leading to an increasing restriction of commerce that ended with the 1962 embargo on all trade between the countries.[53]

During the nineteenth century, the two Cuban wars for independence disrupted its tobacco trade, resulting in considerable benefits to the local leaf growers, merchants, and manufacturers, as already discussed in chapters 2 and 7. This time around, the embargo yielded no discernible benefits. To start with, Havana's share of the US cigar market was negligible. On the eve of the revolution, in 1957 imported Havana exports represented but 0.34 percent of US cigar consumption and 0.37 percent in 1958. Additionally, the largest proportion of imported Havanas belonged to the Class G category, the most expensive ones.[54] H. Upmann's Majestic and Ramón Allones's Ramondo, which were the best-selling Havanas in the United States, then retailed at thirty-five cents each.[55]

All local factories employed machinery that lowered the costs of production, and some relied exclusively on technological advances such as reconstituted sheet as binder and wrapper, to a lesser extent, to replace the more costly natural leaf. Additionally, most manufacturers employed short filler rather than the more expensive long filler. During the early 1960s, local production of General's Tiparillo with its plastic mouthpiece retailed at five cents whereas Consolidated's El Producto sold at two for a quarter in "undistinguished drugstores like Walgreens and Thrifty." Their consumers were so different from Havana smokers that they could not and did not fill the vacuum provoked by the embargo. However, a few of the ATC's plants in New Jersey and some of General's and Bayuk's Tampa factories, which manufactured more expensive cigar styles, were early beneficiaries of the embargo because of their inventories of Cuban leaf.[56]

Despite a strong and protracted presence, General had never manufactured cigars in Caguas or elsewhere in the island. Although Fomento had provided incentives to tobacco ventures and directly courted the firm over a cigar factory, it had been unable to promote one. Negotiations for the factory stalled because the firm wanted greater tax incentives and, above all, an exemption from the use of local tobacco. In 1962, Fomento and other agencies exempted the subsidiary from paying property and income taxes until 1983 and assented to the manufacture of foreign leaf. Three years later, General opened its only cigar factory on a large lot where the 100,000-square-foot building alone required a $4.25 million investment. Established in Utuado, it employed 450, mostly women, operatives mainly in the manufacture of Tiparillos. The fully mechanized plant had just one woman operating each cigar-making device.[57]

While located in Utuado, a significant tobacco-growing municipality, its exemption from locally grown tobacco provoked resentment.[58] This policy stood in sharp contrast to Consolidated's, which in 1963 and 1969, for instance, bought 71 and 92 percent respectively of the local crop.[59]

More than the Cuban embargo, the long-overdue *Smoking and Health* report to the US surgeon general, among other things, assured early success to the Tiparillo and other inexpensive cigars when it concluded unequivocally that: "Cigarette smoking is causally related to lung cancer . . . The risk of developing cancer of the lung for the combined group of pipe smokers, cigar smokers, and pipe and cigar smokers, is greater than for non-smokers, but much less than for cigarette smokers."[60]

The damning conclusions and wide diffusion of the report led the US Congress to enact the Cigarette Labeling and Advertising Act of 1965. This law, according to a Pulitzer-winning book, "watered down" the report and other initiatives of the FTC. Just to identify an instance, the label set to appear on all cigarette packs cautioning that "Cigarette smoking may be hazardous to your health" was an indecisive version of the unambiguous conclusion of the surgeon general.[61]

Consequently, cigar manufacturers increased sales of their less-risky product. The obituary of Edgar Cullman Sr., whose family bought control of General Cigar in 1961, considered the surgeon general's 1964 report to have been the "saving grace" that paved the way for many cigarette consumers to shift to the lesser of two evils.[62] In effect, the *Smoking and Health* report triggered the 1964 US record in cigar consumption, the effects of which lasted four or five years.[63]

Despite the Spanish-sounding names, El Producto and Tiparillo were ready-made cigars, and the latter did not use locally grown tobacco. Both cigars employed short filler and highly processed leaf to substitute the mid-priced Savarona, from the Cayey-Caguas Tobacco Company, and the Ricoro, from PRATCO, of the first decades of the century. The Porto Rico cigar that had played second fiddle to Havanas and Manilas did not have a comeback during the second half of the century. Cigar manufactures of the second half of the century had operations based on Fomento's incentives and a pliant and inexpensive labor force. Neither General nor Consolidated had any special interest in promoting the geographical provenance of the leaf that went into their cigars.

Processing Connecticut Shade-Grown Leaf and R. J. Reynolds

While Consolidated and General became best known for their cigar making, during the 1950s or soon after they started processing Connecticut shade-grown leaf intended as wrapper for cigars. By 1967, six sizable cigar tobacco corporations joined these two behemoths to take advantage of Fomento incentives, low labor costs, and a union-free environment. All but the Universal Cigar Corporation opened factories to import, stem, process, and re-export wrapper leaf.[64] Bayuk Cigars of Philadelphia, Hartman Tobacco and American Sumatra Tobacco of Hartford, Waitt and Bond of Scranton, and the DWG Corporation of Detroit, the latter with two factories, were the other five.

In 1954, Hartman Tobacco leased a 23,125-square-foot building from Fomento in Juncos. A year later it added 11,000 square feet to process more cigar-wrapper leaf from its extensive Connecticut River Valley plantations. At the time of the expansion it already employed some 250 workers, maintaining a level of more than 200 as late as 1971.[65] The company effectively transferred leaf conditioning to Juncos. This included the wetting, sorting according to size, fermentation, drying, fumigation, and baling for export of the shade-grown tobacco imported from its Connecticut plantations. Similarly to Consolidated's factories, the Hartman company air-conditioned the facilities to maintain control over temperature and humidity.[66]

When considered with General's actions, the Hartman transfer led to a thinning of leaf processing in Connecticut that did not go unnoticed.[67] So central was the salary question that, in 1955, the Hartman company joined the Consolidated and General companies to oppose a wage increase and the constitution of the Tobacco Special Industry Committee itself to set the Puerto Rican minimum wage.[68]

Established in 1897 as a partnership, the Bayuk Cigar Company was, by 1929, one of the earliest enterprises to mechanize cigar production on a large scale.[69] As of 1963, the company was the third-largest US cigar manufacturer in sales. Headquartered in Philadelphia, it appropriately named its main brand Phillies; they then retailed for a nickel or a dime each, depending on the size.[70] In sharp contrast to the General and Consolidated companies' long experience with local leaf, the Bayuk firm had only brought small quantities when, in 1961, it opened a factory in Ciales. As in other cases, Fomento provided tax exemptions and built a custom-made factory that processed, similarly to the Hartman company, imported shade-grown leaf and processed it for cigar wrappers.[71]

Henry Deisel and two Wemmer brothers partnered, in 1886, to manufacture cigars in Ohio. A merger with another business led to the Diesel Wemmer Gilbert company in 1929 that shortened its name to in 1946 to DWG.[72] Since the 1940s, if not earlier, its cigar blends included sizable amounts of local tobacco.[73]

As in earlier times, in 1968 it purchased considerable wrapper leaf from the Connecticut River Valley, and its blends kept including significant amounts of local filler.[74] Perhaps seeking to lower production costs, in 1961 the firm moved stemming, sorting, sizing, and selecting wrapper leaf to two Fomento structures in Caguas and Gurabo.[75]

Once a PRATCO subsidiary between 1929 and 1938, Waitt & Bond became the sixth cigar company to establish manufacturing operations when, in 1965, it incorporated Rapaport International and Rapaport Puerto Rico. It inaugurated a two-building, Fomento-sponsored factory of 46,000 square feet in Yabucoa, with an estimated labor force of 175.[76] The Rapaport companies did not manufacture cigars but bought locally grown tobacco to ferment, cure, and grind into a fine powder. Additional processing reconstituted the powder into sheets that they sought to market to cigar manufacturers as wrapper in filter-tipped little cigars.[77] To a lesser extent, the factory sorted, sized, and tied natural wrapper leaf for handmade cigars.[78]

When Waitt & Bond established the Rapaport subsidiaries, it undercapitalized them to a degree that created difficulties when complying with their obligations. Its integrated manufacturing system for reconstituted wrapper had $718,000 worth of machinery, brought with a bank loan with Rapaport International's shares serving as collateral. Rapaport Puerto Rico depended heavily on Fomento incentives, obtained sometime before 1967, that amounted to $69,200 but carried a pledge to provide a specified minimum employment and payroll. Since the parent company, Waitt & Bond, had sold its cigar business at the end of 1966, the subsidiaries' profitability depended exclusively on identifying a market for the reconstituted sheet still under development.[79] To make matters worse, as of December 1967, both subsidiaries owed Fomento $22,000 in unpaid rent.[80] Subsequently, in March 1968, Waitt & Bond settled several liabilities through an issue of preferred stock worth $52,972.[81]

A $49,200 Fomento incentive obliged Rapaport International to maintain specified employment and payroll levels. In July 1969, Fomento gave it a few months' reprieve to fulfill its commitments or return the incentives that by then included another $20,000 forwarded to Rapaport Puerto Rico. When in March 1971 the subsidiaries failed to comply, they pledged 22,715 shares of Waitt & Bond to Edward Rapaport, their president, to guarantee the debt. The president, additionally, waived his $40,000 salary for 1970. The company's reconstituted tobacco sheet was still a work in progress that found its earliest customer in Canada in 1970.[82]

Around 1967, the General Cigar Corporation gained control of the American Sumatra Tobacco Corporation, which later established the Connecticut Shade Leaf Tobacco Packers to handle its local business interests. They conveniently selected Caguas for the firm's factory, most likely because the parent company had significant economic activity there. It stemmed, processed, packed, and reshipped wrapper leaf from the Connecticut River Valley in the same Fomento industrial park where DWG already had one of its factories.[83] The factory appeared for a last time in a 1974 industrial directory.[84]

The New York–based Universal Cigar Corporation became the eighth and last sizable cigar tobacco firm to establish itself during the second half of the twentieth century. Its local subsidiary, Continental Cigar, leased a building in Fomento's Gurabo industrial area sometime in 1968, if not earlier—that is, before it changed its name to the Universal International Cigar Corporation.[85] The parent company was committed, like other large cigar makers, to the manufacture of "small, mild cigars with plastic tips" generally made from reconstituted wrapper and short filler.[86] The firm leased cigar-making machines and enjoyed a fifteen-year exemption from local taxes.[87] Better capitalized than the Rapaport subsidiaries, its retained earnings exceeded $2 million in 1973.[88] During the late 1970s, the factory's payroll had more than 150 employees.[89] Lasting nearly fifteen years, it closed its Gurabo operation around 1982.[90]

The R. J. Reynolds Tobacco Company and others that included PRATCO became independent of the tobacco trust because of a court-mandated breakup in 1911. Soon afterward it became a major cigarette manufacturer with its signature Camel brand.[91] While opening, in 1970, a factory in Yabucoa that was part and parcel of a long expansion in the cigarette industry, it presents a clear and distinct break in local manufacturing. As noted earlier in this chapter, the closing of the Puerto Rico Tobacco Corporation's cigarette department, in 1955, ended their local manufacture. The factory started operations with a 200-strong labor force that manufactured staples such as Winston, Salem, and Camel.[92] By 1977, it operated a daytime shift of approximately 188 workers and a second with about 112 to attend the strong demands for its products and to use intensively the machinery and space.[93] In 1993, the factory employed 450 workers and exported between 65 and 70 percent of the eight billion cigarettes manufactured to Canada and Europe. Winston controlled 60 percent of the local market.[94] Three years later, the firm opened a threshing and leaf treatment installation in an 85,000-square-foot annex that expanded production to include exports to Latin America.[95] By 1997, the Yabucoa factory had become the firm's third largest of its twenty-seven worldwide factories and produced approximately twelve billion cigarettes per year.[96]

While no locally grown tobacco leaf went into its cigarettes, the firm's publicity sought to identify its Winston brand with local culture. Its success as the top-selling brand was partially attributable to the soft cultural nationalist underpinnings of its savvy advertising with slogans such as "I and my Winston, and my Puerto Rico, there is nothing better."[97] Winston's publicity stood in sharp contrast to the rugged individualism of the Marlboro man inspired in the US West.[98]

However, by the turn of the century, the Yabucoa plant ceased to expand and started to face production problems. In spite of having experienced a reduction to three billion cigarettes per year, it still employed some six hundred persons in 2002. Denise Santos, a company officer, ascribed a 15 percent drop in local sales, over a six-month period during the same year, to increased excise taxes. While the short-term reduction might be attributable to taxes, Reynolds's local market share had dropped from 60 percent in 1993 to 41 percent in 2002.[99]

Over the next few years local cigarette consumption maintained an overall downward trend. Increased excise taxes affected both production and a workforce that kept shrinking until 2010, when it reached 600 million cigarettes per year with a sixty-person workforce. The factory, then, ceased operations.[100]

The firm, then known as Reynolds American, did not depart immediately because it maintained a distribution center in Guaynabo that remained in business until 2015. A local distribution company, the Puerto Rico Supply Group, assumed the representation of its remaining brands like Camel because the firm had already sold Winston, Salem, and Kool to the Imperial Tobacco Company.[101]

TECHNOLOGICAL CHANGES IN CIGAR MANUFACTURING

Stemmeries were central to the economy of several tobacco-growing municipalities where, despite a marked slow season, *tiempo muerto,* from January to April, they were the mainstays of thousands of households.[102] For instance, the Puerto Rico Tobacco Marketing Cooperative employed 516 in 1957, and Luis Rivera usually hired about 550 women and 182 men in its Comerío stemmeries.[103]

While artifacts, such as the cigar mold, decomposed the cigar-making craft and the cigar-making machine brought it to an end by the 1920s, the mechanization of leaf stemming took place much later. Up to the late 1940s, the small size of local leaf made it unsuitable for mechanical stemming.[104] In 1948, PRACO installed thirty-two stemming machines where "all the labor of the operator consists in placing the tobacco leaf in a way that the knives of the machine can carry out the function of separating the stem and, then, fold the tobacco strips."[105]

From a technical perspective, neither hand nor mechanical stemmers could remove the midrib from all tobacco leaves. Both types of stemmers could remove it from medium- to large-sized leaf, whether stalk-cut or primed, but could not from short- and narrow-leaf tobaccos, independent of their quality.[106] Cigar makers rolled stemmed strips as filler into the more expensive products than those crafted from "scrap" obtained from shredded, un-stemmed leaf and remnants from manufacture.[107]

Although stemming machine workers earned thirty-six cents per hour, to the thirty-one cents of hand stemmers, their use amounted to a reduction in labor costs, at the expense of hand workers who were, until then, the only stemmers of local tobacco.[108] Bernardo Soler, manager of the Tobacco Marketing Cooperative, held that, by 1957, hand stemming a hundredweight of leaf was worth twenty-two dollars whereas mechanical stemming of the same leaf amounted to only five.[109]

Stemming could be even more economical with a thresher that consisted of a sequence of drums and separators that tore away bits and pieces of strip from the stem, with a technology unlike that of the stemming machine. This labor-saving device, however, failed to maintain the integrity of the strips, breaking them into small pieces appropriate for cigarettes or scrap cigars.[110]

Bernardo Soler considered that the twilight of the hand stemmer was inevitable due to the competition from cigars that used short filler, formerly called scrap. Early in the century, most cigars used stemmed filler and a tobacco residue from manufacture, then called scrap, in the preparation of inferior cigars. Manufacturers additionally shredded leaf that they could not stem in the preparation of not only cigars but also cigarettes. Price-conscious consumers shifted in ever-growing numbers from the more expensive long filler to the newly baptized short filler cigars. Soler estimated that 80 to 85 percent of local tobacco corresponding to the 1958 harvest would end as short filler. By the early 1960s, short filler reached 90 percent of all US cigars consumed.[111]

PRACO's machine stemmers did not have a significant advantage over current hand stemmeries due to the leaf's small size and brief existence of the firm. Perhaps following the lead of PRACO, and in consonance with US manufacturing practices, Consolidated Cigar and other manufacturers introduced threshers and stemming machines.[112] This time, long-term employment of the devices did affect the number of women in the craft. In 1957, Labor Secretary Fernando Sierra Berdecía anticipated that the higher use of short filler would reduce the number of hand stemmers by three thousand in several municipalities.[113]

Hand stemmers were aware of their waning numbers. For instance, in 1959 a commission of 8 women, who identified themselves as mothers, representing some 400 stemmers employed by the Tobacco Growers Cooperative of Utuado, traveled to the governor's office, the Department of Labor, and *El Mundo* newspaper, where they declared that their "only means of earning a living is being eliminated and that they have given us until tomorrow afternoon to do what we can, and not let Utuado die of hunger." They objected to the closing of the cooperative's stemmery, the leaf sale, and its transportation to Cayey, where Consolidated Cigar would thresh it. A few days before the trip to *El Mundo*, a militant group of stemmers and their supporters picketed to prevent the loading of the leaf into the trucks. Consequently, only six trucks succeeded in removing tobacco. Subsequently, the cooperative hired a lawyer to arrange with the police and the legal system the removal of the remaining leaf.[114] In 1950, factories employed 3,106 women, mostly hand stemmers, who were not involved in cigar manufactures. Ten years later, these had collapsed to 934, for a nearly 70 percent reduction.[115]

Cigar manufacturing entered the twentieth century with two major gendered crafts: men rolling cigars and women stemming tobacco, both by hand. The cigar mold, introduced early in the century, started the feminization of cigar making first, and the cigar-making machine after World War I did away, within a decade, with the jobs of thousands doing hand work by creating a few hundred operators who were mostly women. The aftermath of World War II witnessed the diffusion of the stemming machine first and, soon after, the addition of the leaf thresher that made hand stemming an anachronism. A few hundred women working as threshers and mechanical stemmers replaced thousands of hand jobs just in a decade. The trade union militancy, the socialism and anarchism of the craftspeople, women and men, disappeared with the end of their crafts.

DOWNSIZING TOBACCO MANUFACTURES

Cigar exports to the United States, negligible after PRATCO's collapse, soared from 1 million units in 1950 to 137 million units in 1958 when Consolidated's Caguas factory became fully operational. Shipments reached 483 million in 1963 after the Cayey factory started production and a remarkable 1,036 million in 1968 after General Cigar's Utuado factory began operations.[116] During the second half of the century, exports alone reached the absolute maximum of 1,304 million cigars in 1973, a level unheard off.[117] By contrast, cigar manufactures were markedly lower during the first half of the century. For instance, cigars, including both exports and local consumption, reached highs in 1920 and 1926, with 321 and 323 million units respectively.[118]

As discussed earlier, cigars reached extraordinary export levels, by decomposing the cigar-making craft first, outright mechanization of cigar making, and leaf stemming later. Despite record output, the latter-day tobacco manufacturing sector did not employ more workers than it had during the opening decades of the century. As of 1972, total employment in tobacco manufacture reached 4,508, which represented a paltry 3.1 percent of those employed in manufacture and less than 1 percent of gainfully employed.[119] However, employment in tobacco manufactures was 23.8 percent higher in 1919 than in 1973, when it included 5,583 women and men, which represented a formidable 30.3 percent of all jobs in manufacture and 1.4 percent of all duly employed in 1920.[120]

The second half of the 1970s, like the 1910s, were times of retrenchment. By the time that cigar exports reached their zenith in 1973, some smaller factories and those dedicated to stemming and processing Connecticut River Valley leaf had already closed. DWG became the earliest Fomento-sponsored firm to close, perhaps anticipating the trend that followed. Early in his career, Victor Posner, who became "master of the hostile takeover," took control of an ailing DWG that, in 1965, was "deeply in the red."[121] When Posner became chair, he sold most of the firm's tobacco business to the R. R. Dun Corporation late in 1967, which consequently moved the operations of the Caguas and Gurabo factories to Lima, Ohio.[122]

After nearly two decades, Hartman Tobacco's Juncos factory closed in 1971 or soon afterward.[123] According to a company vice president, it abandoned tobacco growing in the Connecticut Valley after the 1978 season for "lack of demand."[124]

Very much like PRATCO, which remained the sole big manufacturer in earlier times, Consolidated Cigar endured as the only large cigar operation. However, the decline of cigar exports affected the major manufacturers as in 1977 Bayuk closed its Ciales factory and Consolidated Cigar shuttered its Caguas factory, effectively consolidating manufacture in Cayey.[125] In line with other manufacturers, General Cigar held that its cigar sales had declined and blamed other problems that continued "to dampen the cigar business."[126] In 1979, it dismissed 330 workers from its Utuado cigar factory and 135 from its Caguas stemmery when, without prior notice, it ceased all local operations.[127] The effect was devastating in Utuado because it had a weaker industrial base than Caguas.[128]

In 1966, Waitt & Bond, by then called the Blackstone Cigar Company, ceased all manufacture in the United States and elsewhere.[129] However, its Rapaport subsidiaries outlived the parent company but, nevertheless, remained a troubled manufacturer until 1976, if not earlier, when an adverse legal decision allowed its major creditor, the Cidanjo Company, to auction the Yabucoa machinery.[130] However, the Fomento industrial directory kept identifying a much-reduced operation, limited to fifteen employees, in Yabucoa until its final shutdown around 1979.[131]

The remaining manufacturers were mostly buckeyes and roll-chewing workshops oriented to the local market. One of the few surviving factories was the Puerto Rico Tobacco Corporation, a PRATCO successor, represented by Nathaniel Pasarell, which maintained operations into the early 1970s on Dr. Veve Street, in Bayamón.[132] A few years later, it shared the same premises with La Restina Tobacco Corporation, where the latter employed between fifty and a hundred hands.[133]

Established in 1971, the Bayamón Tobacco Corporation predated the enormous downsizing of manufactures and plant closings just reviewed. As for continuity, it held the old La Restina brand that it most likely obtained from a corporation named after the brand during the 1970s. With a labor force of fourteen, the Bayamón factory mechanically stemmed and elaborated both hand-rolled and machine-made cigars during the 1990s.[134] It advertised the handmade "La Flor de Cuba" as "Puerto Rico's prestige brand" in an attempt to fill the void left by Consolidated Cigars' Cayey factory with its short filler and reconstituted wrapper products. In fact, the upscale Smoke Shop at Plaza Las Américas shopping center carried only this local cigar.[135] By 2015, it remained the property of José Fernández Crespo, who also owned JFC Tobacco of Mayagüez, but its workforce had diminished to between eight and ten hands.[136]

Finally, in 2016 Consolidated Cigar shuttered its Comerío processing plant, leaving only 420 factory hands working with robotics in Cayey, dwindling to around 300 in 2021.[137] In summary, plant closings responded principally to a retrenchment of the US cigar market.

TRADE UNIONS

The cigar makers' influence extended well beyond their craft unions; it was central to the FLT and the Socialist Party. However, the mechanization of cigar manufacturing, followed by the precipitous drop in cigar exports, brought their unions to an end, leaving mainly those in the stemmeries. While some cigar makers like Emiliano Ramos joined the ranks of the capitalist class, others gained advantage from their finely honed skills in labor organizations and politics. Their presence was so strong that, even after the demise of the cigar-making craft, a US-based labor organizer, with a twist of hyperbole, stated that "most of the leaders in the Free Federation of Labor were former cigar makers."[138]

A case in point is Prudencio Rivera Martínez, who worked in 1904 as a cigar maker in La Turina factory in Caguas while he was a member of the anarchist Centro de Estudios Sociales and a founding member of the *Voz Humana* periodical.[139] His rise was meteoric after he joined the US-based CMIU in 1907 where, by 1913, the union started paying him about $150 a month to work as a full-time labor organizer for several years to come.[140] By 1910, if not earlier, he was a vice president of the FLT.[141] As time went by, he began to distance himself from the craft while retaining positions of leadership in the trade unions.[142]

In 1924, Rivera Martínez was elected to the Worker's Relief Commission.[143] Named commissioner in 1931 of the newly created Department of Labor, he spent the remaining years of the decade at its helm.[144] Upon a major division of the Socialist Party, he became in 1939 the president of the Partido Laborista Puro.[145] Despite the transition to politics and high-level government appointments, the former cigar maker maintained a powerful presence within the FLT for, in 1941, he presided over the organization.[146]

Labor historians generally agree that once the Socialists gained control of the colonial legislature in a coalition with the conservative Union Republicans, during the 1930s, the FLT opted for a nonconfrontational approach to capital that revolved around the concept of "industrial peace" in their negotiation of collective agreements.[147] Rivera Martínez provided a clear statement of the policy in his speech at a meeting of the Association of Sugar Producers and the FLT.[148] He celebrated the encounter to "promote and stimulate the best relations between workers and employers, mediating and conciliating, with a high spirit leaning to preserve industrial peace and the general development and progress in industrial disputes."[149]

Accordingly, the representatives of the FLT and their counterparts from the Association of Sugar Producers, speaking for most sugar mill owners, signed the collective agreement the day before the popular commemoration of the Magi's gifts to the newly born Jesus—Epiphany, the *Día de Reyes*—of 1934. Several signatories might have construed the agreement as an *aguinaldo*, a gift typical of the Epiphany. However, many workers burned sugarcane fields and rose in spontaneous strikes across the land to challenge not only the agreement but, significantly, to disavow their own union representation. Despite the support of the Nationalist Party, the strike petered out by 20 January.[150]

The changing composition of the working class, accompanied with the near disappearance of cigar makers, significant transformations in the sugar industry, and the pursuit of industrial peace, despite some successes, led to other conflicts between workers and the FLT. Thus, some trade unions tested the limits of affiliation to the federation, if sometimes only briefly. One such test started early in May 1937, when some eight hundred cigar machine operatives staged what they called a "seated strike" by ceasing to work while remaining seated at their work benches. A few days later, on 8 May, PRATCO and its operatives, represented by Francisco Colón Gordiany, signed a one-year collective agreement, thus bringing a strike to an end.[151] Nicolás Nogueras Rivera denounced it, claiming its signers behaved "on the margins and behind the back of the Federación Libre."[152] Despite Nogueras Rivera's strong disapproval, both labor leaders cooperated, counseled, and represented about six hundred strikers in the same factory soon after management fired a machine operative in late May.[153] As workers assembled, they listened to Nogueras Rivera, Colón Gordiany, and others who suspended their rivalries for the duration of the second strike. The assembly, held in the Eureka theater of Puerta de Tierra, asked the stemmers in other branches of PRATCO to join the strike and benefitted from the solidarity of the powerful maritime union, which expressed a willingness to consider the possibility of refusing to load the company's exports into the holds of the ships docked in San Juan.[154] However, the independent union lasted less than a month because once the second strike ended in late May, upon the rehiring of Eleuteria Martínez, it became an FLT affiliate.[155]

Despite the failure of the industrial peace policy in the 1934 strike, the policy, forcefully employed, led to a collective agreement in the tobacco industry that avoided large industry-wide strikes. A series of meetings between the FLT and the chamber of commerce, speaking for the workshop owners, accorded in July 1937 an agreement that covered the working conditions of more than ten thousand stemmers and allied workers.[156] The labor federation and the chamber of commerce submitted the agreement to the trade unions and the stemmeries' owners. The FLT celebrated the agreement as an "industrial treaty" by "all peace and justice loving people."[157]

When many shop owners resisted the agreement, a concerned Prudencio Rivera Martínez visited acting governor Rafael Menéndez to inform him of the owners' opposition in Caguas and the danger it signified to the agreement and the policy of cooperation between labor and capital.[158] On the other hand, about 130 stemmers represented by the Unión Protectora del Trabajo struck Rufo Colón's installations in Coamo in defense of the collective agreement that they had already ratified. Colón signed the agreement three days later.[159] An estimated 700 to 900 workers struck three stemmeries because their owners rejected the agreement, claiming that their Caguas counterparts had acquiesced because their employees were more efficient than those based in Aibonito. The eight-day strike came to end when the owners endorsed the agreement and lightened the weight of the bundles, *pesadas*, of unstemmed leaf.[160] In contrast with the 1934 labor conflict, the stemmeries were strike free for the remainder of 1937 and 1938.[161]

Employers and stemmers renewed the collective agreement at least for the following two years, although, in the second semester of 1938, all shop owners refused to pay the wages required by the Wage and Hours Act. Rivera Martínez, commissioner of labor, also admitted that most employers were not complying with the collective agreements they had already endorsed. In spite of the non-compliance, the commissioner maintained an environment of industrial peace in the stemmeries through 1939.[162]

The stevedores' strike of 1938 shook the FLT's hegemony over the trade unions for a second time during the decade.[163] It contributed to the growing gulf between workers and their federation that, with a changing social fabric, created a fertile ground for a new labor organization, the Confederación General de Trabajadores (CGT), that came into being in 1940.[164] Following that lead, local number 4 of the Unión de Trabajadores de la Industria del Tabaco held an early May assembly in Bayamón, where it claimed to be the most "powerful" union in the trade with a membership of eight hundred workers. Claudio Sánchez prided himself for presiding over the largest union in the industry and over its affiliation to the CGT.[165] In a strike since 2 May, seven hundred women and one hundred men who stemmed, wetted leaf, and loaded it demanded and obtained a closed shop, union recognition, and a minimum of twenty-five cents an hour from the successors of San Miguel Hermanos.[166] This Bayamón union seems to have had a more lasting presence than most: it donated $2.09 to *La Voz*, a CGT publication in 1944, two years after the strike.[167] The fact that Juan Sáez Corales, the CGT's secretary, made the agreement public attests to the importance of the strike to the labor federation.[168] During the early 1940s, some stemmers' unions became GGT affiliates in Caguas, Las Piedras, Manatí, San Lorenzo, and, of course, Bayamón.[169]

Sánchez's boast and Sáez Corales's public announcement were likely messages to the rival FLT. During April and May 1942, the FLT was actively negotiating an industry-wide collective agreement with the Asociación de Tabacaleros Unidos, speaking for thirty-two stemmeries. Discussions were underway to use the January agreement with the General Cigar Company, in Caguas and San Lorenzo, as a model for the industry. However, in recognition that unionization rates were precariously low, Rivera Martínez spoke of the need to continue the organization drive.[170]

Unionization rates among stemmers began a slow decline after the 1930s. By 1950, from a total of ninety-three stemmeries, only a single stemmers' union, affiliated with the FLT, had collective agreements with Serafín Inclán and Belarmino "Billy" Suárez, both of whom operated stemmeries in Caguas.[171] If any, the union activities of tobacco stemmers of the 1950s were but marginal. The handwork stemmer, as discussed above in this chapter, suffered the same fate as the cigar makers two decades earlier. Their downfall also brought to an end more than fifty years of an intense and vivid trade union culture in tobacco manufacture.

The stemmers' union activity during the 1960s bore little, if any, continuity with earlier organizations; it was more of an afterthought. As of 1966, only a single unidentified plant, out of seventeen that Fomento promoted in the tobacco sector, had a trade union.[172] A second instance of union activity started to coalesce some years after General Cigar inaugurated its Utuado factory. Management documented and denounced to Fomento what they considered high rates of absenteeism and labor turnover. Fomento responded in 1971 by offering on-site workshops on human relations to rectify the labor problems.[173] The efforts failed to redress the situation, thus creating a fertile ground for the development of an organization to articulate the workers' grievances.

Efforts to organize a union led to clashes with management, such as the police intervention in the 1967 verbal dispute between labor representatives and Isidoro Caldas, who then served as plant manager. The International Association of Machinists and Aerospace Workers and not the CMIU or the FLT, as in earlier times, lent its resources and experience to the effort.[174] Despite the personnel office's disclosure of a doctored survey showing that management would defeat union efforts by a wide margin, the May 1968 election proved otherwise. The election, supervised by the National Labor Relations Board, showed a clear victory for the machinists over the administration.[175]

In August General Cigar petitioned the National Labor Relations Board to annul the election because, among other factors, a female employee had workers smell or come into contact with a potion prepared by a Ponce woman that annulled the will of the workers, forcing them to vote for the machinists. The company's legal representation also claimed that the wife of a union leader paid $150 to a medium who would employ her communications with spirits of the dead to benefit the machinists. Another of the long list of claims had the union paying a male dwarf from Arecibo an unspecified amount for a spell, a *brujo*, on their behalf. The plaintiff claimed that many workers had declared that such external factors directly led them to vote for the machinists.[176]

The company's administration threatened Fomento with closing the factory unless it became union free, a threat that spread throughout Utuado. As late as September 1969, the union and management had not even begun the negotiations for a collective agreement because the Labor Relations Board was still investigating the matter. However, a new initiative effectively turned the tide on the conflict, when, early in 1970, some 375 employees asked the Labor Relations Board for a new election, this time, however, for a union-free factory. In April 1970, the workers massively voted against the machinists, giving management a 380 to 25 victory.[177]

Soon after, in 1972, an officer of the Consolidated Cigar factory in Cayey dismissed Julio Santiago Soto in a dispute over sick leave. The workers staged a two-day stoppage in solidarity with the fired worker. Simultaneously, the Unión de Trabajadores de la Industria Gastronómica, represented by Vitelio Santiago and others, launched an organization drive to secure enough petitions for a labor union to have the Labor Relations Board hold an election over the matter. The Gastronómicas' drive at the entrance of the factory seems to have been unsuccessful.[178]

Sometime before 1977 an unidentified trade union failed twice to represent the workers, this time at the R. J. Reynolds cigarette factory in Yabucoa. Later, in February 1977, a group of workers began discussions with representatives of the Unión General de Trabajadores about the need for a collective agreement. Under the guidance of two labor organizers, Johnny Eliza and Julio Cuadaro [*sic*], the Reynolds factory workers formed a ten-member organizing committee and collected union authorization cards from a majority of the employees. In March the Unión General wrote to the factory's management to demand recognition as the workers' labor representative and simultaneously filed a petition for certification in an election, under the supervision of the Labor Relations Board.[179]

According to a decision by the National Labor Relations Board, management created a hostile environment and practiced "unfair labor practices," infringing on the law in the weeks before the election. These practices included coercive interrogations concerning the union certification, threats to dismiss those who supported the union, and, finally, threats to close the factory if the union gained representation. Aside from the time and effort committed, the union lost the elections held in May.[180]

Despite the same name, the Unión General was not the one in which, as indicated above, Juan Sáez Corales played a decisive role.[181] The labor unrest in General Cigar's Utuado factory, Consolidated Cigar's Cayey branch, and in the

R. J. Reynolds installation in Yabucoa had no identifiable relation with any of the cigar makers' or stemmers' unions of the past. Consequently, these labor union attempts of the 1970s signified a break from earlier labor organizations. Moreover, the failures to organize trade unions pale beside the successes that cigar makers and stemmers had during the early decades of the century, as discussed in chapter 8. Not without certain irony, the weakness of labor organizations in tobacco manufactures proved to be a significant incentive in Fomento's drive for industrial development.[182]

THE ECLIPSE OF TOBACCO AGRICULTURE

Besides the disappearance of the tobacco hacendado and plantation and a reduction of sharecropping, relations of production in the farm remained similar to those of the first half of the century. An ethnographic study of a farming community in the highlands of Arecibo restated that, as in earlier times, small tobacco farms, typically being less than twelve acres, also grew minor crops, often in rotation with the leaf. In consistency with the past, farmers relied heavily on unpaid family labor. However, in contrast with other regions, these growers made little use of the leaf dealer during the 1960s, choosing to finance the crop with a growers' cooperative in Utuado.[183] Elsewhere, growers with small patches relied heavily on unpaid labor whereas those with more extensive sowing fields contracted more sharecroppers, which the Arecibo study did not identify.[184]

A 1976 survey of tobacco growers found that owners operated 70 percent of the farms, lessees another 26 percent, and the remainder in unidentified arrangements. While the study does not mention sharecroppers, it showed a strong reliance on unpaid family labor and, to a lesser degree, on salaried farmhands. A large minority of growers, 28 percent, considered the difficulties in securing wage workers to be their most serious problem. By the late 1970s tobacco farms seem to have already dispensed of sharecroppers and were shedding wage workers, thus unraveling into a family operation based on unpaid labor as in the early nineteenth century.[185]

Tobacco growers gave liens of their crops to dealers and the cooperatives that sought to displace the former starting in the 1920s. Unlike the 1930s, the relations between both groups were civil but not harmonious. For instance, Billy Suárez, while still president of Tabacaleros Unidos, decried the cooperatives for offering fewer services and inferior benefits.[186]

During the 1950s, Antonio Hernández Mejías had liens on the tobacco crops of between 1,000 and 1,200 growers in San Lorenzo and its thereabouts. He typically advanced $300 to $400 per grower and occasionally as much as $6,000.[187] This arrangement repeated itself with Belarmino Súarez in Caguas, Serafín Inclán in

Aguas Buenas, Fernando Álvarez in Cataño, Luis Rivera in Comerío, and others that dotted the tobacco landscape.[188] The leaf dealers' association, "Tabacaleros Unidos," had existed, at the very least, since 1942, when it had thirty-two members.[189] By 1958, it had shrunk to nineteen.[190] As of 1965, the thirteen leaf dealers left financed about two-thirds of the crop planted and harvested by some 7,000 growers.[191]

While, on average, the cooperatives paid higher prices than leaf dealers during the two decades that followed World War II, they financed and marketed about a third of the crop. Three of them, ABC Tabacalera de Aibonito, Cosecheros de Utuado, and the Puerto Rico Tobacco Marketing Cooperative Association, which was the largest, served these growers.[192] However, by 1976, they finally overcame the leaf dealers when a "large majority" of growers financed their tobacco with the last mentioned organization. A minority sold to the Utuado cooperative and individual leaf dealers.[193]

Whereas roll-chewing tobacco had been the most common form of local consumption, it lost its dominance during the early decades of the century. By the early 1960s, leaf committed for roll-chewing accounted for about 2 percent of the crop.[194]

As early as 1959, some tobacco specialists considered that the "Cuban crisis" provoked instability in the leaf markets, leading manufacturers to increase leaf purchases. General Cigar's actions are a case in point. Julian Strauss, the company president, informed the shareholders that the enterprise closed its Cuban stemmeries and shipped its large stocks of leaf to the United States in 1959, thus accumulating an above-average supply.[195] The revolution in 1959, followed by the 1962 US trade embargo, created high expectations for an upturn of tobacco agriculture both locally and in other countries. According to the US Department of Agriculture, the stocks of Cuban leaf in the United States should have lasted until sometime in 1964, giving manufacturers time to search for substitutes.[196]

Government officials, like Miguel Meléndez Ortiz and José A. Hernández, traveled to Tampa to explore the possibilities of having local leaf as a substitute for the Cuban one. The officials invited a group of Tampa manufacturers to visit the island.[197] Despite the high hope, tobacco production statistics did not support the contention for 1959 or 1962. Figure 10.1 shows that local production had an upturn that lasted from 1956 to 1964 before experiencing an abrupt drop in 1965 from which it never recovered. The upturn started three years before the revolution and six years before the embargo. On the other hand, tobacco prices reached a relative maximum of 40.8 cents per pound in 1962 followed by a steep decline, with a low of 33.1 cents in 1966, four years after the embargo went into effect.[198]

This time around, local tobacco was not part of the leaf-substitution process of Cuban leaf as it had during the nineteenth-century wars for independence. Leaf growers from other countries effectively replaced Cuban leaf.[199] Before the Cuban Revolution, Consolidated Cigar's production in its Caguas factory employed 35

Figure 10.1. Puerto Rican tobacco leaf production, 1956–1987

Source: Grise and Griffin, *U.S. Tobacco Industry*, 53.

percent Havana tobacco and the balance from local production.[200] By 1962, the company was seeking replacements for Cuban leaf in Central America and started to participate in the Cameroon auctions held in Paris around 1963.[201]

Meléndez Ortiz offered an explanation for the decrease of tobacco growing. As early as 1959, he held that other agricultural pursuits and particularly the "expansion of manufacturing enterprises," most notably Fomento-sponsored factories, accounted for much of the reduction in Cayey, Caguas, Utuado, Gurabo, Juncos, and Jayuya. Consequently, he maintained that municipalities, such as Aguas Buenas, Cidra, Ciales, Naranjito, Morovis, and Orocovis, lacking these influences, posted increases in production.[202] The reduction in tobacco production presented in figure 10.1 took place when, save for 1964–1966, leaf prices were generally on the rise until 1983.[203]

While the application of science by private companies like PRATCO was frequent during the early decades of the century, the latter half saw a paucity in such investments. In 1971 and 1972, Amchem Products and the Union Carbide Corporation carried out several experiments to inhibit the growth of suckers or runners by spraying a chemical solution over several fields, each planted with a different tobacco cultivar or variety. Eyeing the likely sales to local growers, the companies performed two trials in a Comerío commercial patch planted with a widely used cultivar developed by the Agricultural Experiment Station. The chemical solution successfully inhibited the growth of suckers.[204]

Despite private initiatives, the colonial state, however, carried the burden of the research and development of cultivars with higher yields, disease resistance, and adaptations to the particular soils of the tobacco regions. The Agricultural Experiment Station developed several cultivars for cigar and roll-chewing leaf.[205] To distribute them widely, the Agricultural Extension Service first prepared seedbeds in several municipalities to help growers recuperate from hurricane Santa Clara in 1956.[206] During the following year, the Department of Agriculture and Commerce planted twenty-five cuerdas in seedbeds distributed along eighteen centers to sell seedlings at a low cost.[207] The program was in existence years later, when it still operated eighteen seedbeds across the tobacco regions, which included Isabela in the roll-chewing tobacco area.[208] Despite the media coverage that *El Mundo* provided, a strong 1962 editorial denounced the insufficiency of the incentives to turn around the fate of tobacco production. Among other incentives, it derided the $50,000 allotted for seedbeds as "measly crumbs."[209] Despite the critique, the long-lasting seedling program was still subsidizing their price in 1976 with its best-selling cultivars, PR 4-65 and PR 5-65.[210]

While better cultivars accounted for a partial increase in yields per cuerda, fertilizers also played a role. From 1960 to 1965, the use of fertilizers became more intensive, especially on the larger farms. On average, growers applied 15.4 hundredweights per cuerda in 1965 and 20.1 hundredweights in 1976.[211] However, in spite of the generally higher yields per cuerda and increasing leaf prices, growers kept deserting tobacco agriculture, as shown in figure 10.1.

After 1983, prices began to decline; after 1980, yields started to recede; production shrunk to an extent that the annual reports ceased to publish estimates in 1989; and finally, tobacco stocks in the warehouses of dealers and manufacturers disappeared after 1997.[212] The Puerto Rico Tobacco Marketing Cooperative Association, upon losing its raison d'être, became the Cooperativa Agro Comercial that, among other products and services, purchases, roasts, packs, and markets Café Cibales. "This is the way" that tobacco agriculture "ends not with a bang but a whimper."[213]

After the collapse of tobacco growing, new harvests from patches, at times in combination with manufacture, have become newsworthy. For instance, the Cooperativa Agro Comercial financed and provided seeds, fertilizer, and other incentives during two growing seasons that, in 1998, included fifteen members in Comerío who harvested 598 hundredweights for export.[214] Around 2001, Enrique and Magaly Velázquez planted their own leaf on five cuerdas that they subsequently manufactured into cigars.[215] José Gabriel Cruz Ayala with his wife, Liz Janice López; daughters; and parents grew tobacco in Caguas for their La Hoja del Chan cigar. Hurricane María in 2017 destroyed the patch, but their cigar buckeye weathered the catastrophe.[216] Around 2008, Francisco Castro Barreto started a vegetable farm that ten years later included a patch whose leaf they employ in their own handmade cigars. With his brother Antonio, he organically cultivates seven cuerdas in Río Grande.[217]

CONCLUSION

The "transculturation of tobacco," as Fernando Ortiz called it, unleashed a centuries-long stream of adaptations from Native American cultures to European patterns that initially ranged from medicinal purposes to cut tobacco leaf for pipe smoking and rolls for chewing.[1] Pipe tobacco gained something of a reputation in Europe. Once it made the transatlantic voyage, merchants sold it in crackled earthenware pots of Dutch origin labeled "Porto Rico." For instance, Albert de Morcerf kept one of these, in addition to another from Latakia, in a Parisian smoking salon in Alexandre Dumas's *The Count of Monte Cristo*.

The transculturation has followed adaptations so profound that people who, for instance, smoked pipes centuries ago would feel estranged from the filter-tipped Winston cigarette made from blended tobaccos that R. J. Reynolds once manufactured in Yabucoa. They would not recognize themselves in cigars made from reconstituted wrapper and exhibiting a plastic tip on the Tiparillos that the General Cigar Company used to manufacture in Utuado and sold in nondescript stores. This book has covered the major changes to Puerto Rican tobacco agriculture and manufacture through the *longue durée* from early Spanish colonization to the present.

Overseas commerce evolved from trading small amounts of tobacco, most likely in taverns, for personal use by returnees to Europe. Once the leaf whetted the consumer's appetite, the Dutch and others developed an intense contraband because the Spanish tobacco monopoly had little use for the local product. In a belated effort to contain smuggling, the Spanish crown established a short-lived monopoly (1784–1795) on local export goods to grant a legal character to commerce with the Dutch. Tobacco, which many Europeans chewed but enjoyed mostly in their pipes, became the mainstay of the economy until the 1780s, when it lost its primacy to coffee. The leaf finally entered the concourse of free trade after the Napoleonic wars, with the Spanish monopoly still declining a leaf that the Dutch and the Hanseatic ports eagerly imported.

During the second half of the nineteenth century, export-oriented tobacco farming diffused to the eastern Cordillera, away from the main historical zones along the northern coast and the southwest. Growers from the highlands slowly incorporated Cuban techniques to plant and harvest a leaf appropriate for cigars with that of a lesser quality destined for cigarettes. The new specialty opened new markets where the Cubans took in the best leaf for the manufacture of their cigars and the Spanish monopoly imported the lesser grades for their cigarettes. The orientation to the Cuban paradigm paved the way to the establishment of small shops, *chinchales*, first and later to full-fledged factories employing more than a hundred cigar makers. These factories manufactured cigars for the local market and effectively substituted Cuban imports. The bourgeois impulse continued expanding to the very end of Spanish colonial rule, when three partnerships established modern steam-driven cigarette factories that also substituted the Cuban import.

The invasion in 1898 signified the complete loss of the Cuban and Spanish leaf markets that brought much pain in hardship to tobacco growers, whose deprivation deepened with the 1899 hurricane, San Ciriaco. In conjunction with other cultural factors, this calamitous environment freed segments of the peasantry from their economic obligations and shook social ones, thus laying a solid base for the rise, expansion, and diffusion of latent religious beliefs. These took the form of the messianic Hermanos Cheos with their fiery sermons chastising the abandonment of Marian devotion, living together without the sacrament of matrimony, and other debaucheries in the then most important tobacco area along the northern littoral. In the next few years the Cheos moved their prophecies of hell and brimstone to areas with a substantial tobacco peasantry to the highlands around Caguas, San Lorenzo, and Jayuya and away from the reach of the tobacco hacienda, in Cayey, Comerío, and Utuado.

A few years after the invasion, the collapse of leaf markets gave in to a reorientation and a formidable expansion of leaf and cigar exports to the United States. Local manufacturers sought a niche within the US market by highlighting the provenance of their cigars in newspaper ads and on the box labels themselves. They brought to the fore a new type of cigar, the Porto Rico, that briefly challenged the Havana and Manila archetypes in the United States.

A growing tobacco industry led to the incorporation of thousands of women into farms in the highlands and factories in the urban areas. However, the very high participation rate of women did not lead the way to equal opportunities, despite their militancy and activism in the trade union movement. Women and men did not work side by side because both farms and factories generally followed a strict occupational segregation by gender that included wage disparities.

Soon after the invasion, the tobacco trust established PRATCO, which speedily absorbed a large cigar manufactory and the two largest cigarette factories. Its concentration of manufacture continued unabated by its own growth, the acquisition of other firms, and the disappearance of competitors. The trust's PRLTC tried forefront agricultural innovations with cigar wrappers in thousands of cuerdas, mostly in La Plata Valley. The changes to tobacco farming during the first decades of the century led to an impressive concentration of land in corporate plantations but also in haciendas at the expense of the smallholding and coffee farming.

In 1911, the ATC and PRATCO became independent corporations as a result of the dissolution of the trust by the US Supreme Court. The late 1920s witnessed an acrimonious price-slashing war between two former trust firms, PRATCO and the ATC, over control of locally sold cigarettes. Despite gaining a substantial settlement, the ATC and others displaced the former from the lucrative and expanding cigarette market. They offered an addictive product made from bright leaf and burley, which is comparable to the current electronic cigarette, instead of the locally grown dark tobacco that PRATCO manufactured.[2]

During World War I, local cigar exports ceased expanding to initiate a contraction as smokers began shifting their preference for the cigarette. PRATCO established a foothold in the United States to diversify into other types of cigars and arrest not only declining profits but also labor militancy at home. Individual cigar makers like Bernardo Vega left for New York seeking employment as cigar makers while others established small factories, buckeyes, in the same city. While all other large cigar manufacturers had already gone under, PRATCO's faltering profitability led to bankruptcy in 1939, signifying the collapse of the cigar export market that had provided a livelihood for thousands.

The inauguration of the Consolidated Cigar Company's Caguas factory ended a fourteen-year hiatus without a major manufacturer. Eight large US firms like Consolidated Cigar and General Cigar gave tobacco manufacture a second breath. Their local operations took PRATCO's mechanization of cigar and cigarette manufacture to other dimensions. Their Caguas, Cayey, and Utuado factories used highly processed leaf as cigar wrapper and binder while employing shredders to prepare short filler in their local operations. These cigars fell outside the market for premium cigars that are still handmade and that mostly employ shaded leaf for wrappers, natural leaf for binder, and long filler. Cuba, the Dominican Republic, and others dominate the manufacture of high-grade cigars.

Labor-saving devices such as the cigar mold, mechanical rollers, and machines to stem and thresh leaves, decades in the making, had far-reaching consequences in manufacturing and the organization of production. They led to the substitution of male cigar makers for female team workers who manufacturers then replaced with machine operatives. Decades later, by the mid-twentieth century, the female hand stemmer, who worked at the other major manufacturing occupation, faced the same fate. Part of the history of tobacco manufacture has been the loss of the control that workers had over their own labor process; they stopped being artisans to instead tend machines that automatically roll cigars or thresh tobacco leaves.

The mechanization of manufacture had broad consequences beyond the reorganization of the labor process. It did away with craftspeople who had been for decades a breeding ground for strong trade unions and socialist and anarchist militancy. As the craftspeople gave way to machine operatives, the trade unions withered. Whereas the early decades of the twentieth century mustered powerful labor revindications in the manufacturing sector, the latter decades briefly marshaled a sole trade union and no strikes. Before the advent of mechanization, cigar makers in particular boasted pride and a strong identification with the craft, which echoes José Santana, who held that "once a cigar maker, always a cigar maker. That means that you may get away from the trade for a couple of years, but you always have in your mind the cigar makers."[3] Later tobacco workers, consequently, lacked such a powerful identification.

During the 1960s, the Puerto Rico of Consolidated, General Cigar, and others was not comparable to that of PRATCO and the large independent firms from earlier times. The newly established firms did not employ more workers than the old ones. Despite some of them planting tobacco in the Connecticut River Valley, no large firms ventured into local agriculture. Most of these firms shuttered operations around the 1970s, save for the R. J. Reynolds company, which closed in 2010. Since then, the remaining manufacturers have been Consolidated Cigar in Cayey, the small Bayamón Tobacco Corporation, and a handful of cigar and roll-chewing workshops. Tobacco manufacture lost the centrality that it once enjoyed.

The continuing declines in US cigar consumption that followed World War II led to the unraveling of tobacco agriculture that began shedding sharecroppers, wage workers, and proprietors who migrated or sought jobs in the growing industrial occupations. By 2021, only a few scattered patches remained under cultivation, with a labor force consisting of the owners and their families and few, if any, paid workers. Despite their size, a few have integrated vertically into manufacture.

During the 1950s and 1960s, thousands left for the United States in search of higher incomes and better living conditions, not only in the large urban centers, but in what they did best, farming. Countless became seasonal workers who worked the shaded leaf fields of the Connecticut River Valley well into the 1970s.[4] A few still remain.

The Hermanos Cheos had no second breath. With their base in tobacco agriculture gone, the Cheos remain as the Congregación de San Juan Evangelista, a small association within the Catholic Church, with a house for retreats in Peñuelas.[5] The Madre Elenita maintains a devout following where her former chapel at la Santa Montaña remains an active house of worship.[6] The strong apocalyptic stance of their early preaching is gone, but they have gotten credit for maintaining a good number of Catholics in the rural areas who might have otherwise converted to other beliefs.[7]

Tobacco farming and manufacture have morphed beyond recognition from the start of their transculturation, centuries ago, to the present. Both have reinvented themselves several times over. Current goods are a combination of cigars made by robots from highly processed imported leaf manufactured for a smoker beyond the sea, on the one hand, and handmade ones from natural leaf for domestic consumption, on the other, in a throwback to the nineteenth century. A few small roll-chewing shops, buckeyes, and tobacco patches appear here and there in contrast to the technologically advanced Consolidated Cigar factory in Cayey. It is an environment of opposites between the state-of-the-art mass production and the artisanal model that is closer to the premium cigar that behemoths turn out elsewhere.

However, the current industry is not a shadow of its former self. Gone are the thousands employed in farming and manufacture; gone are the rich working-class culture, trade unions, and other organizations that revolved around tobacco manufacture; gone is the apocalyptical sermon of the Hermanos Cheos. No return to the centrality of times past seems to be looming on the horizon.

NOTES

PREFACE

1. Rivero Muñiz, *Tabaco*; Checo and Sang, *El Tabaco*.

2. Náter, *Redes del Imperio*, 175.

CHAPTER ONE. THE FOUNDATIONS

1. Norton, *Sacred Gifts*, 149, 157; Rodríguez Gordillo, "El tabaco," 188–89.

2. Rodríguez Gordillo, *La creación del estanco del tabaco*, 27, 34; Norton, *Sacred Gifts*, 150.

3. Fuente, García del Pino, and Iglesias Delgado, *Havana and the Atlantic*, 20; Morgan, "Virginia's Other Prototype," 362.

4. Gaskell, "Tobacco, Social Deviance and Dutch Art," 76; Schama, *Embarrassment of Riches*, 193–94.

5. The Kingdom of Castile and León to be precise. Refer to Rodríguez Gordillo, *La creación del estanco del tabaco*, 38–39.

6. Rodríguez Gordillo, *La creación del estanco del tabaco*, 24, 29–30.

7. Melgarejo, "Memoria y descripción de la isla de Puerto Rico," 116.

8. Gil-Bermejo García, *Panorama histórico*, 158. According to Enriqueta Vilá Vilar, the tobacco tax dates from 1621. See Vilá Vilar, *Historia de Puerto Rico*, 21.

9. Torres Vargas, "Descripción de la isla y ciudad," 178.

10. Gil-Bermejo García, *Panorama histórico*, 158–60. For the conflict between tobacco growers and other farmers with cattle ranchers, refer to Moscoso, *Agricultura y sociedad*, 99–100.

11. For the coexistence of large and small farms in Cuban tobacco, refer to Cosner, *Golden Leaf*, 29–67 and López Mesa, *Tabaco, mito y esclavos*. However, the growers in the Lesser Antilles seem to have followed small-scale agriculture more closely. Refer to Morris, "Cultivating Colonies," 172.

12. Gil-Bermejo García, *Panorama histórico*, 159.

13. Stark, *Slave Families and the Hato Economy*, 70, 127.

14. Moscoso, *Agricultura y sociedad*, 205; Nissen, *Reminiscences of a 46 Years' Residence*, 8.

15. Price, *France and the Chesapeake*, 1:76.

16. Jan Steen, *Tavern Scene*, 1661–1665, oil on canvas, 44.3 × 36.8 cm, Museo Nacional Thyssen-Bornemisza, Madrid; Jan Steen, *Peasants Drinking and Cutting Tobacco in an Inn*, 1660, oil on oak panel, 25 × 20.5 cm, private collection; Gaskell, "Tobacco, Social Deviance and Dutch Art," 77.

17. Gil-Bermejo García, *Panorama histórico*, 180.

18. Alonso, *El jíbaro*, 31, 41, 59, 78, 102, 184, 206.

19. Norton, *Sacred Gifts*, 171.

20. Martínez Álvarez, *El último alcalde*, 47; Álvarez Nazario, *El habla campesina del país*, 357; Chanvalon, "De los negros y su conversión," 327; Breen, *Age of Intoxication*, 83.

21. Luxán Meléndez and Bergasa Perdomo, "La institucionalización del modelo tabaquero español," 147.

22. Klooster, *Illicit Riches*, 189–90.

23. Price, *France and the Chesapeake*, 1:44.

24. Luxán Meléndez and Gárate Ojanguren, "La creación de un sistema atlántico," 164–65; Luxán Meléndez, "La defensa global," 198.

25. Klooster, *Illicit Riches*, 80–84, 197–98.

26. Araúz Monfante, "La acción ilegal," 71.

27. López Cantos, *Miguel Enríquez*, 149.

28. Gil-Bermejo García, *Panorama histórico*, 122–23. San Juan–based Pedro Latora (whose last name was a corruption of de la Torre) was another privateer of means. At the very least, he owned two sloops during the 1740s. Refer to "Journal of a Captive," 119–22.

29. Aizpurua Aguirre, "El corso de la Compañía Guipuzcoana," 380–81.

30. Crespo Solana, "Reflections on Monopolies," 79–80.

31. Picó, *Historia general*, 176–77.

32. Gárate Ojanguren, *La Real Compañía Guipuzcoana de Caracas*; Gárate Ojanguren, *Comercio ultramarino e Ilustración*.

33. Pérez Toledo, "Real Factoría Mercantil," master's thesis, 59; Crespo Solana, "Reflections on Monopolies," 79–80. Pérez Toledo published a short article, with the same title, based on his thesis in *Exégesis* 2, no. 6 (January–March 1989): 11–18.

34. Flandreau et al., "Bell Jar," 194–95; Arcila Farías, *Economía colonial de Venezuela*; Crespo Solana, "Reflections on Monopolies," 81.

35. Crespo Solana, "Reflections on Monopolies," 81.

36. Pérez Toledo, "Real Factoría Mercantil," master's thesis, 58–67.

37. Torres, "D. Jaime O'Daly," 50.

38. Chinea, "'Spain Is the Merciful Heavenly Body,'" 3, 16, 24.

39. Espinosa Fernández, *Elites y política colonial*, 64, 70.

40. Gil-Bermejo García, *Panorama histórico*, 175.

41. Espinosa Fernández, *Elites y política colonial*, 58.

42. Pérez Toledo, "Real Factoría Mercantil," master's thesis, 58–59; Jesús, *Tobacco Monopoly*, 10.

43. Pérez Toledo, "Real Factoría Mercantil," master's thesis, 94, 115, 118.

44. Gil-Bermejo García, *Panorama histórico*, 174.

45. Espinosa Fernández, *Elites y política colonial*, 56.

46. Torres Ramírez, *La isla de Puerto Rico*, 102–3.

47. Chinea, "Spanish Immigrant Joseph Martín de Fuentes," 85–109.

48. Sonesson, *Puerto Rico's Commerce*, 32, 51; Pérez Toledo, "Real Factoría Mercantil," master's thesis, 154; Espinosa Fernández, *Elites y política colonial*, 58, 70.

49. Gil-Bermejo García, *Panorama histórico*, 175–76; Lamikiz, *Trade and Trust*, 66.

50. Pérez Toledo, "Real Factoría Mercantil," master's thesis, 147.

51. Sonesson, *Puerto Rico's Commerce*, 29, 31–32.

52. Pacheco Díaz, *Relaciones comerciales*, 56–57.

53. Pérez Morales, *No Limits to Their Sway*; McCarthy, *Privateering*; Santana Peña, "United States and Puerto Rico," 141–99.

54. Géigel, *Corsarios y piratas*; Castleman, *Knickerbocker Commodore*, 75, 77.

55. Picó, *Historia general*, 142, 177; Fradera, *Colonias para después de un imperio*.

56. Sonesson, *Puerto Rico's Commerce*, 45–46; Picó, *Historia general*, 146.

57. Colón, *Historia de Isabela*, 74–75. Isabela's description comes from Ledru, *Voyage aux îles*, 2:101.

58. Acosta, *Cofresí y Ducoudray*, 84.

59. Santana Peña, "United States and Puerto Rico," 285; McCarthy, *Privateering*, 34, 58.

60. Cardona Bonet, *El marinero, bandolero, pirata y contrabandista*, 66; Santana Peña, "United States and Puerto Rico," 335–36.

61. McCarthy, *Privateering*, 37.

62. Roberts, *Schroders*, 21, 50, 56, 96; Reichard de Cancio, *Temas y temitas*, 40, 58; Pacheco Díaz, *Relaciones comerciales*, 163.

63. Pacheco Díaz, *Relaciones comerciales*, 168–69.

64. Colón, *Historia de Isabela*, 133.

65. Roberts, *Schroders*, 24–25; Sonesson, *Puerto Rico's Commerce*, 187, 211.

66. Sonesson, *Puerto Rico's Commerce*, 187, 211.

67. Santiago Méndez, "Los comerciantes," 23.

68. Sonesson, *Puerto Rico's Commerce*, 194.

69. Reichard de Cancio, *Temas y temitas*, 58.

70. Santiago Méndez, "Los comerciantes," 23.

71. Sonesson, *Puerto Rico's Commerce*, 211.

72. Capitanía del Puerto, "Entrada y salida de buques en el presente," *La Gaceta*, 16 June 1842, 288; Capitanía del Puerto, "Entrada y salida de buques en el presente," *La Gaceta*, 21 Sept. 1841, 452; Capitanía del Puerto, "Entrada y salida de buques en el mes presente," *La Gaceta*, 8 Mar. 1841, 116.

73. Reichard de Cancio, *Temas y temitas*, 40.

74. George O. Latimer to James Buchanan, in *Despachos de los cónsules norteamericanos*, 1:197.

75. Computed from US Congress, House, "Statement Showing the Exports and Imports of Tobacco, with the Import into Great Britain, &c," 23 Feb. 1842, 27th Congress, 2nd session, House Document 235, 60, 64.

76. Dávila Cox, *Este inmenso comercio*, 88; Sonesson, *Puerto Rico's Commerce*, 172; Pacheco Díaz, *Relaciones comerciales*, 57.

77. Flinter, *Account of the Present State*, 189.

78. A cuerda is 0.39 of a hectare or 0.97 of an acre. See Russ Rowlett, "A Dictionary of Units of Measurement," University of North Carolina at Chapel Hill, 24 Apr. 2018, http://www.ibiblio.org/units/dictC.html.

79. Picó, *Libertad y servidumbre*, 59.

80. Flinter, *Account of the Present State*, 189–90.

81. Pérez Vega, *Las sociedades mercantiles*, 175–77; Rivero Muñiz, *Tabaco*, 2:123–24; Baud, *Peasants and Tobacco*, 75–76; Kerr-Ritchie, *Freedpeople in the Tobacco South*, 160.

82. Colón, *Historia de Isabela*, 133, 216–20.

83. Nissen, *Reminiscences of a 46 Years' Residence*, 166. In the Isabela of the 1820s, shipments of tobacco rolls for export faced competition from other forms of packaging. Refer to Colón, *Historia de Isabela*, 73–76.

84. US Congress, House, "Statement Showing the Exports," 70.

CHAPTER TWO. FROM HANDCRAFTED TOBACCO ROLLS TO MACHINE-MADE CIGARETTES, 1847–1903

1. González Fernández, "1895–1898," 310–12.

2. Lestina, "Vuelta Abajo, Cuba," 45–46.

3. González del Valle was a director of the Cuban National Commission for the Propaganda and Defense of Havana Cigars and also of the Cuban Association of Tobacco Wholesalers and Growers. González del Valle, *Memorándum presentado*, 1, 61–62. Cayetano Coll y Toste wrote

about some five thousand kilograms of Puerto Rican tobacco seed shipped to Cuba. Refer to "Appendix I, A Review of the Social, Economic, and Industrial Conditions of the Island of Puerto Rico Immediately Preceding Occupation by the United States," in *Annual Reports of the War Department for the Fiscal Year Ended June 30, 1899*, 708.

4. J. M. Ceballos & Co., *Importers and Exporters Pictorial Guide.*

5. Abad, *La República Dominicana*, 317; San Miguel, *Los campesinos del Cibao*, 131–42.

6. Delano, *En busca del maestro Rafael Cordero.*

7. Abad, *La exposición agrícola e industrial*, 96, 97.

8. Braudel, *Civilización material, economía y capitalismo*, 220.

9. Alonso Álvarez, "Pautas de consumo," 255–57; Lluberes Navarro, "La crisis del tabaco cibaeño," 7.

10. Jesús, *Tobacco Monopoly*, 2, 39–40.

11. Havana cigars competed with the aristocratic snuff and the democratic chaw of tobacco but also with a native cigar crafted by farmers in the Connecticut Valley and in Pennsylvania. Robert, *Story of Tobacco*, 95–96.

12. Kiernan, *Tobacco*, 36; Pérez Vidal, *España en la historia del tabaco*, 96; Rodríguez Gordillo, "El personal obrero," 145.

13. Goodman, *Tobacco in History and Culture*, 126, 151.

14. Baud, *Modernidad y luchas sociales*, 250–51; Gottsegen, *Tobacco*, 140–41; Ortiz, *Cuban Counterpoint*, 307–8.

15. Royal decree quoted in Pérez Vidal, *España en la historia del tabaco*, 324.

16. Jesús, *Tobacco Monopoly*, 163, 165.

17. Reid, "From Betel-Chewing to Tobacco-Smoking," 538.

18. García de Torres, *El arriendo de los tabacos filipinos*, 49.

19. Jesús, *Tobacco Monopoly*, 166. Rudyard Kipling extolled their virtues in "The Betrothed," in *Stories and Poems*, 431 while George Sand defied social mores by openly smoking Manilas. Refer to Mirecourt, *George Sand*, 52.

20. Jesús, *Tobacco Monopoly*, 162; Alonso Álvarez, "Pautas de consumo," 257.

21. This is the title of the second to last chapter in Ortiz's *Cuban Counterpoint.*

22. Ortiz, *Cuban Counterpoint*, 309.

23. González Sierra, *Monopolio del humo*, 73–74; Muller, *Cuban Émigrés and Independence*, 50–52. While Mexicans had a strong preference for cigarette smoking, they had a long-standing tradition of cigar manufacturing for the domestic market. See Deans-Smith, *Bureaucrats, Planters, and Workers*, xx, 152.

24. Luxán Meléndez, *La opción agrícola e industrial*, 89–92.

25. Hanusz, *Kretek*, 77; Stoler, *Capitalism and Confrontation*, 14–17.

26. Abad, *La exposición agrícola e industrial*, 96; Gage, *Tobacco Industry*, 17.

27. Sonesson, *Puerto Rico's Commerce*, 210.

28. Abad, *La República Dominicana*, 318; Kimm, "House of Niemeyer," ix; Alexandre Dumas—in *The Count of Monte Cristo*, 386—describes a gentleman's smoking salon as containing, among others, Puerto Rican tobacco stored in a crackled earthenware pot of Dutch origin.

29. Sonesson, *Puerto Rico's Commerce*, 172–73, 209–10; Pacheco Díaz, *Relaciones comerciales*, 168–69, 172–75.

30. Moscoso, *Agricultura y sociedad*, 201–5.

31. Abad, *La exposición agrícola e industrial*, 97. *Boliche* consists of the lower, overripe leaves of the tobacco plant, known as *colas* in Cuba. It also includes the sucker crop, the *segundo corte* in tobacco parlance, which are those obtained when the once-harvested plant is left to sprout. These leaves are unsuitable for the manufacture of long-filler cigars or roll-chewing tobacco because they cannot be stemmed. Refer to John Frese, "Testimony," transcript of record, filed

14 Aug. 1928, Porto Rican American Tobacco Co. v. American Tobacco Company, NARA, New York, Records of the Department of Justice, (Record Group 276), US Court of Appeals for the Second Circuit, case file 10127, 1929, box 3240 and Saavedra, "El cultivo de tabaco en Isabela," 83.

32. Ubeda y Delgado, *Isla de Puerto Rico*, 251–52. Subsequently, Sabana del Palmar changed its name for Comerío. A report from the British consul considered Comerío the best tobacco for cigars. See Dávila Cox, *Este inmenso comercio*, 87.

33. Aguayo, *Manual del cultivo de tabaco*, 64–65.

34. Aguayo, *Manual del cultivo de tabaco*, 58; van Leenhoff, "Tobacco Investigations," 12. The twentieth century witnessed a third harvesting technique called *deshojado*, or primed, where the leaves were picked one by one as they matured individually.

35. Abad, *La República Dominicana*, 353.

36. Infiesta, *La exposición de Puerto Rico*, 214.

37. Abad, *La República Dominicana*, 318.

38. The Pearson product-moment correlation coefficient between tobacco leaf imports and time measured in years is -0.83. The statistic is based on the twenty-three years with available import data. Cutbacks came at Cuban expense primarily and, to a lesser extent, from Virginia. Both handled a superior leaf. Imports of Dominican leaf, considered inferior, show wide fluctuations but no discernible trend during the second half of the nineteenth century.

39. Rivera Rodríguez, "El crecimiento de las importaciones," 195.

40. The Pearson product-moment correlation coefficient between exports of Puerto Rican tobacco leaf and time measured in years is 0.36. Data was complete for 1847–1899.

41. Meléndez Muñoz, *Cayey en el drama del cambio*, 3:127.

42. Sonesson, *Puerto Rico's Commerce*, 173.

43. "Al Congreso," *La Convicción* (Barcelona), 14 July 1871, evening ed., 4289–90.

44. González Fernández, "La manufactura tabacalera cubana," 133.

45. "Tabaco de Puerto Rico," *Boletín Mercantil*, 18 May 1877, 2; "Un nuevo adalid de la prohibición," *Boletín Mercantil*, 22 Aug. 1877, 2.

46. "El asunto del tabaco," *Boletín Mercantil*, 3 Nov. 1876, 2. The contraband might have been more complicated as Pennsylvania fillers apparently found their way to Havana via Puerto Rico. "The Cigar Trade Frauds, How Home Tobacco Reaches Havana and Comes Back," *New York Times*, 15 Mar. 1881, 2.

47. "Tabaco de Puerto Rico," 2.

48. "Noticia importantísima," *Boletín Mercantil*, 6 June 1877, 3; "Porto Rico Tobacco in Cuba," *New York Times*, 7 June 1877, 1.

49. "Noticia importantísima," 3; "Porto Rico Tobacco in Cuba," *New York Times*, 7 June 1877, 1.

50. Delgado y Martín, *La renta de tabacos*, 64–65; Hernández, "Suministradores de tabaco," 360–62.

51. Baldrich, "Cigars and Cigarettes," 20–23.

52. González Fernández, "1895–1898," 310.

53. Rivero Muñiz, *Tabaco*, 2:316; Valle, "Situación económica de Puerto Rico," 568.

54. Gage, *Tobacco Industry*, 43. A few were formerly enslaved people who kept to the trade after emancipation in 1873. Mayo Santana, Negrón Portillo, and Mayo López, "Esclavos y libertos," 39.

55. Ingalls, *Urban Vigilantes*; Westfall, *Key West*.

56. Bureau of Corporations, *Position of the Tobacco Combination*, 150.

57. *La Correspondencia*, 23 Apr. 1892; García, "Las primeras actividades," *Op. Cit.* 246; *La cuestión tabaquera en Puerto Rico*, 5.

58. *La cuestión tabaquera en Puerto Rico*, 5.

59. Abad, *La exposición agrícola e industrial*, 29; Infiesta, *La exposición de Puerto Rico*, 209.

60. *Sketches: Porto Rico.*

61. Infiesta, *La exposición de Puerto Rico*, 214; "Marca de cigarros La Flor de Cayey," 1922, Colección Efraín Archilla Diez; Intendencia General de la Real Casa y Patrimonio, "Concesión de honores de proveedor de la Real Casa," 13 June 1885, Archivo Histórico Nacional, Ultramar, 5122, expediente 2; Intendencia General de la Real Casa y Patrimonio, "Nombramiento de proveedores de tabaco de la Real Casa," 2 Apr. 1886, Archivo Histórico Nacional, Ultramar, 5122, expediente 22.

62. Pérez Moris, *Guía general*, 40.

63. Abad, *Puerto Rico en la feria-exposición*, 127; García, "Primeros fermentos," 12.

64. *La cuestión tabaquera en Puerto Rico*, 5–6.

65. Infiesta, *La Exposición Universal de Barcelona*, 42.

66. Abad, *La exposición agrícola e industrial*, 64.

67. *La Correspondencia*, 28 Apr. 1892, 2; García, "Las primeras actividades," 246.

68. "Tabaquería 'El Escudo Español,'" *La Democracia*, 23 Apr. 1892, 3; Infiesta, *La exposición de Puerto Rico*, 206; M. Paniagua to William H. Hunt, Governor of Puerto Rico, 2 May 1902, AGPR, Fortaleza, caja 103, exp. 2,907.

69. Carroll, *Report on the Island of Porto Rico*, 749.

70. Cámara de Comercio de Puerto Rico, "Tobacco Culture," 62. This partly mechanized factory employed steam by 1899. See J. M. Ceballos & Co., *Importers and Exporters Pictorial Guide*.

71. Hilton, "Retailing History," 131.

72. "Tabaquería 'El Escudo Español.'"

73. Carroll, *Report on the Island of Porto Rico*, 141.

74. Abad, *La exposición agrícola e industrial*, 97.

75. Carroll, *Report on the Island of Porto Rico*, 141.

76. Kutzinski, *Sugar's Secrets*, 43–80; Núñez Jiménez, *Marquillas cigarreras cubanas*.

77. Infiesta, *La exposición de Puerto Rico*, 211–12.

78. Abad, *La exposición agrícola e industrial*, 64, 71.

79. Chandler, *Visible Hand*, 249.

80. Korzeniewicz, "Labor Unrest," 87; Rogoff, "Jewish Proletarians," 141–57.

81. Tennant, *American Cigarette Industry*, 18; Tilley, *Bright Tobacco Industry*, 572–74.

82. Chandler, *Visible Hand*, 249; Porter, "Advertising in the Early Cigarette Industry," 43.

83. Baldrich, "From the Origins of Industrial Capitalism," 80–106.

84. Cayetano Coll y Toste, "El tabaco," *Tobacco*, 29 Dec. 1921, 57–58; Burgos Malavé, "El conflicto tabacalero," 181–91.

85. "Agreement, Fausto Rucabado Vázquez y José Portela Silva and American Tobacco Co.," in *Transcript of Record . . . Supreme Court of the United States. October term, 1908. No. 660. The United States of America, Appellant, vs. the American Tobacco Company, and Others. . . . Appeals from the Circuit Court of the United States for the Southern District of New York . . . Filed December 23, 1908*, ed. United States (New York: Press of Appeal Printed Co., 1908), 5:138–39.

86. Rucabado y Portela, *La Colectiva*, 1899, AGPR, Colecciones Particulares, Junghanns, caja 27, exp. 1111.

87. Abad, *Puerto Rico en la feria-exposición*.

88. Abad, *La exposición agrícola e industrial*; Negociado de Obras Públicas, Construcciones Civiles Montes y Minas, "Á los alcaldes de la Isla—Exposición del tabacos en Ponce," *La Gaceta*, 6 Feb. 1883.

89. They published the petitions as *La cuestión tabaquera* in 1885.

90. *Al gobierno de la nación, a los representantes en Cortes, de la Isla de Puerto Rico* ([San Juan?]: Boletín Mercantil, 1892).

91. Of the three-member commission composed of Mateo Rucabado, Marcelino Solá, and Evaristo San Miguel, the first two were respected tobacco men. See Burgos Malavé, "El conflicto tabacalero"; Coll y Toste, "El tabaco," 57–58; and Torres Grillo, *Historia de la ciudad de Caguas*, 58–59.

92. *La Correspondencia*, 28 Apr. 1892, 2.

93. "Noticias," *La Democracia*, 15 Feb. 1895, 3; García, "Las primeras actividades," 241.

94. Manuel Fernández Juncos, "Crónica de la semana," *La Correspondencia*, 22 Aug. 1897; Iglesias de Pagán, *El obrerismo en Puerto Rico*, 57–58.

95. Carroll, *Report on the Island of Porto Rico*, 764–65.

96. I have used the term *Americanization* rather than *denationalization* since local tobacco factories were the property of foreigners.

97. Carroll, *Report on the Island of Porto Rico*, 765.

98. Cifre de Loubriel, *La formación del pueblo puertorriqueño*, 575–76; Cifre de Loubriel, *La inmigración a Puerto Rico*, 292, 416.

99. Meisel Roca and Viloria de la Hoz, *Los alemanes en el Caribe colombiano*, 21–22; Shechter, "Selling Luxury," 51–75; Rafael León Paz, "Protocolización de venta de fábrica de cigarrillos y tabaco," 22 May 1900, AGPR, PN, Serie de Ponce, Pueblo de Ponce, caja 2057, fols. 1826–1853; Macmillan, *West Indies*, 196; Mayoral Barnés, *Ponce y su historial geopolítico-económico*, 86; Gumersindo Rivas, "Mis lunes," *La Democracia*, 24 Apr. 1899, 2.

100. J. M. Ceballos & Co., *Importers and Exporters Pictorial Guide*. The contract to sell local cigars in the US market, however, did not amount to much. See US Congress, House, *Importers of Goods from Porto Rico*, 56th Cong., 1st sess., H. Doc. 589 (Washington, DC: GPO, 1900) and "Genuine Porto Rican Cigars," *Tobacco*, 8 Mar. 1901, 3.

101. Carroll, *Report on the Island of Porto Rico*, 141.

102. León Paz, "Protocolización de venta de fábrica de cigarrillos y tabaco," fol. 1829.

103. Bureau of Corporations, *Position of the Tobacco Combination*, 180–93. Cox, *Global Cigarette*, 5.

104. León Paz, "Protocolización de venta de fábrica de cigarrillos y tabaco," fols. 1826–1853; Rivas, "Mis lunes," 2; "Portela v. The Porto Rican American Tobacco Co.," *Decisiones de Puerto Rico* 4 (1903): 30–39.

105. Bunker, *Historia de Caguas*, 1:343.

106. Foraker Act (Organic Act of 1900), *US Statutes at Large* 31 (12 Apr. 1900): 77–78.

107. Bunker, *Historia de Caguas*, 2:238; Caliumet III, "Men of Mark in the Trade LI," *Tobacco*, 9 Mar. 1905, 2; García Díaz, *Mi paso*, 37.

108. "Cigars from Porto Rico," *Tobacco*, 29 Dec. 1910, 31.

109. Bunker, *Historia de Caguas*, 2:238; "Puerto Rico," *Diario de Puerto Rico*, 12 Sept. 1900, 1.

110. "A New Line of Porto Rico Cigars," *Tobacco*, 29 Aug. 1902, 1; "Current Comment," *Tobacco*, 19 Sept. 1902, 5.

111. Krout, *United States Directory of Cigar Manufacturers*, 138; 'M. Sola [*sic*] e Hijos," *Tobacco*, 9 Feb. 1905, 21.

112. Caliumet, "Men of Mark in the Trade LI," 3.

113. US Department of Labor, Immigration Service, "List or Manifest of Alien Passengers for the Commissioner or Immigration, S.S. Ponce, Sailing from San Juan, PR," 14–20 Apr. 1903, Ellis Island Passenger Search database; US Department of Labor, Immigration Service, "List or Manifest of Alien Passengers for the US Immigration Officer, S.S. Ponce, Sailing from San Juan, PR," 9–14 June 1903, Ellis Island Passenger Search database.

114. Bunker, *Historia de Caguas*, 2:239.

115. M. Paniagua to William H. Hunt, Governor of Puerto Rico; "Porto Rico Cigars," *Tobacco*, 7 Sept. 1900, 29.

116. "Mateo Rucabado," *Tobacco*, 7 July 1904, 34.

117. *Puerto Rico Ilustrado*, 22 Apr. 1939, 86.

118. Bureau of Corporations, *Position of the Tobacco Combination*, 429.

119. Jean Stubbs refers to this phenomenon, during the 1990s, as the "offshore Havana cigar." See Stubbs, "Turning over a New Leaf?," 235–56.

CHAPTER THREE. THE DEVELOPMENT OF THE "PORTO RICO" CIGAR AND THE INDEPENDENT MANUFACTURERS, 1899–1929

1. Ortiz, *Cuban Counterpoint*, 309.

2. Kipling, "Betrothed," 430–31.

3. Bloch-Dano, *Le dernier amour de George Sand*, 16.

4. My translation of Mirecourt, *George Sand*, 52.

5. Dumas, *Count of Monte Cristo*, 386.

6. Walker, *Masks Outrageous*, 24.

7. Ackerman, *Natural History of the Senses*, 279.

8. Henry, "From Each According to His Ability," 205.

9. Broadway League, "Internet Broadway Database," 2021, https://www.ibdb.com/broadway-cast-staff/louis-massen-51794; "Clubroom Smoking No. 1," *Tobacco World*, 1 Sept. 1913, 21. Savarona was the main trademark of the Cayey-Caguas Tobacco Company, which was a large, US-owned cigar manufacturer. Bunker, "Dos biografías," 338–39.

10. Aiken, "Impulse," 159–60.

11. Kimmel, *Manhood in America*, 207, 210.

12. Morris J. Levi, "The Start and Status of Porto Rico Leaf Tobacco in the United States," *Tobacco Leaf*, 25 Aug. 1921, 15.

13. Levi, "Start and Status of Porto Rico," 25 Aug. 1921, 15.

14. Levi, "Start and Status of Porto Rico," 25 Aug. 1921, 15. Pardo had a tobacco leaf ware house in San Juan. Refer to Blanch, *Directorio comercial e industrial*, N.

15. US Congress, House, *Importers of Goods from Porto Rico*, 56th Cong., 1st sess., 1900, H. Doc. 589sp, 8.

16. Morris J. Levi, "The Start and Status of Porto Rico Leaf Tobacco in the United States," *Tobacco Leaf*, 1 Sept. 1921, 44.

17. US Congress, House, *Importers of Goods*. Decades later, Levi stated that the first shipment took place during the summer of 1899. Refer to Levi, "The Start and Status," 1 Sept. 1921, 44.

18. Levi, "Start and Status," 1 Sept. 1921, 44.

19. "Labels," 955.

20. For a sample, refer to "Buy El Falco Cigars," *Cornell Daily Sun*, 21 Oct. 1912, 5.

21. Lewis Bear Company, "A Cigar that Pleases," *Pensacola Journal*, 16 Mar. 1913, 10. The distributor ran the advertisements in the same newspaper between 8 Dec. 1912 and 27 Jan. 1914.

22. Levi, "Start and Status," 1 Sept. 1921, 43–44.

23. Computed from US Congress, House, *Importers of Goods*. Tobacco leaf shipments, although limited, were more frequent. A case typically contained five thousand cigars. See "From the Firing Line," *Tobacco*, 14 Mar. 1918, 28.

24. US Congress, House, *Importers of Goods*.

25. Sheldon, *Pocket Tariff*; García Muñiz, *Sugar and Power*, 58–59.

26. "Those Cigars from Porto Rico," *Tobacco*, 1 June 1900, 1.

27. Schmidt & Co., "New Porto Rico," 1898, New York, author's collection.

28. Cooper, *Once a Cigar Maker*, 203.

29. "Those Cigars from Porto Rico," 1.

30. Governor of Porto Rico, *Annual Report, 1902*, 10; Salamone, "Constitutional Separation," 76–77.

31. "Maximo Brand of Porto Rican Cigars," *Tobacco*, 22 Mar. 1901, 1. Refer to Baldrich, "From the Origins of Industrial Capitalism," 80–106, for a full discussion of the Rucabado businesses.

32. "The New Maximo Label," *Tobacco*, 26 July 1901, 1. Another label for the same cigar did not sport the map but identified the island by its name along with the municipalities where the firm had a presence. For the latter, refer to the Máximo lithographic proof in the Colección Efraín Archilla Diez.

33. Hemenway and Moser, "Maximo," *Salt Lake Herald*, 8 July 1901, 7.

34. "Porto Rico Cigars," *Tobacco*, 7 Sept. 1900, 29; "Porto Rico Cigars," *Tobacco*, 28 Sept. 1900, 29; "Porto Rico Cigars," *Tobacco*, 1 Mar. 1901, 27.

35. La Ultramarina de Portela y Cª, 17 May 1899, AGPR, Colecciones Particulares, Junghanns, caja 27, expediente 1100.

36. Macy's, "Flor de Cayey," *The Sun* (New York), 28 June 1914, 12.

37. "A $1.75 Box of Cigars," *Pittsburgh Press*, 16 Aug. 1905, 14.

38. "El Toro de la Selva de Toro y Cª," [ca. 1900], author's collection.

39. Weyl, "Labor Conditions," 759; "Porto Rican Tobacco," *Tobacco World*, 30 Sept. 1908, 11.

40. "M. Sola e Hijos," *Tobacco*, 9 Feb. 1905, 21.

41. "A New Aguey-Naba Hanger," *Tobacco World*, 28 May 1902, 7. Agueynaba was a common misspelling of Agüeybaná, who was the main taíno chieftain at the time of the Spanish conquest of Puerto Rico.

42. "The Tantos Cigar," *Tobacco Leaf*, 15 Oct. 1902, 3; Hemenway & Moser, "Formal Opening of Our New Cigar Store," *Ogden Standard*, 15 May 1914, 12; Leadley & Buell, "We Pay Liberally for Our Cigars!," *Daily News* (Batavia, NY), 26 June 1902, 1; "A New Line of Porto Rico Cigars," *Tobacco*, 29 Aug. 1902, 1; Cádiz Cigar Co., "El Resumen," *Tobacco*, 19 Sept. 1902, 26.

43. Bunker, *Historia de Caguas*, 2:238.

44. Bureau of the Census, "Population Census Schedules," 2 Jan. 1920, NARA microfilm publication T625, Censo décimocuarto de los Estados Unidos, 1920, Población Puerto Rico, San Juan, barrio Santurce, Urbano, Hoja 1A, Distrito de Enumeración 20.

45. Moody, *Moody's Manual of Securities*, 2:1106.

46. "El Falcon Damage Suit," *Tobacco Leaf*, 15 Oct. 1902, 3; "El Falco Appeals Dismissed," *Tobacco*, 24 June 1909, 1, 7.

47. AWITCO, "Annual Report," 1901–1906, AGPR, Estado, Corporaciones foráneas con fines de lucro, caja 2, expediente 40.

48. AWITCO, "Written Consent of Agent," 24 Aug. 1901, AGPR, Estado, Corporaciones foráneas con fines de lucro, caja 2, expediente 40; Rivera Martínez, "Santiago Iglesias y yo," 207.

49. La Turina, 1900, inner label in the author's collection.

50. Gardner & Hudgins, "Something Tempting," *Daily Press*(Newport News, VA), 9 Nov. 1906, 5.

51. G. G. Cornwell & Son, "Fine Imported Cigars," *Washington Herald*, 20 Dec. 1906, 12.

52. "Durlach Bros. Win," *New England Tobacco Grower*, Apr. 1905, 11; *Trow's Business Directory*, 353.

53. "Durlach y Springer," *La Correspondencia*, 24 Apr. 1900, 1.

54. "Miscellaneous Imports," *Tobacco*, 8 Nov. 1901, 23.

55. Durlach Bros., "Grand Prize at the 1904 St. Louis Exposition," *Tobacco*, 10 May 1906, 4.

56. A *bogador* is an oarsman, and *rigodón* stands for a baroque dance form.

57. Durlach Bros., "The Cigars that Made 'Porto Rico' Famous," *Tobacco*, 2 May 1902, 21; "Current Comment," *Tobacco*, 2 May 1902, 5.

58. Main Corner, "Cut Rate Cigars," *Seattle Star*, 20 Jan. 1905, 5; New Store, "Cigar Dept.," *Minneapolis Journal*, 25 Aug. 1905, 10.

59. "The Future of the Porto Rico Cigar," *Tobacco*, 25 Apr. 1902, 4.

60. "'Porto Rican' Cigars Now Made Here," *New York Times*, 14 Sept. 1902, 26.

61. "Current Comment," *Tobacco*, 7 Feb. 1902, 5.

62. "The Porto Rico Situation," *Tobacco*, 16 May 1902, 4; "Current Comment," *Tobacco*, 2 May 1902, 5.

63. "La industria tabacalera en Caguas," *La Democracia*, 9 Oct. 1901, 4.

64. Luis Muñoz Morales, "Compraventa (escritura 109)," 10 Nov. 1901, AGPR, PN, Siglo XX, Pueblo: San Juan, Año: 1901, caja 747, fols. 443–46; Bureau of the Census, "Population Census Schedules," 14 June 1900, Brooklyn Ward 25, Kings, New York; Roll 1062; Page 16B; Enumeration District 435; FHL microfilm 1241062.

65. "San Juan, notas por correo," *La Democracia*, 11 Mar. 1902, 2.

66. Porto Rico Export Company of Porto Rico, 15 May 1902, AGPR, Estado, Corporaciones foráneas con fines de lucro, caja 4, expediente 69.

67. "The Exporto Cigar," *Tobacco Leaf*, 18 June 1902, 3. La Industrial factory and trademark used to be the property of Modesto Munitiz, Marcial Suárez, and José Dimas Riera. See Luis Muñoz Morales, "Constitución y disolución de sociedad," 5 Apr. 1902, AGPR, PN, Siglo XX, Pueblo: San Juan, Año: 1902, caja 748, escritura 38, fols. 109–12.

68. "Exporto," 1902, author's collection; "La Industrial," 5 Apr. 1900, AGPR, Colecciones Particulares, Junghanns, caja 27, expediente 1106.

69. "Henry W. Dooley of Porto Rico Dies," *New York Times*, 13 Mar. 1932, 6.

70. "To Test Porto Rican tariff," *New York Times*, 21 Oct. 1900, 6.

71. R. T., "El cabotaje," *La Democracia*, 24 July 1901, 3. For a description of *boliche*, refer to War Department, *Report of the Census of Porto Rico 1899*, 145.

72. "Llegan tabacos de Puerto Rico elaborados con hojas americanas, los tabacos legítimos obtienen difícil venta," *La Correspondencia*, 11 July 1902.

73. For a discussion of the apprenticeship and training of cigar makers, refer to Baldrich, "Gender and the Decomposition of the Cigar-Making Craft," 105–25.

74. "The Future of the Porto Rico Cigar," *Tobacco*, 25 Apr. 1902, 4.

75. "The Porto Rico Situation," *Tobacco*, 16 May 1902, 4.

76. Weyl, "Labor Conditions in Porto Rico," 759.

77. "'Porto Rican' Cigars Now Made Here," 26.

78. "Current Comment," *Tobacco*, 2 May 1902, 5.

79. "The Future of the Porto Rico Cigar," 4.

80. "'Porto Rican' Cigars Now Made Here," 26; "Gossiper's Notebook," *Tobacco Leaf*, 10 June 1903, 5; "Fine Porto Rico Goods in Demand," *Tobacco*, 23 June 1904, 7.

81. "From the Firing Line," *Tobacco*, 27 June 1918, 63; "Atchison, Topeka and Santa Fe," *The Sun* (New York), 3 June 1909, 9; "Changes Are Made by Wall St. Firms," *New York Times*, 1 Oct. 1943, 29.

82. "T. L. Chrystie, 82, Lawyer, Is Dead," *New York Times*, 16 Aug. 1954, 17.

83. Knox, *Who's Who in New York.*

84. Bunker, *Historia de Caguas*, 2:239–40; Bunker, "Dos biografías," 337; "Una 'soiree' en perspectiva," *La Democracia*, 12 Dec. 1901, 3.

85. Cayey-Caguas Tobacco Company, "Informe anual," 1904, AGPR, Estado, Corporaciones foráneas con fines de lucro, caja 5, expediente 86.

86. Bureau of Corporations, "Cayey-Caguas Tobacco Company," 1906, NARA, Washington, DC, FTC, Bureau of Corporations (Record Group 122), box 238, file 3825–11–11; New York State,

"Population Census Schedules,"1905, New York State Archives, Albany, Census Place: Election District 20, Assembly District 12, New York, Kings, 15.

87. Governor of Porto Rico, *Annual Report, 1904*, 47; Cayey-Caguas Tobacco Company, "Informe anual," 1904.

88. "Trade Change at San Juan P.R.," *Tobacco World*, 11 May 1904, 20.

89. Affidavit L. J. Stadeker, 20 Oct. 1904, AGPR, Estado, Corporaciones foráneas con fines de lucro, caja 4, expediente 69.

90. "Porto Rican Conditions," *Tobacco World*, 7 Sept. 1904, 13.

91. "Tobacco Exposition Commences Monday," *Tobacco World*, 7 Dec. 1904, 8; "Exhibitors Are Lining Up," *Tobacco World*, 31 Aug. 1904, 14.

92. "Handsome Exhibits at New York Show," *Tobacco World*, 25 Oct. 1905, 13, 14; "New York Tobacco Exposition," *Tobacco World*, 20 Sept. 1905, 14; "Crowds Are Flocking to the Tobacco Show," *Tobacco World*, 12 Sept. 1906, 12–13, 17; "What the Great Show Is Like and Why the Trade Should Attend," *Tobacco World*, 5 Sept. 1906, 14–19; "The Tobacco Show at Madison Square Garden," *Tobacco World*, 4 Sept. 1907, 16–17; "The Troubles of the Exposition Company," *Tobacco World*, 4 Dec. 1907, 13.

93. "Cayey-Caguas Tobacco Co. Doings," *Tobacco World*, 1 Feb. 1911, 20.

94. Bunker, *Historia de Caguas*, 2:240.

95. "Harrison Johnson Talks of Porto Rico," *Tobacco*, 9 May 1907, 27.

96. "How American Enterprise Has Developed Porto Rican Cigars," *Tobacco World*, 15 Apr. 1910, 11.

97. "Growth Demanded Larger Quarters," *Tobacco*, 8 Feb. 1906, 4; "Cayey Caguas to Move May First," *Tobacco*, 9 Apr. 1908, 5.

98. *Tobacco*, 21 Dec. 1905, 16.

99. Luis Muñoz Morales, "Siembra de tabaco con refacción," 18 Nov. 1913, AGPR, PN, Serie: Siglo XX, Pueblo: San Juan, Año: 1913, caja 760, escritura 77, fols. 777–84; "Cayey Caguas to Move May First," 5; "How American Enterprise Has Developed Porto Rican Cigars," 10.

100. Johnson Development Company, "Annual Report," 9 Oct. 1908, AGPR, Estado, Corporaciones foráneas con fines de lucro, caja 11, expediente 144; Johnson Development Company, "Annual Report," 1 Mar. 1908, AGPR, Estado, Corporaciones foráneas con fines de lucro, caja 11, expediente 144.

101. Benigno Fernández García, "Arrendamiento de fincas rústicas, segregación y rescisión de contrato de siembra y molienda de caña," 10 Jan.1920, AGPR, PN, Serie: San Juan, Siglo XX, Pueblo: Cayey, Año: 1920, caja 337, escritura 22, fols. 63–70.

102. "Profit in Porto Rican Tobacco," *Financial World*, 13 July 1912, 8.

103. "Profit in Porto Rican Tobacco," 8.

104. "Hear'd by Yeway in New York," *Tobacco World*, 15 Oct. 1910, 19.

105. "Profit in Porto Rican Tobacco," 8.

106. "Herbert S. Michael et al., v. Cayey-Caguas Tobacco Company," *Supreme Court of New York, Appellate Division, First Department* 190 (1920): 623.

107. Luis Muñoz Morales, "Siembra de tabaco con refacción y garantía y carta de pago," 1914, AGPR, PN, Serie: Siglo XX, Pueblo: San Juan, Año: 1914, caja 762, escritura 112, fols. 913–20; Luis Muñoz Morales, "Siembra de tabaco con refacción," 1913, AGPR, PN, Serie: Siglo XX, Pueblo: San Juan, Año: 1913, caja 760, escritura 77, fols. 777–84.

108. Asenjo, *Quién es quién en Puerto Rico*, 40.

109. Governor of Porto Rico, *Annual Report, 1918*, 100; "From the Firing Line," *Tobacco*, 23 Jan. 1919, 28.

110. Benigno Fernández García, "Arrendamiento de fincas rústicas, segregación y rescisión de contrato de siembra y molienda de caña," 10 Jan. 1920, AGPR, PN, Serie: San Juan, Siglo XX, Pueblo: Cayey, Año: 1920, caja 337, escritura 22, fols. 63–70.

111. "H. Duys & Co. Enter Porto Rico Trade," *United States Tobacco Journal*, 23 Aug. 1919, 6.

112. Brown's Cigar Store, "Gold or Silver," *Evening Caledonian (VT) Record*, 24 Mar. 1921, 8. The cigar store published twelve identical advertisements in the same newspaper between March 1 and March 24.

113. "To Bring Out a New Brand," *Tobacco*, 7 Sept. 1905, 20.

114. "How American Enterprise Has Developed Porto Rican Cigars," 11.

115. "Knickerbocker's Broadway Jottings," *Tobacco World*, 1 Jan. 1917, 14. In 1914, the Schulte Retail Stores Company was a large chain with forty-one stores in New York. Refer to Cox, *Competition in the American Tobacco Industry*, 246.

116. "Milwaukee," *Tobacco World*, 15 Apr. 1913, 32; "Changes in Milwaukee Firms," *Tobacco World*, 15 Mar. 1910, 31; "With the Trade in Milwaukee," *Tobacco World*, 21 Apr. 1909, 18.

117. "Baltimore Manufacturers Report Trade Active," *Tobacco World*, 1 Apr. 1912, 34.

118. Fumero and Fumero, *Merchant Tokens*, 29.

119. "Reasons for Savarona Success," *United States Tobacco Journal*, 1 Oct. 1910, 5.

120. "How American Enterprise Has Developed," 11.

121. J. M. Greenhut Company, "New York Turn to Greenhut's for Christmas," *Evening World*, 3 Dec. 1914, image 13; Myers-Dillon Drug Co., "Cigars at Cut Rates," *Omaha Daily Bee*, 24 Feb. 1907, 10.

122. Picó, *Los gallos peleados*, 21.

123. Meléndez Badillo, *Voces libertarias*, 174; Shaffer, *Black Flag Boricuas*, 85.

124. PRATCO established a factory in Cayey in 1914. Refer to *La Correspondencia*, 13 Apr. 1914, 6.

125. "Tobacco Partners Disagree," *New York Times*, 8 Apr. 1908, 10.

126. AWITCO, "Certificate of Increase of Capital Stock," 29 July 1908, AGPR, Estado, Corporaciones foráneas con fines de lucro, caja 2, expediente 40.

127. AWITCO, "Annual Report," 1909, AGPR, Estado, Corporaciones foráneas con fines de lucro, caja 2, expediente 40, 2.

128. "Cigars from Porto Rico," *Tobacco*, 4 Jan. 1912, 31.

129. "The Local Tobacco News," *Tobacco World*, 15 July 1908, 12.

130. "Morris J. Levi to Head New House," *Tobacco*, 5 June 1913, 7; "Two Popular Brands of Cigars," *Tobacco*, 13 Oct. 1910, 23.

131. "A $100,000 Failure, the New Orleans Jobbing House of Valloft & Dreux," *United States Tobacco Journal*, 15 June 1912, 1.

132. "Tobacco to Cover $51,000 Note Said to be Worth $15,000," *United States Tobacco Journal*, 28 Aug. 1915, 6.

133. "Tobacco to Cover $51,000 Note," 6; "Plantation Co. Again Attached," *United States Tobacco Journal*, 21 Aug. 1915, 1.

134. "Plantation Co. Again Attached," 1.

135. "Transfers," *Tobacco World*, 1 Dec. 1916, 31; "Transfers," *Tobacco World*, 1 Nov. 1916, 31.

136. Martín Travieso, Treasurer of Puerto Rico, 16 Aug. 1916, AGPR, Estado, Corporaciones foráneas con fines de lucro, caja 2, expediente 40; Governor of Porto Rico, "Annual Report, 1917," 3:77.

137. "Based on Good Tobacco," *Tobacco*, 27 June 1918, 18; *Trow New York*, 221.

138. Luis Muñoz Morales, "Compraventa de fábrica (escritura 26)," 10 de mayo, 1915, AGPR, Fondo: PN, Serie: Siglo XX, Pueblo: San Juan, Año: 1915, caja 763, fols. 127–40.

139. "A. J. Lachman to Retire from Business," *Tobacco World*, 1 May 1917, 23; "Cigars from Porto Rico," *Tobacco*, 25 June 1914, 32. The West Indies Cigar Company formally dissolved itself in 1920–1921. Refer to Governor of Porto Rico, *Annual Report, 1921*, 74.

140. G. W. Sheldon, who appears in table 3.1, was a shipping agent rather than a manufacturer, which, after 1910, occasionally exported small batches of cigars. "Cigars from Porto Rico," *Tobacco*, 7 July 1910, 31; "Imports of Cigars and Leaf Tobacco," *United States Tobacco Journal*, 6 Dec. 1919, 36–37; "Imports of Cigars and Leaf Tobacco," *United States Tobacco Journal*, 17 Apr. 1920, 32.

141. Cox, *Competition in the American Tobacco Industry*, 87–88. A tobacco man appraised PRATCO's share at 95 percent in the same year. Levi, "Start and Status," 1 Sept. 1921, 44.

142. Villar, Lanza y Compañía, "Certificado de disolución por consentimiento unánime de todos los accionistas," 10 Jan. 1924, AGPR, Estado, Corporaciones con fines de lucro, caja 41, expediente 559; "Bosch Bros. now in Wall Street office," *Tobacco Leaf*, 1 Aug. 1931, 5.

143. Bureau of Labor, *Sixth Annual Report, 1918*, 14.

CHAPTER FOUR. THE TOBACCO TRUST IN PUERTO RICO, 1899–1911

1. The census identifies four additional foremen employed in the tobacco farms living in the barrio. Bureau of the Census, Thirteenth Census: Porto Rico, vol. 15, Cayey, 1910, 346, UPR, Centro de Investigaciones Históricas.

2. Rafael B. Díaz, "Incidente en huelga de La Colectiva," 1917, AGPR, Policía, Novedades, Cayey, 19 June 1917, 227–28. Bullock and a number of workers striking the trust subsidiary had an incident along the Carretera Central.

3. Walter Austin Bullock and George Tarry Bullock letters, MSS 00188, Special Collections Research Center, North Carolina State University Libraries, Raleigh, NC.

4. Judith B. Nisbet to author, 3 Sept. 1998; Tilley, *Bright Tobacco Industry*, 184.

5. George returned to Puerto Rico during the twenties as assistant general manager of PRATCO before moving to the sugar industry. During the 1930s, both brothers worked for the Cuban Land and Leaf Tobacco Company, another ATC subsidiary. Refer to "Robert Gans Back from Porto Rico," *United States Tobacco Journal*, 29 Sept. 1923, 47, and "Guide to the Walter Austin Bullock," Walter Austin Bullock and George Tarry Bullock letters, MSS 00188, Special Collections Research Center, NC State University Libraries, Raleigh, NC.

6. Rucabado y Portela, "La Colectiva," 1899, AGPR, Colecciones Particulares, Junghanns, caja 27, expediente 1111.

7. George M. Gales, Declaración jurada de John B. Cobb, 10 May 1901, San Juan Judicial Center, Inactive Archive, Supreme Court, civil case 58, unnumbered pages in the original, but fols. 37–38 in the archive, document no. 3; J. M. Ceballos and Co., *Importers and Exporters Pictorial Guide*.

8. Carroll, *Report on the Island of Porto Rico*, 141; F. Hernández Cancel, "Cigarrillos del país desaparecen al cerrar última firma los hacía," *El Mundo*, 18 Feb. 1956, 8a.

9. Bureau of Corporations, "Porto Rican American Tobacco Company," 29 Aug. 1906, NARA, Washington, DC, FTC, Bureau of Corporations (Record Group 122), Stack 570, Row 7, Compartment 17, Shelf 1, Numerical File, 1903–14, box 237, file 3825-10-10, Report 385, 1. Cobb's saliency within the ATC was such that he was one of the twenty-nine defendants in the Supreme Court decision that finally ordered the dissolution of the firm in 1911. U.S. v. American Tobacco Company, *US Supreme Court Reports* 221 (1911): 189.

10. Gales, Declaración jurada; "Contrato entre Rucabado y Portela, Fausto Rucabado, José Portela y Porto Rican American Tobacco Company," 9 Oct. 1899, San Juan Judicial Center,

Inactive Archive, Supreme Court, civil case 58, unnumbered pages in the original, but fols. 13–16 in the archive, document "A"; Bureau of Corporations, *Position of the Tobacco Combination*, 82.

11. Iglesias de Pagán, *El obrerismo en Puerto Rico*, 57–58.

12. The Bureau of Corporations missed the purchase. "Immense and Continuous Development," *Tobacco*, 25 Dec. 1925, 41. Refer also to chapter 2.

13. Gales was active in the acquisition of the R. J. Reynolds Company in 1899 and by 1907 had joined the National Cigar Stands Company to, in time, preside over it. Bureau of Corporations, *Position of the Tobacco Combination*, 315; Tilley, *R. J. Reynolds Tobacco Company*, 100–101.

14. Durden, *Dukes of Durham*, 69.

15. Bureau of Corporations, *Position of the Tobacco Combination*, 119, 132–33; Bureau of Corporations, "Porto Rican American Tobacco Company."

16. Bureau of Corporations, "Porto Rican American Tobacco Company." For more details refer to chapter 2. "Toro Resigns as Head of Porto Rican-American Co.," *Tobacco Leaf*, 3 Oct. 1931, 3.

17. Turkish cigarettes increased notably only after the turn of the century. Tennant, *American Cigarette Industry*, 44–45.

18. "The New Line of Porto Rico Cigars," *Tobacco*, 12 Oct. 1900, 1. At the time, Becker had a pipes and smokers' articles business in New York that gave way to the presidency of the Manhattan Briar Pipe Company, a trust-owned enterprise. See Financial Directory Association, *Financial Red Book of America*, 206.

19. Bureau of Corporations, *Position of the Tobacco Combination*, 429.

20. These two firms operated steam-driven machinery to manufacture cigarettes. J. M. Ceballos and Co., *Importers and Exporters Pictorial Guide*; Bureau of Corporations, *Position of the Tobacco Combination*, 429.

21. Bureau of Corporations, "Porto Rican American Tobacco Company."

22. Bird Carmona, *Parejeros y desafiantes*, 91–93.

23. Bureau of Corporations, *Capitalization, Investment, and Earnings*, 16, 279, 303.

24. Bureau of Corporations, *Position of the Tobacco Combination*, 329.

25. Cox, "Growth and Ownership," 45; Cox, *Global Cigarette*, 66–77; Bureau of Corporations, *Position of the Tobacco Combination*, 180–93.

26. Concurrent with La Colectiva, the earliest large US investment in tobacco manufactures in the Caribbean was the Havana Commercial Company in 1899, which was an independent firm. The ATC was a latecomer in Cuban tobacco when, in 1902, it became the leading factor through the Havana Tobacco Company. For the ATC in Cuba, refer to Bureau of Corporations, *Position of the Tobacco Combination*, 159–61 and Baldrich, "Cigars and Cigarettes," 27–29.

27. Burns, "Outside Intervention," 53.

28. Bureau of Corporations, *Position of the Tobacco Combination*, 84–85, 150, 418–19.

29. "Cigar Making Firms Unite," *New York Times*, 16 June 1897, 12; Bureau of Corporations, *Position of the Tobacco Combination*, 150–51, 416.

30. For the different types of cigars see Werner, *Tobaccoland*, 243–46. Cooper, *Once a Cigar Maker*, 15–19; Bureau of Corporations, *Position of the Tobacco Combination*, 150.

31. Chandler, *Visible Hand*, 320.

32. Cox, *Competition in the American Tobacco Industry*, 87; Bureau of Corporations, *Position of the Tobacco Combination*, 156; Department of Agriculture, *Annual Book on Statistics*, 140, 142.

33. Industrial Company of Porto Rico, "Certificate of Incorporation," 8 Dec. 1903, AGPR, Estado, Corporaciones foráneas con fines de lucro, caja 5, expediente 88.

34. Industrial Company of Porto Rico, "Annual Report," 29 July 1907, AGPR, Estado, Corporaciones foráneas con fines de lucro, caja 5, expediente 88; Porto Rican American Tobacco

Company, "Informe anual," 1907, AGPR, Estado, Corporaciones foráneas con fines de lucro, caja 2, expediente 37.

35. Bureau of Corporations, *Position of the Tobacco Combination*, 429.

36. As one story goes, two German subjects, H. C. Fritze and Leopold Engelhardt, started in 1897 the business that became a New Jersey corporation by 1904. It claimed to be "completely independent of 'La Colectiva,'" which was PRATCO's popular name. See Macmillan, *West Indies*, 196.

37. "El Timonel," Colección Efraín Archilla Diez. The firm also manufactured cigarettes. For a similar situation see "Tobacco Trust Hides its Control," *New York Times*, 13 July 1907, 3.

38. "Gossiper's Notebook: At Their New," *Tobacco Leaf*, 6 May 1903, 3.

39. "The Demand for Porto Rico Cigars," *Tobacco*, 17 Jan. 1902, 4. See also "Current Comment," *Tobacco*, 7 Feb. 1902, 5.

40. Fiz Jiménez, *Bayamón y su gente*, 123; Bureau of Corporations, *Position of the Tobacco Combination*, 293.

41. Roberto H. Todd, "La antigua cárcel," *El Mundo*, 6 Aug. 1939, 12; Bureau of Corporations, "Porto Rican American Tobacco Company."

42. Bird Carmona, *Parejeros y Desafiantes*.

43. Governor of Porto Rico, *Annual Report, 1907*, 27.

44. Blanco Fernández, *España y Puerto Rico*, 310; Corrada del Río, "Historical-Geographical Development," 77; Moody, *Moodys Analyses of Investments* (1917), 1146.

45. "Las grandes industrias de Puerto Rico," *Puerto Rico Ilustrado*, 9 Mar. 1912.

46. "Porto Ricans at Flat Iron Store," *Tobacco*, 9 Oct. 1913, 11; Bureau of Corporations, *Position of the Tobacco Combination*, 312–14.

47. While the firm was nominally independent, it was heavily indebted to the trust. Its manager, George M. Gales, had been on the payroll for years and had been a director of PRATCO. Bureau of Corporations, *Position of the Tobacco Combination*, 315–16.

48. Gage, *American Tobacco Types*, 73–74.

49. J. R. K., "Holland and Her Tobacco Inscriptions," *Tobacco World*, 15 July 1910, 18–19.

50. Mack, *Cigar Manufacturing Industry*, 19; Whitney, *Tobacco Soils*, 11.

51. Akehurst, *Tobacco*, 269.

52. Mulder, *Cultivation of Tobacco*, 36.

53. Fernández Prieto, *Cuba agrícola*, 227–48.

54. E. A. Schroeder, "The Origin of Shade-Grown Tobacco," *Tobacco World*, 15 Jan. 1902, 16; "How Florida Tobacco Has Become a Factor," *Tobacco World*, 1 Feb. 1905, 3.

55. Stubbs, "El Habano," 50; "Tobacco in Connecticut," *New York Times*, 23 Mar. 1902, 9.

56. Bureau of Corporations, *Position of the Tobacco Combination*, 150–51; Schroeder, "Origin of Shade-Grown Tobacco," 16. These firms and a third one merged in 1902 to form the United Cigar Manufacturers Company. Refer to Chas. D. Barney & Co., *Tobacco Industry*, 1:66.

57. American Cultivator, "Eastern Tobacco Reports, Connecticut Valley," *Tobacco World*, 12 Mar. 1902, 27; "Blame Government for Losses on Shade-Grown," *Tobacco World*, 25 Jan. 1905, 30.

58. The Straiton and Storm firm owned the Owl Commercial Company, which was also known as the Owl Cigar Company. Hain, *Confederate Chronicle*, 214; Schroeder, "Origin of Shade-Grown Tobacco," 16. In 1897, Straiton and Storm merged into Kerbs, Wertheim & Schiffer, and Straiton & Storm Company. Refer to "Cigar Making Firms Unite," 12.

59. Bureau of Corporations, *Position of the Tobacco Combination*, 298, 301.

60. La Plata River gives its name to the narrow valley that lies in its path as it meanders through Cayey, Cidra, and Aibonito. Rafael María González to Chief of the Department of Agriculture, translated by Almont Barnes, 29 June 1901, NARA, Washington, DC, FTC, Bureau of Corporations (Record Group 122), Stack 570, Numerical File, 1903–14, box 304, file 4707/48.

61. J. H. McPike, "Porto Rico as Seen by a Cigar Jobber II: Porto Rico Tobacco," *Tobacco*, 4 Apr. 1902, 1. The experimental harvest had yet to be cured, stemmed, and fermented to establish its aroma and combustibility. González went on to manage plantations for PRLTC from 1902 to 1908. See also "New Cigar Factory in Santurce," *Tobacco*, 25 Dec. 1925, 41.

62. van Leenhoff, "Tobacco Investigations," 17.

63. J. van Leenhoff Jr., "Possibilities of Porto Rico Tobacco," *Tobacco World*, 6 Sept. 1905, 29.

64. *Sketches: Porto Rico.*

65. Garner, *Production of Tobacco*, 151; Mulder, *Cultivation of Tobacco*, 29; Tennant, *American Cigarette Industry*, 180.

66. *Sketches: Porto Rico.*

67. "Cayey-Caguas Co. Gets Good Order," *Tobacco*, 6 June 1907, 7; Luis Muñoz Morales, "Siembra de tabaco con refacción y garantía (escritura 61)," 1913, AGPR, PN, Siglo XX, San Juan, 1913, caja 760, fol. 540. Mendoza owned or rented 2,311 acres of farmland in 1917. Refer to US Congress, Senate, "Real Estate in Excess of 500 Acres Used for Agricultural Purposes in Porto Rico," 1918, 65th Congress, 2d session, 1918, Senate Document 165, 24–25.

68. Bureau of Corporations, *Position of the Tobacco Combination*, 155, 217; Bureau of Corporations, "Porto Rican American Tobacco Company."

69. Bureau of Corporations, "Porto Rican Leaf Tobacco Corporation [*sic*]," 29 Aug. 1906, NARA, Washington, DC, FTC, Bureau of Corporations (Record Group 122), Stack 570, Row 7, Compartment 17, Shelf 1, Numerical File, 1903–14, box 237, file 3825-10-10, Report 388.

70. US Congress, Senate, "Real Estate in Excess of 500 Acres," 40–45, 47. See also chapter 2.

71. "Sobrinos de Ezquiaga v. Munítiz," *Decisiones de Puerto Rico* 8 (1905): 429–38.

72. AGPR, Hacienda, Registro de Tasación de la Propiedad, 1920–1921, Cayey, receipts 657 to 662.

73. Bureau of Corporations, *Position of the Tobacco Combination*, 298–99.

74. Porto Rican Leaf Tobacco Co., "Annual Report," 30 July 1907, AGPR, Estado, Corporaciones foráneas con fines de lucro, caja 3, expediente 65; Bureau of Corporations, "Porto Rican Leaf Tobacco Corporation [*sic*]."

75. Carrasquillo, *Our Landless Patria*; Solá, "Colonialism, Planters, Sugarcane," 349–72. Solá kindly forwarded the author the reference to Herminio Díaz Navarro, "Escritura de venta de la hacienda 'Santa Catalina,' otorgada por Don Francisco Ramis y Borrás á favor de Mr. J. B. Cobb," 27 Aug. 1907, AGPR, PN, Siglo XX, San Juan, 1906, caja 289, fol. 1372.

76. AGPR, Hacienda, Registro de Tasación de la Propiedad, 1910–1911, Cayey, receipt 1188; Bureau of the Census, "Thirteenth Census: Porto Rico," vol. 15, barrio Toíta, Cayey, 1910, 329, lines 24–26, Centro de Investigaciones Históricas, UPR.

77. It was a common trust practice to have all four subsidiaries, which included American Cigar, with operations in Puerto Rico buy farmland. AGPR, Hacienda, Registro de Tasación de la Propiedad, 1920–1921, Cayey, receipt 2156; Luis Muñoz Morales, "Compraventa (escritura 63)," 8 July 1911, AGPR, PN, Siglo XX, San Juan, 1911, caja 756, fols. 472–76.

78. Meléndez Muñoz, "Desarrollo del crédito," 3:314–22.

79. Luis Muñoz Morales, "Siembra de tabaco y refacción (escritura 89)," 1 Oct. 1910, AGPR, PN, Siglo XX, San Juan, 1910, caja 755, fols. 228–39.

80. See his "La crisis tabacalera IV. Otras causas de su origen," *El Mundo*, 18 July 1931, 6.

81. Kerr-Ritchie, *Freedpeople in the Tobacco South*, 160–61; Prince and Simpson, *Long Green*, 39–40; Schwartz, *Radical Protest*, 34–35.

82. Bonnin, "Los contratos de refacción," 123–50.

83. Gage, *Tobacco Industry in Puerto Rico*, 23–29.

84. Fiz Jiménez, *Bayamón y su gente*, 124.

85. Torres Rosario, *Juana Colón*, 17; Governor of Porto Rico, *Annual Report, 1907*, 317.

86. Bureau of the Census, *Electrical Industries of Porto Rico*, 21–22.

87. Corrada del Río, "Historical-Geographical Development," 77.

88. Governor of Porto Rico, *Annual Report, 1907*, 317.

89. Porto Rican Leaf Tobacco Company, "Consejo Ejecutivo de Puerto Rico," May 1906, AGPR, Fortaleza, caja 233, expediente 4328.

90. Bureau of the Census, *Electrical Industries of Porto Rico*, 26.

91. Marchildon, *Profits and Politics*, 58–61, 92–96; Santamaría García, "Los ferrocarriles de servico público," 218–19.

92. "Organization Needed in Porto Rico," *Tobacco*, 9 Aug. 1906, 6; "Trust Defeat in Porto Rico," *Tobacco*, 2 Aug. 1906, 1; Marchildon, *Profits and Politics*, 60–61.

93. "Tobacco Trust Secrets under Secret Inquiry," *New York Times*, 6 May 1905, 1.

94. "Federal Jury Indicts Tobacco Trust Men," *New York Times*, 19 June 1906, 16.

95. "Tobacco Trust Trial Begins," *New York Times*, 19 Dec. 1906, 1; "War on Trusts Will Open To-day," *New York Times*, 10 July 1907, 1.

96. U.S. v. American Tobacco Company, 107–8.

97. United States v. American Tobacco Co. et al., *Federal Reporter* 191 (2d Cir. 1911): 421–22, 424, 429.

98. Computed from Cox, *Competition in the American Tobacco Industry*, 87; Department of Agriculture, *Annual Book on Statistics*, 140, 142; and Bureau of the Census, *Historical Statistics of the United States*, 2:690.

99. Since most US cigar manufacturing statistics did not identify production from Philippine or Puerto Rican firms, the ranking is an interpolation of PRATCO's statistics with those of US-based manufacturers as presented in Baer, *Economic Development*, 257.

100. "Toro and Davis," *Tobacco Leaf*, 19 May 1921, 3; *Moodys Manual of Railroads and Corporation Securities*, vol. 2 "Industrial Section," 1294.

101. "Manifestación del Señor Toro," *La Correspondencia*, 23 Mar. 1914, 1; "Información general," *La Correspondencia*, 1 June 1914, 8.

102. *Moodys Manual of Railroads and Corporation Securities*, vol. 2 "K to Z," 279.

CHAPTER FIVE. "SAILING CLOSE TO THE WIND": THE PORTO RICAN-AMERICAN TOBACCO COMPANY, 1912–1939

1. This New York firm was the forerunner of the United Cigar Manufacturers Company and later the General Cigar Company. "Cigar Making Firms Unite," *New York Times*, 16 June 1897, 12; González del Valle, *Memorándum presentado*, 50–51, 64–67.

2. Bird Carmona, *Parejeros y desafiantes*; Cooper, *Once a Cigar Maker*; Stubbs, *Tobacco on the Periphery*.

3. Cooper, *Once a Cigar Maker*, 166, 256.

4. "Cigars from Porto Rico," *Tobacco*, 29 Sept. 1910, 31; Acting Treasurer of Porto Rico to Henry Winkelmann, 25 Feb. 1916, NARA, Washington, DC, Records of the Bureau of Insular Affairs (Record Group 350), Stack 150, Row 56, Compartment 78, Shelf 1, I3/5B General Classified Index, File 948–37, box 190; "Información de la Isla," *La Correspondencia*, 7 Mar. 1914, 6; "Los últimos sucesos en la Isla," *La Correspondencia*, 7 Apr. 1914, 3; *La Correspondencia*, 13 Apr. 1914, 6.

5. "Manifestación del Señor Toro," *La Correspondencia*, 23 Mar. 1914, 1; "Información general," *La Correspondencia*, 1 June 1914, 8.

6. "A. J. Lachman to Retire from Business," *Tobacco World*, 1 May 1917, 23; "The Continual Development of the Porto Rican American Tobacco Co.," *Tobacco*, 27 June 1918, 40; Picó, *Los gallos peleados*, 118.

7. Baldrich, "Gender and the Decomposition of the Cigar-Making Craft," 105–25.

8. Cox, *Competition in the American Tobacco Industry*, 49–51; Mack, *Cigar Manufacturing Industry*, 52–53.

9. Diffie and Diffie, *Porto Rico*, 96.

10. Cox, *Competition in the American Tobacco Industry*, 91.

11. Evans, *Effects of Mechanization*, 11.

12. Chandler, *Visible Hand*, 297–98.

13. Bureau of Corporations, *Prices, Costs, and Profits*, 2; Baer, *Economic Development*, 258.

14. Roy, *Socializing Capital*, 235.

15. Baer, *Economic Development*, 257–58.

16. Cox, *Competition in the American Tobacco Industry*, 57; Luis Muñoz Morales, "Compraventa de fábrica (escritura 26)," 10 May 1915, AGPR, PN, Siglo XX, San Juan, 1915, caja 763, fols. 127–40.

17. Computed from Baer, *Economic Development*, 258; Cox, *Competition in the American Tobacco Industry*, 87; and Bureau of the Census, *Historical Statistics of the United States*, 2:690. Technically speaking, PRATCO was the fifth-largest US manufacturer with a 4.7 percent market share in 1930 if its ranking and market share include the Congress Cigar Company, a controlled company. Waitt and Bond, another controlled firm, is excluded for lack of data.

18. "Cigars from Porto Rico," *Tobacco*, 7 Oct. 1920, 16.

19. Moody, *Moodys Analyses of Investments*, Public Utilities and Industrials (New York: Moody Investors Service, 1919), 2:1038; *Moodys Manual of Railroads and Corporation Securities*, Industrial Section, 3:1294; "New Cigar Firm Well under Way," *Tobacco Leaf*, 12 May 1921, 3; Industrial Company of Porto Rico, "Annual Report," 1903 to 1917, AGPR, Estado, Corporaciones foráneas con fines de lucro, caja 5, expediente 88.

20. Porto Rican–American Tobacco Company, *Annual Report, 1919* (Jersey City, NJ, 1920).

21. "Toro and Davis," *Tobacco Leaf*, 19 May 1921, 3.

22. *Fitch Bond Book*, 1196.

23. "From Small Business Porto Rican–American Has Had Notable Rise," *United States Tobacco Journal*, 31 May 1924, 194.

24. "Leaf Market Jottings," *Tobacco World*, 1 June 1921, 20–21.

25. "Fred Davis Resigns as Vice-President of P. R. American," *United States Tobacco Journal*, 19 July 1924, 3.

26. Percival R. Lowe Inc., "Leaf Tobacco Brokers," *United States Tobacco Journal*, 31 May 1924, 143. Lowe also brokered purchases for PRATCO, American Cigar Company, General Cigar Company, and other large manufacturers. "Present a Box of United Cigars," *Evening World*, 23 Dec. 1921, 13.

27. "Strike Brings Bankruptcy Proceedings," *Tobacco World*, 1 Dec. 1921, 8.

28. Long, "Open-Closed Shop Battle," 119–20; Veritas, "Tampa," *Tobacco World*, 15 Mar. 1922, 22; Veritas, "Tampa," *Tobacco World*, 1 Apr. 1922, 18.

29. "Strike Brings Bankruptcy Proceedings," 8.

30. Luis Toro appointed Pendás, in April 1921, as the official in charge of cigar production in Puerto Rico. Soon after, in June 1921, he was in the employ of New York–Tampa Cigar Company. Harwood Hull, "Toro Announces Open Shop Policy," *Tobacco Leaf*, 21 Apr. 1921, 4; "Pendas Joins N. Y.–Tampa Cigar Co.," *Tobacco Leaf*, 23 June 1921, 3.

31. Porto Rican–American Tobacco Company, "Informe anual," 1923, AGPR, Estado, Corporaciones domésticas con fines de lucro, caja 30, expediente 363.

32. "Fred Davis Resigns as Vice-President," 3.

33. "N.Y. & Tampa Cigar Company Bought by Leon Schwab and Fred Davis," *Tobacco World*, 1 Mar. 1925, 8; "Porto Rican–American Issues $8,000,000 Bonds," *Tobacco World*, 15 Jan. 1927, 5.

34. John Frese, "Testimony," Filed 14 Aug. 1928, Porto Rican American Tobacco Co. v. American Tobacco Company, NARA, New York, Records of the Department of Justice, (Record Group 276), US Court of Appeals for the Second Circuit, case file 10127, 1929, box 3240.

35. Bird Carmona, *Parejeros y desafiantes*, 91–93; Nathaniel F. Pasarell, "Testimony," Filed 14 Aug. 1928, Porto Rican American Tobacco Co. v. American Tobacco Company, NARA, New York, Records of the Department of Justice, (Record Group 276), US Court of Appeals for the Second Circuit, case file 10127, [1929?], box 3240, 384.

36. Tilley, *R. J. Reynolds Tobacco Company*, 210–11; Cox, *Competition in the American Tobacco Industry*, 33–34, 41.

37. Muñoz Morales, "Compraventa de fábrica," fols. 127–40; "Only Cigarette Factory in Porto Rico Purchased," *Tobacco World*, 1 June 1915, 32.

38. The Universal Leaf gained, in 1916, a 45 percent participation in the firm. FTC, *Report of the Federal Trade Commission on the Tobacco Industry*, 53–54.

39. Pasarell, "Testimony," 384; Duke and Jordan, *Tobacco Merchant*, 54.

40. PRATCO's market loss was so closely associated with increasing imports that the Pearson correlation coefficient reaches -0.907 for the seventeen years spanning from 1924 to 1940, with data on both variables. PRATCO's data in figure 5.2 includes manufactures for both the local market and for export. Exports, however, constituted a small portion of manufacture that ranged from less than 1 percent, in years like 1920 and 1923, to just more than 9 percent in 1939.

41. "Porto Rican American Tobacco Co. of Porto Rico v. American Tobacco Co.," *Federal Reporter*, 2d series 30 (2d Cir. 1929): 237.

42. "American Tobacco Price War Enjoined," *New York Times*, 11 Feb. 1928, 36.

43. "Porto Rican American Tobacco Co. v. American Tobacco Co.," 235.

44. J. D. Woodward, "Testimony," Filed 14 Aug. 1928, Porto Rican American Tobacco Co. v. American Tobacco Company, NARA, New York, Records of the Department of Justice (Record Group 276), US Court of Appeals for the Second Circuit, case file 10127, box 3240, 259; "Porto Rican American Tobacco Co. v. American Tobacco Co.," 237.

45. "American Tobacco Price War Enjoined," 36.

46. "Porto Rican American Tobacco Co. v. American Tobacco Co.," 237.

47. Luis Toro testified that the cigarette division had yearly profits of some $200,000, which turned into losses of $20,000 to $25,000 a month once the price war began. Luis Toro, "Testimony," filed 14 Aug. 1928, Porto Rican American Tobacco Co. v. American Tobacco Company, NARA, New York, Records of the Department of Justice, (Record Group 276), US Court of Appeals for the Second Circuit, case file 10127, box 3240, 186; "Sues Over Cigarette War, Porto Rican Concern Asks $900,000 from American Tobacco," *New York Times*, 24 June 1928, 18; "Porto Rican American Tobacco Co. v. American Tobacco Co.," 236.

48. "Sues Tobacco Company, Porto Rican Concern Says Lucky Strikes Sell There for 12 Cents," *New York Times*, 21 Sept. 1927, 4; "Court Refuses Injunction against American Tobacco Company," *Tobacco World*, 1 Nov. 1927, 4.

49. "A. T. Co. Appeals from P. R. Injunction," *Tobacco World*, 1 May 1929, 10; "American Tobacco Price War Enjoined,"36.

50. "Porto Rican American Tobacco Co. v. American Tobacco Co."

51. "A. T. Co. Appeals from P. R. Injunction," *Tobacco World*, 1 May 1929, 10; "Porto Rican American Tobacco Co. v. American Tobacco Co."

52. "Sues over Cigarette War," 18.

53. American Tobacco Co., "Fiscal Statement," 31 Dec. 1932, 508, Bates: ATX01 0282372-ATX01 0283082, accessed 20 Dec. 2018, http://tobaccodocuments.org/atc/1433024.html. PRATCO, however, disclosed a different sum, amounting to $392,251, to the FTC. FTC, *Investigation of Concentration of Economic Power*, 17716.

54. Flue-cured bright leaf cigarettes, blended with artificially sweetened burley, burn with a smoke that is slightly acidic and not alkaline, as that of other tobacco products. The reversal of the pH balance allows the consumer of the blended cigarette to inhale smoke into the lungs, which speeds and increases the absorption of nicotine into the bloodstream. This cigarette is powerfully addictive, more so than other types of tobacco consumption, and herein lies a fundamental reason for its extensive diffusion and the eclipse of other tobacco products. Refer to Brandt, *Cigarette Century*, 24; Proctor, *Golden Holocaust*, 33.

55. Luis Muñoz Morales, "Compraventa (escritura 53)," 25 June 1915, AGPR, PN, Siglo XX, San Juan, 1915, caja 763 fols. 255–60.

56. US Congress, Senate, "Real Estate in Excess of 500 Acres Used for Agricultural Purposes in Porto Rico," 1918, 65th Congress, 2d session, 1918, Senate Document 165, 47.

57. Frese, "El cultivo de tabaco," 576–77.

58. Gage, *Tobacco Industry in Puerto Rico*, 18.

59. Carlos Nieves Rivera, "¿Por qué la Isla no produce un tabaco propio para capa?," *El Mundo*, 14 Aug. 1949, 23.

60. Nolla, "Primer informe anual," 27.

61. J. D. Stubbe, "La situación tabacalera en Puerto Rico," *El Agricultor Puertorriqueño*, 15 Feb. 1928, 30.

62. American Tobacco Co., "Fiscal Statement," 31 Dec. 1932, 425.

63. The Cuban Land and Leaf Tobacco Company planted both shade- and sun-grown tobacco for wrapper and filler respectively. Nelson, *Rural Cuba*, 131–32.

64. Neither Luis Toro nor any PRATCO official bore any relation to the new firm. Manuel Domenech to C. Gallardo, Secretario Ejecutivo de Puerto Rico, 3 Oct. 1934, AGPR, Estado, Corporaciones foráneas con fines de lucro, caja 3, expediente 65.

65. At the onset of the Great Depression, the ATC embarked on the reorganization of its leaf-procurement departments and subsidiaries with the stated purpose of saving on operation costs. Absorbing the American Cigar Company in 1931, the ATC then established American Suppliers as a companywide procurement subsidiary for both cigar and cigarette leaf. "American Tobacco to Merge Cigar Unit," *New York Times*, 26 Feb. 1932, 27; Tennant, *American Cigarette Industry*, 327.

66. Chapter 6 briefly identifies the movement that I discuss fully in *Sembraron la no siembra*.

67. AGPR, Policía, Novedades, Cayey, 20 Aug. 1931, 193. AGPR, Policía, Novedades, Cidra 24 Aug. 1931, 80; 25 Aug. 1931, 81.

68. AGPR, Policía, Novedades, Cayey, 13 Oct. 1931, 121; 15 Oct. 1931, 135; 16 Oct. 1931, 143–44; *El Mundo*, 15 Oct. 1931, 3; 16 Oct. 1931, 1, 6.

69. AGPR, Policía, Querellas, Cidra (fuego), 13 Oct. 1931, caja 18; 13 Oct. 1931, caja 15, expediente 18037; AGPR, Policía, Novedades Cidra, 20 Oct. 1931, 182, 183.

70. AGPR, Policía, Querellas Cidra (fuego), 12 Dec. 1931, caja 18.

71. Cámara de Comercio de Puerto Rico, "Tobacco Culture," *Boletín Oficial* 10, no. 6 (1934): 63.

72. Porto Rican Leaf Tobacco Company, "Planilla de contribuciones," 1934–1935, AGPR, Hacienda, Planillas de Corporaciones, 1934–1935, tomo 5, planilla 263.

73. Descartes, "Land Reform," 404; Picó, "Land Tenure," 143.

74. "Tobacco Products Corp. to Take over Porto Rican American, Reports State," *United States Tobacco Journal*, 10 Mar. 1923, 3; Cox, *Competition*, 334.

75. Porto Rican–American Tobacco Company, *Annual Report*, 1917–1919 (Jersey City: n.p., 1918–1920); FTC, *Investigation of Concentration of Economic Power*, 17714–17715.

76. "Porto Rican–American Issues $8,000,000 Bonds," 5; Sally Bedell Smith gave the selling price at 13,750,000. Refer to Smith, *In All His Glory*, 631.

77. Department of Agriculture, *Annual Book on Statistics of Puerto Rico*, 142; "Porto Rican–American Issues $8,000,000 Bonds," 5.

78. Congress Cigar Co., "Annual Report," 1932, AGPR, Estado, Corporaciones foráneas con fines de lucro, caja 33, expediente 385; "Paleys Retire from Congress Co.; Jas. M. Porter Elected President," *Tobacco Leaf*, 4 July 1931, 3, 7.

79. Mack, *Cigar Manufacturing Industry*, 71.

80. US Congress, Senate, Stock Exchange Practices. *Hearings before the Committee on Banking and Currency [Pecora Hearings]*, 23–25 May, 1933, 73rd Cong., 1st sess., 1933, 260.

81. "Blackstone Transfer Now Completed," *Tobacco World*, 1 Aug. 1929, 12.

82. Joseph Henry Melhado, "Readjustment in the Cigar Industry: Machine Manufacture, Extensive Advertising, and Concentration of Brands Eliminate Weak Units," *Barron's*, 20 July 1931, 18; Mack, *Cigar Manufacturing Industry*, 70.

83. Porto Rican–American Tobacco Company, *Annual Report, 1931* (Jersey City: n.p., 1932).

84. Joseph Henry Melhado, "The Prospects for Tobacco Companies," *Barron's*, 11 Apr. 1932, 11.

85. "Porto Rican American Tobacco—Consolidation with Congress Cigar Will Save $1,000,000—How Earnings Figure Out on Stock," *Barron's*, 17 Jan. 1927, 12.

86. "La Palina Gets Leaf Department; Absorbs Max Gans' Sons," *United States Tobacco Journal*, 23 Aug. 1924, 3.

87. C. Matos Colón, "Declaradas en huelga ayer en Bayamón trabajadoras," *La Correspondencia*, 23 June 1936, 1.

88. "Philip M. Forristall to Head La Palina Sales Department," *Tobacco Leaf*, 12 Dec. 1931, 5.

89. "Congress New York Branch Distributes 'El Toro' and 'Blackstone,'" *Tobacco World*, 1 Oct. 1931, 10; "Klauber-Wangenheim Take on 'El Toro,'" *Tobacco World*, 1 Mar. 1931, 6.

90. Cox, *Competition in the American Tobacco Industry*, 352, 357.

91. "Ricoro Cigars," 11; "United Cigar Sale Carries Control," *New York Times*, 26 Oct. 1935, 23.

92. "Luis Toro in Porto Rico," *Tobacco World*, 15 May 1931, 16.

93. "Ricoro," *Harvard Illustrated Magazine*, 28 Feb. 1918, 4; "Porto Ricans at Flat Iron Store," *Tobacco*, 9 Oct. 1913, 11.

94. "El Toro Cigar Well Represented," *Tobacco Leaf*, 5 Sept. 1931, 12; "P. R. American Launches Ad Campaign," *Tobacco World*, 1 Apr. 1931, 3; "Trade Notes," *Tobacco World*, 15 July 1932, 6.

95. El Toro faced stiff competition in the inexpensive cigar category that was one of the few expanding cigar categories at the time. Melhado, "Prospects for Tobacco Companies," 11.

96. "Porto Rican American Tobacco Lost $238,200 before Inventory Depreciation of $189,729," *Barron's*, 11 Apr. 1932, 15; "Bonds Inviting," *Barron's*, 29 July 1935, 14.

97. FTC, *Investigation of Concentration of Economic Power*, 17717.

98. The correlation between net sales and year is -0.916 between 1920 and 1937. Using a lower base year, PRATCO suffered an 82.5 percent decline between 1921 and 1937. Bureau of the Census, *Historical Statistics of the United States*, 2:689–90.

99. Porto Rican–American Tobacco Company, *Annual Report* (Jersey City: n.p., 1917–1938).

100. Differences within the management of the combination never went public.

101. "Paleys Retire from Congress Co.," 3.

102. "Toro Resigns as Head of Porto Rican-American Co.," *Tobacco Leaf*, 3 Oct. 1931, 3.

103. Porto Rican American Tobacco Company, "Annual Report," 1932, AGPR, Estado, Corporaciones foráneas con fines de lucro, caja 36, expediente 423; Congress Cigar Co., "Annual

Report," 1932, AGPR, Estado, Corporaciones foráneas con fines de lucro, caja 33, expediente 385; "Blackstone Transfer Now Completed," 12.

104. "'La Colectiva' en proceso de traslado a los Estados Unidos," *El Mundo*, 10 Aug. 1937, 1.

105. "El embarque de máquinas de la 'La Colectiva,'" *El Mundo*, 15 Sept. 1937, 1. Notwithstanding, a New York spokesman held that an increase in local taxes was responsible for the situation. Refer to "Taxes Shift Cigar Plant: But Porto Rican American Co. Will Continue to Buy Tobacco," *New York Times*, 17 Sept, 1937, 3.

106. "'La Colectiva' casi totalmente paralizada," *El Mundo*, 13 Sept. 1937, 1, 5; "'La Colectiva' continúa embarcando máquinas," *El Mundo*, 24 Sept. 1937, 4. The mechanization of cigar making had decimated the ranks of hand rollers.

107. "'La Colectiva' casi totalmente paralizada," 1, 5; "El embarque de máquinas de la 'La Colectiva,'" 1.

108. "Porto Rican American Tobacco Co. v. City Bank Farmers Trust Co. et al.," *Federal Reporter D.* 1 (S. D. NY 1939): 20–22.

109. "Waitt & Bond Quits Tobacco Combination at Request of Two Associated Concerns," *New York Times*, 10 Mar. 1938, 29.

110. "In re Porto Rican American Tobacco Co. v. Brown v. Rican Corporation et al.," *Federal Reporter*, 2d series 117 (2d. Cir. 1941): 599.

111. "In re Porto Rican American Tobacco Co. Porto Rican American Tobacco Co. [*sic*] v. Glidden et al.," *Federal Reporter*, 2d series 117 (2d Cir. 1940): 655–57. The firm left a thin paper trail. Gordon Auchincloss, the court-appointed trustee, became its president from 1940 to 1943. "Obituary Record of Graduates of Yale University Deceased during the Year," *Bulletin of Yale University* 40, no. 1 (1944): 98–99.

CHAPTER SIX. TOBACCO LEAF DEALERS, STEMMERS, AND MERCHANTS AFTER THE INVASION

1. Baldrich, "Tobacco Leaf Dealers," 1–11.

2. Baldrich, "Tobacco Leaf Dealers," 7.

3. "Movimiento de buques," *Boletín Mercantil*, 31 Jan. 1892, 3.

4. "Movimiento de buques," *Boletín Mercantil*, 8 Apr. 1899, 2; "Cigars from Porto Rico," *Tobacco*, 21 Feb. 1902, 7.

5. "Porto Rico Cigars," *Tobacco*, 7 Sept. 1900, 29; "Genuine Porto Rican Cigars," *Tobacco*, 8 Mar. 1901, 3.

6. Morris J. Levi, "The Start and Status of Porto Rico Leaf Tobacco in the United States," *Tobacco Leaf*, 25 Aug. 1921, 15.

7. Levi, "Start and Status," 25 Aug. 1921, 15.

8. AWITCO, "Certificate of Incorporation," 9 Sept. 1898, AGPR, Estado, Corporaciones foráneas con fines de lucro, caja 2, expediente 40; AWITCO, "Verified Statement," 7 Aug. 1901, AGPR, Estado, Corporaciones foráneas con fines de lucro, caja 2, expediente 40.

9. US Congress, House, *Importers of Goods from Porto Rico*, 56th Cong., 1st sess., H. Doc. 589 (Washington, DC: GPO, 1900) incorrectly identified Levi Blumenstiel as Levi Blumenthal in some shipments. For the mistake, compare "Tobacco Partners Disagree," *New York Times*, 8 Apr. 1908, 10 and "Levi, Blumenthal & Co. Ask Extension," *New York Times*, 10 Aug. 1908, 3.

10. "Sumatra by the Rotterdam," *Tobacco World*, 11 June 1902, 20; US Congress, House, *Importers of Goods*, 4; "Cigars from Porto Rico," *Tobacco*, 2 May 1902, 6.

11. "Foraker Act (Organic Act of 1900)," *US Statutes at Large* 31 (12 Apr. 1900): 77–78.

12. White, "Allie Lewis Sylvester," 15:111. In 1907, Allie partnered with Maximilian Stern and renamed the firm Sylvester and Stern. "Lewis Sylvester & Son Becomes Sylvester & Stern," *United States Tobacco Journal*, 2 Mar. 1907, 6.

13. Porto Rican Leaf Tobacco Co., "Annual Report," 1912–1928, AGPR, Estado, Corporaciones foráneas con fines de lucro, caja 3, expediente 65; White, "Allie Lewis Sylvester," 15:111.

14. Krout, *United States Directory*, 137–38.

15. "Some Fine Old Porto Rico Comes to Light," *Tobacco Leaf*, 26 May 1921, 9.

16. Krout, *United States Directory*, 138.

17. Levi, "Start and Status," 25 Aug. 1921, 11, 44.

18. "Tobacco Partners Disagree," 10.

19. "Tobacco Partners Disagree," 10.

20. "Experts from Havana in Porto Rico," *Tobacco*, 5 Apr. 1906, 5.

21. "Morris J. Levi to Head New House," *Tobacco*, 5 June 1913, 7.

22. Levi, "Start and Status," 25 Aug. 1921, 43. Exports of stemmed leaf ranged from a minimum of 57.4 percent of all unmanufactured tobacco in 1924 to a maximum of 80.9 percent in 1923 for data that ranged from 1923 to 1936. Refer to Gage, *Tobacco Industry in Puerto Rico*, 39. Unfortunately, earlier statistics are not available.

23. "H. Duys & Co. Enter Porto Rico trade," *United States Tobacco Journal*, 23 Aug. 1919, 6; "Handsome New Headquarters in New York Mark 20th year of H. Duys & Co's Notable Success," *United States Tobacco Journal*, 17 Apr. 1920, 6–7.

24. Frese, "El cultivo de tabaco," 576.

25. *Tobacco World*, 15 Apr. 1918, 10.

26. "L. F. Theyskens in New Export Firm," *Tobacco World*, 15 Mar. 1922, 22; "Theyskens & Shaw," *United States Tobacco Journal*, 12 July 1924, 18.

27. US Congress, Senate, "Real Estate in Excess of 500 Acres Used for Agricultural Purposes in Porto Rico," 1918, 65th Congress, 2d session, 1918, Senate Document 165, 2–3.

28. AGPR, Hacienda, Registro de Tasación de la Propiedad, 1920–1921, Cayey, receipts 127–31.

29. "R. A. Echevarria in Porto Rico for Firm," *United States Tobacco Journal*, 21 July 1923, 7; US Department of Labor, Immigration Service, "List or Manifest of Alien Passengers for the United States Immigration Officer, S. S. San Lorenzo, Sailing from San Juan, PR," 2–6 Aug. 1923, Ellis Island Passenger Search database.

30. "Hurto de la nómina de Aragunde y Co.," 17 July 1920, AGPR, Policía, Novedades, Pueblo de Cayey, 17 July 1920, 156–57, 158 and 21 July 1920, 171.

31. "Theyskens & Shaw, Inc.," *Tobacco*, 25 Dec. 1925, 44; US Department of Labor, Immigration Service, "List or Manifest of Alien Passengers for the United States Immigration Officer, S. S. Brazos, Sailing from San Juan, PR," 12–17 Feb. 1919, Ellis Island Passenger Search database.

32. Independent Tobacco Growers Corporation, "Certificado de disolución por consentimiento," 20 Apr. 1926, AGPR, Estado, Corporaciones con fines de lucro, caja 38, expediente 506; Independent Tobacco Growers Corporation, "Artículos de incoporación," 14 Apr. 1921, AGPR, Estado, Corporaciones con fines de lucro, caja 38, expediente 506. This was another short-term company, established in 1921 and dissolved in 1926.

33. US Department of Labor, Immigration Service, "List or Manifest of Alien Passengers for the United States Immigration Officer, S. S. Carolina, Sailing from San Juan, PR," 7 to 11 Feb. 1924, Ellis Island Passenger Search database; "Durlach Bros. win," *New England Tobacco Grower*, Apr. 1905, 11.

34. Bureau of the Census, "Population Census Schedules," 16–17 Jan. 1920, Cayey, Puerto Rico, citing sheets 11B and 12A, NARA microfilm publication T625 (Washington, DC: NARA, n.d.), FHL microfilm 1,822,051.

35. AGPR, Hacienda, Registro de Tasación de la Propiedad, 1910–1911, Cayey, receipts 7–8 and 1920–1921, Cayey, receipt 29.

36. US Bureau of the Census, "Population Census Schedules," 22–23 Jan. 1920, Cayey, Puerto Rico, citing sheets 27B, NARA microfilm publication T625 (Washington, DC: NARA, n.d.), FHL microfilm 1,822,051.

37. AGPR, Hacienda, Registro de Tasación de la Propiedad, 1920–1921, Cayey, receipts 1723–1729.

38. In consonance with Rivera's lack of warehouses, the police reported (albeit in 1926) two tobacco leaf thefts from loaded trucks of his left overnight in a garage. "Hurto de tabaco de rama de un camión," 6 Feb. 1926, AGPR, Policía, Novedades, Cayey, 23 and 24 Feb. 1926, 296–99.

39. Benigno Fernández García, "Aclaración haciendo constar que ciertos contratos celebrados a favor," 30 Oct. 1922, AGPR, PN, Serie: San Juan, Siglo XX, Pueblo: Cayey, 1922, caja 339, fols. 579–84v.

40. Benigno Fernández García, "Siembra y cultivo de tabaco, refacción e hipoteca," 1922, AGPR, PN, Serie: San Juan, Siglo XX, Pueblo: Cayey, 1922, caja 339, fols. 495–98.

41. Benigno Fernández García, "Cumplimiento de contrato de refacción y carta de pago," 1922, AGPR, PN, Serie: San Juan, Siglo XX, Pueblo: Cayey, 1922, caja 339, fols. 585–86.

42. Benigno Fernández García, "Aclaración," 1923, AGPR, PN, Serie: San Juan, Siglo XX, Pueblo: Cayey, 1923, caja 340, fols. 603–6.

43. "Galo Rivera, Jr., Joins Durlach Bros.," *United States Tobacco Journal*, 15 Dec. 1923, 7.

44. US Department of Labor, Immigration Service, "List of United States Citizens, S. S. Porto Rico, Sailing from San Juan, PR," 11 Sept. 1920, Ellis Island Passenger Search database.

45. "Durlach Bros. Win," 11; *Trow's Business Directory*, 353; Bureau of the Census, "Population Census Schedules," 4–5 June 1880, New York City, wards 19 and 12 (ED 592, sheet 1-ED 612, sheet 50) (NARA Series T9, Roll 896).

46. "The Cigars from Porto Rico," *Tobacco*, 25 June 1914, 32.

47. Cámara de Comercio de Puerto Rico, "Tobacco Culture," 68; Durlach Bros., "Porto Rico Tobacco," 63.

48. Luis Muñoz Morales, "Escritura de cuenta de participación," 3 May 1915, AGPR, PN, Serie: Siglo XX, Pueblo: San Juan, Año: 1915, caja 763, fols. 121–40.

49. "Durlach Bros. Incorporate," *United States Tobacco Journal*, 27 Sept. 1919, 6; "N. I. Durlach Dies Suddenly," *Tobacco World*, 15 Dec. 1910, 26.

50. Gallart, *Tabacalero y socialista en Cayey*, 68.

51. FTC, *Report*, 53.

52. Duke and Jordan, *Tobacco Merchant*, 54.

53. FTC, *Report*, 56.

54. "Consolidation of Two Big Tobacco Concerns," *Tobacco*, 1 Jan. 1920, 1, 3.

55. "Maximilian Stern Dies in 53rd Year," *United States Tobacco Journal*, 28 Feb. 1920, 10.

56. "Louis Bornemann," *Tobacco*, 22 Jan. 1920, 4; "Jos. Mendelsohn Back in New York," *Tobacco Leaf*, 30 July 1932, 5.

57. "Stern-Mendelsohn Co. Inc.," *Tobacco*, 24 Mar. 1921, 8; Wertenbaker, *Mister Junior*, 70–78.

58. "Fernando Alvarez Visits New York," *United States Tobacco Journal*, 11 Nov. 1922, 5; "Fern. Alvarez P. R. Pioneer Dies in Spain," *Tobacco Leaf*, 25 July 1936, 3.

59. Benigno Fernández García, "Promesa de venta de tabaco," AGPR, PN, Serie: San Juan, Siglo XX, Pueblo: Cayey, Año: 1923, caja 340, fols. 43–44. In another instance, Álvarez had a 1927 lien worth $11,250 on the tobacco that Julio Esteves Solá grew on 150 cuerdas in Caguas. Refer to Levy, *Puerto Ricans in the Empire*, 90.

60. Mack, *Cigar Manufacturing Industry*, 30–32, 60–64; Cox, *Competition in the American Tobacco Industry*, 91.

61. Evans, *Effects of Mechanization*, 11.

62. Max Gans' Sons, "Annual Report," 11 Apr. 1924, AGPR, Estado, Corporaciones foráneas con fines de lucro, caja 30, expediente 340; "Max Gans' Sons, Inc., One of Oldest Leaf Houses in Business," *United States Tobacco Journal*, 31 May 1924, 190.

63. Max Gans & Son, "Porto Rico Tobacco."

64. "Max Gans & Sons Will Incorporate," *United States Tobacco Journal*, 6 Dec. 1919, 10. With offices on Water Street, Elias Bach's tobacco interests lay in Pennsylvania and Connecticut. Refer to "Hartford Packers Happy over the Excellent Curing Weather," *United States Tobacco Journal* 11 Oct. 1919, 38 and "No Buying Yet in Lancaster Co.," *United States Tobacco Journal*, 25 Oct. 1919, 10.

65. "Max Gans & Son to Sever Association with Bach," *Tobacco Leaf*, 24 Nov. 1921, 8.

66. "La Palina Gets Leaf Department; Absorbs Max Gans' Sons," *United States Tobacco Journal*, 23 Aug. 1924, 3.

67. "Max Gans' Sons to Move to 142 Water St.," *United States Tobacco Journal*, 1 Mar. 1924, 7.

68. Congress Cigar Co., "Annual Report," 1926, AGPR, Estado, Corporaciones foráneas con fines de lucro, caja 32, expediente 373; "La Palina Gets Leaf Department," 3.

69. Baer, *Economic Development*, 258; Smith, *In All His Glory*, 31.

70. Cullman, *I'm a Lucky Guy*, 37; Baer, *Economic Development*, 258.

71. Percival R. Lowe, "Leaf Tobacco Brokers," *United States Tobacco Journal*, 31 May 1924, 143.

72. Baer, *Economic Development*, 258.

73. "Gans in Porto Rico," *Tobacco World*, 1 June 1928, 14; "Una comisión de industriales tabacaleros visitó ayer al Gobernador para tratar sobre el movimiento huelgario," *El Mundo*, 8 Aug. 1933, 1.

74. Baer, *Economic Development*, 155–60.

75. Cámara de Comercio, "Tobacco Culture," 64.

76. "Personals," *United States Tobacco Journal*, 13 Mar. 1937, 6.

77. "Heavy Buying in Puerto Rico Mart," *Tobacco Leaf*, 29 June 1935, 7; Department of Labor Wage and Hour Division, *Puerto Rico*, 41.

78. Extensively discussed in my *Sembraron la no siembra*.

79. "Agricultural Credits Act of 1923," *Federal Reserve Bulletin (Final edition)* (Mar. 1923): 303; Miguel Meléndez Muñoz, "La crisis tabacalera V. Extensión a Puerto Rico del plan cooperativo-agrícola federal," *El Mundo*, 20 July 1931, 6, 14; "Ley 70 de ventas cooperativas," *Leyes de Puerto Rico* (4 Aug. 1925): 370–73.

80. J. Córdova Chirino, "Los acaparadores de tabaco," *La Correspondencia*, 28 July 1931, 1; "Los cosecheros de tabaco," *El Agricultor Puertorriqueño*, 23 Jan. 1926, 7.

81. Miguel Meléndez Muñoz, "La crisis tabacalera VII," *El Mundo*, 22 July 1931, 6. The G. H. P. Cigar Company was one of the "leading" cigar manufacturers on the East Coast in 1926 according to Mack, *Cigar Manufacturing Industry*, 71.

82. "'General' Buys Large Quantity Puerto Rico" *United States Tobacco Journal*, 29 May 1937, 3; "Vendieron 14 millones de lbs. de tabaco," *El Mundo*, 26 Sept. 1945, 1.

83. For the specialization of the intermediary along one or two product lines see Chandler, *Visible Hand*, 15.

CHAPTER SEVEN. THE SOCIAL ORGANIZATION OF TOBACCO GROWING, 1899–1950

1. "Sosa, demandante y apelante, v. Cardona et al., demandados y apelados," *Decisiones de Puerto Rico* 30 (1922): 274–81; Santamaría García, "Los ferrocarriles de servicio público," 214.

2. Sosa, for his part, filed a claim for the return of the rolls or $460 besides the legal costs. He lost the claim in the district court and, upon appeal, in the Supreme Court. "Sosa v. Cardona," 274–81. The result of the criminal case against Gutiérrez is unknown.

3. Torres, *No quiero decir adiós*, 20.

4. Abad, *La exposición agrícola e industrial*, 96–98; Rogler, *Comerío*, 49.

5. Batchelder, "Land Use Problems," 141, 144. Unsuitable leaves for tobacco rolls, which were considerable, had other uses in the manufacture of cigarettes, pipe tobacco, and short-filler cigars. Gage, *Tobacco Industry*, 17.

6. Gage, *Tobacco Industry*, 43; Rogler, *Comerío*, 49.

7. Rogler, *Comerío*, 49.

8. Martínez Álvarez, *El último alcalde*, 47.

9. Manners, "Tabara," 121. The quotation and the description of the country huckster follow Torres, *No quiero decir adiós*, 20.

10. Computed from Bureau of the Census, *Fifteenth Census*, 232–37.

11. Coll y Toste, *Reseña del estado social*.

12. Bureau of the Census, *Fifteenth Census*, 232–37.

13. Gage, *Tobacco Industry*, 17

14. Dietz, *Economic History*, 116; Levy, *Puerto Ricans in the Empire*, 17.

15. Coll y Toste, *Reseña del estado social*, 8; War Department, *Report of the Census of Porto Rico 1899*, 356; Bureau of the Census, *Fifteenth Census*, 232.

16. Computed from Coll y Toste, *Reseña del estado social* and Bureau of the Census, *Fifteenth Census*, 232–37.

17. John P. Augelli coined the phrase in reference to the boom in tobacco agriculture between 1898 and 1932. Refer to Augelli, "Sugar Cane and Tobacco," 65.

18. Computed from Coll y Toste, *Reseña del estado social* and Bureau of the Census, *Fifteenth Census*, 232–37

19. Dietz, *Economic History*, 99.

20. Ayala and Bergad, *Agrarian Puerto Rico*, 229, 235; Picó, *Los gallos peleados*, 19; Schwartz, *Sea of Storms*, 253–55.

21. Picó, *Amargo café*, 39; Wolf, "San José," 233–34. The phrase comes from Picó, *Los gallos peleados*, 21.

22. Gulick, "Occupance Summary," 383.

23. This research estimated the percentage of all farmland planted with tobacco and coffee in 1897 and 1929 in each municipality. The first column of table 7.1 presents the differences between the percentage of farmland planted with tobacco in 1897 and the respective percentage in 1930. The second column follows the same logic with coffee.

24. Meléndez Muñoz, "La prosperidad," 1:727.

25. Computed from Coll y Toste, *Reseña del estado social* and Bureau of the Census, *Fifteenth Census*, 232–37.

26. O'Neil, "Memoir," 185.

27. "Cambio de nombre del pueblo Sabana del Palmar," 23 Sept. 1894, Archivo Histórico Nacional, Ministerio de Ultramar, legajo 5147, expediente 19. The ministerio approved the requested change in December.

28. Computed from Coll y Toste, *Reseña del estado social* and Bureau of the Census, *Fifteenth Census*, 232–37.

29. "The Sensation of Moving, while Standing Still," *American Ethnologist* 16 (1989): 792.

30. Benigno Fernández García, "Testamento," 22 Jan. 1918, AGPR, PN, Serie: San Juan, Siglo XX, Pueblo: Cayey, 1918–1919, caja 336, fols. 13–14; Bureau of the Census, "Thirteenth Census: Porto Rico," vol. 15, Cayey, 1910, 337, UPR, Centro de Investigaciones Históricas; "Acta de

matrimonio de Ramón Gómez Nieves y Felia Coto," 5 May 1916, Registro Civil y Demográfico de Puerto Rico, Cayey, Libro de Matrimonios 1907–1928, fol. 80, no. 50.

31. The reports of Inocencia's age are not consistent. Her birth dates stretch from 1875 to 1884, according to Bureau of the Census, "Thirteenth Census: Porto Rico," 1910, 337 and Bureau of the Census, "Population Census Schedules," NARA microfilm publication T625, Censo Décimocuarto de los Estados Unidos, 1920, Población Puerto Rico, Cayey, barrio Toíta, Hoja 26 B.

32. Bureau of the Census, "Population Census Schedules," 1920, Hoja 26 B.

33. "Acta de matrimonio de Ramón Gómez Nieves y Felia Coto."

34. For the quotation see Manners, "Tabara," 114. Baud, *Peasants and Tobacco*, 121.

35. Censo décimocuarto de los Estados Unidos, 1920, Población, Puerto Rico, Cayey, barrio Rincón, Hoja 22 A.

36. Fernández García, "Testamento," "Acta de defunción de Susana Soler Mendoza," 20 Aug. 1926, Registro Civil y Demográfico de Puerto Rico, Cayey, Libro de Defunciones 1921–1927, fol. 252, no. 421.

37. Mintz, "Cañamelar," 380.

38. Meléndez Muñoz, *El jíbaro en el siglo XIX*, 3:523.

39. "Acta de matrimonio de Rafael Jiménez Díaz y Rosa María Mendoza Carattini," 9 Nov. 1923, Registro Civil y Demográfico de Puerto Rico, Cayey, Libro de Matrimonios 1907–1928, fol. 372, no. 165; Fernández García, "Testamento." "Certificado de defunción de José Mendoza Rodríguez," 6 Feb. 1958, Registro Civil y Demográfico de Puerto Rico, Cayey, Libro de Defunciones 1956–1965, series no. 1627.

40. "Certificado de defunción de Baltasar Mendoza Martínez," 3 Apr. 1932, Registro Civil y Demográfico de Puerto Rico, Cayey, Libro de Defunciones 1931–1934, no. 158.

41. José Fernando Mendoza's date of death and will are a courtesy that Fernando Picó obtained from Cayey's "Libro décimo de defunciones."

42. "Acta de matrimonio de Baltazar Mendoza con Irene Carattini," [1] Aug. 1894, Registro Civil, Aibonito, Libro de matrimonios 1890–1895, acta 15, fol. 122.

43. AGPR, Hacienda, Registro de Tasación de la Propiedad, 1910–1911, Cayey, receipts 625–33.

44. Luis Muñoz Morales, "Siembra de tabaco con refacción e hipoteca y cancelación (escritura 98)," AGPR, PN, Siglo XX, San Juan, 1914, caja 762, fols. 811–24 and "Siembra de tabaco con refacción y garantía (escritura 61)," AGPR, PN, Siglo XX, San Juan, 1913, caja 760, fols. 536–45; "Destrucción parcial de un rancho," AGPR, Policía, Novedades, Cayey, 1 Dec. 1925, 273, 275–76. For a discussion of the crop lien refer to chapter 4.

45. US Congress, Senate, "Real Estate in Excess of 500 Acres Used for Agricultural Purposes in Porto Rico," 65th Congress, 2d session, 1918. Senate Document 165, 24–25.

46. Benigno Fernández García, "Agrupación de fincas rústicas e hipoteca voluntaria (escritura 130)," 19 Aug. 1925, "Siembra y cultivo de tabaco con refacción (escritura 149)," 11 Sept. 1925, "Siembra y cultivo de tabaco y refacción (escritura 153)," 19 Sept. 1925, AGPR, PN, San Juan, Siglo XX, Pueblo: Cayey, caja 342, fols. 407–14, 479–82, and 491–96 respectively.

47. AGPR, Hacienda, Registro de Tasación de la Propiedad, 1931–1932, Aibonito, fol. 20; Caguas, fol. 116; Cidra, fol. 16; Cayey, fols. 34, 79, and others; "Certificado de defunción de Baltasar Mendoza Martínez."

48. Concejo Municipal de Cayey, "Actas," 14 Jan. 1907, AGPR, Fondo Municipal de Cayey, caja 10, expediente 51, fol. 1; Commonwealth Board of Elections, *Results of Elections*.

49. Picó, *Cayeyanos*, 132; Junta Insular de Elecciones, *Estadísticas de las elecciones celebradas en Puerto Rico el 6 de noviembre de 1928* and *Estadísticas de las elecciones celebradas en Puerto Rico el 4 de noviembre de 1924*; Asamblea Municipal de Cayey, "Actas," 10 Jan. 1921, AGPR, Fondo Municipal de Cayey, caja 12, expediente 58, fols. 138–39.

50. "Modelo oficial de papeleta electoral," 1914, AGPR, Fortaleza, caja 595, expediente 2336; Meléndez Muñoz, "Benigno Fernández García," 3:845; Picó, *Cayeyanos*, 108.

51. "Oración fúnebre de Benigno Fernández García en el sepelio de don Baltazar Mendoza," *La Democracia*, 8 Apr. 1932, 4.

52. US Congress, Senate, "Real Estate," 24–25.

53. "Acta de matrimonio de Tomás Rodríguez Rivera y Angelina Mendoza Díaz," 29 Oct. 1917, Registro Civil y Demográfico de Puerto Rico, Cayey, Libro de Matrimonios 1907–1928, fol. 80, no. 50.

54. US Congress, Senate, "Real Estate," 30–31.

55. Tabacaleros de Cayey, "Informe Anual," 19 Aug. 1926, AGPR, Estado, Corporaciones domésticas con fines de lucro, caja 47, expediente 676.

56. "Acta de matrimonio de Modesto Cobián Rivera y Josefa Espina Rivera," 24 May 1896, Registro Civil y Demográfico de Puerto Rico, Comerío, Libro de Matrimonios 1892–1902, fols. 7–8; "Acta de matrimonio de Rafael Solares Solares y Manuela Espina Rivera," 3 Sept. 1914, Registro Civil y Demográfico de Puerto Rico, Comerío, Libro de Matrimonios 1911–1918, fol. 281, no. 111.

57. Bureau of the Census, "Population Census Schedules," 1930, NARA microfilm publication, Fifteenth Census of the United States, Puerto Rico, Comerío, pp. 2A, 8A.

58. US Congress, Senate, "Real Estate," 8–9.

59. Tabacaleros de Comerío, "Informe Anual," 22 Jan. 1926, AGPR, Estado, Corporaciones domésticas con fines de lucro, caja 47, expediente 678.

60. "Acta de matrimonio de Modesto Cobián Rivera" and "Acta de matrimonio de Rafael Solares Solares."

61. Rogler, *Comerío*, 42–43.

62. Miguel Meléndez Muñoz directly characterizes this form of labor as serfdom in "La crisis tabacalera XXIX. Continuación del examen de la situación general de los productores de tabaco. Motivos finales de la abstención de siembra," *El Mundo*, 19 Aug. 1931, 6.

63. Rogler, *Comerío*, 47; Meléndez Muñoz, *El jíbaro en el siglo XIX*, 483–84.

64. Manners, "Tabara," 115.

65. Rogler, *Comerío*, 44.

66. Bureau of the Census, "Population Census Schedules," 1930, Comerío, 2A, 8A, 19A.

67. US Department of Labor, Immigration Service, "List of United States Citizens, S.S. Brazos, Sailing from San Juan, PR," 14–19 July 1920, Ellis Island Passenger Search database; Fiz Jiménez, *Comerío y su gente*, 53.

68. Manners, "Tabara," 162.

69. Manners and Steward, "Cultural Studies," 128.

70. Augelli, "Rural Settlement Types," 325–36.

71. Augelli, "Sugar Cane and Tobacco," 63. For instance, US Congress, Senate, "Real Estate," identifies four men with more than five hundred acres of land in San Lorenzo and other municipalities that grew tobacco, among other staples, in 1917.

72. Ayala and Bergad, *Agrarian Puerto Rico*, 179.

73. Miguel Meléndez Muñoz, "La crisis tabacalera XXVIII," *El Mundo*, 18 Aug. 1931, 6.

74. Abad, *La exposición agrícola e industrial*, 98.

75. Baldrich, "From the Origins of Industrial Capitalism," 80–106; Solá, "Colonialism, Planters, Sugarcane," 357.

76. Baldrich, *Sembraron la no siembra*, 47–53.

77. Colón Torres, "Estudio económico," 42–44.

78. Meléndez Muñoz, "La crisis tabacalera XXVIII," 6 and "La crisis tabacalera XXIX," 6. Fernando Picó makes a similar argument but referring to local coffee agriculture during the

twentieth century. Coffee haciendas proved more vulnerable than *estancias* to fluctuations and external elements. The estancias persisted long after the end of the former due to their capacity to reduce their dependance on market forces by shifting to subsistence farming. Refer to Picó, *Amargo café*, 160–61.

79. Manners, "Tabara," 122.

80. Levy, *Puerto Ricans in the Empire*, 90.

81. Francisco M. Zeno to Benigno Fernández García, *La Correspondencia*, 6 Sept. 1933, 6.

82. Thomas, "Do Not Go Gentle," 463.

83. Baldrich, *Sembraron la no siembra.*

84. Abad, *La exposición agrícola e industrial*, 93.

85. Meléndez Muñoz, *El jíbaro en el siglo XIX*, 486.

86. Bureau of the Census, *Sixteenth Census*, 48.

87. Ángel Cruz Cruz, "El tabacal se desangra," *El Mundo*, 28 Jan. 1945, 12, 16; Manners, "Tabara," 112. The patterns were similar to those found in the neighboring Dominican Republic. Refer to Baud, *Peasants and Tobacco*, 59.

88. Clark et al., *Porto Rico and Its Problems*, 682.

89. Manners, "Tabara," 111. Sharecropping occurred when a landholder provided land, seeds, oxen to plow, and economic resources to support a tenant over the planting, cultivation, harvest, and drying of the leaf. Upon selling the leaf, the landowner deducted his expenses to divide the remainder, if any, with the tenant, usually in halves. Refer to Rosario, "Porto Rican Peasant," 561.

90. Manners, "Tabara," 141.

91. Manners, "Tabara," 148.

92. The sharecropping and unpaid farm labor variables consisted of the percentage of the population, aged more than fourteen years old, active in each of these two types of agricultural labor.

93. Torres Rosario, *Juana Colón*; "Huelga firme en Comerío," *Unión Obrera*, 16 Nov. 1918; "Huelga en Comerío," *Unión Obrera*, 5 Nov. 1918.

CHAPTER EIGHT. STRIKES AND THE INSTITUTIONALIZATION OF TRADE UNIONS IN TOBACCO MANUFACTURE, 1892–1927

1. Juan C. Velázquez, "Meeting socialista," AGPR, Policía, Novedades, Cayey, 2 Apr. 1920, 60.

2. José F. Quiles, "Labor Day en Cayey," *Unión Obrera*, 9 Sept. 1922, 1.

3. J. Ramón Collazo Aponte, "Desde Cayey," *Justicia*, 8 Oct. 1923, 6.

4. Demetrio Guzmán, Interview with author, Fajardo, Puerto Rico, 18 July 1989.

5. Guzmán, Interview.

6. Shorter and Tilly, "Shape of Strikes," 60–86.

7. Snyder, "Early North American Strikes," 328.

8. Moore, *Injustice*, 472.

9. Moore, *Injustice*, 502.

10. Perrot, *Workers on Strike*, 26.

11. Perrot, *Workers on Strike*, 24.

12. Moore, *Injustice*, 191, 502.

13. Refer to Baldrich, "Gender and the Decomposition of the Cigar-Making Craft," 105–25 and Quintero Rivera, "Socialista y tabaquero," 29–84.

14. The names of the occupations follow Department of Labor, *Dictionary of Occupational Titles*.

15. Oxford University Press, "Lexico.com Online English Dictionary," 2021, https://www.lexico.com.

16. Early cigar and cigarette workers combined the march and the riot with strike-like actions. Refer to Deans-Smith, *Bureaucrats, Planters, and Workers*, 237–44 and Candela Soto, *Cigarreras madrileñas*, 169–73.

17. "Las Dos Antillas," *La Correspondencia*, 23 Apr. 1892; García, "Las primeras actividades," 246.

18. Abad, *La exposición agrícola e industrial*, 29.

19. *La Correspondencia*, 28 Apr. 1892, 2.

20. José Rodríguez Fuentes, "'Las Dos Antillas' se cierran," *La Correspondencia*, 28 Apr. 1892, 2.

21. Stubbs, *Tobacco on the Periphery*, 101–4; Scott, "'Unión Obrera Democrática,'" 158–62.

22. Cruz Monclova, *Historia de Puerto Rico*, 40–41; García, "Las primeras actividades," 230.

23. Dávila Santiago, *El derribo de las murallas*, 36.

24. The distraught owner published his account, but unfortunately, the cigar makers' version does not seem to exist. One of the earliest reported strikes affected a sugar plantation in 1891. Ramos Mattei, *La sociedad del azúcar*, 120. For the "modularity" of collective gatherings see Tilly, "Contentious Repertoires," 33–34.

25. Cruz Monclova, *Historia de Puerto Rico*, 222–23; Rosenberg, "Foundations of United States International Power," 172–73.

26. Álvarez Curbelo, "El Motín de los Faroles," 140–6; García, "Las primeras actividades," 237–42; Cruz Monclova, *Historia de Puerto Rico*, 224–25. On the non-working-class social base of the riot, as opposed to that of the strike, refer to Álvarez Curbelo, "El Motín de los Faroles," and to Gould, "Trade Cohesion," 723.

27. "Huelga de tabaqueros," *La Correspondencia*, 28 Jan 1895, 3; *La Correspondencia*, 16 Feb. 1895.

28. "Noticias," *La Democracia*, 15 Feb.1895, 3.

29. Manuel Fernández Juncos, "Crónica de la semana," *La Correspondencia*, 22 Aug. 1897; *La Correspondencia*, 17, 19, and 20 Aug. 1897.

30. Guilds and mutual aid societies, at times, funded strikes. See Perrot, *Workers on Strike*, 31.

31. Iglesias de Pagán, *El obrerismo en Puerto Rico*, 57–58.

32. Negociado del Trabajo, *Informe especial*, 87.

33. Iglesias de Pagán, *El obrerismo en Puerto Rico*, 57, 92.

34. Silvestrini de Pacheco, "La mujer puertorriqueña," 90.

35. "Huelga," *Diario de Puerto Rico*, 4 May 1900, [7]; "Otra huelga," *Diario de Puerto Rico*, 8 Sept. 1900, 3; "Huelga concluida," *Diario de Puerto Rico*, 11 Sept. 1900, 5; Schwartz, "Hurricane of San Ciriaco," 316.

36. García and Quintero Rivera, *Desafío y solidaridad*, 49.

37. "Cabos sueltos," *La Huelga*, 4 Aug. 1900, 3–4.

38. Strikes exhibited variations with respect to their beginning, strategies, and outcomes. Charles Tilly has a useful image to explain the variation when he holds that a particular form of collective action, the strike here, comprises a "repertoire in something like the theatrical or musical sense of the word but the repertoire in question resembles that of commedia dell'arte or jazz more than that of a strictly classical ensemble," leaving ample room for improvisation within the form. See Tilly, *Contentious French*, 390.

39. Perrot, *Workers on Strike*, 27–28.

40. García and Quintero Rivera, *Desafío y solidaridad*, 46.

41. Gremio de Tabaqueros de Comerío, "Reglamento," 1901, AGPR, Estado, Corporaciones sin fines de lucro, caja 2, exp. 206.

42. Gremio Unión de Rezagadores, "Reglamento," 1903, AGPR, Estado, Corporaciones sin fines de lucro, caja 19, exp. 360.

43. Perrot, *Workers on Strike*, 35.

44. Unión de Torcedores de Tabaco, Caguas, "Reglamento," 1902, AGPR, Estado, Corporaciones sin fines de lucro, caja 19, exp. 364.

45. Iglesias de Pagán, *El obrerismo en Puerto Rico*, 196–98.

46. Gremio de Tabaqueros de Comerío, "Acta," 1902, AGPR, Estado, Corporaciones sin fines de lucro, caja 2, exp. 206.

47. Gremio de Tabaqueros de Comerío, "Reglamento."

48. Unión de Torcedores, San Juan, "Reglamento," 1902, AGPR, Estado, Corporaciones sin fines de lucro, caja 19, exp. 362; Unión de Torcedores de Tabaco, Caguas, "Reglamento"; Unión de Torcedores de Tabaco, Cayey, "Reglamento," 1902, AGPR, Estado, Corporaciones sin fines de lucro, caja 19, exp. 363.

49. Samuel Gompers to Santiago Iglesias, AFL organizer, 6 May [*sic*] 1903, *Unión Obrera*, 15 Feb. 1903, 1.

50. The FLT identified affiliates in San Juan and Caguas in 1902 and in Ponce a year later. "Directorio Obrero," *Obrero Libre*, 14 June 1903.

51. "Directorio Obrero."

52. Santiago Iglesias, "Los tabaqueros de Puerto Rico y la Unión Internacional de Tabaqueros de los Estados Unidos," *Unión Obrera*, 15 Feb. 1903, 1.

53. Iglesias, "Los tabaqueros de Puerto Rico," 1.

54. Gremio Unión de Rezagadores, "Reglamento."

55. Moore, *Injustice*, 472.

56. "Reorganización del gremio de torcedores de Utuado," *La Correspondencia*, 16 Sept. 1902; "En la Unión de Torcedores de Ponce," *Unión Obrera*, 14 June 1903, 1; "Otra unión que se afilia," *Unión Obrera*, 12 July 1903.

57. Dávila Santiago, *El derribo de las murallas*, 147–48.

58. "Huelga que dignifica," *Voz Humana*, 2 Sept. 1906; Dávila Santiago, *El derribo de las murallas*, 145–55.

59. Dávila Santiago, *El derribo de las murallas*, 133.

60. "Directorio Obrero"; Córdova Iturregui, *Ante la frontera del infierno*, 25; Meléndez Badillo, "Imagining Resistance," 36; FLT, *Actuaciones de las segunda y tercera asambleas regulares*, 32.

61. Dávila Santiago, *El derribo de las murallas*, 146.

62. "Huelga pacífica," *La Correspondencia*, 20 Jan. 1902, 4.

63. "Huelga de los torcedores de la fábrica 'La Ultramarina,'" *La Correspondencia*, 16 Apr. 1902, 2; "Huelga de tabaqueros," *Boletín Mercantil*, 16 Apr. 1902, 1.

64. "Huelga en Cayey," *La Democracia*, 26 Nov. 1902, 4; "Cayey," *Boletín Mercantil*, 25 Nov. 1902, 2. The strike may have had some support from the new trade union in town. See Unión de Torcedores de Tabaco, Cayey, "Reglamento."

65. "San Juan, notas por correo," *La Democracia*, 3 July 1902, 2.

66. "Decisión sobre huelga," *La Democracia*, 31 July 1902, 2; "San Juan, notas por correo," *La Democracia*, 31 July 1902, 3.

67. "Huelga de tabaqueros," *La Correspondencia*, 2 Aug. 1902, 3.

68. Braulio López, "La Unión de Torcedores de San Juan," *La Democracia*, 8 Aug. 1902, 1.

69. H. A. C., "Strike in Porto Rico," *Tobacco*, 5 Sept. 1902, 6; "Huelga en Aguadilla," *La Correspondencia*, 5 Sept. 1902, 2.

70. "Información local," *La Correspondencia*, 22 Sept. 1902, 3; "Huelga terminada," *Boletín Mercantil*, 23 Sept. 1902, 3; "Manifestación de torcedores," *La Democracia*, 23 Sept. 1902, 3.

71. "Reorganización del gremio de torcedores de Utuado," *La Correspondencia*, 16 Sept. 1902.

72. Unión de Torcedores, San Juan, "Reglamento."

73. "Unión y Trabajo," *La Correspondencia*, 3 Sept. 1902.

74. Unión de Torcedores, San Juan, "Reglamento"; Unión de Torcedores de Tabaco, Caguas, "Reglamento"; Unión de Torcedores de Tabaco, Cayey, "Reglamento."

75. "Esta mañana se declararon en huelga los tabaqueros de 'La Internacional,'" *La Correspondencia*, 11 Nov. 1903, 2; "Los obreros de 'La Colectiva' declarados en huelga, presentan á los dueños de la fábrica un pliego," *La Correspondencia*, 17 Nov. 1903, 1; Iglesias de Pagán, *El obrerismo en Puerto Rico*, 231–32.

76. Iglesias de Pagán, *El obrerismo en Puerto Rico*, 358–73; Torcedores del taller Johnson, "A los torcedores de Caguas," *Voz Humana*, 2 Sept. 1906.

77. "Huelga que dignifica," *Voz Humana*, 2 Sept. 1906; Rivera Martínez, "Santiago Iglesias y yo," 210.

78. Dávila Santiago describes the Solidaridad center in detail in *El derribo de las murallas*, 154–55. La Comisión, "Victoria segura: Los tabaqueros de Cayey robustecen la huelga," *Voz Humana*, 30 Sept. 1906.

79. La Comisión, "Victoria segura," n.p.

80. Perrot, *Workers on Strike*, 26.

81. For instance, José Ferrer, president of a cigar makers' union, played a prominent role in the strike. See Córdova Iturregui, *Ante la frontera del infierno*, 24–25; Ramos Mattei, *La sociedad del azúcar*, 124–27; Meléndez Badillo, "Imagining Resistance," 33–81.

82. Quintero Rivera, "El Partido Socialista," 60–61.

83. Ojeda Reyes, "¿Colonialismo sindical o solidaridad internacional?" 318–44.

84. Sanabria, *Puerto Rican Labor History*, 115.

85. García and Quintero Rivera, *Desafío y solidaridad*, 35–41, discuss the motivations for US-based labor to cooperate with their comrades in Puerto Rico.

86. FLT, *Libro de actuaciones de la asamblea magna*, 13.

87. Eugenio Sánchez López, "Comisión de Propaganda Especial de la Organización de los Tabacaleros," *Unión Obrera*, 4 Mar. 1907; Eugenio Sánchez López, "Informe general," *Unión Obrera*, 3 June 1907, 1; Eugenio Sánchez López, "Cigar Makers' International Union of America: Circular," *Unión Obrera*, 15 Aug. 1907.

88. "Habla el organizador Padilla lo que ha hecho, lo que hace y lo que hará," *Unión Obrera*, 5 Mar. 1907.

89. Baldrich, "Gender and the Decomposition of the Cigar-Making Craft," 105–25.

90. FLT, *Libro de actuaciones de la primera asamblea regular*, 14; "Notas de Cayey . . . en Cidra," *Unión Obrera*, 30 Sept. 1907.

91. Unión de Torcedores de San Juan, "Acta." 28 Jan. 1906, AGPR, Estado, Corporaciones sin fines de lucro, caja 19, exp. 362.

92. Unión de Torcedores de Bayamón N° 1, "Reglamento," 1906, AGPR, Estado, Corporaciones sin fines de lucro, caja 19, exp. 361; Lucas Martínez to Secretary of Porto Rico, Feb. 1907, AGPR, Estado, Corporaciones sin fines de lucro, caja 19, exp. 361.

93. García and Quintero Rivera, *Desafío y solidaridad*, 45.

94. FLT, *Actuaciones de las segunda y tercera asambleas*, 69–70.

95. Samuel Gompers to Santiago Iglesias, 6 May 1903 [*sic*], *Unión Obrera*, 15 Feb. 1903, 1.

96. See the frustrated attempt of the San Juan–based Asociación de Torcedores in 1906. Its potential constituency joined an FLT-sponsored union. Florencio Calderón to Secretary of Porto Rico, 31 July 1906, AGPR, Estado, Corporaciones sin fines de lucro, caja 2, exp. 32.

97. FLT, *Actuaciones de las segunda y tercera asambleas*, 44–47.

98. Tirado, "Cigar Workers" 195.

99. Dorothee Schneider documents a similar proposition during the large cigar makers' strike in New York during 1877. She holds that "the community of workers, it seemed, were in charge of their own future unencumbered by union rules and a pre-existing leadership." Refer to Schneider, *Trade Unions and Community*, 76.

100. Virgilio Meana Colón, "Asamblea de organización," *Unión Obrera*, 4 May 1907; Corresponsal, "Desde Cayey," *Unión Obrera*, 8 June 1907.

101. Corresponsal, "Desde Cayey," *Unión Obrera*, 13 June 1907.

102. The factory identified as "Mr. Mendoza" is Las Riberas del Plata. Corresponsal, "Desde Cayey," *Unión Obrera*, 19 June 1907; Corresponsal, "De Cayey," *Unión Obrera*, 6 July 1907.

103. Corresponsal, "Desde Cayey," *Unión Obrera*, 26 June 1907.

104. Eusebio Colón, "Desde Río Piedras," *Unión Obrera*, 6 Aug. 1907; Corresponsal, "Una huelga," *Unión Obrera*, 27 July 1907, 1; Corresponsal, "Notas de Caguas," *Unión Obrera*, 27 Aug. 1907.

105. Corresponsal, "Notas de Cayey," *Unión Obrera*, 7 Aug. 1907.

106. Corresponsal, "Notas de Cayey," *Unión Obrera*, 20 Aug. 1907.

107. Corresponsal, "Huelga acabada," *Unión Obrera*, 5 Sept. 1907.

108. Luis González, "Una acta," *Unión Obrera*, 10 Oct. 1907.

109. FLT, *Actuaciones de las segunda y tercera asambleas*, 56. The number of cigar makers comes from the manuscript census. See Bureau of the Census, Thirteenth Census: Porto Rico, vol. 15, Cayey, 1910.

110. "Notas de Cayey," *Unión Obrera*, 23 Oct. 1907; Felipe Olivieri and Luis Meana, "Acta de Constitución," *Unión Obrera*, 8 Oct. 1910, 1. The meeting place was now solely in the hands of the cigar makers. The carpenters' union with whom they had shared it failed.

111. FLT, *Actuaciones de las segunda y tercera asambleas*, 89; Luis Barrera, "Los jóvenes obreros," *Unión Obrera*, 22 Nov. 1911, n.p.

112. Corresponsal, "Notas Cayeyanas," *Unión Obrera*, 7 Jan. 1910, 1; Corresponsal, "Notas de Cayey," *Unión Obrera*, 9 Apr. 1910.

113. FLT, *Actuaciones de las segunda y tercera asambleas*, 69–70.

114. Ramón L. Fraguada, "Desde Cayey," *Unión Obrera*, 31 Aug. 1910; Luis González, "Una acta," *Unión Obrera*, 10 Oct. 1907.

115. Ramón L. Fraguada, "Desde Cayey," *Unión Obrera*, 29 Aug. 1910.

116. Titán, "De Cayey," *Unión Obrera*, 22 Dec. 1910.

117. Don Guipe, "Sobre Rompe Huelgas," *Unión Obrera*, 29 July 1911; El hombre que Canta, "Rompe huelgas," *Unión Obrera*, 2 Aug. 1911, 1.

118. Analysis from this perspective is vital because the board endorsement was necessary to petition the CMIU home office for strike funds. See also Cooper, *Once a Cigar Maker*, 99.

119. Reproduced in FLT, *Actuaciones de las segunda y tercera asambleas*, 41–42.

120. "Viaje del organizador E. Sánchez López," *Unión Obrera*, 13 Apr. 1907; Eugenio Sánchez López, "Informe general del trabajo en la comisión de organizador especial de la Unión Internacional de los Tabaqueros de América," *Unión Obrera*, 3 June 1907, 1.

121. FLT, *Actuaciones de las segunda y tercera asambleas*, 42; García and Quintero Rivera, *Desafío y solidaridad*, 46; Comité de la Huelga, "Asamblea local de los tabaqueros de San Juan," 11 May 1907, UPR, Río Piedras, Colección Puertorriqueña, "Periódicos obreros puertorriqueños," microfilm S-95A.

122. FLT, *Actuaciones de las segunda y tercera asambleas*, 30.

123. FLT, *Libro de actuaciones de la primera asamblea regular*, 19.

124. Unless otherwise specified the sources for this strike are Dávila Santiago, *El derribo de las murallas*, 181–209 and FLT, *Actuaciones de las segunda y tercera asambleas*, 30–34.

125. "Enfermo en San Lorenzo," *La Correspondencia*, 1 Apr. 1911, 1.

126. "Crisis industrial en Caguas," *La Correspondencia*, 4 Apr. 1911, 1.

127. Rivera Martínez, "Santiago Iglesias y yo," 209; Shaffer, *Black Flag Boricuas*, 85.

128. George R. Shanton to George R. Colton, Governor of Porto Rico, 21 Mar. 1911, AGPR, Fortaleza, caja 516, exp. 1849.

129. FLT, *Actuaciones de las segunda y tercera asambleas*, 34–35.

130. FLT, *Actuaciones de las segunda y tercera asambleas*, 39–41.

131. Ramón Delgado, "A los rompe huelgas," *Unión Obrera*, 2 Nov. 1911; Ramón L. Fraguada, "Notas de Cayey," *Unión Obrera*, 9 Nov. 1911; Arnaldo Ramírez, "Qué vergüenza!" *Unión Obrera*, 14 Oct. 1911, 1.

132. FLT, *Actuaciones de las segunda y tercera asambleas*, 35.

133. FLT, *Actuaciones de las segunda y tercera asambleas*, 68–70.

134. Union officials referred to the tradition of spontaneity as the *movimiento de taller*, the shop movement. See FLT, *Actuaciones de las segunda y tercera asambleas*, 42.

135. FLT, *Actuaciones de las segunda y tercera asambleas*, 68–70.

136. FLT, *Actuaciones de las segunda y tercera asambleas*, 68.

137. Tilly, *Contentious French*, 314.

138. Ansell, "Symbolic Networks," 374; Laurie, *Artisans into Workers*, 186–87.

139. Calero Amor, *Historia del movimiento obrero*, 139–40; Hobsbawm, *Rebeldes primitivos*, 138; Casanovas, *Bread, or Bullets!*, 205–20; Poyo, *"With All,"* 91–92.

140. García, "Las primeras actividades," 239–40.

141. Córdova Iturregui, *Ante la frontera del infierno*; Ramos Mattei, *La sociedad del azúcar*, 124–27.

142. García and Quintero Rivera, *Desafío y solidaridad*, 49.

143. FLT, *Actuaciones de las segunda y tercera asambleas*, 21, 28, 89, 107–8.

144. "Noticias," *Boletín Mercantil*, 18 Feb. 1914, 8; "Otra huelga: Lo que piden los tabaqueros," *La Correspondencia*, 26 Feb. 1914, 4.

145. "El estado de la huelga," *La Correspondencia*, 30 Mar. 1914, 1.

146. Santiago Iglesias to Drew Carrell, 2 Mar. 1914, *La Correspondencia*, 3 Mar. 1914, 3.

147. Comité de Huelga, "La huelga de las despalilladoras," *La Correspondencia*, 20 Feb. 1914, 4.

148. "El estado de la huelga," *La Correspondencia*, 30 Mar. 1914, 1; "La huelga de tabaqueros," *La Correspondencia*, 3 Apr. 1914, 1; "Rumores y noticias," *La Correspondencia*, 15 Apr. 1914, 1; "Información general," *La Correspondencia*, 29 Apr. 1914, 8; "La huelga en la Isla," *La Correspondencia*, 1 May 1914, 7; "Información general," *La Correspondencia*, 25 May 1914, 8.

149. "Manifestación del Señor Toro," *La Correspondencia*, 23 Mar. 1914, 1; "Información general," *La Correspondencia*, 1 June 1914, 8; Acting Treasurer of Porto Rico to Henry Winkelmann, 25 Feb. 1916, NARA, Washington, DC, Records of the Bureau of Insular Affairs, (Record Group 350), file 948–37; "Información de la Isla," *La Correspondencia*, 7 Mar. 1914, 6; "Los últimos sucesos en la Isla," *La Correspondencia*, 7 Apr. 1914, 3.

150. *La Correspondencia*, 13 Apr. 1914, 6; "Información general," *La Correspondencia*, 13 June 1914, 8.

151. Negociado del Trabajo, *Tercer informe anual, 1914*, 20; *La Correspondencia*, 14 Apr. 1914, 3; "Los últimos sucesos," *La Correspondencia*, 25 Apr. 1914, 3; "Agresión a un capataz," *La Correspondencia*, 2 May 1914, 8; "Información general," *La Correspondencia*, 27 May 1914, 8.

152. "'Leaders' obreros americanos en San Juan," *La Correspondencia*, 26 Mar. 1914, 1.

153. Prudencio Rivera Martínez to Luis Toro, 15 May 1914, *La Correspondencia*, 16 May 1914, 1.

154. "Movimiento Obrero," *La Correspondencia*, 2 May 1914, 8.

155. Comité Central de la Huelga, *Informe general de cuentas* (San Juan: Porto Rico Progress Publishing Co., 1914), 17, AGPR, Fortaleza, caja 593, expediente 746, documento 20.

156. "Información general," *La Correspondencia*, 29 Apr. 1914, 8; "Movimiento Obrero," *La Correspondencia*, 2 May 1914, 8.

157. "Terminación de la huelga," *La Correspondencia*, 11 June 1914, 8.

158. Prudencio Rivera Martínez to Samuel Gompers, 29 July 1914, in Comité Central de la Huelga, *Informe general de cuentas*, 28.

159. While the best basis for comparison would be actual union membership for tobacco workers overall, reliable statistics for this group are not readily available. The statistics refer to CMIU membership because it kept strict accountability of its finances and membership. FLT, *Actuaciones de las segunda y tercera asambleas*, 68–70. The 1915 membership information comes from CMIU, "Annual Financial Report," *Cigar Makers Official Journal* 40, no. 4 (1916): 55–90.

160. "El Pueblo, v. Porto Rican American Tobacco Company," *Decisiones de Puerto Rico* 30 (1922): 795–802; Comité General, "La huelga de tabaqueros," *Justicia*, 19 Aug. 1916, 9–11; Luis Muñoz Morales, "Exposición del caso," in *Alegato de la parte acusada apelante y transcripción del record*, 27–41, Centro Judicial de San Juan, Archivo Inactivo, Tribunal Supremo, Criminal, Caso 1845, El Pueblo de Puerto Rico vs. Porto Rican American Tobacco Co.

161. Negociado del Trabajo, *Quinto informe anual, 1916*, 33.

162. "Huelga de torcedores en Cayey," *Unión Obrera*, 16 Mar. 1916.

163. "A los tabaqueros del Branch, Cayey," *Unión Obrera*, 16 Mar. 1916.

164. Negociado del Trabajo, *Quinto informe anual, 1916*, 33; Retama, "Movimiento tabacalero," *Justicia*, 2 Sept. 1916, 15; Comité General, "La huelga de tabaqueros," 9; Prudencio Rivera Martínez to PRATCO, *Justicia*, 19 Aug. 1916, 1–3; "Los representantes de los tabaqueros vigilantes," *Justicia*, 9 Sept. 1916, 15.

165. Ángel Figueroa, "Desde Cayey: Notas de la huelga," *Justicia*, 2 Sept. 1916, 8.

166. Negociado del Trabajo, *Quinto informe anual, 1916*, 33.

167. The sources for the strike are the extensive police coverage in AGPR, Policía, Novedades, Cayey, 5 June 1917 to 14 July 1917, 208–58 and Eugenio Vega, "La huelga de las escogedoras de tabaco en rama," *Justicia*, 7 July 1917, 4.

168. Manuel F. Rojas, "La gran huelga de torcedores triunfa," *Unión Obrera*, 26 Dec. 1917, 3. My estimate, computed from government data, places it around 8,500 strikers. Refer to Bureau of Labor, *Special Bulletin of the Bureau of Labor on Strikes in Porto Rico during the Fiscal Year 1917–1918*, 29–32.

169. Cuerpo Consultivo Conjunto, "Proclama de huelga," 31 Oct. 1917, UPR, Río Piedras, Colección Puertorriqueña, Microfilm S-95A.

170. Cuerpo Consultivo Conjunto de tabaqueros de P. R., "Información oficial sobre la probable huelga de tabaqueros," *Unión Obrera*, 27 Sept. 1917, 1.

171. "Huelga general de torcedores," *Unión Obrera*, 24 Sept. 1917, 1.

172. "Huelga general de torcedores," *Unión Obrera*, 24 Sept. 1917, 1; Arturo Bird Carmona provides a good representation of the working-class milieu in *Parejeros y desafiantes*.

173. [Comisiones de los talleres del distrito tabacalero de San Juan], "A todos los tabaqueros que laboran para el Trust P. R. A. T. Co." *Unión Obrera*, 28 Sept. 1917, 1.

174. Cuerpo Consultivo Conjunto de tabaqueros de P. R., "Información oficial sobre la probable huelga de tabaqueros," *Unión Obrera*, 27 Sept. 1917, 1.

175. Cuerpo Consultivo Conjunto de la Uniones de Tabaqueros de Puerto Rico, "A todos los empleados por la Porto Rican American Tobacco Co.," *Unión Obrera*, 15 Oct. 1917, 3.

176. Cuerpo Consultivo Conjunto de la Uniones de Tabaqueros de Puerto Rico. "A todos los empleados por la Porto Rican American Tobacco Co.," *Unión Obrera*, 15 Oct. 1917, 3.

177. Cuerpo Consultivo Conjunto de la Uniones de Tabaqueros de P. R., "A todos los tabaqueros de San Juan y la Isla," *Unión Obrera*, 20 Oct. 1917, 1.

178. Cuerpo Consultivo Conjunto de la Uniones Tabaqueros de Puerto Rico, "Proclama de huelga general," *Unión Obrera*, 1 Nov. 1917, 1, 2.

179. "La huelga general de los tabaqueros de Puerto Rico," *Unión Obrera*, 28 Oct. 1917, 2.

180. "Informe oficial de la huelga de tabaqueros," Dec. 1917, UPR, Río Piedras, Colección Puertorriqueña, Microfilm S-95A; "Huelgas de tabaqueros vigorosas, *Unión Obrera*, 30 Oct. 1917, 3. For the strike funds disbursed by the AFL, refer to Sanabria, *Puerto Rican Labor History*, 117–18.

181. Cuerpo Consultivo Conjunto, "La huelga del trust del tabaco," 7 May 1919, AGPR, Junghanns, caja 37, exp. 1588; PRATCO, *Annual Report, 1917* (Jersey City: n.p., 1918).

182. "El Pueblo, v. Porto Rican American Tobacco Company."

183. Bureau of Labor, *Sixth Annual Report, 1918*, 25–26; El Jíbaro Pernicioso, "Acusaciones de Cayey," *Unión Obrera*, 6 Mar. 1918.

184. Comité Central, "La huelga del trust del tabaco, manifiesto de información," *Unión Obrera*, 28 Jan. 1919, 1–3.

185. Luis Toro, "Proposition Made by the Porto Rican American Tobacco Company to its Employees and Workmen," 20 Dec. 1918, NARA, Washington, DC, Records of the Bureau of Insular Affairs (Record Group 350), file 27430-5.

186. Cuerpo Consultivo Conjunto, "La huelga del trust del tabaco," 7 May 1919, AGPR, Junghanns, caja 37, exp. 1588; "Huelga del trust del tabaco," *Unión Obrera*, 11 Feb. 1919.

187. Unión de despalilladoras número 12,439, "Importante asamblea a las 2 de la tarde del miércoles 15 enero de 1919, en los salones de la Fed. Libre," *Unión Obrera*, 15 Jan. 1919, 1; Unión de secadores y mojadores no. 15,206, "Importante asamblea a las 9 de la mañana del martes 14 de enero de 1919, en los salones de la Fed. Libre," *Unión Obrera*, 13 Jan. 1919, 1; Unión Internacional de Tabaqueros de America, "Importante asamblea general de uniones el miércoles 22 de enero a las 2 de la tarde en el Cine Real de Puerta de Tierra," *Unión Obrera*, 21 Jan. 1919, 1.

188. Comité Central, "La huelga del trust del tabaco, manifiesto de información," 1.

189. "El Pueblo, Demandante y Apelado, v. Álvarez, Acusado y Apelante," *Decisiones de Puerto Rico* 28 (1920): 937–47; José María González to Pedro Giusti, 28 May 1919, Juan Giusti Cordero Collection.

190. Sanabria, *Puerto Rican Labor History*, 117–18; Unión de secadores y mojadores no. 15,206, "Importante asamblea," 1.

191. Muñoz Morales, "Exposición del caso," 40; "Porto Rico Strike Ended Monday," *Tobacco Leaf*, 3 July 1919, 6; "El Pueblo, v. Porto Rican American Tobacco Company."

192. Muñoz Morales, "Exposición del caso," 40.

193. Governor of Porto Rico, *Annual Report, 1920*, 557.

194. Comité Central de la Huelga General de los Tabaqueros, *Manifiesto* (San Juan: La Democracia, 1926), 1; Muñoz Morales, "Exposición del caso," 38–39.

195. Cuerpo Consultivo de las Uniones de Tabaqueros y Ramas Aliadas, "Manifiesto," 30 Jan. 1921, UPR, Río Piedras, Colección Puertorriqueña, Microfilm S-95A.

196. Governor of Porto Rico, *Annual Report, 1920*, 557–58; AGPR, Policía, Novedades, Cayey, 15 Mar. 1920 to 26 Apr. 1920, 23–122.

197. Governor of Porto Rico, *Annual Report, 1920*, 558.

198. AGPR, Policía, Novedades, Cayey, 9 Mar. 1920, 6.

199. Stubbs, *Tobacco in the Periphery*, 89, 104; Shaffer, *Anarchism and Countercultural Politics*.

200. Baldrich, "Gender and the Decomposition of the Cigar-Making Craft," 105–25.

201. Baldrich, *Sembraron la no siembra*, 39–56; Evans, *Effects of Mechanization*.

202. Department of Agriculture, *Annual Book on Statistics*, 142.

203. Governor of Porto Rico, *Annual Report, 1923*, 259. The timing of the strike benefitted management enormously because it began during the slow season that spanned winter and spring when employment decreased between one-third to one-half of the high season during late fall. See Negociado del Trabajo, *Informe especial, 1912*, 62 and Mack, *Cigar Manufacturing Industry*, 90.

204. Comité Central de la Huelga General de los Tabaqueros, *Manifiesto*, 2; Muñoz Morales, "Exposición del caso," 38–39.

205. For instance, refer to the complaint of a tobacco workers' union. Unión de Tabaqueros No. 460 de San Juan, "A los torcedores y al pueblo de San Juan," 24 June 1921, AGPR, Junghanns, caja 20, exp. 746-A.

206. Governor of Porto Rico, *Annual Report, 1921*, 498; Comité Central de la Huelga General de los Tabaqueros, *Manifiesto*, 2–3.

207. Comité Central de la Huelga General de los Tabaqueros, *Manifiesto*, 4–5.

208. Prudencio Rivera Martínez, "Los tabaqueros se mueven para defenderse," *Unión Obrera*, 12 July 1922, 1; "Luchas de tabaqueros," *Unión Obrera*, 19 July 1922.

209. Governor of Porto Rico, *Annual Report, 1923*, 259–60; Comité Central de la Huelga General de los Tabaqueros, *Manifiesto*, 5.

210. Negociado del Trabajo, *Noveno informe anual*, 72.

211. Prudencio Rivera Martínez, "Invitación a los tabaqueros de San Juan," *Unión Obrera*, 18 July 1922, 1; Prudencio Rivera Martínez, "Huelga de tabaqueros terminada," *Unión Obrera*, 25 July 1922.

212. Negociado del Trabajo, *Noveno informe anual*, 72.

213. Governor of Porto Rico, *Annual Report, 1925*, 614.

214. Sociedad de Escogedores, "Certificate of Filing of Certificate of Consent to Dissolution," 6 Nov. 1924, AGPR, Estado, Corporaciones sin fines de lucro, caja 12A, expediente 147.

215. "Marca de cigarros *Ribosch* de Bosch Brothers," 28 Feb. 1929, Estado, División de Marcas de Fábrica, Domestic Trade Marks, vol. 4, 3219.

216. AGPR, Policía, Novedades, Cayey, 29 Oct. 1926, 216; Evangelio Collazo, "Se intensifica la lucha. Nuevo brote de protesta en Cayey," *Unión Obrera*, 11 Nov. 1926.

217. AGPR, Policía, Novedades, Cayey, 6 Nov. 1926, 257.

218. AGPR, Policía, Novedades, Cayey, 14 Nov. 1926, 292.

219. Governor of Porto Rico, *Annual Report, 1927*, 43.

220. Comité Central de la Huelga General de los Tabaqueros, *Manifiesto*, 6–8.

221. Antonio Villafañe, "Un llamamiento a los tabaqueros en huelga," *La Correspondencia*, 31 Mar. 1927, 10.

222. Luis Toro to Antonio Villafañe and Eugenio Andrade, 2 Apr. 1927, *La Correspondencia*, 5 Apr. 1927, 7. Tadeo Rodríguez García, "Grito de indignación y protesta," *La Correspondencia*, 28 Mar. 1927, 8.

223. Antonio Villafañe, "El Comité Central de la Huelga de Tabaqueros somete a referéndum las proposiciones últimas," *La Correspondencia*, 22 Mar. 1927, 1, 7.

CHAPTER NINE. THE HERMANOS CHEOS: RELIGIOUS RESISTANCE TO THE BREAKDOWN OF ORDER AND MARKET FORCES, 1898–1938

1. Domingo Castro, "Algo de la predicación de 'San Francisco de Sena' en el barrio Real, casa de Pedro Rivera," 17 July 1906, Congregación de San Juan Evangelista, Archivo.

2. The name Hermanos Cheos derives, in part, from the practice of the missionaries to address their congregation and themselves as *hermanos*, brothers. José de los Santos Morales

and his namesake, José Rodríguez, became the most influential preachers in the movement and some nicknames for José are *Cheo* and *Che.*

3. For the incorporation of the Cheos into the Catholic Church, refer to Hernández Aponte, *La Iglesia Católica,* 356–57.

4. Diacon, *Millenarian Vision,* 7–8.

5. Bastide, preface to *Historia y etnología,* 8, 11.

6. Levine, *Vale of Tears,* 94, 206, 226.

7. Barkun, *Disaster and the Millennium,* 1, 62.

8. Hobsbawm, *Rebeldes primitivos,* 107; E. J. Hobsbawm, "Epílogo a la edición española," in *Rebeldes primitivos,* 305–6.

9. Lundius and Lundahl, *Peasants and Religion,* 25–26, 673–74.

10. Pessar, "Three Moments," 95–116.

11. Diacon, *Millenarian Vision,* 102–14.

12. Harris, *Lourdes.*

13. Christian, *Visionaries.*

14. The miracle of Sábana Grande in 1953 is the more salient apparition of the Virgin Mary in Puerto Rico. Román, *Governing Spirits,* 160–93.

15. Vidal, *La Monserrate negra,* 6; Zayas Micheli, *Catolicismo popular,* 13–16; Parrilla Bonilla, *Estampas Monserratinas,* 11–12.

16. Lange, "Santos de Palo," 43–65; Quintero Rivera, "Vueltita, con mantilla, al primer piso," 9–100.

17. Domingo Castro, "Prédicas del elegido: Tomado del Apóstol San Juan Evangelista," 15 Jan. 1907, Congregación de San Juan Evangelista, Archivo.

18. Traba, *La rebelión,* 30; Wolf, "San José," 214.

19. Curbelo de Díaz González, "Apéndice D," 159; Lange, "Santos de Palo," 43; and Vidal, *Santeros puertorriqueños,* 10, prepared a list and two maps identifying the municipalities with abundant *santos.* Based on these sources, I prepared an index of the presence of wooden saints. The correlation coefficient between the presence of the household saints and the logarithm of the new Cheo preachers was 0.213 with a 0.086 significance level for a two-tailed test and data for sixty-six municipalities.

It is very likely that the social acceptance and encouragement of the preachings of a single missionary might serve as a model to other potential preachers. Thus, to a certain extent, each additional preacher, in some fashion, found a model to emulate in already successful preachers. A logarithmic transformation is a standard procedure to manage such an effect. The logarithm—plus one because the logarithm of zero is undefined—of the number of first preachings in each municipality acknowledges a declining marginal effect of each additional preacher. Refer to Oneal and Russett, "Kantian Peace," 16.

20. Moore, *Injustice,* 470. While not referring to religious movements, he elaborates themes pertinent to them.

21. Several researchers of religious phenomena have identified the invasion and Protestantism as the triggering phenomenon of the Cheo movement. Refer to Agosto Cintrón, *Religión y cambio social,* 77; Silva Gotay, *Protestantismo y política,* 168; Zayas Micheli, *Catolicismo popular,* 66–86.

22. Carlos Torres, "Historia de la fundación de la Congregación Misionera de San Juan Evangelista," [1975?], 1, Congregación de San Juan Evangelista, Archivo; Santaella Rivera, *Historia de los Hermanos Cheos,* 49–52.

23. Silva Gotay, *Protestantismo y política,* 112, 183–84.

24. Barragán, "El clero de la diócesis," 99, 104–5.

25. Harris, *Lourdes;* Santaella Rivera, *Historia de los Hermanos Cheos,* 35–40.

26. The number of priests per parish comes from "Clero parroquial," *Boletín Eclesiástico* 29, no. 1 (20 Jan. 1899): 5–8. I aggregated the parish data for each municipality. One priest, from an illegible parish name, remains unassigned. The clergy from the "Clero parroquial" numbers 105, which is fewer than the 110 that Barragán's "El clero de la diócesis de San Juan" identifies for 1899.

27. The correlation coefficient between the logarithm of the number of preachers with the number of priests per ten thousand inhabitants is -0.348. The population data in 1899 comes from the 1910 census for the sixty-six municipalities recognized by the census. If the data were drawn form a random sample, this correlation would have been significant at the 0.004 level for a two-tailed test.

28. Barkun, *Disaster and the Millennium*, 62–90.

29. Computed from Aráez y Ferrando, *Historia del ciclón del día de San Ciriaco*. G. G. Groff combines deaths by wind and flooding to present a similar picture in "Appendix D. Report on Hurricane," in *Appendices to the Report*, ed. Military Government of Porto Rico (Washington, DC: GPO, 1901), 141. Health officials did not collect mortality statistics from disease from the date of San Ciriaco to October. See Hoff, "Report of Superior Board of Health of Porto Rico," 119–20.

30. Ashford, *A Soldier in Science*, 39.

31. Reyes, *La Santa Montaña*, 25.

32. Reyes, *La Santa Montaña*, 32, 49.

33. The correlation coefficient between the logarithm of the number of preachers with the mortality rate is 0.355. The population data in 1899 comes from the 1910 census and reflects the sixty-six municipalities recognized by the census. If the data were drawn form a random sample, this correlation would have been at the 0.003 level for a two-tailed test. Yabucoa is the significant exception to this pattern with a mortality rate of 16.18 and no preachers whatsoever.

34. Hobsbawm, *Rebeldes primitivos*, 107; Levine, *Vale of Tears*, 89–94; Diacon, *Millenarian Vision*; Lundius and Lundahl, *Peasants and Religion*, 675–77.

35. Foraker Act (Organic Act of 1900), *US Statutes at Large* 31 (12 Apr. 1900): 77–78; Salamone, "Constitutional Separation," 39.

36. Ramos Mattei, "Las inversiones norteamericanas," 60–64.

37. Department of Commerce and Labor, *Commercial Porto Rico in 1906*, 54.

38. Giusti Cordero, "Hacia otro 98," 72–124; García Muñiz, *Sugar and Power*.

39. Picó, "El café," 70. The Cuban government practically eliminated coffee imports with high customs duties in 1898. Baralt, *Buena Vista*, 167.

40. Schwartz, "Hurricane of San Ciriaco," 330–32.

41. Baralt, *Buena Vista*, 167.

42. Computed from Department of Commerce and Labor, *Commercial Porto Rico*, 54.

43. Computed from Department of Commerce and Labor, *Commercial Porto Rico*, 54.

44. Colón, *Datos sobre la agricultura*, 290–91.

45. D. Santiago Estrago to Director of *El Ideal Católico*, 25 Mar. 1901, in Rodríguez Pérez, "La obra de los Hermanos Cheos," 202.

46. "Los ángeles enviados" (1906), in Rodríguez Pérez, "La obra de los Hermanos Cheos," 208; Santaella Rivera, *Historia de los Hermanos Cheos*, 63; "Acta de matrimonio de José de los Santos Morales Rodríguez con María Eulalia Núñez Padilla," 1 Apr. 1928, Registro Civil y Demográfico de Puerto Rico, Ponce, Libro de Matrimonios 1921–1928, fol. 436, no. 145; "Acta de matrimonio de José de los Santos Morales Rodríguez con Micaela Reyes Jesús," 21 Oct. 1906, Registro Civil y Demográfico de Puerto Rico, Utuado, Libro de Matrimonios 1896–1906, fol. 61, no. 268; "Acta de defunción de Nicolás Morales Rodríguez," 14 Nov. 1917, Registro Civil y Demográfico de Puerto Rico, Jayuya, Libro de Defunciones 1910–1931, no. 320.

47. The Pearson product moment correlation for the raw version of the number of first preachings and the percentage of tobacco area planted primarily for roll-chewing is 0.471, while the coefficient for the logarithmic transformation of the preacher's variable is 0.392. These coefficients pertain to the data before recoding the tobacco variable into the three categories presented in the table.

48. Coll y Toste, *Reseña del estado social*; Bureau of the Census, *Thirteenth Census*, 77–77; Bureau of the Census, *Thirteenth Census, Statistics for Porto Rico*, table 4.

49. Although never joining the movement, she was close to the Cheos. The Pearson product moment correlation for the percentage of tobacco area planted primarily for cigar filler and wrapper and the number of first preachings is -0.103. The version with the logarithmic transformation is -0.108.

50. Santaella Rivera, *Historia de los Hermanos Cheos*, 56–57.

51. Santiago Estrago to Director, 202.

52. Torres, "Historia de la fundación de la Congregación," 17–18.

53. Santaella Rivera, *Historia de los Hermanos Cheos*, 52–53, 56–57. Quiles was a farmer who preached in the same language as his wife, coarse and peasant-like, but with great effect. He was reputed for his description of events that he had not witnessed to enhance and make his missions more effective.

54. José Rodríguez Medina, "Historia de los Hermanos Cheos en Puerto Rico," [1975?], 8, Congregación de San Juan Evangelista, Archivo; Santaella Rivera, *Historia de los Hermanos Cheos*, 121–24, 126; Laboy left Barranquitas for Ponce to offer his children a better education. In 1939, he became president of the congregation on the death of Morales.

55. Santaella Rivera, *Historia de los Hermanos Cheos*, 61–94, 235.

56. "Predicador bígamo," *Puerto Rico Eagle*, 24 Sept. 1909, 1; "Noticias locales: Bígamo preso," *Puerto Rico Eagle*, 30 Sept. 1909, 7. Rodríguez was accused of bigamy and jailed after he remarried, in a religious ceremony, without divorcing his first wife.

57. Rodríguez Medina, "Historia de los Hermanos Cheos en Puerto Rico," 1, 6, 8–9, 15; Santaella Rivera, *Historia de los Hermanos Cheos*, 102.

58. Torres, "Historia de la fundación de la Congregación," 11; Santaella Rivera, *Historia de los Hermanos Cheos*, 163.

59. 11 Apr. 1915, Redemptorist Provincial Archives, San Juan, Puerto Rico, House Chronicles, Dulce Nombre de Jesús, Caguas, 1 Mar. 1915 to 4 Oct. 1918, 24–25.

60. Santaella Rivera, *Historia de los Hermanos Cheos*, 72–74. The Hermano Che added two lateral aisles to the chapel to accommodate the pilgrims attending spiritual exercises. See José Dimas Soberal, *Los Hermanos Cheo* (N.p., n.d.), 25.

61. Torres, "Historia de la fundación de la Congregación," 3.

62. Picó, *Libertad y servidumbre*, 133–34. Years later, during the 1940s, Eric R. Wolf described the interplay of the solemn Holy Week processions with the gambling and drinking that went on in and around the town square of Ciales in the highlands. See Wolf, "San José," 243.

63. Santaella Rivera, *Historia de los Hermanos Cheos*, 74. The duress of the trip and the stay must have tested the faith of the pilgrims. Most arrived on foot while the privileged few traveled on horseback. According to some, it took as much as five days for those traveling from afar. During the trip and upon arrival, the well-off might stay at the small hotels in the towns along the route; the fortunate might stay in the homes of pious families; but most would carry hammocks and would sleep in the open fields. All carried provisions such as baked sweet potatoes, cassava bread, ground coffee, sugar, and cornmeal fritters—similar in appearance to the croquette and known as *sorullos*—in cloth bags identified as *alforjas*. As at home, women did whatever cooking needed to be done.

64. "Hay en Patillas una religiosa que predica el Evangelio," *La Correspondencia*, 21 Aug. 1903, 4.

65. Reyes, *La Santa Montaña*, 49, 50; Santaella Rivera, *Historia de los Hermanos Cheos*, 45.

66. The marriage dates are from Fernando Picó, email to author, 8 Apr. 2003. Elenita gave missions in Luciano and Faustina's home in barrio Guavate that was close to the Santa Montaña. See Reyes, *La Santa Montaña*, 38, 46.

67. Ponce, despite its size, evokes images of its urban area, the coastal plain, and closeness to the Caribbean. In contravention to the stereotype, most Cheo chapels in Ponce were in the northern barrios of the municipality that were firmly embedded in the highlands. Thus, the Cheos built three chapels in barrio San Patricio, which borders Jayuya and Utuado, and another in barrio Guaraguao, which adjoins Adjuntas. Chapels in barrios such as Tibes, Maragüez, Monte Llano, and Real also fell to the north of the municipality.

68. A parish priest reported that assistance to Catholic services in rural Caguas was higher in and around the feast of this Virgin. See 11 July 1915, Redemptorist Provincial Archives, San Juan, Puerto Rico, House Chronicles, Dulce Nombre de Jesús, Caguas, 1 Mar. 1915 to 4 Oct. 1918, 41.

69. The Pearson correlation coefficient reinforces this interpretation of map 9.2. The first variable is the number of chapels in each of the seventy-seven municipalities while the second refers to the minimum linear distance from the town squares of each town to Jayuya and San Lorenzo that were the municipalities that housed the two main chapels. The correlation for these two variables is -0.373 that is significant at the 0.001 level for a two-tailed test if the data were drawn from a random sample, which they are not. However, the linear relation expressed by -0.373 is not the best statistical explanation of the relationship between the variables because the number of chapels presents a statistical difficulty corrected by a logarithmic transformation. The logarithmic transformation yields a correlation coefficient of -0.463 that is significant at the 0.000 level for a two-tailed test. The correlation suggests most chapels were close to either the Santa Montaña or the Throne chapel and that, as distance increased, there was a lesser likelihood of chapels.

70. McCook, *States of Nature*, 72; "Tobacco Growers Association," *Porto Rico Progress*, 26 Jan. 1911, 27.

71. Fernández, "La Asociación de Cosecheros de Tabaco," 584, 586.

72. Manners, "Tabara," 115, 150–51, 162. Robert Manners did his field study in rural "Tabara," which is the fictitious name he gave to Barranquitas. A criterion for choosing Barranquitas was that it was "representative" of the tobacco sector but not "an important processing and servicing" center for the area as in Comerío. See Manners, "Tabara," 96. Consequently, it was more "representative," then, of the Cheo zone but not of the zone where organized tobacco growers prevailed.

73. From a comparative perspective, Patricia Pessar argues that the end of servitude obligations contributed to the emergence of early forms of Brazilian millenarianism. Refer to Pessar, *From Fanatics to Folk*, 87–88.

74. The indicator must be considered with the proviso that the heyday of the chapels took place in the teens while the maturity of the cooperatives corresponds to the late twenties. Nonetheless, one must point out that the marketing cooperatives themselves were outgrowths from a decades-old process of institution building that ran concurrently with the peak of Cheo chapels. The municipalities with long-standing *bancos tabacaleros* were Aibonito, Cayey, Comerío, San Lorenzo, and Utuado.

75. The correlation coefficient between the distance from the town squares of municipalities with tobacco cooperatives and the number of chapels in a municipality is -0.186.

However, the linear relation expressed by this coefficient is not the best statistical explanation of the relationship between the variables because the number of chapels presents a statistical difficulty attenuated and corrected by a logarithmic transformation. The logarithm of the chapels yields a correlation coefficient of -0.288 that would have been significant at the 0.01 level—for a two-tailed test and data for seventy-seven municipalities—if the data were drawn from a random sample.

76. Bishop of Puerto Rico to Padre Puras, 1911, in Reyes, *La Santa Montaña*, 215–16; Padre Puras to Bishop of San Juan, 212–14

77. Comisión para Proteger el Tabaco de Puerto Rico, "Informe anual, 1932–1933," *La Correspondencia*, 12 Sept. 1933, 5; Tabacaleros de San Lorenzo, "Informe Anual," 1926–1932; AGPR, Estado, Corporaciones domésticas con fines de lucro, caja 47, expediente 675; US Congress, *Real Estate in Excess of 500 Acres Used for Agricultural Purposes in Porto Rico* 65th Congress—Second Session, Document Number 165 (Washington, DC: GPO, 1918), 22–23.

78. Reyes, *La Santa Montaña*, 60–61.

79. Francisco M. Zeno, *El obrero agrícola o de los campos* (San Juan: La Correspondencia de Puerto Rico, [1922]), 68; Asociación de Cosecheros de Tabaco de Puerto Rico, "Informe anual," 1922—1925, AGPR, Estado, Corporaciones sin fines de lucro, caja 17A, expediente 239.

80. Previous research has identified 192 distinct events during 1931 and 1932 associated to the boycott that involved the attempt or actual destruction of property. Refer to Baldrich, *Sembraron la no siembra*, 109.

81. The Pearson correlation for the ungrouped version of both variables is 0.290 for the seventy-seven municipalities of the island. This coefficient would have been significant at the 0.010 level for a two-tailed test if the data were drawn from a random sample. The correlation coefficient of the logarithmic version of both variables is 0.280, which would have been significant at the 0.014 level. Fifty-six municipalities experienced no damage at all.

82. Santaella Rivera, *Historia de los Hermanos Cheos*, 160, 249. The ways through which the faithful became missionaries experienced significant changes. Initially (1) God's calling was enough; (2) afterward the calling needed the approval of the Hermano Che; (3) then came a period with a dearth of vocations; (4) after the Church took over the movement, it began the rationalization of recruitment and the formation, schooling, preparation of lay preachers.

83. For the routinization of charisma see Max Weber, *Economy and Society*, 2:1121.

84. Justo Zayas, interview with author accompanied by Humberto García Muñiz, barrio Sonadora, Aguas Buenas, 12 May 1984.

85. Picó, "Land Tenure," 143–44.

86. Levy, *Puerto Ricans in the Empire*, 102–4; "A. A. A. gives out acreage set up for Puerto Rico," *Tobacco Leaf*, 3 Mar. 1934, 5; Nolla, "Primer informe anual," 34.

87. Pessar, "Three Moments in Brazilian Millenarism," 95.

CHAPTER TEN. THE UNRAVELING OF AN INDUSTRY

1. "'La Colectiva' casi totalmente paralizada," *El Mundo*, 13 Sept. 1937, 1, 5.

2. Puerto Rico Tobacco Corporation, "¡Lotería gratis!" *El Mundo*, 20 Sept. 1938, 14.

3. Esteva, *Annual Report*, 8. Pasarell was the local agent for both Congress Cigar Company and the PRATCO parent company in 1938. See Congress Cigar Co., "Annual Report," 1938, AGPR, Estado, Corporaciones foráneas con fines de lucro, caja 33, cxpediente 385; Porto Rican American Tobacco Company, "Annual Report," 1938, AGPR, Estado, Corporaciones foráneas con fines de lucro, caja 36, expediente 423.

He had also been the secretary of PRATCO's local subsidiary in 1937. Refer to "Los Directores de 'La Colectiva' en Tesorería," *La Correspondencia*, 16 Sept. 1937, 1.

4. Department of Labor Wage and Hour Division, Special Industry Committee, "Report, Findings of Fact, and Recommendations for the Tobacco Industry in Puerto Rico," 1955, Archivo Central, Recinto de Río Piedras, UPR, Oficina del Rector, Correspondencia General I-N, 1949–1957, localización 3–193–3, caja 202, 7.

5. Wage and Hour and Public Contracts Division, *Cigar and Cigarette Industry*, 2.

6. F. Hernández Cancel, "Cigarrillos del país desaparecen al cerrar última firma los hacía," *El Mundo*, 18 Feb. 1956, 8a.

7. J. M. Ceballos & Co., *Importers and Exporters*.

8. *Puerto Rico Ilustrado*, 22 Apr. 1939, 86.

9. Luis Muñoz Morales, "Compraventa de fábrica (escritura 26)," 10 May 1915, AGPR, PN, Serie: Siglo XX, Pueblo: San Juan, caja 763, fols. 127–40.

10. "Where Buyer and Seller Meet," *Tobacco Leaf*, 2 Feb. 1935, 35; Infanzon and Rodriguez, "Manufacturers," *Tobacco Leaf*, 5 Jan. 1935, 32.

11. "Transfers," *Tobacco World*, 15 Mar. 1931, 18. M. Solá e Hijos had initially registered the brand in 1902.

12. Departamento de Agricultura y Comercio, *Commercial and Industrial Directory*, 363.

13. "Where to Buy . . . Where to Sell," *United States Tobacco Journal*, 16 Jan. 1937, 43.

14. "Personals," *United States Tobacco Journal*, 27 Feb. 1937, 6; "Infanzon & Rodriguez Brands Show Good Gain," *Tobacco Leaf*, 3 Mar. 1934, 7; Cayey-Caguas Tobacco Company, "Informe anual," 1904–1917, AGPR, Estado, Corporaciones foráneas con fines de lucro, caja 5, expediente 86.

15. Carlos Nieves Rivera, "Uso de papel no desplazaría tabaco, dice R. Rodríguez Ema," *El Mundo*, 20 July 1948, 11; "Penn Tobacco Buys Rosedor Company," *Tobacco World*, 15 Jan. 1933, 4.

16. Wage and Hour and Public Contracts Division, *Leaf Tobacco Industry*, 25.

17. Department of Labor Wage and Hour Division, "Report, Findings of Fact," 7.

18. Ley de la Compañía Agrícola de Puerto Rico, ley número 31, *Leyes de la Asamblea Legislativa de Puerto Rico*, 24 Apr. 1945, 74. PRACO's scope of action was wide ranging. For example, it sought to revive the agriculture of the offshore island of Vieques after the US Navy started to return to the US Department of the Interior large tracts of land it had expropriated only a few years earlier. Refer to Ayala Casás and Bolívar Fresneda, *Battleship Vieques*.

19. José M. García Calderón, "CA tiene máquina que despalilla 60 libras de tabaco en 8 horas," *El Mundo*, 4 Feb. 1948, 22.

20. García Calderón, "CA tiene máquina que despalilla," 22. Although unable to identify his standing in the tobacco industry before joining PRACO, he went on to become a factory manager for the DWG Corporation in Ohio. Refer to *Lima (OH) News*, 29 June 1960, 18.

21. "Comenzó a operar la fábrica de cigarros de Compañía Agrícola," *El Mundo*, 15 Jan. 1948, 1, 12; "Fennell acelerará instalación de fábrica de cigarros este año," *El Mundo*, 14 Nov. 1947, 5, 20. Lynn Baker specialized in "packaged goods accounts, with emphasis on merchandise sold through variety, drug and food stores." Refer to "Lynn Baker Opens Agency," *New York Times*, 31 Jan. 1940, 26.

22. "Fábrica de la PRACO lista a comenzar," *El Mundo*, 25 Nov. 1947, 1; Nieves Rivera, "Uso de papel no desplazaría tabaco," 11; Akehurst, *Tobacco*, 265.

23. Wage and Hour and Public Contracts Division, *Cigar and Cigarette Industry*, 2.

24. "Ley de la Compañía de Fomento de Puerto Rico, ley número 188," *Leyes de la Asamblea Legislativa de Puerto Rico*, 11 May 1942, 942.

25. Dietz, *Puerto Rico*, 44–50; Teodoro Moscoso, "Sobre la industrialización, sus metas y problemas actuales," *Fomento de Puerto Rico, Revista Trimestral* no. 1 (1951): 4.

26. R. Torres Mazzorana, "La fábrica de cigarros Consolidated Cigar proporcionará empleo a 1,000 obreros," *Fomento de Puerto Rico, Revista Trimestral* no. 1 (1951): 15, 23–25; Alfredo Margenat, "Fomento aprueba ampliación operaciones de fábrica de cigarros," *El Mundo*, 12 Feb. 1955, 20.

27. "Creen fábrica cigarros esté lista en marzo," *El Mundo*, 19 Sept. 1952, 1, 16.

28. Alfredo Margenat, "Para curar tabaco—Fomento dará préstamos para 10 ranchos modelos," *El Mundo*, 4 Nov. 1953, 4; "Anuncian un programa insular para almacenamiento tabaco," *El Mundo*, 9 Aug. 1952, 22, 28.

29. Alfredo Margenat, "El Gobernador y el Obispo tienen incidente en Caguas," *El Mundo*, 1 June 1953, 36.

30. Carlos Quesada, "La inversión extranjera: un país, Puerto Rico," *Revista de Ciencias Sociales* 14, no. 4 (1970): 506.

31. "Fábrica daría $5,000 al día al gobierno," *El Mundo*, 9 Feb. 1953, 14; "Colocan mañana la 1ra piedra en fábrica cigarros de Caguas," *El Mundo*, 2 Jan. 1952, 14.

32. "G. H. P. Company Will Remain Unchanged despite Merger with Consolidated," *Tobacco World*, 15 Sept. 1926, 5; "Una comisión de industriales tabacaleros visitó ayer al Gobernador para tratar sobre el movimiento huelgario," *El Mundo*, 8 Aug. 1933, 1, 6, 13.

33. Department of Labor Wage and Hour Division, *Puerto Rico*, 50; "Hicieron dos ventas grandes de tabaco," *El Mundo* 21 Sept. 1949, 4, 20.

34. Margenat, "Para curar tabaco," 4.

35. Margenat, "Fomento aprueba ampliación operaciones," 20.

36. PRIDCO, *13th Anniversary Report*, 12.

37. "La Consolidated establecerá fábrica cigarros en Comerío," *El Mundo*, 1 Aug. 1958, 26.

38. "How Consolidated Cigar Revitalized Puerto Rico Trade," *Tobacco*, 25 Dec. 1959, 14, 16; Luis M. Escribano, "En la Consolidated Cigar, como se trataba de reunión 'no política' Muñoz cambió la frase a 'cuesta arriba,'" *El Mundo*, 7 Oct. 1960, 1, 18.

39. "La Consolidated hará en Comerío un despalillado," *El Mundo*, 6 Apr. 1959, 1, 30.

40. Rafael Santiago Sosa, "Emplearía más de 1,000 fábrica cigarros Caguas planea sucursal Cayey," *El Mundo* 19 June 1957, 1, 27.

41. López Martínez, *Historia de Cayey*, 128; "Nueva fábrica en Cayey producirá 200 millones de cigarros al año," *El Mundo*, 27 June 1959, 20.

42. Nathaniel Soltero, "En Caguas abrirán otra planta despalillar," *El Mundo*, 19 Aug. 1959, 14; "Consolidated dará empleo 3,100 obreros," *El Mundo*, 27 June 1959, 19.

43. "How Consolidated Cigar Revitalized," 14.

44. Douglas D. Richards, "Aumenta en EU uso de tabaco produce isla," *El Mundo*, 3 Oct. 1964, 32.

45. Bureau of the Census, *Census of Population: 1960*, table 106, "Detailed industry of the experienced civilian labor force and of the employed by sex," 337.

46. Rivera Díaz, *Historia de la General Cigar*, 57–62; Departamento de Agricultura y Comercio, *Informe anual, 1954–1955*, 163.

47. Rivera Díaz, *Historia de la General Cigar*, 79.

48. Wage and Hour and Public Contracts Division, *Hearing in the Matter of the Minimum Wage Recommendations of Special Industry Committee no. 17-D for the Tobacco Industry in Puerto Rico*, reported by James A. Brownlee (Washington, DC: n.p., 6–8 Sept. 1955), 49–50; Tobacco Products Manufacturing Corporation of Puerto Rico, "Articles of Incorporation," 22 Dec. 1953, Estado, División de Corporaciones, registro número 4102, transacciones.

49. Rivera Díaz, *Historia de la General*, 95–98.

50. L. Castillo to Mojica, 22 Feb. 1971, Estado, División de Corporaciones, registro número 4102, transacciones; Price, Waterhouse and Co., "Auditor's Report Tobacco Products

Manufacturing Corporation of Puerto Rico," 8 Feb. 1963, Estado, División de Corporaciones, registro número 4102, transacciones.

51. "Mayer y Levis General Cigar elige nuevos ejecutivos," *El Mundo*, 29 May 1968, 52; Rivera Díaz, *Historia de la General*, 94.

52. R. Santiago Sosa, "General Cigar, en Caguas, coloca la primera piedra nuevo edificio $1,200,000," *El Mundo*, 19 Aug. 1964, 22; Joaquín O. Mercado, "General Cigar Co. Plan expansión incluye fábrica en Utuado a un costo de $4 millones," *El Mundo* 10 Apr. 1964, 4.

53. Purcell, "Cuba," 37–39.

54. US Consumer and Marketing Service, Tobacco Division, *Annual Report*, 49.

55. Shanken, "Richard DiMeola."

56. David A. Loehwing, "A Good Five-Cent Cigar," *Barron's National Business and Financial Weekly*, 11 Nov. 1963, 3, 10; Akehurst, *Tobacco*, 265, 479. Reconstituted sheets employ ground tobacco that gets spread over a processed leaf stem adhesive then covered with a final layer of dust that machines wind into sheet rolls. Refer to Akehurst, *Tobacco*, 485–86.

57. Mercado, "General Cigar Co.," 4. Price, Waterhouse and Co., "Auditor's Report General Cigar of Utuado," 28 Jan. 1970, Estado, División de Corporaciones, registro número 1836, transacciones; Marlén Rojas Daporta, "En Utuado mujeres predominan en personal que trabaja en fábrica de cigarros," Saturday Supplement, *El Mundo*, 18 Sept. 1965, 3.

58. Aníbal Díaz Montero, "Tabaco importado," *El Mundo*, 27 Sept. 1965, 6.

59. "Consolidated compra 92% cosecha tabaco," *El Mundo*, 12 Aug. 1969, 12a.

60. Surgeon General's Advisory Committee, *Smoking and Health*, 37. For the context of the report, refer to Brandt, *Cigarette Century*, 211–40.

61. Kluger, *Ashes to Ashes*, 286, 784.

62. Magalit Fox, "Edgar M. Cullman Sr., Who Helped Turn Cigars into Objects of Desire, Is Dead at 93," *New York Times*, 29 Aug. 2011, A25.

63. Grise and Griffin, *U.S. Tobacco Industry*, 9; Shanken, "Interview with Edgar Cullman Jr."

64. "La agricultura de Puerto Rico," 124.

65. PRIDCO, *12th Annual Report*, 9; PRIDCO, *13th Annual Report*, 12. Richard Mourey, "Firm Shifts Work to Puerto Rico, Thinning Ranks of 'Tobacco Row,'" *Hartford Courant*, 5 May 1954, 1; Economic Development Administration, *Puerto Rico Official*, G-100.

66. "Hartman Tobacco Company of Puerto Rico v. Secretario de Hacienda," 81 *Decisiones de Puerto Rico* 620.

67. Mourey, "Firm Shifts Work to Puerto Rico," 1.

68. Luis Sánchez Cappa, "Industria tabaco vuelva a impugnar comité salarios," *El Mundo*, 7 Sept. 1955, 1; Wage and Hour and Public Contracts Division, *Hearing in the Matter of the Minimum Wage Recommendations*.

69. Mack, *Cigar Manufacturing Industry*, 72.

70. Loehwing, "Good Five-Cent Cigar," 10; Edward Hopper's *Nighthawks*, an oil painting of a diner, immortalized the brand in 1942.

71. PRIDCO, *19th Annual Report*, 5, 12; Newman with Miller, *Cigar Family*, 111; Price, Waterhouse and Co., "Auditor's Report Bayuk Caribe, Inc.," 3 Feb. 1976, Estado, División de Corporaciones, registro número 4378, transacciones.

72. "A Salute to DWG Cigar Corporation," *Lima (OH) News*, 7 Oct. 1964, 9.

73. Department of Labor Wage and Hour Division, *Puerto Rico*, 49.

74. Hope Strong, "His Ole' Stogie Gets Lovin' Touch," *Lima (OH) News*, 25 Feb. 1968, C-3.

75. PRIDCO, *19th Annual Report*, 5; "Certificates Authorizing the Employment of Learners at Special Minimun Wages," *Federal Register* 30, no. 188 (29 Sept. 1965): 12,437.

76. Joaquín O. Mercado, "Fomento hará 2 edificios," 8; "Certificates Authorizing the Employment of Learners at Special Minimun Wages," *Federal Register* 30, no. 126 (1 July 1965): 8,428;

R. T. Prior, "Department of State," 9 Apr. 1965, Estado, División de Corporaciones, registro número 1994, transacciones.

77. Waitt & Bond, *Tobacco Wrapper*.

78. Mercado, "Fomento hará 2 edificios," 8.

79. Aníbal Muñoz, "Rapaport International, Inc.," 6 Apr. 1967, Estado, División de Corporaciones, registro número 1993, transacciones.

80. Aníbal Muñoz, "Rapaport Puerto Rico, Inc.," 17 June 1968, Estado, División de Corporaciones, registro número 1994, transacciones.

81. Aníbal Muñoz, "Rapaport International, Inc.," 17 June 1968, Estado, División de Corporaciones, registro número 1993, transacciones.

82. Lybrand, Ross Bros, & Montgomery, "Rapaport International, Inc.," 8 Apr. 1971, Estado, División de Corporaciones, registro número 1993, transacciones; "Allied Cigar's Test of Waitt & Bond's Wrapper a Success," *United States Tobacco Journal*, 11 Feb. 1971, 1, 13.

83. Hochstein, *Cigars and Other Passions*, 180; Economic Development Administration, *Official Industrial & Trade Directory*, 72. See also Shanken, "Interview with Edgar M. Cullman Sr."

84. Economic Development Administration, *Puerto Rico Official Industrial Directory*, 6th ed., 363

85. Gloria I. Silva de Díaz, "O'Connor, Calabria & Barney," 27 Sept. 1968, Estado, División de Corporaciones, registro número 2461, transacciones.

86. "Universal Cigar Files for Secondary," *Securities and Exchange Commission News Digest*, no. 64-8-18 (27 Aug. 1964): 1.

87. Ernst & Whinney, "Balance Sheets," 29 Jan. 1974, Estado, División de Corporaciones, registro número 2461, transacciones.

88. Universal International Cigar Corporation, "Informe de corporaciones foráneas," 15 Apr. 1974, Estado, División de Corporaciones, registro número 3355, transacciones.

89. Economic Development Administration, *Puerto Rico Official Industrial Directory*, 9th ed., 186; Economic Development Administration, *Puerto Rico Official Industrial Directory* (1979), 190.

90. Ana Luisa Santo Domingo to José L. Calabria, 23 Mar. 1983, Estado, División de Corporaciones, registro número 3355, transacciones.

91. Tilley, *R. J. Reynolds Tobacco Company*, 187–225.

92. B. Olavarría García, "R. J. Reynolds abrirá fábrica cigarrillos aquí," *El Mundo*, 6 Nov. 1970, 6B.

93. "R. J. Reynolds Tobacco Co. and Unión General de Trabajadores," *Decisions and Orders of the National Labor Relations Board* 240, no. 89 (7 Feb. 1979): 620.

94. Mariano Mier, "Pero expande operaciones acá," *El Nuevo Día*, 16 Sept. 1993, 140.

95. "Planta de tratamiento de tabaco," *El Nuevo Día*, 22 Nov. 1995, 144.

96. Lida Estela Ruaño, "R. J. Reynolds Investing $40 Million Here," *Caribbean Business*, 20 Feb. 1997, 9.

97. Dávila, *Sponsored Identities*, 180.

98. Guevara Monge, "Estudio evaluativo," 24–26.

99. Taína Rosa, "R. J. Reynolds Copes with Excise Tax Increase," *Caribbean Business*, 12 Dec. 2002, 14.

100. "Reynolds to Shut Yabucoa Cigarette Plant, Cut 60 Jobs," *Caribbean Business*, 3 June 2010, 58; Marian Díaz, "Cierra RJ Reynolds en Yabucoa," *El Nuevo Día*, 29 May 2010, 43.

101. Andrea Martínez, "R. J. Reynolds pasa el batón en la Isla," *El Nuevo Día*, 29 Oct. 2015, 44; Michael J. de la Merced and Chad Bray, "To Compete with Altria, Reynolds American is Buying Lorillard," *New York Times*, 15 July 2014.

102. Luis Sánchez Cappa, "De mayo a noviembre prevén 3,000 ociosos en los despalillados," *El Mundo*, 19 Dec. 1957, 1, 20.

103. Pedro Hernández, hijo, "Situación 'caótica': Comerío cierra almacenes despalillados y 1,248 personas quedan desempleadas," *El Mundo*, 4 Dec. 1957, 4.

104. David S. Campbell, "Puerto Rico Tobacco Region Area Analysis," 1942, University of Florida Archives, Raymond E. Crist Papers.

105. My translation of José M. García Calderón, "CA tiene máquina que despalilla 60 libras de tabaco en 8 horas," *El Mundo*, 4 Feb. 1948, 22. A strip refers to the sides of the leaf that remain after the removal of the stem or midrib.

106. "Explican servicios de la P.M.A a los productores de tabaco," *El Mundo*, 19 Jan. 1953, 11.

107. Akehurst, *Tobacco*, 477–78.

108. Department of Labor Wage and Hour Division, "Report, Findings of Fact," 1.

109. Pedro Hernández, hijo, "Realizan aquí gestión pro despalillados: Tratan aplazar mecanización," *El Mundo*, 19 Nov, 1957, 18.

110. Akehurst, *Tobacco*, 186, 475.

111. Akehurst, *Tobacco*, 301, 478; Hernández, "Realizan aquí gestión pro despalillados," 1, 18.

112. Department of Labor Wage and Hour Division, "Report, Findings of Fact," 2, 5; "How Consolidated Cigar Revitalized," 16.

113. Sánchez Cappa, "De mayo a noviembre prevén 3,000 ociosos," 1, 20.

114. Antonio Miranda, "Afectaría a 400: Tratan evitar se elimine despalillado en Utuado," *El Mundo*, 24 Nov. 1959, 1, 15.

115. Bureau of the Census, *Census of Population: 1960*, table 106, "Detailed industry of the experienced civilian labor force and of the employed by sex," 337.

116. Grise and Griffin, *U.S. Tobacco industry*, 9.

117. Grise and Griffin, *U.S. Tobacco Industry*, 9.

118. Department of Agriculture, *Annual Book on Statistics*, 142

119. Bureau of the Census, *Statistical Abstract*, 889, 891.

120. Bureau of the Census, *Fourteenth Census, Reports for States, with Statistics for Principal Cities*, 9:1692; Bureau of the Census, *Fourteenth Census, Population 1920 Occupation*, 4:1286.

121. Frederick Andrews, "Sharon Steel Appears the Loser in Fight for Foremost-McKesson," *New York Times*, 3 Apr. 1977, 45; Kenneth N. Gilpin, "Victor Posner, 83, Master of Hostile Takeover," *New York Times*, 13 Feb. 2002, A00029; John Slatter, "Vanishing Indians? Cigar Manufacturers Are Seeking to Diversify," *Barron's National Business and Financial Weekly*, 12 June 1967, 11.

122. Strong, "His Ole' Stogie Gets Lovin' Touch," C-3; "DWG Chief Quits, Cites Policy Strife, Posner Replaces Gordon," *Lima (OH) News*, 17 June 1966, 17.

123. Economic Development Administration, *Puerto Rico Official Industrial* (1971), G-100. The factory fails to appear in subsequent editions of the directory.

124. John S. Rosenberg, "Shade-Tobacco Growers Face Uncertain Future," Connecticut Weekly, *New York Times*, 1 June 1980, 8.

125. "Bayuk to Close Plant," *New York Times*, 18 May 1977, 87; Harrigan, *Declining Demand*, 256.

126. General Cigar Company, *1975 Annual Report*, 12.

127. Business International Corporation, *Puerto Rico, Critical Choices*, 60, 74; Clarence Beardsley, "General Cigar cierra plantas: 465 sin empleo," *El Mundo*, 14 July 1979, 1, 12A; Ariel Ortiz Tellechea, "Timaron a Fomento," *El Mundo*, 14 July 1979, 2.

128. Hernández Paralitici, *Utuado*, 96.

129. Aníbal Muñoz, "Rapaport International, Inc.," 6 Apr. 1967, Estado, División de Corporaciones, registro número 1993, transacciones; "Cigar Maker Changes Name," *New York Times*, 16 June 1964, 54.

130. "Compañía de Fomento Industrial de Puerto Rico, demandante, vs. Rapaport International de Puerto Rico, Inc., demandada. Cidanjo Company, interventora," 10 Mar. 1976, Tribunal Superior de Puerto Rico, Sala de San Juan; J. Adrián Rebollo, "Rapaport International de P.R.," 27 Apr.1976, Estado, División de Corporaciones, registro número 1994, transacciones.

131. Economic Development Administration, *Puerto Rico Official Industrial Directory* (1979), 224. The factory fails to appear in subsequent editions of the directory.

132. Economic Development Administration, *Official Industrial & Trade Directory*, 2nd. ed., 70; Economic Development Administration, *Puerto Rico Official Industrial Directory*, 5th ed., 159.

133. Economic Development Administration, *Puerto Rico Official Industrial Directory*, 5th ed., 156, 159.

134. Amanda Díaz de Hoyo, "Tabacos con sabor de aquí," *El Nuevo Día*, 12 June 1997, 92–93; Ruth N. Tellado Domenech, "Un oficio que no muere," *El Nuevo Día*, 7 Dec. 2003, 8, 21; Economic Development Administration, *Puerto Rico Official Industrial Directory* (1972–1973), 474; Economic Development Administration, *Puerto Rico Official Industrial Directory* (1977), 142.

135. Larry Luxner, "Will Cigar Industry Rise from the Ashes?," *San Juan Star*, 11 Apr. 1993, 8.

136. Michelle González Paonessa, "Sigue en pie tabaquería de Bayamón," *El Todo*, 29 Jan.–4 Feb. 2015, 4; J. F. C. Tobacco Corp., "Certificado de incorporación," 10 Jan. 1996, Estado, División de Corporaciones, registro número 93447, transacciones.

137. Sharon Minelli Pérez, "La impresionante fábrica de Cayey donde se hacen 2,600 cigarros por hora," *El Nuevo Día*, 20 Jan. 2020, 16; "La fábrica de cigarros Congar invertirá $23 millones en cuatro años," *Sin Comillas*, 26 May 2021, https://sincomillas.com/la-fabrica-de-cigarros-congar-invertira-23-millones-en-cuatro-anos.

138. Baldrich, prologue to *Voces libertarias*, 11–17; Pesotta, *Bread upon the Waters*, 130.

139. Dávila Santiago, *El derribo de las murallas*, 133, 146; Rivera Martínez, "Santiago Iglesias y yo," 207, 209.

140. "Expenditures for August, 1913," *Cigar Makers Official Journal* 37, no. 8 (Sept. 1913): 34; "Death Benefits Paid, March, 1916," *Cigar Makers Official Journal* 40, no. 8 (Aug. 1916): 36.

141. Secretary of Porto Rico, *Register of Porto Rico for 1910*, 218.

142. Pérez Velasco, "La condición obrera," 167.

143. Junta Insular de Elecciones, *Estadísticas de las elecciones celebradas en Puerto Rico el 4 de noviembre de 1924*.

144. Silvestrini de Pacheco, *Los trabajadores puertorriqueños*, 29; Industrial Commission, *Annual Report*, 8.

145. Badillo and Soltero, "Se constituye el Partido Laborista Puro," 603.

146. American Federation of Labor, *Report of the Proceedings*, 223.

147. Quintero Rivera, "La clase obrera," 279; Silvestrini de Pacheco, *Los trabajadores puertorriqueños*, 108–9; Taller de Formación Política, *¡Huelga en la caña!*, 10, 19, 71.

148. Taller de Formación Política, *¡Huelga en la caña!*, 69.

149. "Los obreros y patronos de la industria de la azúcar acordaron ayer iniciar conversaciones a través de sendos comités," *El Mundo*, 16 Sept. 1933, 11.

150. Taller de Formación Política, *¡Huelga en la caña!*, 71–72, 79–87, 177.

151. "La huelga de la fábrica de tabacos se mantiene firme," *La Correspondencia*, 7 May 1937, 1; Francisco Colón Gordiany, "Arreglada la huelga en los talleres de 'La Colectiva,'" *El Mundo*, 10 May 1937, 4.

152. Nicolás Nogueras Rivera, "El Lcdo. Colón Gordiany silenció ante la trabajadoras," *La Correspondencia*, 25 May 1937, 5.

153. Francisco Colón Gordiany, "Las partes en controversia no se abroquelan en actitudes," *La Correspondencia*, 25 May 1937, 8.

154. Evaristo Echevarría, "Celebran asamblea esta tarde," *El Mundo*, 27 May 1937, 6; Ana María Luciano, "Las obreras de 'La Colectiva,'" *El Mundo*, 25 May 1937, 4.

155. "Se afilia a la Federación Libre," *El Mundo*, 1 June 1937, 18.

156. F. Paz Granela, "Se espera que los propietarios de todos los despalillados firmarán el convenio ya en vigor en la industria," *La Correspondencia*, 27 Sept. 1937, 1, 8; "Progresan las conversaciones," *El Mundo*, 26 Aug. 1937, 8.

157. Departamento del Trabajo, "'El convenio de la industria del tabaco beneficia a diez mil 618 trabajadores de ambos sexos,'" *La Correspondencia*, 25 Sept. 1937, 1, 9.

158. "Rivera Martínez le informa al Gobernador," *El Mundo*, 17 July 1937, 5.

159. Nicolás Santiago, "Conflicto huelgario resuelto en Coamo," *El Mundo*, 23 Aug. 1937, 15. For the number of strikers see Commissioner of Labor, *Annual Report, 1937–1938*, 58.

160. "Huelga de 700 mujeres en los despalillados de Aibonito," *La Correspondencia*, 20 Aug. 1937, 1; "Protesta de Francisco Ortiz Lebrón," *El Mundo*, 21 Aug. 1937, 4; Commissioner of Labor, *Annual Report, 1937–1938*, 58; "Los patronos de Aibonito ausentes," *El Mundo*, 23 Aug. 1937, 7.

161. Commissioner of Labor, *Annual Report, 1937–1938*, 58–59; Commissioner of Labor, *Annual Report, 1938–1939*, 46–47.

162. Commissioner of Labor, *Annual Report, 1938–1939*, 11; Commissioner of Labor, *Annual Report, 1939–1940*, 12–13.

163. Taller de Formación Política, *No estamos pidiendo el cielo*.

164. García and Quintero Rivera, *Desafío y solidaridad*; Lugo del Toro, *Nacimiento y auge*.

165. José M. Santiago and Claudio Sánchez, "Tabaqueros respaldan al gobernador Tugwell," *El Imparcial*, 6 May 1942, 7.

166. Commissioner of Labor, *Annual Report, 1941–1942*, 87.

167. Lugo del Toro, *Nacimiento y auge*, 260.

168. "Firmaron un convenio colectivo ayer," *El Mundo*, 20 May 1942, 5; "Huelga de despalilladoras resuelta," *El Mundo*, 14 May 1942, 7.

169. Lugo del Toro, *Nacimiento y auge*, 357–59.

170. Junta de Salario Mínimo, *La industria del tabaco en rama*, 25–26; "Se celebrará reunión tabaqueros," *El Mundo*, 1 May 1942, 7; "Un convenio sobre despalillado de tabaco," *El Mundo*, 20 Apr. 1942, 1, 3.

171. Wage and Hour and Public Contracts Division, *Leaf Tobacco Industry*, 22, 25.

172. Quesada, "La inversión extranjera," 510.

173. Rivera Díaz, *Historia de la General*, 247–48.

174. As the FLT and the CGT withered, US-based trade unions, like the Machinists here, started an intense organizational drive. Ayala and Bernabe, *Puerto Rico in the American Century*, 232–33.

175. Miguel A. Santín, "Trasfondo," *El Mundo*, 27 Sept. 1968, 7; Rivera Díaz, *Historia de la General*, 241–42.

176. Santín, "Trasfondo," 7; Rivera Díaz, *Historia de la General*, 258.

177. Rivera Díaz, *Historia de la General*, 258–59.

178. Ferdinand Torres, "Gastronómica intenta organizar primer paro en Consolidated Cigar," *La Hora*, 8 Sept. 1972, 5.

179. "R. J. Reynolds Tobacco Co. and Unión General de Trabajadores," 620.

180. "R. J. Reynolds Tobacco Co. and Unión General de Trabajadores," 621, 624.

181. Arbona Martínez and Núñez Miranda, *Pedro Grant*, 102–3, 149.

182. Félix Córdova Iturregui extended this point to all Fomento-sponsored enterprises. Refer to Córdova Iturregui, "La Confederación General de Trabajadores: Una vida corta y deslumbrante," *Claridad*, 28 Mar.–3 Apr. 2003, 22–23.

183. Buitrago Ortiz, *Esperanza*, 14–15.

184. "La agricultura de Puerto Rico," 115.

185. González Villafañe and Espinet, "Análisis económico," 3–4, 6.

186. Billy Suárez, "Función social del traficante de tabaco," *El Mundo*, 23 May 1956, 15.

187. Wage and Hour and Public Contracts Division, *Hearing*, 129.

188. Wage and Hour and Public Contracts Division, *Leaf Tobacco Industry in Puerto Rico*, 25–28; Pedro Hernández, hijo, "En Comerío: Lunes vuelven a operar los despalillados," *El Mundo*, 16 June 1956, 1,18.

189. Junta de Salario Mínimo, *La industria del tabaco en rama*, 26.

190. D. Douglas Richard, "En vista salarios señalan hay una baja en elaboración tabaco," *El Mundo*, 24 Oct. 1958, 4.

191. "La agricultura de Puerto Rico," 124.

192. Piñero, "Study of the Puerto Rico Tobacco Marketing Cooperative Association," 63; "La agricultura de Puerto Rico," 124.

193. González Villafañe and Espinet, "Análisis económico," 5.

194. "La agricultura de Puerto Rico," 120.

195. "Report Made on Cuba, General Cigar Sees Most at Investment Salvaged," *New York Times*, 5 Nov. 1960, 37.

196. Pat Munroe, "Agricultura Federal, augura buen mercado en EU para cigarros de Pto. Rico," *El Mundo*, 1 Oct. 1963, 24.

197. Ignacio Duarte Alfonso, "Esperan visita de grupo compraría tabaco de aquí," *El Mundo*, 7 Mar. 1962, 25.

198. Grise and Griffin, *U.S. Tobacco Industry*, 53.

199. "La agricultura de Puerto Rico," 124–26.

200. Shanken, "Richard DiMeola."

201. Gordon Mott, "A Century Mark," *Cigar Aficionado*, Spring 1995; "Sanciones EU favorecerán tabaco Isla," *El Mundo*, 17 Feb. 1962, 39.

202. Miguel Meléndez Ortiz, "Puerto Rico's Changing Tobacco Trade Scene," *Tobacco*, 25 Dec. 1959, 12.

203. Grise and Griffin, *U.S. Tobacco Industry*, 53.

204. Anson Richard Cooke and George Robert Starke, Method for Inhibiting the Growth of Tobacco Suckers, US Patent 3,880,643, filed 12 Aug. 1972, and issued 29 Apr. 1975; Anson Richard Cooke and George Robert Starke, Method for Inhibiting the Growth of Tobacco Suckers, US Patent 4,077,795, filed 12 Feb. 1975, and issued 7 Mar. 1978.

205. For the number and identification of several cultivars refer to the Agricultural Research Service, *Plant Inventory no. 200, Part II, Plant Materials Introduced May 1 to August 31, 1991 (nos. 550931 to 555395)* (Beltsville, Maryland: US Department of Agriculture, 1991), 266.

206. Rafael Santiago Sosa, "Explican ayuda Gobierno dará a tabacaleros," *El Mundo*, 15 Sept. 1956, 22.

207. Alfredo Margenat, "Plan agencias agrícolas, se sembrarán semilleros en 18 zonas tabacaleras," *El Mundo*, 9 Aug. 1957, 32.

208. A. Quiñones Calderón, "Agricultura dispone de plantitas tabaco," *El Mundo*, 7 Nov. 1967, 14.

209. "Secretario Agricultura: Objeta editorial critica cuotas producción tabaco," *El Mundo*, 7 Aug. 1962, 13.

210. González Villafañe and Espinet, "Análisis económico," 4.

211. "La agricultura de Puerto Rico," 115; González Villafañe and Espinet, "Análisis económico," 4.

212. Agricultural Marketing Service, *Annual Report on Tobacco Statistics, 1990*, 6–7; Agricultural Marketing Service, *Annual Report on Tobacco Statistics, 1998*, 23; Grise and Griffin, *U.S. Tobacco Industry*, 53.

213. Eliot, "Hollow Men," 108.

214. "Dan gran apoyo a la siembra de tabaco en Comerío," *El Nuevo Día*, 22 June 1998, 93; "Exitosa cosecha de tabaco," *Boletín Informativo del Comité de Educación de la Cooperativa Agro Comercial* 1 (July 1998): 1; Cooperativa Agro Comercial de Puerto Rico, *Folleto informativo*, 7, 13.

215. Frances Rosario, "Vivo el cultivo del tabaco boricua," *El Nuevo Día*, 15 Apr. 2001, 60.

216. Rut N. Tellado Domenech, "La Hoja del Chan," *El Nuevo Día*, 15 Feb. 2021, 24.

217. Cesiach López Maldonado, "Hermanos Castro emprenden proyecto familiar agrícola en la Finca NeoJibairo," *Primera Hora*, 12 Aug. 2018, https://www.primerahora.com/noticias/puerto-rico/nota/hermanoscastroemprendenproyectofamiliaragricolaenlafincaneojibairo-1297080/.

CONCLUSION

1. Ortiz, *Cuban Counterpoint*, 183–253.

2. St. Helen et al., "Differences in Nicotine Intake," 757–67.

3. Cooper, *Once a Cigar Maker*, viii.

4. García Colón, *Colonial Migrants*.

5. Agustín Muñoz Santiago, "Los Hermanos Cheos en búsqueda de la juventud," *El Sol*, 4–17 Mar. 2021, 6.

6. Eusebio Ramos Morales, "Decreto sobre asuntos devocionales relacionados con la Santa Montaña," *El Visitante*, 13–19 Jan. 2019, 18.

7. Silva Gotay, *Catolicismo y política*, 313–23.

BIBLIOGRAPHY

Abad, José Ramón. *La exposición agrícola e industrial de tabaco realizada en Ponce durante el mes de diciembre de 1883*. Ponce, PR: El Vapor, 1884.

Abad, José Ramón. *Puerto Rico en la feria-exposición de Ponce en 1882*. Ponce, PR: El Comercio, 1885.

Abad, José Ramón. *La República Dominicana: Reseña general geográfico-estadística*. Santo Domingo, DR: Imprenta de García Hermanos, 1888.

Ackerman, Diane. *A Natural History of the Senses*. New York: Random House, 1990.

Acosta, Úrsula. *Cofresí y Ducoudray: Hombres al margen de la historia*. Río Piedras, PR: Editorial Edil, 1991.

Agosto Cintrón, Nélida. *Religión y cambio social en Puerto Rico (1898–1940)*. Río Piedras, PR: Ateneo Puertorriqueño and Ediciones Huracán, 1996

"La agricultura de Puerto Rico: Situación y posibilidades." *Revista de Agricultura de Puerto Rico* 53, nos. 1–2 (January–December 1966): 1–205.

Agricultural Marketing Service. *Annual Report on Tobacco Statistics, 1990*. Washington, DC: Agricultural Marketing Service, 1991.

Agricultural Marketing Service. *Annual Report on Tobacco Statistics, 1998*. Washington, DC: Agricultural Marketing Service, 1999.

Aguayo, Ricardo C. *Manual del cultivo de tabaco, precedido de su historia, su monografía y caracteres botánicos, y otros conocimientos generales que conducen a aquel objeto*. Ponce, PR: Establecimiento Tipográfico El Vapor, 1876.

Aiken, Conrad. "Impulse." In *Collected Short Stories of Conrad Aiken*, 159–72. 1934. Reprint, London: Heinemann, 1966.

Aizpurua Aguirre, Ramón. "El corso de la Compañía Guipuzcoana: Los casos de la lancha San Fernando y de la balandra Nuestra Señora de Aránzazu." *Itsas Memoria: Revista de Estudios Marítimos del País Vasco* no. 5 (2006): 379–92.

Akehurst, B. C. *Tobacco*. New York: Humanities Press, 1968.

Alonso Álvarez, Luis. "Pautas de consumo y cambio tecnológico: La evidencia del tabaco en España, 1735–1886." In *El tabaco en la historia económica: Estudios sobre fiscalidad, consumo y empresa (siglos xvii–xx)*, edited by Luis Alonso Álvarez, Lina Gálvez Muñoz and Santiago de Luxán, 247–70. Madrid: Fundación Altadis, 2006.

Alonso, Manuel A. *El jíbaro*. 1849. Reprint, Río Piedras, PR: Colegio Hostos, 1949.

Álvarez Curbelo, Silvia. "El Motín de los Faroles y otras luminosas protestas: Disturbios populares en Puerto Rico, 1894." *Historia y Sociedad* 2 (1989): 120–46.

Álvarez Nazario, Manuel. *El habla campesina del país: Orígenes y desarrollo del español en Puerto Rico*. San Juan: Editorial de la UPR, 1990.

American Federation of Labor. *Report of the Proceedings of the 61st Annual Convention of the American Federation of Labor Held at Seattle, Washington, 1941*. Washington, DC: Ransdell, 1941.

Ansell, Christopher K. "Symbolic Networks: The Realignment of the French Working Class, 1887–1894." *American Journal of Sociology* 103, no. 2 (1997): 359–90.

Aráez y Ferrando, Román. *Historia del ciclón del día de San Ciriaco.* San Juan: Imprenta del Heraldo Español, 1905.

Araúz Monfante, Celestino Andrés. "La acción ilegal de los holandeses en el Caribe y su impacto en las Antillas y Puerto Rico durante la primera mitad del siglo XVIII." *Revista/Review Interamericana* 14, nos. 1–4 (1984): 67–79.

Arbona Martínez, Ramón, and Armindo Núñez Miranda. *Pedro Grant: La vida una lucha, una lucha la vida: Memorias de un líder sindical.* San Juan: Ediciones Callejón, 2005.

Arcila Farías, Eduardo. *Economía colonial de Venezuela.* Mexico City: Fondo de Cultura Económica, 1946.

Asenjo, Conrado. *Quién es quién en Puerto Rico, 1936–37.* San Juan: Real Hermanos, 1936.

Ashford, Bailey K. *A Soldier in Science: The Autobiography of Bailey K. Ashford, Colonel M.C., U.S.A.* 1934. Reprint, Río Piedras: Editorial de la UPR, 1998.

Augelli, John P. "Rural Settlement Types of Interior Puerto Rico: Sample Studies from the Upper Loíza Basin." In *Symposium on the Geography of Puerto Rico*, edited by Clarence F. Jones and Rafael Picó, 325–36. Río Piedras: University of Puerto Rico Press, 1955.

Augelli, John P. "Sugar Cane and Tobacco: A Comparison of Agricultural Types in the Highlands of Eastern Puerto Rico." *Economic Geography* 29, no. 1 (1953): 63–73.

Ayala Casás, César, and José L. Bolívar Fresneda. *Battleship Vieques: Puerto Rico from World War II to the Korean War.* Princeton, NJ: Markus Wiener Publishers, 2011.

Ayala, César J., and Laird W. Bergad. *Agrarian Puerto Rico: Reconsidering Rural Economy and Society, 1899–1940.* Cambridge: Cambridge University Press, 2020.

Ayala, César J., and Rafael Bernabe. *Puerto Rico in the American Century: A History since 1898.* Chapel Hill: University of North Carolina Press, 2007.

Badillo, Samuel E., and Nathaniel Soltero. "Se constituye el Partido Laborista Puro." In *Puerto Rico: Cien años de lucha política*, edited by Reece B. Bothwell González, 603–12. Vol. 1 *Programas y Manifiestos*, bk. 1 (1869–1952). 1939. Reprint, Río Piedras, PR: Editorial Universitaria, 1979.

Baer, Willis N. *The Economic Development of the Cigar Manufacturing Industry in the United States.* Lancaster, PA: Art Printing Company, 1933.

Baldrich, Juan José. "Cigars and Cigarettes in Nineteenth Century Cuba." *Revista/Review Interamericana* 24, nos. 1–4 (1994): 8–35.

Baldrich, Juan José. "From the Origins of Industrial Capitalism in Puerto Rico to Its Subordination to the U.S. Tobacco Trust: Rucabado and Company, 1865–1901." *Revista Mexicana del Caribe* 3, no. 5 (1998): 80–106.

Baldrich, Juan José. "Gender and the Decomposition of the Cigar-Making Craft in Puerto Rico, 1899–1931." In *Puerto Rican Women's History: New Perspectives*, edited by Félix V. Matos Rodríguez and Linda C. Delgado, 105–25. Armonk, NY: M. E. Sharpe, 1998.

Baldrich, Juan José. Prologue to *Voces libertarias: Los orígenes del anarquismo en Puerto Rico*, rev. ed., by Jorell A. Meléndez Badillo, 11–17. Lajas, PR: Editorial Akelarre, 2015.

Baldrich, Juan José. *Sembraron la no siembra: Los cosecheros de tabaco puertorriqueños frente a las corporaciones tabacaleras, 1920–1934.* Río Piedras, PR: Huracán, 1988.

Baldrich, Juan José. "Tobacco Leaf Dealers in Puerto Rico in the Twilight of the Colony with Spain, 1860–1898." In *Actas del XXIII Coloquio de Historia Canario-Americana, celebrado del 8 al 12 de octubre de 2018*, 1–11. Las Palmas, Spain: Cabildo de Gran Canaria, 2020.

Baralt, Guillermo. *Buena Vista: Life and Work on a Puerto Rican Hacienda, 1833–1904.* Chapel Hill: University of North Carolina Press, 1999.

Barkun, Michael. *Disaster and the Millennium.* New Haven, CT: Yale University Press, 1974.

Barragán, Feliciano. "El clero de la diócesis de San Juan de Puerto Rico (1874–1924)." *Anuario de Historia de la Iglesia* 7 (1998): 85–125.

Bastide, Roger. Preface to *Historia y etnología de los movimientos mesiánicos: Reforma y revolución en las sociedades tradicionales*, by Maria Isaura Pereira de Queiroz, 3–13. Mexico City: Siglo Veintiuno Editores, 1969.

Batchelder, Robert B. "Land Use Problems in the Minor Commercial Agricultural Region of the Hinterland of Isabela." In *Symposium on the Geography of Puerto Rico*, edited by Clarence F. Jones and Rafael Picó, 129–53. Río Piedras: University of Puerto Rico Press, 1955.

Baud, Michiel. *Modernidad y luchas sociales en la sociedad dominicana, siglos XIX y XX*. Santo Domingo: Academia Dominicana de la Historia, 2020.

Baud, Michiel. *Peasants and Tobacco in the Dominican Republic, 1870–1930*. Knoxville: University of Tennessee Press, 1995.

Bird Carmona, Arturo. *Parejeros y desafiantes: La comunidad tabaquera de Puerta de Tierra a principios del siglo XX*. San Juan: Huracán, 2008.

Blanch, José. *Directorio comercial e industrial de Puerto-Rico para 1894 formado con relaciones oficiales remitidas por los Sres. alcaldes de cada localidad y compilados por José Blanch*. [San Juan?]: La Correspondencia, 1894.

Blanco Fernández, Antonio. *España y Puerto Rico, 1820–1930*. San Juan: Cantero Fernández y Co., 1930.

Bloch-Dano, Evelyne. *Le dernier amour de George Sand*. Paris: Éditions Grasset et Fasquelle, 2010.

Bonnin, María Isabel. "Los contratos de refacción y el decaimiento de la hacienda tradicional en Ponce: 1865–1880." *Op. Cit.* no. 3 (1987–1988): 123–50.

Brandt, Allan M. *The Cigarette Century: The Rise, Fall and Deadly Persistence of the Product that Defined America*. New York: Basic Books, 2007.

Braudel, Fernand. *Civilización material, economía y capitalismo, siglos XV–XVIII*. Vol. 1, *Las estructuras de lo cotidiano: lo posible y lo imposible*. Madrid: Alianza Editorial, 1984.

Breen, Benjamin. *The Age of Intoxication: Origins of the Global Drug Trade*. Philadelphia: University of Pennsylvania Press, 2019.

Bryan, William S., ed. *Our Islands and Their People*. Saint Louis, MO: N. D. Thompson Publishing, 1899.

Buitrago Ortiz, Carlos. *Esperanza: An Ethnographic Study of a Peasant Community in Puerto Rico*. Tucson: University of Arizona Press, 1973.

Bunker, Héctor R. "Dos biografías: Harrison Johnson y Franklin H. Bunker." In *Antología histórica de Caguas: Año del Bicentenario, 1975*, edited by Enrique Lugo Silva, 337–39. Caguas, PR: Ediciones Club de Leones de Caguas, 1976.

Bunker, Oscar L. *Historia de Caguas*. 2 vols. Barcelona: M. Pareja, 1975–1981.

Bureau of Corporations. *Capitalization, Investment, and Earnings*. Report of the Commissioner of Corporations on the Tobacco Industry, part 2. Washington, DC: GPO, 1911.

Bureau of Corporations. *Position of the Tobacco Combination in the Industry*. Report of the Commissioner of Corporations on the Tobacco Industry, part 1. Washington, DC: GPO, 1909.

Bureau of Corporations. *Prices, Costs, and Profits*. Report of the Commissioner of Corporations on the Tobacco Industry, part 3. Washington, DC: GPO, 1915.

Bureau of the Census. *Census of Population: 1960*. Vol. 1, *Characteristics of the Population*, part 53, Puerto Rico. Washington. DC: GPO, 1963.

Bureau of the Census. *Electrical Industries of Porto Rico, 1907*. Washington, DC: GPO, 1909.

Bureau of the Census. *Fifteenth Census of the United States: 1930. Outlying Territories and Possessions*. Washington, DC: GPO, 1932.

Bureau of the Census. *Fourteenth Census of the United States: 1920*. Vol. 4, *Population 1920 Occupation*. Washington, DC: GPO, 1923.

Bureau of the Census. *Fourteenth Census of the United States: 1920*. Vol. 9, *Reports for States, with Statistics for Principal Cities*. Washington, DC: GPO, 1923.

Bureau of the Census. *Historical Statistics of the United States, Colonial Times to 1970, Bicentennial Edition*. Vol. 2. Washington, DC: GPO, 1975.

Bureau of the Census. *Sixteenth Census of the United States: 1940, Puerto Rico*. Vol. 2. *Characteristics of the Population*. Washington, DC: GPO, 1943.

Bureau of the Census. *Statistical Abstract of the United States: 1980*. 101st ed. Washington, DC: GPO, 1980.

Bureau of the Census. *Thirteenth Census of the United States, 1910. Statistics for Porto Rico*. Washington, DC: GPO, 1913.

Bureau of the Census. *Thirteenth Census of the United States: 1910*. Vol. 4, *Occupation Statistics*. Washington, DC: GPO, 1914.

Bureau of Labor. *Sixth Annual Report, 1918*. San Juan: Bureau of Supplies, Printing, and Transportation, 1919.

Bureau of Labor. *Special Bulletin of the Bureau of Labor on Strikes in Porto Rico during the Fiscal Year 1917–1918*. San Juan: Bureau of Supplies, Printing and Transportation, 1918.

Burgos Malavé, Eda M. "El conflicto tabacalero entre Cuba y Puerto Rico." *Revista de Estudios Generales* 4, no. 4 (1989–1890): 181–91.

Burns, Malcolm R. "Outside Intervention in Monopolistic Price Warfare: The Case of the 'Plug War' and the Union Tobacco Company." *Business History Review* 56, no. 1 (1982): 33–53.

Business International Corporation. *Puerto Rico, Critical Choices for the 1980s*. New York: Business International Corporation, 1980.

Calero Amor, Antonio María. *Historia del movimiento obrero en Granada (1909–1923)*. Madrid: Tecnos, 1973.

Cámara de Comercio de Puerto Rico. "Tobacco Culture." *Boletín Oficial* 10, no. 6 (1934): 59–70.

Candela Soto, Paloma. *Cigarreras madrileñas: Trabajo y vida (1888–1927)*. Madrid: Tecnos, 1997.

Capetillo, Luisa. *Nation of Women: An Early Feminist Speaks Out: Mi opinión sobre las libertades, derechos y deberes de la mujer*. Edited by Félix Matos Rodríguez. Houston, TX: Arte Público Press, 2004.

Cardona Bonet, Walter A. *El marinero, bandolero, pirata y contrabandista, Roberto Cofresí (1819–1825)*. San Juan: self-published, 1991.

Carrasquillo, Rosa. *Our Landless Patria: Marginal Citizenship and Race in Caguas, Puerto Rico, 1880–1910*. Lincoln: University of Nebraska Press, 2006.

Carroll, Henry K. *Report on the Island of Porto Rico*. Washington, DC: GPO, 1899.

Casanovas, Joan. *Bread, or Bullets! Urban Labor and Spanish Colonialism in Cuba, 1850–1898*. Pittsburgh: University of Pittsburgh Press, 1998.

Castleman, Bruce A. *Knickerbocker Commodore: The Life and Times of John Drake Sloat, 1781–1867*. Albany: State University of New York Press, 2016.

Chandler, Alfred D., Jr. *The Visible Hand: The Managerial Revolution in American Business*. Cambridge, MA: Belknap Press, 1977.

Chanvalon, Thibault de. "De los negros y su conversión al cristianismo; de la resistencia que éstos oponen a la esclavitud; de sus costumbres y usos; de las enfermedades y otras noticias curiosas." In *Crónicas de las poblaciones negras en el Caribe francés*, edited by Eugenio Fernández Méndez, 315–28. 1763. Reprint, San Juan: Centro de Estudios Avanzados de Puerto Rico y el Caribe y Editorial de la UPR, 1996.

Chas. D. Barney & Co. *The Tobacco Industry*. Vol. 1. New York: Chas. D. Barney, 1924.

Checo, José Chez, and Mu-kien Adriana Sang. *El tabaco: Historia general en la República Dominicana*. 3 vols. Santo Domingo: Grupo León Jimenes, 2008.

Chinea, Jorge Luis. "'Spain Is the Merciful Heavenly Body Whose Influence Favors the Irish': Jaime O'Daly y Blake." *Tiempos Modernos: Revista Electrónica de Historia Moderna* 7, no. 25 (2012): 1–33.

Chinea, Jorge Luis. "The Spanish Immigrant Joseph Martín de Fuentes: A Self-styled Reformer, Imperial Watchdog and Nativist in Puerto Rico at the End of the Eighteenth Century." *Revista Mexicana del Caribe* 6, no. 12 (2001): 85–109.

Christian, William A., Jr. *Visionaries: The Spanish Republic and the Reign of Christ*. Berkeley: University of California Press, 1996.

Cifre de Loubriel, Estela. *La formación del pueblo puertorriqueño. Contribución de los gallegos, asturianos y santanderinos*. Río Piedras: Editorial de la UPR, 1989.

Cifre de Loubriel, Estela. *La inmigración a Puerto Rico durante el siglo XIX*. San Juan: Instituto de Cultura Puertorriqueña, 1966.

Clark, Victor S., et al. *Porto Rico and Its Problems*. Washington, DC: Brookings Institution, 1930.

Coll y Toste, Cayetano. "Appendix I. A Review of the Social, Economic, and Industrial Conditions of the Island of Puerto Rico Immediately Preceding Occupation by the United States." In *Annual Reports of the War Department for the Fiscal Year Ended June 30, 1899*, edited by US War Department, 703–16. Washington: GPO, 1900.

Coll y Toste, Cayetano. *Reseña del estado social, económico e industrial de la Isla de Puerto Rico al tomar posesión de ella los Estados Unidos*. San Juan: La Correspondencia, 1899.

Colón Torres, Ramón. "Estudio económico de 270 fincas de tabaco en Puerto Rico, 1936–37." *Boletín Estación Experimental Agrícola* 50 (1939): 1–54.

Colón, Edmundo D. *Datos sobre la agricultura de Puerto Rico antes de 1898*. San Juan: Tipografía de Cantero, Fernández y Co., 1930.

Colón, María Judith. *Historia de Isabela y su desarrollo urbano, 1750–1850*. Carolina, PR: Tipografía Misces, 1988.

Commissioner of Labor. *Annual Report, 1937–1938*. San Juan: Bureau of Supplies, Printing, and Transportation, 1938.

Commissioner of Labor. *Annual Report, 1938–1939*. San Juan: Bureau of Supplies, Printing, and Transportation, 1939.

Commissioner of Labor. *Annual Report, 1939–1940*. San Juan: Bureau of Supplies, Printing, and Transportation, 1940.

Commissioner of Labor. *Annual Report, 1941–1942*. San Juan: Bureau of Supplies, Printing, and Transportation, 1942.

Commissioner of Patents. *Annual Report*. Washington, DC: GPO, 1921.

Commonwealth Board of Elections. *Results of Elections November 6, 1906. Statistics for Votes Elections of 1908, 1910 1912, 1912 1914*. [San Juan?]: Commonwealth Board of Elections, [1965?].

Cooperativa Agro Comercial de Puerto Rico. *Folleto informativo*. San Juan: Cooperativa Agro Comercial de Puerto Rico, 2008.

Cooper, Patricia A. *Once a Cigar Maker: Men, Women, and Work Culture in American Cigar Factories, 1900–1919*. Urbana: University of Illinois Press, 1987.

Córdova Iturregui, Félix. *Ante la frontera del infierno: El impacto social de las huelgas azucareras y portuarias de 1905*. San Juan: Huracán, 2007.

Corrada del Río, Ramón S. "The Historical-Geographical Development of Santurce, 1582–1930." PhD diss., Johns Hopkins University, 1994.

Cosner, Charlotte. *The Golden Leaf: How Tobacco Shaped Cuba and the Atlantic World*. Nashville: Vanderbilt University Press, 2015.

Cox, Howard. *The Global Cigarette: Origins and Evolution of British American Tobacco, 1880–1945*. New York: Oxford University Press, 2000.

Cox, Howard. "Growth and Ownership in the International Tobacco Industry: BAT 1902–27." *Business History* 31, no. 1 (1989): 44–67.

Cox, Reavis. *Competition in the American Tobacco Industry, 1911–1932*. New York: Columbia University Press, 1933.

Crespo Solana, Ana. "Reflections on Monopolies and Free Trade at the End of the Eighteenth Century: A Tobacco Trading Company between Puerto Rico and Amsterdam in 1784." *Itinerario* 29, no. 2 (2005): 73–90.

Cruz Monclova, Lidio. *Historia de Puerto Rico (Siglo XIX)*. Vol. 3, *Segunda parte (1885–1898)*. [Río Piedras?]: Editorial Universitaria, UPR, 1962.

Cullman, Joseph F., III. *I'm a Lucky Guy*. New York: Philip Morris, 1998.

Curbelo de Díaz González, Irene. "Apéndice D, Mapa de Puerto Rico." In *La rebelión de los santos*, edited by Marta Traba, 159. Río Piedras, PR: Ediciones Puerto, 1972.

Dávila Cox, Emma Aurora. *Este inmenso comercio, las relaciones mercantiles entre Puerto Rico y Gran Bretaña, 1844–1898*. San Juan: Editorial de la UPR, 1996.

Dávila Santiago, Rubén. *El derribo de las murallas: Orígenes intelectuales del socialismo en Puerto Rico*. Río Piedras, PR: Editorial Cultural, 1988.

Dávila, Arlene M. *Sponsored Identities: Cultural Politics in Puerto Rico*. Philadelphia: Temple University Press, 1997.

Deans-Smith, Susan. *Bureaucrats, Planters, and Workers: The Making of the Tobacco Monopoly in Bourbon Mexico*. Austin: University of Texas Press, 1992.

Delano, Jack. *En busca del maestro Rafael Cordero/In Search of Maestro Rafael Cordero*. Río Piedras: Editorial UPR, 1994.

Delgado y Martín, Eleuterio. *La renta de tabacos*. Madrid: Tipografía de Manuel Ginés Hernández, 1892.

Departamento de Agricultura y Comercio. *Commercial and Industrial Directory of Puerto Rico*. San Juan: N.p., [1934?]).

Departamento de Agricultura y Comercio. *Informe anual, 1954–1955*. San Juan: Administración General de Suministros, Oficina de Servicios, División de Imprenta, 1955.

Department of Agriculture. *Annual Book on Statistics of Puerto Rico, 1934–35*. [San Juan?]: N.p., 1935.

Department of Commerce and Labor. *Commercial Porto Rico in 1906*. Washington, DC: GPO, 1907.

Department of Labor. *Dictionary of Occupational Titles*. 4th ed. Washington, DC: GPO, 1991.

Department of Labor Wage and Hour Division. *Puerto Rico: The Leaf Tobacco Industry*. Washington, DC: N.p., 1941.

Descartes, Sol Luis. *Basic Statistics on Puerto Rico*. Washington, DC: Office of Puerto Rico, 1946.

Descartes, Sol Luis. "Land Reform in Puerto Rico." *Journal of Land and Utility Economics* 19, no. 4 (November, 1943): 397–417.

Diacon, Todd Alan. *Millenarian Vision, Capitalist Reality: Brazil's Contestado Rebellion, 1912–1916*. Durham, NC: Duke University Press, 1991.

Dietz, James L. *Economic History of Puerto Rico: Institutional Change and Capitalist Development*. Princeton, NJ: Princeton University Press, 1986.

Dietz, James L. *Puerto Rico: Negotiating Development and Change*. Boulder, CO: Lynne Rienner, 2003.

Diffie, Bailey W., and Justine Whitfield Diffie. *Porto Rico: A Broken Pledge*. New York: Vanguard Press, 1931.

Dinwiddie, William. *Puerto Rico, Its Conditions and Possibilities*. New York: Harper and Brothers Publications, 1899.

Duke, Maurice, and Daniel P. Jordan, *Tobacco Merchant: The Story of Universal Leaf Tobacco Company*. Lexington: University Press of Kentucky, 1995.

Dumas, Alexandre. *The Count of Monte Cristo*. 1844. Reprint, New York: Oxford University Press, 2008.

Durden, Robert F. *The Dukes of Durham, 1865–1929*. Durham, NC: Duke University Press, 1975.

Durlach Bros. "Porto Rico Tobacco." In *Directory of the Jobbing Trade in Cigars, Cigarettes and Manufactured Tobacco*, 2nd ed., edited by United States Tobacco Journal. New York: United States Tobacco Journal, 1912.

Economic Development Administration. *Official Industrial & Trade Directory to Puerto Rico*. 2nd ed. San Juan: Publishers Group, 1967.

Economic Development Administration. *Puerto Rico Official Industrial & Trade Directory*. 4th ed. San Juan: Witcom Group, 1971.

Economic Development Administration. *Puerto Rico Official Industrial & Trade Directory*. 5th ed. San Juan: Witcom Group, 1972–1973.

Economic Development Administration. *Puerto Rico Official Industrial & Trade Directory*. 6th ed. San Juan: Witcom Group, 1974.

Economic Development Administration. *Puerto Rico Official Industrial & Trade Directory*. 9th ed. San Juan: Witcom Group, 1977.

Economic Development Administration. *Puerto Rico Official Industrial & Trade Directory*. San Juan: Witcom Group, 1979.

Economic Development Administration and Department of Agriculture. *Annual Book on Statistics of Puerto Rico, 1949–50*. [San Juan?]: N.p., 1950.

Eliot, T. S. "The Hollow Men." In *T. S. Eliot*, edited by Harold Bloom, 97–112. Philadelphia: Chelsea House Publishers, 2003.

Espinosa Fernández, José Manuel. *Elites y política colonial en los márgenes del imperio: Puerto Rico, 1765–1815*. Seville: Escuela de Estudios Hispano-Americanos, Universidad del Norte, Asociación Cultural La Otra Andalucía, 2015.

Esteva, Carlos, Jr. *Annual Report of the Tobacco Institute, Fiscal Years 1939–40, 1940–41*. San Juan: Bureau of Supplies, Printing, and Transportation, 1942.

Esteva, Carlos, Jr. *Tercer informe anual del Instituto del Tabaco*. San Juan: Negociado de Materiales, Imprenta y Transporte, 1940.

Evans, W. D. *Effects of Mechanization on Cigar Manufacturing*. Philadelphia: GPO, 1938.

Federación Libre de Trabajadores de Puerto Rico. *Actuaciones de las segunda y tercera asambleas regulares de las uniones de tabaqueros*. San Juan: Porto Rico Progress Publishing, 1914.

Federación Libre de Trabajadores de Puerto Rico, *Libro de actuaciones de la asamblea magna de los tabaqueros de Puerto Rico, 22 y 23 de enero de 1907* (San Juan: Tipografía El Alba, 1907).

Federación Libre de Trabajadores de Puerto Rico. *Libro de actuaciones de la primera asamblea regular de las uniones de tabaqueros, celebrada en Caguas, julio de 1908*. N.p.: Cuerpo Consultivo de las Uniones de Tabaqueros en Puerto Rico, 1910.

Federal Trade Commission. *Investigation of Concentration of Economic power*. Washington, DC: GPO, 1941.

Federal Trade Commission. *Report of the Federal Trade Commission on the Tobacco Industry*. Washington, DC: GPO, 1921.

Fernández, Agustín. "La Asociación de Cosecheros de Tabaco de Puerto Rico." In *El libro de Puerto Rico*, edited by Eugenio Fernández García, 584–86. San Juan: El Libro Azul Publishing Company, 1923.

Fernández Prieto, Leida. *Cuba agrícola: Mito y tradición, 1878–1920*. Madrid: Consejo Superior de Investigaciones Científicas, 2005.

Financial Directory Association. *The Financial Red Book of America*. New York: Financial Directory Association, 1905.

The Fitch Bond Book. New York: Fitch Publishing Company, 1922.

Fiz Jiménez, Epifanio. *Bayamón y su gente*. Barcelona: Rumbos, 1960.

Fiz Jiménez, Epifanio. *Comerío y su gente*. Barcelona: Ediciones Rumbos, 1957.

Flandreau, Marc, et al. "The Bell Jar: Commercial Interest Rates between Two Revolutions, 1688–1789." In *The Origins and Development of Financial Markets and Institutions from the Seventeenth Century to the Present*, edited by Jeremy Atack and Larry Neal, 161–208. Cambridge: Cambridge University Press, 2009.

Flinter, George D. *An Account of the Present State of the Island of Puerto Rico*. London: Longman, Rees, Orme, Brown, Green, and Longman, 1834.

Fradera, Josep María. *Colonias para después de un imperio*. Barcelona: Edicions Bellaterra, 2005.

Frese, John. "El cultivo de tabaco en Puerto Rico." In *El libro de Puerto Rico*, edited by Eugenio Fernández García, 570–78. San Juan: El Libro Azul Publishing Company, 1923.

Fuente, Alejandro de la, César García del Pino, and Bernardo Iglesias Delgado. *Havana and the Atlantic in the Sixteenth Century*. Chapel Hill: University of North Carolina Press, 2008.

Fumero, Félix J., and Félix R. Fumero. *Merchant Tokens of Puerto Rico*. N.p., 2012.

Gage, Charles E. *American Tobacco Types, Uses, and Markets*. Washington, DC: GPO, 1933.

Gage, Charles E. *The Tobacco Industry in Puerto Rico*. Washington, DC: GPO, 1939.

Gallart, Mary Frances. *Tabacalero y socialista en Cayey: Salvador Gallart Alonso*. San Juan: Editorial Postdata, 2011.

Gárate Ojanguren, Montserrat. *Comercio ultramarino e Ilustración: La Real Compañía de La Habana*. Donostia-San Sebastián, Spain: Real Sociedad Bascongada de los Amigos del País, 1993.

Gárate Ojanguren, Montserrat. *La Real Compañía Guipuzcoana de Caracas*. San Sebastián, Spain: Sociedad Guipuzcoana de Publicaciones, 1990.

García Colón, Ismael. *Colonial Migrants at the Heart of Empire: Puerto Rican Workers on U.S. Farms*. Berkeley: University of California Press, 2020.

García de Torres, Juan. *El arriendo de los tabacos filipinos*. Madrid: Montoya, 1881.

García Díaz, Gervasio A. *Mi paso por la alcaldía de Caguas*. Edited by María de los Ángeles Castro Arroyo. San Juan: Editorial Luscinia, 2018.

García Muñiz, Humberto. *Sugar and Power in the Caribbean*. San Juan: University of Puerto Rico Press, 2010.

García, Gervasio Luis. "Las primeras actividades de los honrados hijos del trabajo." *Op. Cit.* no. 5 (1990): 179–247.

García, Gervasio Luis. "Primeros fermentos de organización obrera en Puerto Rico, 1873–1898." 2nd ed., Cuadernos de CEREP: Investigación y análisis. San Juan: Centro de Estudios de la Realidad Puertorriqueña, 1983.

García, Gervasio L., and A. G. Quintero Rivera. *Desafío y solidaridad: Breve historia del movimiento obrero puertorriqueño*. Río Piedras, PR: Huracán, 1982.

Garner, Wightman W. *The Production of Tobacco*. Philadelphia: Blakiston, 1946.

Gaskell, Ivan. "Tobacco, Social Deviance and Dutch Art in the Seventeenth Century." In *Looking at Seventeenth-century Dutch Art: Realism Reconsidered*, edited by Wayne Franits, 68–77. Cambridge: Cambridge University Press, 1998.

Gaztambide Báez, José A. "La historia del tabaco en Puerto Rico," *Agricultura al Día* 15, nos. 1–2 (1968): 6–13.

Géigel, Fernando J. *Corsarios y piratas de Puerto Rico: Episodios en Puerto Rico durante la guerra de los Estados Unidos con los piratas de las Indias Occidentales, 1819–1825*. San Juan: Cantero Fernández, 1946.

General Cigar Company. *1975 Annual Report*. New York: N.p., 1975.

Gil-Bermejo García, Juana. *Panorama histórico de la agricultura en Puerto Rico*. Seville: Instituto de Cultura Puertorriqueña, Escuela de Estudios Hispano-americanos, 1970.

Giusti Cordero, Juan A. "Hacia otro 98: El 'grupo español' en Puerto Rico, 1890–1930 (azúcar, banca y política)." *Op. Cit.* no. 10 (1998): 72–124.

González del Valle, Ángel. *Memorándum presentado a la Comisión Nacional de Propaganda y Defensa del Tabaco Habano*. Havana: Imprenta "El Siglo XX," 1929.

González Fernández, Doria C. "1895–1898. La guerra económica y su efecto en el tabaco." In *La nación soñada: Cuba, Puerto Rico y Filipinas ante el 98*, edited by Consuelo Naranjo Orovio, Miguel Angel Puig-Samper and Luis Miguel García Mora, 305–16. Madrid: Ediciones Doce Calles, 1996.

González Fernández, Doria C. "La manufactura tabacalera cubana durante la segunda mitad del siglo XIX." *Revista de Indias* 52, no. 194 (1992): 129–56.

González Sierra, José. *Monopolio del humo (Elementos para la historia del tabaco en México y algunos conflictos de tabaqueros veracruzanos: 1915–1930)*. Xalapa, Veracruz: Centro de Investigaciones Históricas, Universidad Veracruzana, 1987.

González Villafañe, Edgardo, and Gabriel R. Espinet. "Análisis económico de la producción de tabaco en Puerto Rico, 1976." *Boletín Estación Experimental Agrícola* no. 118 (January 1978): 1–21.

Goodman, Jordan, ed. *Tobacco in History and Culture: An Encyclopedia*. Vol. 1, *Addiction—Music, Popular.* Detroit: Charles Scribner's Sons, 2004.

Gottsegen, Jack J. *Tobacco: A Study of Its Consumption in the United States*. New York: Pitman Publishing, 1940.

Gould, Roger V. "Trade Cohesion, Class Unity, and Urban Insurrection: Artisanal Activism in the Paris Commune." *American Journal of Sociology* 98, no. 4 (1993): 721–54.

Governor of Porto Rico. *Annual Report, 1902*. Washington, DC: GPO, 1902.

Governor of Porto Rico. *Annual Report, 1904*. Washington, DC: GPO, 1904.

Governor of Porto Rico. *Annual Report, 1907*. Washington, DC: GPO, 1907.

Governor of Porto Rico. "Annual Report, 1917." In *Annual Reports, 1917*, edited by War Department, 1–585. Vol. 3. Washington, DC: GPO, 1918.

Governor of Porto Rico. *Annual Report, 1918*. Washington, DC: GPO, 1918.

Governor of Porto Rico. *Annual Report, 1920*. Washington, DC: GPO, 1920.

Governor of Porto Rico. *Annual Report, 1921*. Washington, DC: GPO, 1921.

Governor of Porto Rico. *Annual Report, 1923*. Washington, DC: GPO, 1923.

Governor of Porto Rico. *Annual Report, 1925*. Washington, DC: GPO, 1926.

Governor of Porto Rico. *Annual Report, 1927*. San Juan: Bureau of Supplies, Printing, and Transportation, 1927.

Grise, Verner N., and Karen F. Griffin, *The U.S. Tobacco Industry*. Washington, DC: US Department of Agriculture, Economic Research Service, 1988.

Guevara Monge, Maribel. "Estudio evaluativo de las tendencias en el mercado de cigarrillos en Puerto Rico." Master's thesis, UPR, 1992.

Gulick, Luther H., Jr. "Occupance Summary of Rural Utuado and Jayuya." In *Symposium on the Geography of Puerto Rico*, edited by Clarence F. Jones and Rafael Picó, 369–401. Río Piedras: UPR Press, 1955.

Hain, Pamela Chase. *A Confederate Chronicle: The Life of a Civil War Survivor.* Columbia: University of Missouri Press, 2005.

Hanusz, Mark. *Kretek: The Culture and Heritage of Indonesia's Clove Cigarettes*. Jakarta: Equinox Publishing, 2000.

Harrigan, Kathryn Rudie. *Declining Demand, Divestiture, and Corporate Strategy*. Washington, DC: Beard Books, 2003.

Harris, Ruth. *Lourdes: Body and Spirit in the Secular Age*. New York: Viking, 1999.
Hartmann, Heidi I. "The Family as the Locus of Gender, Class, and Political Struggle: The Example of Housework." *Signs* 6, no. 3 (1981): 366–94.
Henry, O. "From Each According to His Ability." In *The Voice of the City*, 205–14. Garden City, NY: Doubleday, Doran, 1908.
Hernández Aponte, Gerardo Alberto. *La Iglesia Católica en Puerto Rico ante la Invasión de Estados Unidos de América: Lucha, sobrevivencia y estabilización (1898–1921)*. San Juan: Tiempo Nuevo, 2013.
Hernández Paralitici, Pedro H. *Utuado: Notas para su historia*. San Juan: Oficina Estatal de Preservación Histórica de la Fortaleza, 1983.
Hernández, Telesforo M. "Suministradores de tabaco y acaparamiento de contratas: El ejemplo del Marqués de Campo, 1860–1887." In *El tabaco en la historia económica: Estudios sobre fiscalidad, consumo y empresa (siglos xvii–xx)*, edited by Luis Alonso Álvarez, Lina Gálvez Muñoz and Santiago de Luxán, 335–62. Madrid: Fundación Altadis, 2006.
Hilton, Matthew. "Retailing History as Economic and Cultural History: Strategies of Survival by Specialist Tobacconists in the Mass Market." *Business History* 40, no. 4 (1998): 114–37.
Hobsbawm, E. J. *Rebeldes primitivos: Estudio sobre las formas arcaicas de los movimientos sociales en los siglos XIX y XX*. Barcelona: Editorial Ariel, 1974.
Hochstein, Peter. *Cigars and Other Passions: The Biography of Edgar M. Cullman*. [Bloomington, IN?]: Trafford Publishing, 2010.
Hoff, John van R. "Report of Superior Board of Health of Porto Rico." In *Appendices to the Report*, edited by Military Government of Porto Rico, 7–175. Washington, DC: GPO, 1901.
Iglesias de Pagán, Igualdad. *El obrerismo en Puerto Rico: Época de Santiago Iglesias (1896–1905)*. Palencia de Castilla, Spain: Ediciones Juan Ponce de León, 1973.
Industrial Commission. *Annual Report, 1930–31*. San Juan: N.p., 1931.
Infiesta, Alejandro. *La exposición de Puerto Rico*. San Juan: Boletín Mercantil, 1895.
Infiesta, Alejandro. *La Exposición Universal de Barcelona, 1888*. [San Juan?]: Boletín Mercantil, 1889.
Ingalls, Robert P. *Urban Vigilantes in the New South: Tampa, 1882–1936*. Gainesville: University Press of Florida, 1993.
J. M. Ceballos & Co. *The Importers and Exporters Pictorial Guide and Business Directory of Porto Rico, 1899*. New York: Pictorial Guide Publishing Company, 1899.
Jesús, Ed. C. de. *The Tobacco Monopoly in the Philippines: Bureaucratic Enterprise and Social Change, 1766–1880*. Quezon City, Philippines: Ateneo de Manila University Press, 1980.
"The Journal of a Captive, 1745–1748." In *Colonial Captivities*, edited by Isabel M. Calder, 3–136. Baltimore: Waverly Press, 1935.
Junta de Salario Mínimo. *La industria del tabaco en rama*. San Juan: Junta de Salario Mínimo, 1942.
Junta Insular de Elecciones. *Estadísticas de las elecciones celebradas en Puerto Rico el 4 de noviembre de 1924*. [San Juan?]: N.p., 1924.
Junta Insular de Elecciones. *Estadísticas de las elecciones celebradas en Puerto Rico el 6 de noviembre de 1928*. [San Juan?]: N.p., 1928.
Kerr-Ritchie, Jeffrey R. *Freedpeople in the Tobacco South: Virginia, 1860–1900*. Chapel Hill: University of North Carolina Press, 1999.
Kiernan, Victor Gordon. *Tobacco: A History*. London: Hutchinson Radius, 1991.
Kimm, Tiemen H. "The House of Niemeyer, or, the History of a Leading Firm of Tobacco-Manufacturers in the Netherlands." In *Nicotiana Tabacum: The History of Tobacco and Tobacco Smoking in the Netherlands*, edited by Georg A. Brongers, i–xx. Haarlem, Netherlands: Joh. Enschedé, 1964.

Kimmel, Michael. *Manhood in America: A Cultural History*. 2nd ed. New York: Oxford University Press, 2006.

Kipling, Rudyard. "The Betrothed." In *Stories and Poems*, 430–32. 1886. Reprint, New York: Oxford University Press, 2015.

Klooster, Wim. *Illicit Riches: Dutch Trade in the Caribbean, 1648–1795*. Leiden, Netherlands: KITLV Press, 1998.

Kluger, Richard. *Ashes to Ashes: America's Hundred-Year Cigarette War, the Public Health, and the Unabashed Triumph of Philip Morris*. New York: Knopf, 1996.

Knox, Herman W., ed. *Who's Who in New York*. 7th ed. New York: Who's Who Publications, 1917–1918.

Korzeniewicz, Roberto P. "Labor Unrest in Argentina, 1887–1907." *Latin American Research Review* 24, no. 3 (1989): 71–98.

Krout, Jay Y. *United States Directory of Cigar Manufacturers, Leaf Tobacco Importers, Packers and Dealers*. Philadelphia: Jay Y. Krout, 1902.

Kutzinski, Vera M. *Sugar's Secrets: Race and Erotics of Cuban Nationalism*. Charlottesville: University Press of Virginia, 1993.

"Labels." *Official Gazette of the United States Patent Office* 97 (29 October 1902): 955.

La cuestión tabaquera en Puerto Rico. Madrid: Imprenta y fundición de Manuel Tello, 1885.

Lamikiz, Xabier. *Trade and Trust in the Eighteenth-Century Atlantic World: Spanish Merchants and Their Overseas Networks*. Woodbridge, UK: Boydell and Brewer, 2010.

Lange, Yvonne. "Santos de Palo: The Household Saints of Puerto Rico." *Clarion* 16, no. 4 (1991–1992): 43–65.

Latimer, George O. to James Buchanan, Secretary of State. In *Despachos de los cónsules norteamericanos en Puerto Rico*, 197. Vol. 1. 4 February 1848. Reprint, Río Piedras: Editorial de la UPR, 1982.

Laurie, Bruce. *Artisans into Workers: Labor in Nineteenth-Century America*. Urbana: University of Illinois Press, 1997.

Ledru, André Pierre. *Voyage aux îles de Ténériffe, la Trinité, Saint-Thomas, Sainte-Croix et Porto Ricco: Exécuté par ordre du gouvernement français, depuis le 30 septembre 1796 jusqu'au 7 juin 1798, sous la direction du capitaine Baudin, pour faire des recherches et des collections relatives à l'histoire naturelle*. Vol. 2. Paris: Arthus Bertrand, 1810.

Lestina, Mildred Letitia. "Vuelta Abajo, Cuba: A Study of its Tobacco Industry." *Journal of Geography* 39, no. 2 (1940): 45–55.

Levine, Robert M. *Vale of Tears: Revisiting the Canudos Massacre in Northeastern Brazil, 1893–1897*. Berkeley: University of California Press, 1992.

Levy, Teresita. *Puerto Ricans in the Empire: Tobacco Growers and U.S. Colonialism*. New Brunswick, NJ: Rutgers University Press, 2014.

Lluberes Navarro, Antonio. "La crisis del tabaco cibaeño, 1879–1930." In *Tabaco, azúcar y minería*, edited by Antonio Lluberes Navarro, José del Castillo, and Ramón Alburquerque, 3–22. Santo Domingo: Banco de Desarrollo Interamérica, S. A. and Museo Nacional de Historia y Geografía, 1984.

Long, Durward. "The Open-Closed Shop Battle in Tampa's Cigar Industry, 1919–1921." *Florida Historical Quarterly* 47, no. 2 (1968): 101–21.

López Cantos, Ángel. *Miguel Enríquez*. San Juan: Ediciones Puerto, 1998.

López Martínez, Pío. *Historia de Cayey*. San Juan: N.p., 1972.

López Mesa, Enrique. *Tabaco, mito y esclavos: Apuntes cubanos de historia agraria*. Havana: Editorial de Ciencias Sociales, 2015.

Lugo del Toro, Kenneth. *Nacimiento y auge de la Confederación General de Trabajadores, 1940–1945*. San Juan: Universidad Interamericana, 2013.

Lundius, Jan, and Mats Lundahl. *Peasants and Religion: A Socioeconomic Study of Dios Olivorio and the Palma Sola Movement in the Dominican Republic*. London: Routledge, 1999.

Luxán Meléndez, Santiago de. "La defensa global del imperio y la creación de los monopolios fiscales del tabaco americanos en la segunda mitad del siglo XVIII." In *Política y hacienda del tabaco en los imperios ibéricos (siglos XVII–XIX)*, edited by Santiago de Luxán Meléndez, 177–230. Madrid: Centro de Estudios Políticos y Constitucionales, 2015.

Luxán Meléndez, Santiago de. *La opción agrícola e industrial del tabaco en Canarias, una perspectiva institucional, los orígenes 1827–1939*. Las Palmas de Gran Canaria, Spain: Sociedad Canaria de Fomento Económico, 2006.

Luxán Meléndez, Santiago de, and Montserrat Gárate Ojanguren. "La creación de un sistema atlántico del tabaco (siglos XVII–XVIII): El papel de los monopolios tabaqueros, una lectura desde la perspectiva española." *Anais de História de Além-Mar* 11 (2010): 145–75.

Luxán Meléndez, Santiago de, and Óscar Bergasa Perdomo. "La institucionalización del modelo tabaquero español 1580–1636: La creación del estanco del tabaco en España, nota y discusión." *Vegueta* no. 7 (2003): 135–53.

Mack, Russell Herbert. *The Cigar Manufacturing Industry*. Philadelphia: University of Pennsylvania Press, 1933.

Macmillan, Allister. *The West Indies*. London: W. H. & L. Collingridge, 1911.

Manners, Robert A. "Tabara: Subcultures of a Tobacco and Mixed Crops Municipality." In *The People of Puerto Rico*, edited by Julian H. Steward, et al., 93–170. Urbana: University of Illinois Press, 1956.

Manners, Robert A., and Julian H. Steward. "The Cultural Studies of Contemporary Societies: Puerto Rico." *American Journal of Sociology* 59, no. 2 (1953): 123–30.

Marchildon, Gregory P. *Profits and Politics: Beaverbrook and the Gilded Age of Canadian Finance*. Toronto: University of Toronto Press, 1996.

Martínez Álvarez, Rafael. *El último alcalde español en las Américas*. Mexico City: [Imprenta Manuel León Sánchez], 1947.

Max Gans & Son. "Porto Rico Tobacco." In *Directory of the Jobbing Trade in Cigars, Cigarettes and Manufactured Tobacco*, edited by United States Tobacco Journal. 2nd ed., New York: United States Tobacco Journal, 1912.

Mayo Santana, Raúl, Mariano Negrón Portillo, and Manuel Mayo López. "Esclavos y libertos: El trabajo en San Juan pre y post-abolición." *Revista de Ciencias Sociales* 30, nos. 3–4 (1995): 3–48.

Mayoral Barnés, Manuel. *Ponce y su historial geopolítico-económico y cultural con el árbol genealógico de sus pobladores*. Ponce, PR: N.p., 1946.

McCarthy, Matthew. *Privateering, Piracy and British Policy in Spanish America, 1810–1830*. Woodbridge, UK: Bodywell Press, 2013.

McCook, Stuart. *States of Nature: Science, Agriculture, and Environment in the Spanish Caribbean, 1760–1940*. Austin: University of Texas Press, 2002.

Meisel Roca, Adolfo, and Joaquín Viloria de la Hoz. *Los alemanes en el Caribe colombiano: El caso de Adolfo Held, 1880–1927*. Cartagena: Banco de la República, 1999.

Meléndez Badillo, Jorell A. *Voces libertarias: Los orígenes del anarquismo en Puerto Rico*. Rev. ed. Lajas, PR: Editorial Akelarre, 2015.

Meléndez Badillo, Jorell A. "Imagining Resistance: Organizing the Puerto Rican Southern Agricultural Strike of 1905." *Caribbean Studies* 43, no. 2 (2015): 33–81.

Meléndez Muñoz, Miguel. "Benigno Fernández García: El hombre y el humanista." In *Ensayos cortos y otros artículos*, 840–46. Vol. 3, *Obras completas*. San Juan: Instituto de Cultura Puertorriqueña, 1963.

Meléndez Muñoz, Miguel. *Cayey en el drama del cambio de soberanía (año 1898)*, 113–48. Vol. 3, *Obras completas*. San Juan: Instituto de Cultura Puertorriqueña, 1963.

Meléndez Muñoz, Miguel. "Desarrollo del crédito en Puerto Rico." In *Una oración en Montebello*, 314–22. Vol. 3, *Obras completas*. 1925. Reprint, San Juan: Instituto de Cultura Puertorriqueña, 1963.

Meléndez Muñoz, Miguel. *El jíbaro en el siglo XIX: Ensayo mínimo sobre una realidad máxima*, 453–612. Vol. 3, *Obras completas*. San Juan: Instituto de Cultura Puertorriqueña, 1963.

Meléndez Muñoz, Miguel. "La prosperidad (1919–1920)." In *Cuentos del Cedro*, 723–28. Vol. 1, *Obras completas*. 1927. Reprint, San Juan: Instituto de Cultura Puertorriqueña, 1963.

Melgarejo, Joan. "Memoria y descripción de la isla de Puerto Rico mandada a hacer por S. M. el Rey don Felipe II." In *Crónicas de Puerto Rico*, edited by Eugenio Fernández Méndez, 107–34. 2nd ed., 1582. Reprint, Río Piedras: Editorial UPR, 1969.

Meyer, Gerald. *Vito Marcantonio: Radical Politician, 1902–1954*. Albany: State University of New York Press, 1989.

Mintz, Sidney W. "Cañamelar: Rural Sugar Plantation Proletariat." In *The People of Puerto Rico*, edited by Julian H. Steward et al., 314–417. Urbana: University of Illinois Press, 1956.

Mintz, Sidney W. "The Sensation of Moving, while Standing Still." *American Ethnologist* 16 (1989): 786–96.

Mirecourt, Eugène de. *George Sand*. Paris: Gustave Havard, 1859.

Moody, John. *Moodys Analyses of Investments*. Vol. 2 Public Utilities and Industrials. New York: Moody's Investors Service, 1917.

Moody, John. *Moodys Analyses of Investments*. Vol. 2 Public Utilities and Industrials. New York: Moody Investors Service, 1919.

Moody, John. *Moody's Manual of Securities*. Vol. 2. New York: John Moody, 1901.

Moodys Manual of Railroads and Corporation Securities. Vol. 3, *Industrial Section*. New York: Moody Manual Company, 1918.

Moodys Manual of Railroads and Corporation Securities. Vol. 2, *K to Z*. New York: Poor's Publishing Company, 1922.

Moore, Barrington, Jr. *Injustice: The Social Bases of Obedience and Revolt*. White Plains, NY: M. E. Sharpe, 1978.

Morgan, Philip D. "Virginia's Other Prototype: The Caribbean." In *The Atlantic World and Virginia, 1550–1624*, edited by Peter C. Mancall, 342–82. Chapel Hill: University of North Carolina Press, 2007.

Morris, Melissa N. "Cultivating Colonies: Tobacco and the Upstart Empires, 1580–1640." PhD diss., Columbia University, 2017.

Moscoso, Francisco. *Agricultura y sociedad en Puerto Rico, siglos 16 al 18*. San Juan: Instituto de Cultura Puertoriqueña, Colegio de Agrónomos de Puerto Rico, 1999.

Mulder, Emile. *Cultivation of Tobacco in Sumatra*. Washington, DC: GPO, 1898.

Muller, Dalia Antonia. *Cuban Émigrés and Independence in the Nineteenth-Century Gulf World*. Chapel Hill: University of North Carolina Press, 2017.

Náter, Laura. *Redes del Imperio: Análisis de gobernabilidad a partir del sistema de monopolios de tabaco en la monarquía española (siglos XVII y XVIII)*. Santo Domingo: Archivo General de la Nación, 2018.

Negociado del Trabajo. *Informe especial, 1912*. San Juan: Bureau of Supplies, Printing, and Transportation, 1913.

Negociado del Trabajo. *Noveno informe anual, 1922*. San Juan: Negociado de Materiales, Imprenta y Transporte, 1923.

Negociado del Trabajo. *Quinto informe anual, 1916*. San Juan: Bureau of Supplies, Printing, and Transportation, 1917.

Negociado del Trabajo, *Tercer informe anual, 1914*. San Juan: Bureau of Supplies, Printing, and Transportation, 1915.

Nelson, Lowry. *Rural Cuba*. Minneapolis: University of Minnesota Press, 1950.

Newman, Stanford J., with James V. Miller. *Cigar Family: A 100 Year Journey in the Cigar Industry*. New York: Forbes Custom Publishing, 1999.

Nissen, Johan Peter. *Reminiscences of a 46 Years' Residence in the Island of St. Thomas in the West Indies*. Nazareth, PA: Senseman, 1838.

Nolla, J. A. B. "Primer informe anual del Instituto del Tabaco de Puerto Rico." *Revista de Agricultura de Puerto Rico* 29, no. 1 (1937): 1–50.

Norton, Marcy. *Sacred Gifts, Profane Pleasures: A History of Tobacco and Chocolate in the Atlantic World*. Ithaca, NY: Cornell University Press, 2008.

Núñez Jiménez, Antonio. *Marquillas cigarreras cubanas*. [Madrid?]: Ediciones Tabapress, 1989.

Ojeda Reyes, Félix. "¿Colonialismo sindical o solidaridad internacional? Las relaciones entre el movimiento obrero puertorriqueño." *Revista de Ciencias Sociales* 26, nos. 1–4 (1987): 311–44.

Oneal, John R., and Bruce Russett. "The Kantian Peace: The Pacific Benefits of Democracy, Interdependence, and International Organizations, 1885–1992." *World Politics* 52, no. 1 (1999): 1–37.

O'Neil, J. T. "Memoir of the Island of Porto Rico." In *The Spanish West Indies: Geographic, Political and Industrial*, edited by Richard S. Fisher, 133–90. New York: J. H. Colton, 1855.

Ortiz, Fernando. *Cuban Counterpoint: Tobacco and Sugar*. New York: Alfred A. Knopf, 1947.

Pacheco Díaz, Argelia. *Relaciones comerciales entre Hamburgo, Puerto Rico y St. Thomas: 1814–1867*. Morelia, Mexico: Universidad Michoacana de San Nicolás de Hidalgo, Instituto de Investigaciones Históricas, 2012.

Parrilla Bonilla, Antulio. *Estampas Monserratinas: Una crónica y tres cuentos*. Hormigueros, PR: Editorial Cuarto Siglo, 1989–1990.

Pérez Morales, Edgardo. *No Limits to Their Sway: Cartagena's Privateers and the Masterless Caribbean in the Age of Revolutions*. Nashville: Vanderbilt University Press, 2018.

Pérez Moris, José. *Guía general de la Isla de Puerto Rico*. [San Juan?]: Establecimiento Tipográfico del Boletín, 1879.

Pérez Toledo, Edgar. "La Real Factoría Mercantil: Contribución a la historia de las instituciones económicas de Puerto Rico 1784–1795." *Exégesis* 2, no. 6 (January–March 1989): 11–18.

Pérez Toledo, Edgar. "Real Factoría Mercantil: Contribución a la historia de las instituciones económicas de Puerto Rico (1784–1795)." Master's thesis, UPR, 1983.

Pérez Vega, Ivette. *Las sociedades mercantiles de Ponce, 1816–1830*. San Juan: Academia Puertorriqueña de la Historia and Ediciones Puerto, 2015.

Pérez Velasco, Erik J. "La condición obrera en Puerto Rico (1898–1920)." *Plural* 3, nos. 1–2 (1984): 157–70.

Pérez Vidal, José. *España en la historia del tabaco*. Madrid: Consejo Superior de Investigaciones Científicas, 1959.

Perrot, Michelle. *Workers on Strike: France, 1871–1890*. New Haven, CT: Yale University Press, 1987.

Pesotta, Rose. *Bread upon the Waters*. New York: Dodd, Mead and Company, 1944.

Pessar, Patricia R. *From Fanatics to Folk: Brazilian Millenarianism and Popular Culture*. Durham, NC: Duke University Press, 2004.

Pessar, Patricia R. "Three Moments in Brazilian Millenarism: The Interrelationship between Politics and Religion." *Luso-Brazilian Review* 28, no. 1 (1991): 95–116.

Picó, Fernando. *Amargo café (los pequeños y medianos caficultores de Utuado en la segunda mitad del siglo xix)*. Río Piedras, PR: Ediciones Huracán, 1981.

Picó, Fernando. *Cayeyanos: Familias y solidaridades en la historia de Cayey*. Río Piedras, PR: Huracán, 2007.

Picó, Fernando. "El café y el inicio de la agricultura comercial en la montaña puertorriqueña, 1855–1928." In *Al filo del poder: Subalternos y dominantes en Puerto Rico, 1739–1910*, edited by Fernando Picó, 61–72. Río Piedras: Editorial de la UPR, 1993.

Picó, Fernando. *Historia general de Puerto Rico*. 4th ed. Río Piedras, PR: Huracán, 2008.

Picó, Fernando. *Libertad y servidumbre en el Puerto Rico del siglo XIX: Los jornaleros utuadeños en vísperas del auge del café*. Río Piedras, PR: Huracán, 1979.

Picó, Fernando. *Los gallos peleados*. Río Piedras, PR: Ediciones Huracán, 1983.

Picó, Rafael. "Land Tenure in the Leading Types of Farming of Puerto Rico." *Economic Geography* 15, no. 2 (1939): 135–45.

Piñero, José. "A Study of the Puerto Rico Tobacco Marketing Cooperative Association." Master's thesis, Cornell University, 1952.

Porter, Patrick G. "Advertising in the Early Cigarette Industry." *North Carolina Historical Review* 48 (Winter 1971): 31–43.

Poyo, Gerald Eugene. *"With All, and for the Good of All": The Emergence of Popular Nationalism in the Cuban Communities of the United States, 1848–1898*. Durham, NC: Duke University Press, 1989.

Price, Jacob M. *France and the Chesapeake: A History of the French Tobacco Monopoly, 1674–1791, and of Its Relationship in the British and American Tobacco Trades*. Vol. 1. Ann Arbor: University of Michigan Press, 1973.

Prince, Eldred E., and Robert R. Simpson, *Long Green: The Rise and Fall of Tobacco in South Carolina*. Athens: University of Georgia Press, 2000.

Proctor, Robert N. *Golden Holocaust: Origins of the Cigarette Catastrophe and the Case for Abolition*. Berkeley: University of California Press, 2011.

Puerto Rico Industrial Development Company. *19th Annual Report, 1961*. [San Juan?]: N.p., n.d.

Puerto Rico Industrial Development Company. *13th Anniversary Report for the Fiscal Year 1954–1955*. New York: Aldus Printers, n.d.

Puerto Rico Industrial Development Company. *12th Annual Report: 1953–1954*. New York: Aldus Printers, n.d.

Purcell, Susan Kaufman. "Cuba." In *Economic Sanctions and American Diplomacy*, edited by Richard N. Haass, 35–56. New York: Council on Foreign Relations, 1998.

Quintero Rivera, Ángel G. "El Partido Socialista y la lucha política triangular de las primeras décadas bajo la dominación norteamericana." *Revista de Ciencias Sociales* 19, no. 1 (1975): 47–100.

Quintero Rivera, Ángel G. "La clase obrera y el proceso político en Puerto Rico." *Revista de Ciencias Sociales* 19, no. 3 (1975): 261–300.

Quintero Rivera, Ángel G. "Socialista y tabaquero: La proletarización de los artesanos." In *La danza de la insurrección: Para una sociología de la música latinoamericana*, 29–84. 1978. Reprint, Buenos Aires: CLACSO, 2020.

Quintero Rivera, Ángel G. "Vueltita, con mantilla, al primer piso: Sociología de los santos." In *Vírgenes, magos y escapularios: Imaginería, etnicidad y religiosidad popular en Puerto Rico*, edited by Ángel G. Quintero Rivera, 9–100. San Juan: Fundación Puertorriqueña de las Humanidades, 1998.

Ramos Mattei, Andrés A. "Las inversiones norteamericanas en Puerto Rico y la Ley Foraker, 1898–1900." *Caribbean Studies* 14, no. 3 (1974): 53–69.

Ramos Mattei, Andrés A. *La sociedad del azúcar en Puerto Rico: 1870–1910*. Río Piedras: UPR, 1988.

Reichard de Cancio, Haydée E. *Temas y temitas*. 2nd ed. Mayagüez, PR: Imprenta RUM, 2006.

Reid, Anthony. "From Betel-Chewing to Tobacco-Smoking in Indonesia." *Journal of Asian Studies* 44, no. 3 (1985): 529–47.

Reyes, Jaime. *La Santa Montaña de San Lorenzo, Puerto Rico, y el misterio de Elenita de Jesús (1898–1909)*. San Lorenzo, PR: Santuario de la Virgen del Carmen, 1992.

Rivera Díaz, Roberto. *Historia de la General Cigar de Utuado*. Utuado, PR: Self-published, 2018.

Rivera Martínez, Prudencio. "Santiago Iglesias y yo." In *Santiago Iglesias Pantín*, edited by Juan Carreras, 207–12. 2nd ed. San Juan: Club de Prensa, 1970.

Rivera Rodríguez, Irene. "El crecimiento de las importaciones de mercancía a Puerto Rico, 1875–1897." PhD diss., UPR, 1998.

Rivero Muñiz, José. *Tabaco, su historia en Cuba*. 2 vols. Havana: Instituto de Historia, Academia de Ciencias de la República de Cuba, 1964–1965.

Robert, Joseph C. *The Story of Tobacco in America*. 1949. Reprint, Chapel Hill: University of North Carolina Press, 1964.

Roberts, Richard. *Schroders: Merchants & Bankers*. London: Macmillan, 1992.

Rodríguez Gordillo, José Manuel. "El personal obrero en la Real Fábrica de Tabaco." In *La difusión del tabaco en España: Diez estudios*, edited by José Manuel Rodríguez Gordillo, 141–50. Seville: Universidad de Sevilla and Fundación Altadis, 2002.

Rodríguez Gordillo, José Manuel. "El tabaco: Del uso medicinal a la industrialización." In *La difusión del tabaco en España: Diez estudios*, edited by José Manuel Rodríguez Gordillo, 181–220. Seville: Universidad de Sevilla and Fundación Altadis, 2002.

Rodríguez Gordillo, José Manuel. *La creación del estanco del tabaco en España*. Madrid: Fundación Altadis, 2002.

Rodríguez Pérez, Lillian del Carmen. "La obra de los Hermanos Cheos (1902–1927)." Master's thesis, Centro de Estudios Avanzados de Puerto Rico y el Caribe, 1994.

Rogler, Charles C. *Comerío, A Study of a Puerto Rican Town*. Lawrence: University of Kansas, 1940.

Rogoff, Leonard. "Jewish Proletarians in the New South: The Durham Cigarette Rollers." *American Jewish History* 82, nos. 1–4 (1994): 141–57.

Román, Reinaldo L. *Governing Spirits: Religion, Miracles, and Spectacles in Cuba and Puerto Rico, 1898–1956*. Chapel Hill: University of North Carolina Press, 2007.

Rosario, José Colombán. "The Porto Rican Peasant and His Historical Antecedents." In *Porto Rico and Its Problems*, edited by Victor S. Clark et al., 537–75. Washington, DC: Brookings Institution, 1930.

Rosenberg, Emily S. "Foundations of United States International Power: Gold Standard Diplomacy, 1900–1905." *Business History Review* 59, no. 2 (1985): 169–202.

Roy, William G. *Socializing Capital: The Rise of the Large Industrial Corporation in America*. Princeton, NJ: Princeton University Press, 1997.

Saavedra, Emilio F. "El cultivo de tabaco en Isabela: Manera de elaborar rollos de verdadera calidad." *Revista de Agricultura de Puerto Rico* 23, no. 2 (1929): 83.

Salamone, Paul. "Constitutional Separation and the Foraker Act: How They Influenced Puerto Rico's Tax Reform from 1898–1901 and Led to the Adoption of the Import Excise and Property Tax." *Revista del Colegio de Abogados de Puerto Rico* 64, no. 2 (April–June 2003): 34–113.

Sanabria, Carlos. *Puerto Rican Labor History 1898–1934: Revolutionary Ideals and Reformist Politics*. Lanham, MD: Lexington Books, 2018.

Sánchez Korrol, Virginia. *From Colonia to Community: The History of Puerto Ricans in New York City, 1917–1948*. Westport, CT: Greenwood Press, 1983.

San Miguel, Pedro L. *Los campesinos del Cibao: Economía de mercado y transformación agraria en la República Dominicana, 1880–1960*. Río Piedras: Editorial de la UPR, 1997.

Santaella Rivera, Esteban. *Historia de los Hermanos Cheos: Recopilación de escritos y relatos.* 2nd ed. Rincón: M. B. Publishers de Puerto Rico, 2003.
Santamaría García, Antonio. "Los ferrocarriles de servicio público de Puerto Rico (1870–1990)." *Revista Complutense de Historia de América* 20 (1994): 207–28.
Santana Peña, Arturo. "The United States and Puerto Rico, 1797–1830." PhD diss., University of Chicago, 1953.
Santiago Méndez, Helen. "Los comerciantes alemanes en Aguadilla en el siglo XIX." In *Tertulias aguadillanas*, edited by Haydée E. Reichard de Cancio, 21–28. Aguadilla, PR: Comité de Aguadilla para la Celebración del 5to Centenario del Descubrimiento de Puerto Rico, 1993.
Schama, Simon. *The Embarrassment of Riches: An Interpretation of Dutch Culture in the Golden Age.* Berkeley: University of California Press, 1988.
Schneider, Dorothee. *Trade Unions and Community: The German Working Class in New York City, 1870–1900.* Urbana: University of Illinois Press, 1994.
Schwartz, Michael. *Radical Protest and Social Structure: The Southern Farmers' Alliance and Cotton Tenancy, 1880–1890.* Chicago: University of Chicago Press, 1988.
Schwartz, Stuart B. "The Hurricane of San Ciriaco: Disaster, Politics and Society in Puerto Rico, 1899–1901." *Hispanic American Historical Review* 72, no. 3 (1992): 303–34.
Schwartz, Stuart B. *Sea of Storms: A History of Hurricanes in the Greater Caribbean from Columbus to Katrina.* Princeton, NJ: Princeton University Press, 2015.
Scott, William Henry. "The 'Unión Obrera Democrática,' First Filipino Labor Union." *Philippine Social Sciences and Humanities Review* 47, nos. 1–4 (1983): 131–92.
Secretary of Porto Rico. *Register of Porto Rico for 1910.* San Juan: Bureau of Printing and Supplies, 1911.
Shaffer, Kirwin R. *Anarchism and Countercultural Politics in Early Twentieth-Century Cuba.* Gainesville: University Press of Florida, 2005.
Shaffer, Kirwin R. *Black Flag Boricuas: Anarchism, Antiauthoritarianism, and the Left in Puerto Rico, 1897–1921.* Urbana: University of Illinois Press, 2013.
Shanken, Marvin R. "An Interview with Edgar Cullman Jr., President and Chief Executive Officer, Culbro Corporation." *Cigar Aficionado* (Autumn 1996).
Shanken, Marvin R. "An Interview with Edgar M. Cullman Sr." *Cigar Aficionado* (Autumn 1994).
Shanken, Marvin R. "Richard DiMeola, Executive Vice President, Chief Operating Officer, Consolidated Cigar Corporation." *Cigar Aficionado* (Summer 1996).
Shechter, Relli. "Selling Luxury: The Rise of the Egyptian Cigarette and the Transformation of the Egyptian Tobacco Market, 1850–1914." *International Journal of Middle East Studies* 35, no. 1 (2003): 51–75.
Sheldon, G. W. *Pocket Tariff of the United States Customs Duties.* Chicago: G. W. Sheldon, 1909.
Shorter, Edward, and Charles Tilly. "The Shape of Strikes in France, 1830–1960." *Comparative Studies in Society and History* 13, no. 1 (1971): 60–86.
Silva Gotay, Samuel. *Catolicismo y política en Puerto Rico bajo España y Estados Unidos, Siglos XIX y XX.* San Juan: La Editorial, UPR, 2005.
Silva Gotay, Samuel. *Protestantismo y política en Puerto Rico: 1898–1930: Hacia una historia del protestantismo evangélico en Puerto Rico.* Río Piedras: Editorial de la UPR, 1997.
Silvestrini de Pacheco, Blanca. "La mujer puertorriqueña y el movimiento obrero en la década de 1930." *Cuadernos de la Facultad de Humanidades* 3 (1979): 84–104.
Silvestrini de Pacheco, Blanca. *Los trabajadores puertorriqueños y el Partido Socialista, 1932–1940.* Río Piedras: Editorial de la UPR, 1979.
Sketches: Porto Rico. N.p.: Porto Rican-American Tobacco Company, 1904.
Smith, Sally Bedell. *In All His Glory: The Life of William S. Paley, the Legendary Tycoon and His Brilliant Circle.* New York: Simon and Schuster, 1990.

Snyder, David. "Early North American Strikes: A Reinterpretation." *Industrial and Labor Relations Review* 30, no. 3 (1977): 325–41.

Solá, José O. "Colonialism, Planters, Sugarcane, and the Agrarian Economy of Caguas, Puerto Rico, between the 1890s and 1930." *Agricultural History* 85, no. 3 (2011): 349–72.

Sonesson, Birgit. *Puerto Rico's Commerce, 1765–1865: From Regional to Worldwide Market Relations*. Los Angeles: University of California, Los Angeles, Latin American Center, 2000.

Stark, David Martin. *Slave Families and the Hato Economy in Puerto Rico*. Gainesville: University Press of Florida, 2015.

St. Helen, Gideon, Natalie Nardone, Newton Addo, Delia Dempsey, Christopher Havel, Peyton Jacob, and Neal L. Benowitz. "Differences in Nicotine Intake and Effects from Electronic and Combustible Cigarettes among Dual Users." *Addiction* 115, no. 4 (2020): 757–67.

Stoler, Ann Laura. *Capitalism and Confrontation in Sumatra's Plantation Belt, 1870–1979*. 2nd. ed. Ann Arbor: University of Michigan Press, 1995.

Stubbs, Jean. "El Habano and the World It Has Shaped: Cuba, Connecticut, and Indonesia." *Cuban Studies* 41 (2010): 39–67.

Stubbs, Jean. *Tobacco on the Periphery: A Case Study in Cuban Labour History, 1860–1958*. Cambridge: Cambridge University Press, 1985.

Stubbs, Jean. "Turning over a New Leaf? The Havana Cigar Revisited." *New West Indian Guide* 74, nos. 3–4 (2000): 235–56.

Surgeon General's Advisory Committee. *Smoking and Health: Report of the Advisory Committee to the Surgeon General of the Public Health Service*. Washington, DC: GPO, 1964.

Taller de Formación Política. *¡Huelga en la caña!* Río Piedras, PR: Huracán, 1982.

Taller de Formación Política. *No estamos pidiendo el cielo, huelga portuaria de 1938*. Río Piedras, PR: Huracán, 1988.

Tennant, Richard B. *The American Cigarette Industry: A Study in Economic Analysis and Public Policy*. New Haven, CT: Yale University Press, 1950.

Thomas, Dylan. "Do Not Go Gentle into That Good Night." In *The English Reader: What Every Literate Person Needs to Know*, edited by Diane Ravitch and Michael Ravitch, 463. New York: Oxford University Press, 2006.

Thompson, E. P. *The Making of the English Working Class*. New York: Vintage Books, 1966.

Tilley, Nannie May. *The Bright Tobacco Industry, 1860–1929*. Chapel Hill: University of North Carolina Press, 1948.

Tilley, Nannie May. *The R. J. Reynolds Tobacco Company*. Chapel Hill: University of North Carolina Press, 1985.

Tilly, Charles. *The Contentious French*. Cambridge, MA: Belknap Press, 1986.

Tilly, Charles. "Contentious Repertoires in Great Britain, 1758–1834." In *Repertoires and Cycles of Collective Action*, edited by Mark Traugott, 15–42. Durham, NC: Duke University Press, 1995.

Tirado, Amílcar. "Cigar Workers and the History of the Labor Movement in Puerto Rico, 1890–1920." PhD diss., City University of New York, 2012.

Torres, Bibiano. "D. Jaime O'Daly: Propulsor del cultivo del tabaco en Puerto Rico." *Revista del Instituto de Cultura Puertorriqueña* 15 (1962): 49–52.

Torres Grillo, Herminio. *Historia de la ciudad de Caguas: La invicta del Turabo*. Barcelona: Rumbos, 1965.

Torres Ramírez, Bibiano. *La isla de Puerto Rico (1765–1800)*. San Juan: Instituto de Cultura Puertorriqueña, 1968.

Torres Rosario, Wilson. *Juana Colón: Combatiente en el tabacal puertorriqueño*. Comerío, PR: Self-published, 2011.

Torres Vargas, Diego de. "Descripción de la isla y ciudad de Puerto-Rico, y de su vecindad y poblaciones, presidio. Gobernadores y obispos; frutos y minerales." In *Crónicas de Puerto*

Rico, edited by Eugenio Fernández Méndez, 171–218. 2nd ed. 1647. Reprint, Río Piedras: Editorial UPR, 1969.

Torres, Víctor M. *No quiero decir adiós: Memorias de un hablador*. Río Piedras: Editorial de la UPR, 2000.

Traba, Marta. *La rebelión de los santos*. Río Piedras: Ediciones Puerto, 1972.

Trow New York Copartnership and Corporation, 1918–19. New York: R. L. Polk, 1919.

Trow's Business Directory. New York: Trow Directory, 1898.

Ubeda y Delgado, Manuel. *Isla de Puerto Rico. Estudio histórico, geográfico y estadístico de la misma*. [San Juan?]: Tipografía del Boletín, 1878.

US Consumer and Marketing Service, Tobacco Division. *Annual Report on Tobacco Statistics*. Washington, DC: Department of Agriculture, Consumer and Marketing Service, Tobacco Division, 1965.

Valle, José F. del. "Situación económica de Puerto Rico en 1899." In *Crónicas de Puerto Rico*, edited by Eugenio Fernández Méndez, 559–68. 2nd ed., 1907. Reprint, Río Piedras: Editorial UPR, 1969.

Valle Ferrer, Norma. *Luisa Capetillo, Pioneer Puerto Rican Feminist*. New York: Peter Lang, 2006.

van Leenhoff, J., Jr. "Tobacco Investigations in Porto Rico during 1903–4." *Bulletin Agricultural Experiment Station* 5 (1905): 8–44.

Vidal, Teodoro. *La Monserrate negra con el Niño blanco*. San Juan: Ediciones Alba, 2003.

Vidal, Teodoro. *Santeros puertorriqueños*. San Juan: Ediciones Alba, 1979.

Vilá Vilar, Enriqueta. *Historia de Puerto Rico 1600–1650*. Seville: Escuela de Estudios Hispano-Americanos, 1974.

Waitt & Bond. *The Tobacco Wrapper*. [New York?]: N.p., 1969.

Wage and Hour and Public Contracts Divisions. *The Cigar and Cigarette Industry in Puerto Rico*. Washington, DC: Division of Wage Determinations, 1950.

Wage and Hour and Public Contracts Divisions. *The Leaf Tobacco Industry in Puerto Rico*. Washington, DC: Division of Wage Determinations, 1950.

Walker, Cheryl. *Masks Outrageous and Austere: Culture, Psyche, and Persona in Modern Women Poets*. Bloomington: Indiana University Press, 1991.

War Department. *Report of the Census of Porto Rico 1899*. Washington, DC: GPO, 1900.

Weber, Max. *Economy and Society*. Edited by Guenther Roth and Claus Wittich. Vol. 2. Berkeley: University of California Press, 1978.

Werner, Carl Avery. *Tobaccoland*. New York: Tobacco Leaf Publishing, 1922.

Wertenbaker, Lael Tucker. *Mister Junior*. Patterson, NJ: Pageant Books, 1960.

Westfall, L. Glenn. *Key West: Cigar City U.S.A.* Key West, FL: Historic Key West Preservation Board, 1984.

Weyl, Walter. "Labor Conditions in Porto Rico." *Bulletin of the Bureau of Labor* 61 (1905): 723–856.

White, James B. "Allie Lewis Sylvester." In *The National Cyclopedia of American Biography*, 111. Vol. 15. New York: James B. White, 1916.

Whitney, Milton. *Tobacco Soils*. Washington, DC: GPO, 1898.

Wolf, Eric R. "San José: Subcultures of a 'Traditional' Coffee Municipality." In *The People of Puerto Rico*, edited by Julian H. Steward et al., 171–264. Urbana: University of Illinois Press, 1956.

Zayas Micheli, Luis O. *Catolicismo popular en Puerto Rico:—una explicación sociológica*. Ponce, PR: N.p., 1990.

Zeno, Francisco M. *El obrero agrícola o de los campos*. San Juan: La Correspondencia de Puerto Rico, [1922?].

INDEX

ABOUT THE AUTHOR

Photo by Estelle L. Vilar

Juan José Baldrich is a retired professor from the Department of Sociology and Anthropology at the University of Puerto Rico. He is author of *Sembraron la no siembra* and has been published in numerous journals, including *Agricultural History* and *CENTRO: Journal of the Center for Puerto Rican Studies*. He has also contributed chapters to edited volumes such as *El tabaco en la historia económica* and *Puerto Rican Women's History: New Perspectives*.

www.ingramcontent.com/pod-product-compliance
Lightning Source LLC
Chambersburg PA
CBHW020241290326
41929CB00045B/1439
* 9 7 8 1 4 9 6 8 4 2 1 1 4 *